ONE WEEK LOAN

The Modern British State

An Historical Introduction

Philip Harling

Polity

The right of Philip Harling to be identified as author of this work has been asserted in accordance with the Copyright, Designs and Patents Act 1988.

First published in 2001 by Polity Press in association with Blackwell Publishers Ltd

Editorial Office:
Polity Press
65 Bridge Street
Cambridge CB2 1UR, UK

Marketing and production:
Blackwell Publishers Ltd
108 Cowley Road
Oxford OX4 1JF, UK

Published in the USA by
Blackwell Publishers Inc.
350 Main Street
Malden, MA 02148, USA

A catalogue record for this book is available from the British Library.

Library of Congress Cataloging-in-Publication Data

Harling, Philip.
  The modern British state: an historical introduction / Philip Harling.
    p.   cm.
Includes bibliographical references and index.
  ISBN 0-7456-2192-9 (acid-free paper) – ISBN 0-7456-2193-7 (pbk.: acid-free paper)
  1. Great Britain – Politics and government – 18th century.   2. Great Britain – Politics and government – 19th century.   3. Great Britain – Politics and government – 20th century.   4. Great Britain – Politics and government – 1689–1702.   I. Title.
  DA470.H29   2001
  941 – dc21

00-012557

Typeset in 10 on 12 pt Palatino
by Best-set Typesetter Ltd., Hong Kong
Printed in Great Britain by MPG Books Ltd, Bodmin, Cornwall

This book is printed on acid-free paper.

Contents

Acknowledgements

My first debt of gratitude is to Polity. It was Petra Moll, then of Polity, who came to me with the idea for this book. As it has turned out, that was virtually the only idea that the staff at Polity have brought to my notice, and I shall be eternally grateful for their indulgence in permitting me to shape the manuscript as I saw fit. They have almost entirely restricted themselves to seeing it through the press, and Louise Knight deserves my particular thanks for her guidance in this respect.

I am deeply indebted to several of my friends and colleagues for taking the time to read and comment on complete drafts of the manuscript. Peter Mandler went over it with his accustomed perceptiveness and tact. Jeremy Popkin read it diligently and intelligently, and offered a great deal of welcome advice. My own graduate students, Rebecca Bates and Erin Shelor, provided a number of most helpful suggestions and at the same time assured me that writing this book was indeed a worthwhile enterprise. I also received important moral support from two other graduate students in my department, Pat Mullins and Jules Sweet, who read drafts of a couple of chapters as part of the preparation for their doctoral examinations. It was only because my nerves failed me that I did not share the manuscript with Mark Summers. I hope they do not fail me next time, because while he tends to offer me more suggestions than I can possibly know what to do with, they are always on the mark, and they stem from a boundless passion for history and a commitment to intellectual honesty that I shall always admire. I cherish his companionship, as I do that of several other friends who have made Lexington a pleasant and stimulating place in which to work and live, most notably Dan Gargola, Richard Greissman, Lori and Sakah Mahmud, Joanne Melish, Jeff Peters, Karen Petrone, Sue Roberts, Dan Rowland, Rich Schein, Kristin Seymour, Al Shapere, Gretchen Starr-LeBeau, and Tony Thompson.

All historians rely on the work of their predecessors. But in putting together a synthetic overview, I have relied very much indeed on the rich historiography of British state formation. Several scholars have influenced my thoughts heavily enough to deserve recognition here at the outset: John Brewer, James Cronin, Joanna Innes, Jose Harris, Ross McKibbin, and Pat Thane.

Neither this nor any of my other endeavours would have seen the light of day were it not for the abiding love and companionship of my wife, Bettina Morrish, and my sons, Nate and Nick. Every day truly is a new adventure with them, and each one sweeter than the last. Bettina's family – Bill and Eva-Marie Morrish, Ken, Mia, Max, and Marian Morrish – is very much my own, not least in the abiding support they have provided me over the last decade. It is to my own parents and siblings that I wish to dedicate this book: Ray and Betty Harling, Carolyn Mensch, and Jeff Harling. There will be no getting over the loss of my brother Jeff. But perhaps the most fitting memorial to such a genuinely good person is that in death he continues to bind the rest of us closer together with each other, and with his wife, Noelle. His time with us was all too brief, but his life's work was and remains well done.

Lexington, Kentucky
September 2000

Introduction

The structure and social impact of the national state have generated a great deal of scholarly interest over the last quarter-century or so.[1] In line with this trend, a rich literature now attests to the centrality of the British state to social life as far back as the eighteenth century, when until recently the state was thought to have had a scarcely discernible impact on the lives of its subjects.[2] But there is still no broad synthesis of the historical literature that offers an explanation of how and why the contours of the British state have changed over the last three centuries. My goal here is to offer just such a synthetic account, in the hope that it will provide a coherent introduction to the changing shape and role of that state for students of history, politics, and sociology, and a useful overview for specialists who are already familiar with the rich but fragmentary literature on modern British state formation.

How does one describe something as amorphous and potentially all-encompassing as 'the state'? One way is to try to define what it *is*, in the manner of the historian John Brewer:

> A territorially and jurisdictionally defined political entity in which public authority is distinguished from (though not unconnected to) private power, and which is manned by officials whose primary (though not sole) allegiance is to a set of political institutions under a single, i.e. sovereign and final, authority.[3]

Another way, as Brewer goes on to say, is to try to describe what the state *does* – the functions it performs, how it performs them, the constituencies it serves, and how all of these things change over time. It is in this latter sense that I shall be examining the British state here, in a chronological account that makes no claim to theoretical rigour.

The most obvious theme of the book is the broadening of the state's functions over the last three centuries, and most noticeably over the last one. Thatcherism and the rise of New Labour might at first glance suggest for Britain what President Clinton memorably suggested for the United States: that 'the era of big government is over'. But on both sides of the Atlantic, the contemporary state continues to have a far more palpable impact on the lives of its citizens than it did three or four generations ago; it extracts far more in the shape of taxes than it did then, but in return it also gives far more back in the shape of services. As late as 1870, most Britons assumed that the only tasks that should be entrusted to the central and local authorities were the defence of the realm, the maintenance of public order, the prevention of destitution, a modicum of workplace and sanitary regulation, and the provision of basic amenities such as street lighting. Today, they assume that these tasks ought to extend – and of course they do extend – to the provision of education, retirement benefits, unemployment insurance, affordable housing for the underprivileged, health care, labour arbitration, and a host of other services. Defence spending and debt service, which routinely accounted for well over four-fifths of central government expenditure during the eighteenth century, now account for under a fifth of it. Social security, health, and education – items of expenditure that were scarcely perceptible to taxpayers a century ago – now cost them four times as much as the armed services. The cost of the state has multiplied along with its functions. Central and local government spending now accounts for well over four times as much of the gross domestic product as it did two centuries ago, and government expenditure measured in constant prices is at least a couple of hundred times more now than it was then.[4]

Obviously, a great many factors must be taken into account in order to understand something as complicated and immense as the broadening scope of the British state over the last three hundred years. Drawing up a preliminary laundry-list of factors here would defeat the main purpose of the rest of the text, which is to place them in their proper chronological setting. Hence this deliberately brief introduction will simply highlight, in chronological order, some of the main issues that will be discussed in greater length in the body chapters.

The first is the emergence of a parliamentary monarchy in the eighteenth century, and its consequences for the state's traditional war-making role. After the Hanoverian succession of 1714, it was even more clear in practice than it was in law that sovereignty resided not in the king *per se*, but in king-and-parliament. While the monarch continued to enjoy certain prerogative powers, the authority of his ministers rested on their ability to maintain the support of a majority in the House of Commons. The establishment of parliamentary sovereignty had a profound impact on one of the British state's only well-established responsibilities: the defence of the realm. In an era of chronic warfare on an ever vaster scale, defending the realm became a hugely expensive proposition. Parliamentary control of the national finances provided Britain with a great advantage in war-making. For it made the enormous growth in taxes that was necessary to pay for the British war machine more tolerable by making it the responsibility of an elected assembly, and it enabled the state to borrow on comparatively favourable terms by providing a parliamentary guarantee for the swift payment of interest.

The second issue is the political controversy inspired by the expansion of the state's war-making functions during the eighteenth century. Critics insisted that the massive growth of taxes and government offices required to prosecute war was actually threatening the political independence of the House of Commons by furnishing the king and his ministers with the means to purchase the support of MPs. The effort to make the colonists foot part of the bill for the escalating costs of imperial defence helped to foment the American rebellion. 'No taxation without representation' became a catchphrase on both sides of the Atlantic, as the disgust of English radicals with the seeming waste and extravagance of the British war effort in America prompted them to endorse parliamentary reform as the only means of ridding the political system of its putative corruption. The military struggles with revolutionary and Napoleonic France inspired rebellion in and annexation of Ireland, made Britons the most heavily taxed people in Europe, and inspired a widespread perception that the wartime state furnished too many opportunities for privileged insiders to profit at taxpayers' expense. Finally, the perceived excesses of the wartime state helped to guarantee that the post-Napoleonic era would be one of dramatic retrenchment. Growing affluence and the 'Pax Britannica' made the state's traditional military function a far less expensive burden on the mid-Victorian generation than it had been on their eighteenth-century forebears.

The third issue is the uneven and deliberate pace with which the local and central authorities assumed new regulatory duties during the middle quarters of the nineteenth century. It is true that by 1880 they were involved in many spheres of social life with which they had scarcely interfered before 1815, most notably through factory and sanitary regulation and primary education. But this widening of the responsibilities of the state was not a sudden or even always an orderly or logical response to the new needs of a rapidly growing and increasingly urban population. The Victorians considerably broadened the points of contact between government and society, but they did so grudgingly and haltingly. There were many reasons why they sought to make state intervention the exception rather than the rule: a perception that a fair and disinterested government was by definition a frugal and unobtrusive one; a widespread fear that social reform might trench upon 'respectable' propertied interests; a persistent suspicion of the potentially corrupting influence of an over-mighty central government; and a deep respect for local autonomy. It is true that this era was just as remarkable for its violations of *laissez-faire* principles as it was for its efforts to uphold them; in terms of factory or sanitary reform, for instance, Britain was one of the most 'progressive' nations in the world by the 1870s. But such reforms tended to be limited in practice, the piecemeal results of a series of battles between formidable interest groups. The Victorians' respect for the authority of local government, moreover, meant that these results varied greatly from one town to the next; by no means all localities were keen to exercise the growing range of permissive regulatory powers that parliament put into their hands. In short, most Victorians remained content with a government that generally left people to look after themselves. Those who were deemed unwilling to do so, however – most notably paupers, prostitutes, and prisoners – were severely dealt with by a Victorian state that, however 'minimal' in some respects, was armed with formidable disciplinary powers.

The fourth issue is the dramatic broadening of central and local responsibilities in the late-Victorian and Edwardian eras into areas of social and economic life from which government had hitherto been excluded. By 1914 the authorities were helping to provide unemployment insurance, health insurance, old-age pensions, and public housing to millions of Britons, and all of these programmes greatly expanded during the interwar years. In 1880 the state scarcely intervened in the economy, save for the limitation of factory working hours for women and children and the enforcement of a narrow range of workplace safety laws. By the eve of World War II it was providing labour exchanges for the unemployed, arbitrating industrial disputes, setting minimum wages, controlling rents, and rationalizing smoke-stack industries that had fallen into decline. In short, by 1939 the state reached far more deeply into the daily lives of Britons than it had done fifty years earlier. There were several closely related reasons why this was so: the growing recognition at the turn of the century that poverty was even more a social than it was a moral problem, and that the state thus had a responsibility to take more active measures to fight it; the quest for greater 'national efficiency' and combat-readiness in an age of imperial competition; fear of social upheaval; the (often mistaken) assumption of elite politicians that the new mass electorate of the 1880s and the truly democratic electorate of the interwar years looked to more continuous state intervention to enhance the quality of their lives;

and, last but by no means least, the full-scale mobilization of World War I, which gave the state unprecedented control over the lives and livelihoods of its citizens and greatly enhanced its fiscal capacities. These capacities were not entirely scaled back after the Armistice; while military spending greatly declined between 1918 and 1938, social spending rose considerably, mainly thanks to the spiralling cost of unemployment insurance during the interwar Slump.

The fifth issue is the growth and the limits of the welfare state in the decades after World War II. After hostilities broke out in 1939 there was a rapid commitment to total war that led to a more efficient and extensive government intervention than the Great War had brought about. Whitehall coordination of capital and labour and the enormous budgetary commitments of the war years indicated that, for the first time, the central government assumed a permanent role for itself in economic planning. The experience of the Blitz and the successful wartime experiments in central coordination broadened public trust in the social utility of government initiatives and inspired rising expectations about what the state could and should do for its citizens. At the 1945 general election the two major parties committed themselves to the provision of a truly comprehensive system of social security that included universal health, unemployment, and old-age benefits as rights of citizenship. Public spending on these and other entitlements grew considerably over the next several decades. But the postwar welfare state did not inspire a dramatic social revolution, nor did many of its advocates intend it to do so. What it did help to ensure for its poorer citizens was simply that their (still relatively low) incomes would keep pace with rising living standards during the boom years of the 1950s and 1960s.

The sixth and final set of issues concerns the mixed results of the backlash against the perceived excesses of the welfare state from 1979 onward. It is true that the Conservative governments of the 1980s and 1990s 'liberated' the state from a number of the interventionist assumptions and practices of the previous thirty years: that the chief goal of fiscal policy ought to be the maintenance of full employment; that the 'commanding heights' of industry should be owned and managed by the state; that economic stability depended on the government's willingness to cooperate with producer groups, most notably the trade unions; and that welfare spending should continue to rise indefinitely. Still, it can hardly be said that the Thatcher and Major governments succeeded in their efforts to 'roll back' the welfare state. Overall public spending was scarcely lower in 2000 than it had been in 1970. While a combination of tax and welfare reforms helped to widen an income gap that had only slightly narrowed over the previous thirty years, spending on most social entitlements continued to grow. At the same time, the Conservative effort to subject local government and a broad range of other public services to fiscal discipline and market competition concentrated ever more power in the hands of the central government; thus under the Tories the centralizing tendencies of the postwar welfare state were reinforced rather than reversed. At present, a combination of related forces appears to be challenging the traditional notion that sovereignty ought to reside solely at Westminster: the communications revolution, economic globalization, the growing influence of the European Union over the domestic policies of its member states, devolutionist sentiment within the United Kingdom, and the rise to power of a New Labour government that sees some advantages in transferring to the British regions and to transnational institutions some of the immense power concentrated in Westminster and Whitehall.

Now that we have highlighted the basic themes of the book in rough chronological order, let us briefly reflect on some of the key points that we will be relying on in this effort to map the trajectory of British state development over the last three centuries or so. What were the pivotal moments in modern British state formation, and how adequately do the various theoretical approaches to state-building (whiggish-progressive, Marxist, war-centred, bureaucratic-rational, Foucauldian, and the like) take them into account? Like most other volumes that seek to stress the complexity and contingency of historical events, this book does not adhere to any one set of theoretical precepts. Indeed, one of its underlying premisses is that the historical record is simply too complicated and contradictory to fit comfortably within even the most capacious of theoretical models. That being the case, proponents of any one theory of state formation are bound to disagree with a good many of the generalizations and unarticulated assumptions to be found in the following chapters. But most of them, at least, are also likely to find plenty of grist for their respective mills, as the following brief sketch of the salient episodes in modern British state formation will probably make clear.

The first of those episodes is what for the sake of convenience is still commonly described as the 'Glorious Revolution'. Historians now generally agree that this was a much more gradual and deeply contested affair than the Whig interpretation bequeathed by the nineteenth century made it out to be. But there remains common agreement that a series of political events from 1688 to 1715 did indeed considerably enhance the powers of parliament at the expense of the crown, and in so doing created a new constitutional framework for the development of the state. Whether or not it established the 'rule of law' is much more debatable; the legal restriction of civil liberties that accompanied the Hanoverian succession, for instance, does not easily accord with a straightforward notion of libertarian 'progress'. But the 'Glorious Revolution' does accommodate a war-centred approach to state-building, for there is no doubt that it helped greatly to enhance the state's fiscal capacity for war-making. Britain's 'rise to greatness' during the 'long' eighteenth century (i.e. 1688–1815) owed virtually everything to its remarkable military success. In turn, its unrivalled ability to wage war over long periods of time and on an ever greater scale owed virtually everything to the establishment of a sound system of public finance. The key to that system's success was the prompt payment of interest to state creditors, and it was the relatively consensual means through which parliamentary government managed to raise taxes to unprecedented heights that kept the system creditworthy. Of course, the parliamentary tax regime provoked serious dissent, most spectacularly in the American colonies. But if the American rebellion is scarcely imaginable without that tax regime, so too is Britain's success in virtually every other major military conflict between 1689 and 1815.

A second major episode is the expansion of the state's role as a protector and facilitator of absolute property rights, particularly in the second half of the eighteenth century. The spectacular growth of parliamentary legislation indicates that the state came to the aid of a wide range of propertied interests in this era. Much of this was enabling legislation that benefited a great many people indeed by encouraging local interests to improve the economic infrastructure through the development of turnpikes and canals, and to provide what we would now consider basic amenities such as street-lighting and -cleaning. This sort of state-sanctioned activity squares with a rational/progressive model of development in which the state gives its seal of approval to a broad range of widely beneficial local initiatives. But other such initiatives were and remain more controversial, and more readily assimilable to a Marxist notion of development which highlights the role of the state as an enforcer of market mechanisms that privileged the patricians at the expense of the plebs. Many of the customary rights that had traditionally made the lot of the poor more endurable came under legal assault in this era, such as access to common lands, local controls on the price of bread, and apprenticeship regulations. At the same time, a growing volume of property offences became punishable by death. It would be too crude to damn the Georgian legal code as a blunt instrument of class oppression, however. Humbler folk could and readily did use it to seek redress of their grievances and to protect what little property they possessed. In short, war-centred, progressive, and Marxist explanations can all help us to make sense of eighteenth-century state formation, but only if they are employed selectively and (in so far as it is possible) complementarily.

Much the same can be said of the nineteenth century. Here, there are two broad issues that need to be taken into account: the uneven development of central and local government's regulatory functions in response to unprecedented population pressure and urban-industrial development, and the dramatic broadening of central and local responsibilities between roughly 1880 and the outbreak of World War I. After Waterloo, the waging of war was no longer the single-minded preoccupation of the state that it had been during the previous century. But the accretion of new state responsibilities to help meet the needs of a rapidly growing, urbanizing, and industrializing population was neither immediate nor uncontested. There was no popular mandate for government intervention in an age when most people, including the new voters created by the Reform Acts of 1832 and 1867, felt that the central and even the local authorities should be unobtrusive, inexpensive, and chiefly concerned with enforcing a minimal framework of law that allowed 'respectable' folk to get on with the business of living. Thus, for instance, there was nothing 'rational' or 'inevitable' about the halting process of factory regulation, which featured a series of protracted struggles that pitted powerful interests against each other. At the same time, this was by no means an era of untrammelled *laissez-faire*. Over the long run, central and local authorities did assume a fairly broad range of new regulatory powers in order to promote social discipline and to shield Britons partially from the impact of market forces. But they did so from a complicated mix of motives that is not easily assimilated to any one model of state formation: altruism; evangelical religiosity; the need to legitimate the power of what was still a narrow ruling elite; a Benthamite dedication to public utility and bureaucratic rationality; a disciplinary ethos that sought to root out fecklessness among the idle rich and the idle poor alike; and so on.

There were similarly complicated and sometimes contradictory reasons why the scope and cost of central and local government rather suddenly grew by an order of magnitude towards the very end of the century: imperial rivalry and the arms build-up precipitated by it; the widespread (and largely mistaken) notion within the political elite that a truly mass electorate needed to be bribed with primitive social entitlements; the political influence of well-entrenched pressure groups; and a pseudo-scientific preoccupation with the ostensible threat posed to the fitness of the nation by the unhealthy environment of the urban slums and the unhealthy habits of 'deviant' groups such as vagrants and homosexuals. All of these factors fit comfortably within one or another model of state development – elite legitimation within a

Marxist model, for instance, or the preoccupation with social 'deviance' within a Foucauldian one. But no single model can readily accommodate all of them.

Obviously, Britain's participation in the two world wars of the first half of the twentieth century had a profound impact on the size and scope of the state. Waging modern warfare on a truly global scale required full-scale mobilization, and with it the accretion to the state of powers over the property and the very lives of its citizens that would scarcely have been permitted to it under any other circumstances. Hence a war-centred theory of state development seems particularly apt for the period between 1914 and 1945. Yet the interwar period was marked by strenuous efforts to roll back the interventionist state that the Great War had brought into being. The military budget shrank precipitously, and so too did the regulatory mechanisms that had been furnished to the state in wartime. While social spending remained buoyant after the war, this was not so much a reward to humble Britons for their wartime sacrifices as it was a means of pacifying the millions of them who suffered from the chronically high unemployment levels of the Slump years. It is likewise possible to exaggerate the impact of World War II on the postwar extension of social insurance. There is little doubt that, this time round, full-scale mobilization prompted a widespread political commitment to enhancing the state's role as a social provider in the postwar world. In this limited sense, it is probably still accurate to talk of a 'consensus' that broader welfare provision ought to be a high priority at the central and local levels. But how much broader it should be was a deeply controversial question to which there was never a definitive answer. Certainly the legislative enshrinement of the principle of 'cradle-to-grave' social security as a right of citizenship marked a sharp break from prewar practices. Still, it can hardly be said that the 'Blitz experience' turned British state-building into a triumphal exercise in social solidarity. For the 'classic' welfare state of the late 1940s to the late 1960s did little to promote income redistribution, and therefore did little to promote egalitarianism. This came as no surprise, however, since most of its advocates simply wished to ensure that *relative* poverty did not substantially increase in an era of general affluence.

Even that more modest goal came into question during the economic crisis of the 1970s, when the perception of economic decline and an increasingly 'ungovernable' society helped to pave the way for the Conservative electoral victory of 1979. The rise to power of Margaret Thatcher and her supporters marks the last major episode in modern British state formation, and this episode is no more readily assimilated than its predecessors to any one theory of state formation. It is plausible to interpret the Conservatives' efforts to discipline the trade unions and free-spending local authorities, their eagerness to prop up sterling at the expense of industrial jobs, and their aggressive promotion of entrepreneurial values in both the private and public sectors as features of an ambitious effort to place the levers of state in the hands of a triumphal free-market capitalism. It is likewise possible to view their commitment to tougher policing, to preserving state secrecy, and to enhancing Westminster's and Whitehall's powers at local expense as evidence that moral authoritarianism remained as marked a feature of the state towards the end of the twentieth century as it had been at its beginning. But it is also worth stressing that, for all their rhetoric, the Conservative governments of the 1980s and 1990s were unable to cut the overall level of public spending, or even significantly to reduce the social-security functions of the state. Popular support for entitlements such as unemployment insurance and the National Health Service fortified them against frontal assaults, suggesting that even the most determined of governments in affluent western democracies cannot decisively reform the mechanisms of state unless they manage to overcome the habitual centrism of swing voters. In any case, however one wishes to interpret Thatcherism, or, for that matter, New Labour, it is safe to say that the British state continues to exert a far more palpable and widespread influence on its citizens than it did at any point before World War II. How it has become such a conspicuous presence in Britons' daily lives is the main story here. Now let us turn to the details of that story.

1

The Revolution Settlement and the Rise of the Fiscal–Military State

1688–1715

By the latter half of the eighteenth century Britons routinely spoke of 'the state' in a variety of contexts.[1] More often than not they used it as a shorthand for the three branches of the central government – King, Lords, and Commons – and the agencies that did their bidding. Commentators agreed that the chief responsibility of the state was to protect the lives and property of its subjects from tyranny. This the 'balanced constitution' of King, Lords, and Commons was alleged to do supremely well, precisely because the balance established among them prevented any one branch from sacrificing the nation to its own selfish interests. '[H]erein consists the true excellence of the English government', the Georgian jurist William Blackstone noted,

> that all the parts of it form a mutual check upon each other. . . . Thus every branch of our civil polity supports and is supported, regulates and is regulated, by the rest. . . . Like three distinct powers in mechanics, they jointly impel the machine of government in a direction different from what either, acting by itself, would have done; but at the same time in a direction partaking of each, and formed out of all; a direction which constitutes the true line of the liberty and happiness of the community.[2]

According to Blackstone and many others, it was the Glorious Revolution that had achieved this unique balance by subordinating the prerogative of the king to the rule of law. What set the British state apart from virtually all of its major counterparts on the Continent was that the monarch was statutorily obliged to manage it in cooperation with a permanent representative assembly that enjoyed real legislative power. One need not assume along with Blackstone and the Whig historians of the nineteenth century that the revolution settlement marked the Triumph of Liberty to agree with them that it ensured that the eighteenth-century British state would develop within a new political framework, in which sovereignty was vested in crown and parliament jointly rather than in the crown alone. Thus we need to examine that settlement in some detail before we trace the lineaments of that state. Five main points will be made about it here. The first is that the 'revolution' which disposed of James II was tentative and limited. Only after years of royal provocation did Anglican landed support for the Stuart regime collapse, and even then it was as much the military ambition of William of Orange as the rebelliousness of England's 'natural rulers' that brought about a change of kings. The ensuing transfer of power from throne to parliament, moreover, took decades to work itself out, and was incomplete. Secondly, the gradual growth in parliamentary influence was largely the result of massive involvement in foreign wars between 1690 and 1713. The wartime need to raise money on an unprecedented scale obliged the monarchy to trade a good deal of its executive authority for parliamentary support of the war effort. Thirdly, the waging of war led to massive increases in debt, taxes, and central offices, and thus a palpable growth in the state's involvement in the lives of its subjects. Fourthly, these same wartime trends prompted fears that parliament's independence was in peril. For it allegedly provided the crown and its ministers with enough patronage to bribe MPs into doing their bidding. Finally, the revolution settlement was central to the forging of a British and not simply an English state that relied on the use of force to stabilize its Scottish and Irish peripheries. A discussion of these five themes will demonstrate the messy complexity of the revolution settlement while introducing a number of salient issues that we will pursue more thoroughly in the next chapter.

A tentative transfer of power

While the 'Glorious Revolution' was but a propaganda slogan coined shortly after the event to justify the cashiering of James II in 1688,[3] it did indeed mark a major turning point in English constitutional development. As the relationship between crown and parliament evolved, it became obvious that the revolution settlement had created a parliamentary monarchy in which the royal prerogative was hedged in by a formidable body of statutes and customs. Indeed, by 1690 the only discretionary power that the king still enjoyed over the legislative actions of parliament was the royal veto, and while William III used this weapon several times, no subsequent monarch ever resorted to it again after 1708.[4] While the monarch retained the power to dissolve parliament, since the 1690s there has never been any doubt that it would be called back; parliament has convened in every year since 1689. The idea of parliamentary permanence was a novel one in the late seventeenth century. On the Continent, most representative institutions were dead or dying. Indeed, the main reason for the chronic political strife in England was that a series of Stuart kings treated parliament as an expendable institution, while the Anglican landed gentlemen who sat in it generally saw it as a crucial check on royal power.[5] The landed gentlemen decisively won this argument in 1688–9, and the legal framework of the 'balanced constitution' grew out of their victory. By 1716 it was illegal for the king to legislate outside of parliament, to dispense with acts that had been passed by parliament, or to supplement his ordinary revenue through the collection of taxes that had not been approved by parliament.[6] Still, it needs to be stressed that this dramatic shift in the balance of power was the result of a long series of piecemeal measures. It took much provocation to persuade England's 'natural rulers' that James II posed such a dire threat to their property and religion that he had to go. Having in effect cashiered him and denied the principle of hereditary succession, they could not bring themselves to admit what they had done. Having accepted William as *de facto* sovereign, they were initially reluctant to divest him of customary sovereign powers.

Prerogative power was in a flourishing state when Charles II died in 1685. The coronation of an openly Catholic monarch provoked no palpable unrest, despite the widespread Anglican belief that Catholicism and absolutism were two sides of the same coin. It was only James II's adoption of a long series of controversial measures in a short span of time that triggered rebellion against him. His chief blunder was to offend the religious sensibilities and to threaten the property of the Anglican political elite. He forced his policy of official toleration on Anglican gentlemen who truly believed that Catholics and Dissenters were fanatical enemies of the establishment in church and state, suspending penal laws against Catholics and Dissenters and appointing Catholic advisors at court and Catholic officers to the army. He dissolved parliament in 1687, mainly because of MPs' resistance to his religious policies, and then endeavoured to govern without it. The judiciary generally upheld James's power to suspend or dispense with parliamentary statutes, not least because it was packed with judges who were amenable to the king's wishes. Thus he feared no serious legal setbacks when he proceeded with an extensive remodelling of borough charters and the wholesale replacement of Anglican magistrates.[7] Here was an unprecedented assault on the Anglican gentry's accustomed monopoly of local government, and they viewed it as a threat to their sense of personal property in office, to their local status, to their religion, and to their liberty.[8] To many of them, the most alarming development of all was the birth of a Catholic heir to the throne in June 1688, and the thought of what a Catholic succession might portend. It is thus no coincidence that within three weeks of the birth, six noblemen and one bishop wrote to William of Orange, the Protestant Stadtholder of Holland and the husband of James II's Protestant daughter Mary, and invited him to come to England and help them deal with James.

William was all too happy to accept, because as the arch-enemy of Louis XIV he was eager to enlist England in his struggle to contain the French king's seemingly boundless territorial ambitions. In fact, it was Dutch military decisiveness even more than the resentment of the Anglican political elite that sealed James's fate and paved the way for a new constitutional settlement. William forced the issue in October 1688 by setting sail for England with an army of 15,000 men. The invasion guaranteed that France would declare war on the Dutch Republic, but William assumed that war with France was in any case inevitable, so it was best to take an enormous risk in hopes of enlisting England in the anti-French cause while Louis XIV's armies were preoccupied in an invasion of the Rhineland.[9] Fortunately, James II fled to France rather than staying to fight. With James thus conveniently out of the way, and with the country in a state of anarchy, it was obvious that William and Mary would succeed to the throne.

Their claim to sovereignty remained open to question, however, as did the extent to which that sovereignty would have to be shared with parliament. The initial phase of the revolution settlement was marked by controversy and confusion. The question of legitimacy, like the question of the subject's right to resist a hereditary monarch, was endlessly debated in 1689. In declaring William and Mary to be joint sovereigns, the Convention parliament preserved the blood connection to the Stuart dynasty. But the Stuart king had neither been deposed nor had he abdicated, and the legitimate heir to his throne was with him in France. In the end, most apologists for William and Mary embraced an explanation for what had happened that conveniently ignored the troubling issue of William's invasion: that James had 'vacated the throne', leaving the country in chaos and its 'natural leaders' with little choice but to sanction the accession of William and Mary as an act of self-defence.[10] 'Solving' the problem of legitimacy by avoiding it altogether made it easier for the more reluctant members of the Anglican elite to accept the necessity of a change of regime, because it absolved them of responsibility for what they had in fact acquiesced in: the cashiering of a hereditary monarch.[11]

The only thing clear at the outset of the new reign was that the balance of power between crown and parliament was as yet unclear. The Bill of Rights, enacted in 1689, was more a reflection on past events than a binding agreement that clearly subordinated the monarchy to the wishes of parliament. It declared illegal James II's use of the dispensing and suspending powers,[12] but there was no certainty that the law courts would agree, or that future monarchs would refrain from using them. There were, moreover, plenty of formidable royal powers that the Bill of Rights did not dispute, even though it was widely felt that the later Stuarts had systematically abused them: the king's right to name his own ministers, to make foreign and domestic policy, to veto legislation, and to summon, prorogue, and dissolve parliament.[13]

The most radical aspect of the Bill of Rights was the rejection of strict hereditary succession enshrined in the principle that future English monarchs could neither be Catholic themselves nor married to Catholics. But of course even this dictum stemmed from the assumption that the Stuart family would never regain the throne, and this was not an entirely safe assumption until the middle of the eighteenth century. Just as the Bill of Rights had declared that Mary's Protestant sister, Anne, would succeed to the throne after William and Mary died, the Act of Settlement (1701) vested the succession in the heirless Anne's nearest Protestant relatives in the German House of Hanover, and stated that future monarchs would have to be Anglican communicants. Through these two measures, parliament asserted its authority over the terms of the royal succession. There were fifty-seven Catholic Stuarts who had a stronger hereditary claim to the throne when George, the Elector of Hanover, ascended to it in 1714.[14] But while it was parliament that determined George's succession, the Stuarts felt they had good reason to contest it, and contest it they did. Ultimately, parliamentary statute had to be backed by the use of force to guarantee the Protestant succession.

The religious settlement of 1689 encompassed in the Toleration Act was just as limited and pragmatic as the political settlement between crown and parliament. The Act did not apply to Catholics, Jews, or Unitarians. What it did for Protestant Dissenters who believed in the Trinity was to remove the legal restraints on their civil liberty and freedom to worship that had been imposed on them shortly after the Restoration. Yet Dissenters would remain second-class citizens for another 150 years. They were not permitted to take degrees from Oxford or Cambridge, they were still legally obliged to pay tithes, and those who wished to qualify for political office had to demonstrate their 'occasional conformity' to the doctrines of the Church of England by taking Anglican communion. Dissenters would henceforth enjoy a freedom of worship that had been emphatically denied to them in the 1660s. Still, the 'toleration' granted under the terms of the Act was a far cry from the well-nigh universal religious freedom that James II had sought to secure for his non-Anglican subjects. The point was to mollify Dissenters while upholding the connection between the Anglican Church and the state by refusing to acknowledge that non-Anglicans had a *right* to equal treatment under the law.[15] By no means all Anglicans felt that the new regime was properly maintaining that connection, however. The establishment of the new regime had made a mockery of the doctrines of passive obedience and non-resistance to the monarch that many High-Churchmen still endorsed. When in 1690 clergymen were required to take oaths of supremacy and allegiance to William and Mary, some 400 of them refused to do so, along with six bishops, and open schism ensued between these so-called 'non-jurors' and the church majority.[16] Ultimately, the pragmatic religious settlement of 1689 helped to foster political stability by encouraging a relatively permissive environment in which the Anglican political monopoly remained intact while other sects were left unmolested. But in the short term, it was anything but stabilizing. For it left non-Anglicans feeling aggrieved and High Anglicans feeling politically and spiritually compromised.

War and the growth of parliamentary authority

The consequences of the 'Glorious' Revolution were thus not immediately clear. While the monarch had been replaced, the monarchy was still largely in control of the apparatus of state. William III (to whom Mary deferred when it came to political decision-making) still held formidable powers, and he had no qualms about using them. This was particularly true in the realm of foreign policy. Ultimately, he was less interested in England itself than in enlisting English resources in a military effort to stymie French territorial ambitions on the Continent.[17] For England, the ensuing Nine Years War (1689–97) was a war on an unprecedented scale. It had been centuries since the English had participated in a long series of campaigns on the Continent, and never had they fought in such large numbers: some 48,000 troops, along with another 20,000 or so foreign mercenaries in the pay of William's government. The struggle at sea was equally vast, with naval tonnage increasing by 60 per cent over the nine years of warfare. The British military effort only intensified thereafter, because Europe was at peace for only five years before a second coalition went to war to prevent Louis XIV seizing control of Spain and its empire. William III died shortly before the War of the Spanish Succession broke out in 1702. But he had been instrumental in forging the new Grand Alliance, and would have taken satisfaction in knowing that the Peace of Utrecht which ended the war in 1713 ensured that the French and Spanish thrones would remain separate, left France in very bad financial shape, and secured for Britain valuable colonies in North America and the Caribbean. This was arguably the first truly global conflict; British soldiers fought in the West Indies and Canada as well as the German states and the Iberian peninsula. The average number of troops involved in all theatres came close to 100,000 a year. By 1710, Britain's armed forces surpassed the combined population of the seven largest cities in the kingdom after London.[18]

Waging war on an unprecedented scale required an unprecedented financial effort. Simply provisioning William's continental armies was hugely expensive. For each year of war, William's troops in the Low Country required about 400,000 tons of provisions.[19] Supplying the navy was an even more complicated and expensive business. It was thus obvious from the outset of the war that William's chief domestic political task would be to find ways of raising enough money to keep his soldiers in the field and his sailors at sea.

The waging of war had long been the chief responsibility of European states. Over the course of the sixteenth and seventeenth centuries, technological innovations (muskets, reliable field artillery, etc.) combined with ever larger armies and war-making bureaucracies to make warfare a vastly more expensive business than it had ever been before.[20] Mainly in response to the growing demands of war, more centralized states emerged that extracted ever larger sums from their subjects.[21] In England's case, the Nine Years War marked a quantum leap in the state's tax-raising power. Taxes in England had remained at more or less the same level for some 300 years before the outbreak of the civil war. Cromwell managed to increase the tax burden very significantly, and it continued slowly to climb under the late Stuarts. But William III's war against France initiated a dramatic rise in the tax burden that continued right through the eighteenth century, a trend that we shall examine more closely in chapter 2.[22]

It was the war, far more than the statutory settlement of 1689–90, that limited royal authority and gave parliament joint control of the instruments of state. William desperately needed extra revenue, and the only feasible means of obtaining it was through parliamentary sanction.[23] First of all, even before the outbreak of war, it was clear that MPs had learned from the past and were not willing to grant William and Mary a sufficient ordinary revenue at the beginning of their reign to enable them to try to 'live of their own' and dispense with parliament altogether. With the onset of war, it was obvious that the crown would have no choice but to summon parliament annually, if for no other reason than to request the raising of additional revenues to keep the war machine in working order. MPs quickly got into the habit of appropriating new taxes to specific purposes, thus furnishing themselves with a potent new instrument of financial control. The principle of appropriation soon gave rise to the principle of 'annuality', by which the king's ministers would submit formal estimates of their financial needs for the year and the Commons would subject these estimates to careful scrutiny and then vote the sums they deemed adequate to supply them. The debates on the estimate and the 'supply' quickly became the main highlights of the annual session, serving as potent reminders that it was only through parliamentary consent that the machinery of state would be paid for.[24]

Parliament's control of the purse strings got tighter as war continued. The Public Accounts commissions of the House of Commons (1690–7, 1702–3) that were charged with the task of rooting out waste and corruption in wartime spending were vivid reminders that the Commons took seriously its new role as the government's permanent financial watchdog.[25] The crown and its ministers likewise had to get accustomed to the ritual indignity of asking parliament for additions to the Civil List – the list of sums appropriated for the payment of the civil expenditures of the crown – which MPs had deliberately underfunded in 1689. Thus the once commonplace notion that the crown should enjoy an independent revenue was a casualty of the war years.[26]

Parliament's financial assertiveness helped to win for it *de facto* control over the armed forces. This was technically still a prerogative of the crown, but by the late 1690s it was clear that it was a prerogative that could only be exercised effectively with parliamentary approval. It had already been undermined by the 1689 Mutiny Act (passed for one year only, but annually renewed thereafter), which placed under statutory control the martial law that was at the root of military discipline. But the question was not definitively settled until the late 1690s, when fierce parliamentary opposition forced William III to scuttle his plans for a larger peacetime army and settle for a small permanent force of 7,000 native-born soldiers to be funded exclusively from specific appropriations. William's acceptance of this humiliating compromise was a vivid illustration of parliament's new authority. Most of the major continental monarchies retained their control over the military until the end of World War I. But in peacetime Britain the army existed only on parliamentary sufferance, and whether at peace or at war its size and cost were ultimately determined by parliament.[27]

The rise of the fiscal–military state

The vast expense of the Nine Years War and the War of the Spanish Succession (1702–13) not only magnified the power of parliament at the expense of the crown. It also marked the first phase in the growth of a 'fiscal–military' state[28] that demanded ever greater sacrifices from its subjects. The state's main responsibilities had long been to protect private property, to conduct foreign policy, and to defend the realm. But the last of these responsibilities grew by leaps and bounds after 1689, as Britain continually found itself at war, more often than not with France. The social and political consequences of war-related government growth over the course of the eighteenth century are complicated, and will receive more detailed treatment in chapter 2. But since the growth of the fiscal–military state was triggered by William's military strategy, it should also be seen in part as a consequence of the revolution settlement and thus deserves some brief analysis here.

First of all, the two wars led to new intrusions into the lives of Britons in the shape of new taxes. Between the 1670s and 1715 British tax income *trebled*, a rate of increase far higher than that of the other major belligerents.[29] There were three types of levy that the Treasury relied on in this era, and indeed throughout the eighteenth century: the land tax, excise, and customs duties. The land tax, first imposed in 1692, fell heavily on landowners, as it was mainly assessed on the rents and produce of their estates.[30] It provided about 40 per cent of all tax revenue during the wars at the turn of the century.[31] Landed gentlemen acquiesced in the land tax because they enjoyed considerable control over it. A House of Commons dominated by landowners raised it to the hefty rate of four shillings in the pound during war, but unfailingly lowered it to minuscule levels in peacetime. The tax, moreover, was locally administered, so landowners did not feel they were being forced to pay up by the crown's revenue officers. In the long run, local control of the land tax meant frequent and in some regions chronic under-assessment as well as relatively high collection costs. But early in the century it hit some landowners very hard indeed, amounting to over 17 per cent of the rental value of the enormous Coke estates in Norfolk at the height of the War of the Spanish Succession, an immense tax bill for the time.[32] Not until the Napoleonic Wars would landowners again be obliged to carry a tax load of comparable weight.

Taken together, the two main indirect taxes, customs duties on imported goods and excise duties on a growing variety of domestic products, added up to over half of the state's tax income by the end of the Nine Years War. The war years saw a steep rise in the general level of import tariffs, but an even more noticeable rise in the number and rate of excise taxes. Excises were widely perceived as a grievous invasion of privacy and a potentially despotic weapon in the hands of the central government. They were first introduced in 1643 and mainly devoted to the upkeep of the widely despised standing army during the civil war. Unlike the land-tax collector, who was a familiar local man, or the customs agent, who imposed upon the mercantile community but was invisible to everyone else, the exciseman was an anonymous, perambulating, centrally appointed symbol of state authority, and a source of chronic irritation for the small business-people whose premises he inspected. The excise tax was a favourite of the central government, despite its bad reputation, because its yield was reliable, it was relatively 'invisible' to consumers (if not to producers), and its collection was comparatively efficient. Thus the excise lived on after the Restoration, and it grew by leaps and bounds during the war years at the turn of the century. Over the course of the 1690s, additional excises were laid on beer and other alcoholic beverages, on spices, malt, coffee, tea, tobacco, coal, timber, even salt. The extension of excise duties to items of mass consumption made even more obvious what some observers had noted as early as the civil war years: the abandonment of the custom that the poor should be exempt from the payment of taxes.[33] By the turn of the century the state was taking money out of all its subjects' pockets in order to fulfil its ancient but now greatly more burdensome task of waging war.

The enormous cost of war made it impossible for the government to pay for it out of taxes alone. Waging war on an ever more massive scale was dependent on the government's ability to raise loans through the accumulation of a permanent national debt. Tax receipts accounted for only 49 per cent of the extra revenue raised to finance the Nine Years War, and an increasingly smaller percentage thereafter: from 26 per cent during the War of the Spanish Succession down to only 19 per cent during the American War of Independence (1775–83).[34] The British state's success in war-making rested on the development of the so-called funding system, by which parliament 'funded' debts by earmarking specific taxes for the payment of interest to government creditors. As time passed, the government became an ever safer credit risk for investors, who became increasingly confident that parliament's allocation of tax money guaranteed them a safe return on their investments.

It took time for the funding system to establish itself. Long-term, funded borrowing was still only experimental during the Nine Years War, accounting for under 10 per cent of wartime expenditure. Funded loans, moreover, were not yet the bargain for the government that they would later become. Their average rate of interest was over 8 per cent, well above the legal maximum of 6 per cent that could be charged to individual debtors.[35] But the important point is that for the first time, parliament guaranteed the payment of interest on government debts, making them truly 'national' debts. The creation of the Bank of England by act of parliament in 1694, moreover, not only enhanced the supply of reliable paper money, but also helped to mobilize public credit in wartime. From the outset the Bank looked upon war finance as one of its chief items of business, regularly lending to the Treasury, under-writing Exchequer bills, and even remitting large sums of money to William's armies in the Low Country.[36]

It was not just the growth of debt and taxes that made the state increasingly perceptible to its subjects; it was also the rapid growth of a central bureaucracy to administer it. The number of government employees roughly trebled between 1660 and 1714. By the mid-1720s, there were over 12,000 state servants, and well over half of them were involved in the intrusive business of taxing the public.[37] Thus, while the responsibilities of the state were still few and the range of official tasks narrow by modern standards, the greatly expanded traditional task of war-making was now being met by a formidable central admin-istration whose presence was felt throughout the country. The eighteenth-century bureaucracy was far from being a 'civil service' in the modern sense of the term. Many of the principles that we now asso-ciate with public administration had not yet been firmly established: the concept that office was a public trust rather than private property, for instance, or that officers should be recruited via competitive exam-ination and paid strict salaries while they worked and pensions after retirement. Still, many important administrative tasks were already being efficiently performed, and often by officers whose terms of service were recognizably modern. The employees of the new depart-ments created at the turn of the century all worked under 'rational' terms of service: they held their appointments 'during the king's plea-sure' rather than for life, so it was possible to dismiss them; they were all paid realistic salaries; and they were all forbidden to top up those salaries through the taking of fees or other 'irregular' emoluments.[38] Thus a spirit of professionalism was already discernible in administrative ranks. The emergence of the fiscal–military state facilitated its growth by making value for money an even higher priority than it had been hitherto.[39]

By 1715, the size and scope of the central government were still minuscule by modern standards. But if the chronic warfare that stemmed directly from the revolution settlement did little to add to the state's responsibilities, it made its traditional responsibility to defend the realm far more extensive. The permanent and generally consensual partnership established between crown and parliament after 1688 made it possible for the state to meet the wartime challenge without provoking serious unrest. The Stuart efforts to collect relatively modest taxes without parliamentary consent helped to trigger civil war in the mid-seventeenth century. In contrast, the parliamentary monarchy forged in the 1690s was able to use a veritable army of tax collectors to bring in vastly greater sums without causing serious political disturbance.

Warfare, the 'influence of the crown', and the 'rage of party'

While the size and cost of the wartime state never came close to inspiring a civil war, it did become a source of serious conflict. Indeed, the period between 1690 and 1715 is notorious for its ferocious political partisanship, and most of the partisan issues related in one way or another to the growth of the wartime state. There are two ways of looking at the political schisms of these years. One is through the increasingly bitter party-political contest between the Whigs and the Tories. The second is through the ideological contest between the 'court' and the 'country'. Both types of schism deserve a brief examination here, because each of them stemmed from controversies surrounding the revolution settlement and the ensuing growth of the fiscal–military state.

Let us begin by looking at the 'rage of party', the dispute between Whigs and Tories that was increasingly preoccupied with issues pertaining to the state's war-making capacity. The terms 'Whig' and 'Tory' were pejoratives that stemmed from Scottish and Irish religious disputes, the two words denoting respectively the Protestant and Catholic extremists of those countries.[40] The terms first entered English political discourse during the Exclusion crisis (1679–81), when the MPs who sought to bar the Catholic James from the throne became known as Whigs and his staunchest defenders as Tories. The confessional and dynastic divisions between the two factions lived on into the 1690s. Tories sought to bolster the influence of the Anglican episcopacy and were keen to enforce the penal laws against Dissenters. Whigs, on the other hand, generally sought to play down the connection between church and state and favoured a more thorough toleration of Dissenters. Generally speaking, Tories had been considerably more reluctant to see James II go than had their Whig counterparts. Many of them had embraced the principles of passive obedience and non-resistance, if for no other reason than to preserve the sanctity of hereditary succession, and thus had difficulty living with the accession of William and Mary. Some of them longed for the return of the Stuarts. Whigs, on the other hand, were warm advocates of the Protestant succession.

Whigs and Tories were no less divided over the military consequences of the Revolution settlement than they were over its confessional and dynastic results. Early in his reign William III had sought to bring leaders of both factions into his counsels, but it quickly became obvious that the Whigs shared his enthusiasm for continental war while the Tories did not. The Whigs did not question William's broader strategic objectives, and did what they could to furnish him with the financial means to meet them. Most of the government's major creditors were impeccably whiggish in their politics. Many Tories, on the other hand, came to believe that the commitment to continental warfare was intolerably expensive, that it imposed a disproportionate share of the fiscal burden on land, and that the wartime growth of taxes and central offices was putting a dangerously large amount of patronage in the hands of the government, which to their minds seemed all too keen on using it to compromise the independence of the House of Commons. Considering this Tory suspicion of continental entanglements and the nefarious political consequences of government growth, it was not surprising that a Tory administration under the leadership of the Earl of Oxford pulled Britain out of the War of the Spanish Succession before the salient question of who would sit on the Spanish throne had been settled.

There was virtually no aspect of political life that was left untouched by the party disputes of this era. The Whig–Tory rivalry heated up the political atmosphere throughout the country, and enhanced the power of voters by giving them frequent opportunities to participate in parliamentary elections that offered them a real choice between parties. The electorate in England and Wales had been growing ever since Tudor times, thanks in large part to inflation, one effect of which was to vault more and more men over the relatively low property requirement for the franchise in some of the more open boroughs and in the counties. The intensive canvassing activities of the two parties pushed the size of the electorate upwards, and encouraged high rates of voter turnout. Indeed, at the three elections of 1710, 1715, and 1722, a higher percentage of the English male population cast votes than at any other election before the passage of the Second Reform Act in 1867.[41] At times the party strife grew so acrimonious that it threatened to split the normally unshakable social solidarity of the governing elite, spawning rival Whig and Tory balls and dinner parties.[42] The number of justices of the peace in most counties skyrocketed as the party in power sought to drown its opponents in a sea of partisan magistrates.[43] Bitter invective was rampant at election time, with Tories lambasting Whigs as the sleek minions of corruption while Whigs pilloried Tories as the instruments of the pope.[44] Thus, while the revolution settlement finally resolved the interminable dispute between the crown and the propertied elite over the balance of power between them, the ensuing party struggle within the elite split the political nation from top to bottom. The fiscal–military state helped to inspire the struggle, because that struggle centred on several war-related issues, most notably the extent of Britain's commitment to continental warfare, the growth of government patronage, and the incidence of war taxes.

The party battle was closely related to but never indistinguishable from the ideological battle at the turn of the century between 'court' and 'country'. By the mid-1690s, it is safe to say that most Tories were advocates of 'country' principles in opposition to wartime ministries that were dominated by Whigs. Still, there were always a good many gentlemen of whiggish principles in the House of Commons who could be relied on to vote in favour of 'country' measures from time to time. 'Country ideology' was never the sole preserve of either party, nor was the 'country' critique of the state ever as systematic or coherent as the word 'ideology' implies. Yet historians have adopted the phrase as a convenient shorthand for the main sources of opposition to the executive government in the decades in which the revolution settlement was taking shape. It betrayed an abiding fear that the executive government – the king, his ministers, and the central bureaucracy that was accountable to them – sought to establish a tyranny not by doing away with parliament, as the Stuarts had ostensibly tried to do, but by undermining parliament's independence through systematic corruption. According to 'country' observers, there were two especially potent sources of executive corruption: the use of patronage to purchase the support of MPs, and the growth of a politically dependent 'moneyed interest' at the expense of independent landowners. More than anything else it was the experience of war that shaped the 'country' line of argument, because both forms of 'corrupt influence' were seen to expand in tandem with the growth of the fiscal–military state.

'Country' critics first and foremost insisted that the growth of the wartime bureaucracy was enabling the government to bribe more and more MPs with the gift of lucrative offices and/or pensions. They assumed that placemen and pensioners – MPs who held public office or otherwise drew annual (and often very hefty) emoluments from the crown – had sacrificed their political independence in return for a regular income from the government, and that their number was swelling during the war years. These assumptions were not entirely accurate. While placemen and pensioners were likely to vote with government on most issues, this was mainly because many of them had been given places not as a bribe intended to convert them from opposition, but as a reward for an established track record of loyalty to the ministry of the day. Some of these loyalists, moreover, occasionally found themselves voting against ministers when their consciences prompted them to do so. Even so, the number of placemen and pensioners grew to worrisome levels during the war years. While between a fifth and a quarter of all MPs profited from a place or a pension in virtually every late-Stuart House of Commons, this percentage may have risen to as much as a third by 1714, while almost half of the peers had come to enjoy government patronage of one sort or another.[45]

'Country' measures to reduce the number of placemen in the Commons enjoyed some Whig as well as staunch Tory support, and the crown and its ministers had to fight hard to preserve this important form of the 'influence of the crown'. While general place bills invariably failed, efforts to exclude broad groups of government revenue officers succeeded, and their effect was to prevent by far the largest cadre of government employees from serving as MPs. Another 'country' effort to safeguard the independence of the Commons took the shape of bills to limit the duration of parliaments, thus narrowing the interval between elections in which the government could seek to purchase the support of additional MPs. This initiative bore fruit with the passage of the Triennial Act (1694).[46] In sum, the 'country' effort to curb the government's influence in the House of Commons was a dominant feature of parliamentary politics at the turn of the century, and more than anything else it was the growth of crown patronage in wartime that made this influence such a salient issue.

A second form of allegedly 'corrupt' influence that 'country' critics crusaded against within parliament and without was the influence of the 'moneyed interest' on the wartime state. The growing power of the Whig financiers of the City was seen to be nefarious because they were government dependants who owed their fortunes to the war machine constructed by William III and his advisors. Country gentlemen, in contrast, were the paragons of virtue because they were independent, deriving both their fortunes and their political influence from the possession of broad acres, a commodity over which the government exercised no control. While this 'country' obsession with landownership as the source of public virtue had ancient roots,[47] it was the frantic growth of a stock market that was increasingly devoted to the buying and selling of government securities that gave it particular force in the 1690s. 'Country' observers perceived the City as a threatening world where fortunes were mysteriously lost as quickly as they were made, where government officials abused their power in order to make a killing, and where a handful of greedy financiers, many of them foreigners or Jews, grew fat off the interest payments that a debt-ridden government had transferred to them from hard-pressed taxpayers. Politically speaking, the denizens of the City were thought to be utterly dependent on the ministers in power, because, as Bishop Burnet of Salisbury put it, 'whoever were Lenders to the Government, would by the surest Principle be obliged to support it'.[48] The government rewarded them handsomely for their services, however, allegedly at the direct expense of the country's 'natural rulers', who groaned under the weight of the wartime land tax and whose virtuous political influence was gradually being supplanted by that of the new money men.

There was just enough truth to the caricature of the City man as a privileged alien who profited immensely from his connections to the state to make it resonant. While there were probably at least 30,000 people investing in the stock market by 1720, many of them country gentlemen, professionals, and even shopkeepers, prominent City men probably did own a large percentage of total investments. As late as 1750, for instance, 93 per cent of the holders of five major stocks lived in London and the home counties, including City plutocrats such as the government financier Sampson Gideon, who left at his death the then colossal sum of almost £600,000.[49] Finally, there is little question that one reason why men like Gideon were able to accumulate such enormous personal wealth was because the tax system did not tap it to nearly the same extent as it did landed fortunes. The proceeds of the land tax that were earmarked for the servicing of the national debt *did* divert income from landed estates to City fundholders, although we have no way of knowing how much. Meanwhile, fundholders generally enjoyed a considerably higher return on their investments than the 5 per cent that the ownership of land was usually thought to yield.[50] There was thus a kernel of truth to the extravagant claims of 'country' polemicists that the state's heavy investment in warfare had spawned the rise of a new sectional interest that directly benefited from the wartime burdens imposed on taxpayers in general and the landed classes in particular.

The 'country' effort to cleanse the nation of 'corruption' fell short in many respects. But it did help to ensure that parliament would remain a more or less independent check on the power of the court and its ministers. The Triennial Act and the several different place acts limited the growth of the 'influence of the crown' in the House of Commons, just as close scrutiny of the government's finances and statutory reduction of the standing army made it clear that the revolution settlement would not end with the creation of a new sort of over-mighty executive power. As John Brewer has noted, the 'Glorious' Revolution was just as much a 'country' as it was a Protestant 'revolution', the point of which was to limit the central government's ability to meddle in the lives of its citizens as well as to save the country from the perceived dangers of Catholic absolutism. But protecting that 'revolution' from its foreign enemies required acquiescence in a war effort that necessitated an enormous growth of state power. 'Country' critics were able to accept this basic fact and still manage to assert themselves in ways that served notice to the court and its ministers that parliament was jealous of its hard-won sovereign powers and was not about to hand them back.[51]

The forging of a British state

Thus far, this story of the revolution settlement has been a bloodless and English one in which crown and parliament managed peacefully to forge a series of formal and informal power-sharing arrangements over the instruments of state. The story looks radically different from an Irish or Scottish perspective. In these countries, the Glorious Revolution was marked by sectarian strife and full-scale warfare. It led to a Protestant monopoly of political power in Ireland which was actively encouraged by an English government that enjoyed extensive powers over Irish political affairs. It also led to the extinction of an independent Scottish state, enshrined in the terms of the 1707 Act of Union that fused England and Scotland together in a British state within which many Scots felt they held only second-class citizenship. In retrospect, the victory of Williamite forces in Ireland and Scotland marked a huge step in the long process of expansionism within the British Isles by which the English sought simultaneously to exploit and to protect themselves from their neighbours.

English expansionism was of course already a very well-established theme in the history of the British Isles prior to 1688. In the sixteenth century the Tudor kings had forced the institutional and even the linguistic integration of Wales with England in response to the perceived threats posed by brigandage in the border counties and by the power of the Marcher lords. There had been English invasions of Ireland as early as the twelfth century, and the establishment of Anglo-Scottish settlements there had had the blessing of the late Tudors and early Stuarts. Ireland's political autonomy had already been undermined by Poynings' Law of 1494, which granted the English Privy Council effective control over Irish legislation. English political control was built into the structure of the executive branch of the Irish government at Dublin Castle, which was headed by a viceroy appointed by the English government, and who was himself usually an Englishman.[52]

From the Restoration onward, the twin goals of English policy towards Ireland and Scotland were to prevent any foreign powers using the Celtic lands as a back door for the invasion of England and to foster the growth of English agriculture and manufactures by legally discriminating against potential Scottish and Irish rivals. As far as the court and the Westminster parliament were concerned, the point remained the same before and after 1688: to manipulate Scotland and Ireland for the sake of English security and of the English economy. But if English ends remained the same, English means changed radically in the wake of William's invasion. For the invasion itself spawned events in Ireland and Scotland that led to massive English intervention.

In Ireland, Protestants who felt even more threatened than their English counterparts by James II's catholicizing efforts enthusiastically raised troops for William III and seized several walled towns, most notably Derry. The war in Ireland escalated in March 1689 when James II arrived there from France, hoping to invade England with French assistance after defeating the Williamite forces in Ireland. William stymied these plans, landing in Ireland with a large army and defeating James's forces at the Boyne in July. James fled back to France, where he remained for good, but the war in Ireland raged on for another year.

The Treaty of Limerick finally signed in 1691 gave decent terms to the Jacobites (i.e. Catholic supporters of James), including a measure of religious toleration and protection for the property of the Jacobite soldiers who remained in the country. But the Irish parliament refused to honour it. Many Irish Protestants felt that repression and not lenity was required in order to guarantee the future security of their lives and property against the perceived Catholic threat. So in the next several decades the Dublin parliament passed a series of penal laws making it illegal for Catholics to buy land, forcing partible inheritance on Catholic families, barring Catholics from the professions and from the right to vote or to hold political office, disarming them, forbidding them to open Catholic schools or to arrange for the education of their children abroad, banishing Catholic bishops and requiring Catholic priests to register and take an oath of loyalty to the state. Only 14 per cent of all Irish land remained in Catholic hands in 1700, and a mere 5 per cent eighty years later.[53] The virtual destruction of the Catholic nobility and gentry meant that for many years there was no leadership for a Catholic alternative to the Protestant Ascendancy.[54] In short, the Williamite revolution in Ireland was hugely divisive. It of course remains so to this day in Northern Ireland, where King Billy's victory at the Boyne stirs up proud memories of Protestant triumph on one side and bitter ones of confiscation and disenfranchisement on the other.[55] The sectarian feud that culminated in the penal laws was by no means the invention of the English state. But there is no question that the projection of English state power in Ireland during the reigns of James II and William III made it that much fiercer.

In Scotland, the revolution settlement ultimately led to the elimination of a separate political identity. The immediate results of William's invasion were more dramatic north of the Tweed than they were south of it. The Scottish Convention parliament, called by William and dominated by Whigs and Presbyterians, declared that James had forfeited his crown, and it abolished Episcopalianism in favour of an established Presbyterian Church. Obviously, as the hereditary king of Scotland and nominal head of clan Stewart, James II enjoyed a great deal of support in Scotland, and Scottish Jacobites, many of them Highland clansmen, responded to the excesses of the Convention parliament by taking up arms against William. The ensuing Highland War continued for nearly two years, featuring numerous acts of treachery, most notably the massacre of some forty Glencoe Macdonalds by Williamite Campbells.

The outcome of the struggle in Scotland was chronic political instability. The establishment of a rigid Presbyterian regime did nothing to salve the wounds of the defeated Jacobites. William's English ministers habitually sought but often failed to control the Edinburgh parliament through patronage and bribery. A terrible famine in 1696–8, responsibility for which Jacobites sought to lay on the shoulders of the new men who ruled in Edinburgh, deprived Scotland of perhaps a full third of its population through death and emigration. Scottish politicians who lost their shirts in a futile attempt to found a trading company on the isthmus of Darien in Spanish America insisted that the English government had gone out of its way to foil the scheme. While Lowland Scots pressed for greater access to English markets, the Westminster parliament laid stiff tariffs on some of the Lowlands' leading products – coal, salt, and linen. Finally, in 1704, the Edinburgh parliament declared that it would exercise what it perceived to be its right to pick its own successor to Queen Anne if Scotland were not granted free trade with England. More than anything else, it was this declaration that led to the creation of a unified British state. MPs at Westminster, fearful of a Stuart restoration in Scotland, sought first and foremost to force their counterparts at Edinburgh to acknowledge the Elector of Hanover's claim to the joint crowns of England and Scotland. They started out by talking tough, threatening to ban the import of Scottish cattle and to treat all Scots in England as aliens if Scotland refused to negotiate a treaty of union. Ultimately, the English offered several carrots along with this stick, but the 1707 Act of Union was nevertheless highly controversial in Scotland. The prospective advantages of free trade and a liberal application of English patronage prompted a majority in the Edinburgh parliament to vote for its dissolution. But that Scotland had actually gained from the voluntary cession of its political autonomy was long a matter of debate.

The creation of a free-trade zone that covered the entire island was a singular achievement in a Europe whose economic structure was still dominated by internal tariffs, and it was certainly a better deal for Scottish enterprise than the alternative: an economic war with England that it had no hope of winning.[56] But free trade yielded few discernible short-term benefits north of the Tweed, while it was obvious to many from the very beginning that Scotland would be under-represented in a British parliament in which it was given only forty-five MPs and sixteen peers. It was true that the Act of Union enabled Scotland to preserve its own institutional distinctiveness in several important respects, most notably in the perpetuation of a separate state church and legal structure. The British parliament incorporated the Scottish parliament, but not the Scottish nation, which thus retained some important badges of a separate identity.[57] Still, even many Scottish proponents of the treaty would have preferred to see it sanction a looser federation that gave Scotland greater control over its own political destiny. Meanwhile, other Scots expressed their opinion of the terms of the treaty by rioting in the streets of Edinburgh while the parliament determined its own fate. Clearly, the Union did not inspire an immediate sense of British national consciousness. A few years after it was consummated, even such an enthusiastic supporter as Daniel Defoe would conclude that 'a firmer union of policy with less union of affection has hardly been known in the whole world'.[58]

In any case, it was immediately obvious that the English had got what they wanted. The Act of Union made Scotland a much smaller security risk than it would have been had a separate Scottish parliament been in a position to dispute the Hanoverian succession; incorporation made the political management of the Scottish magnates considerably easier than it hitherto had been; and the free-trade zone gave English producers the easiest possible access to Scottish markets.[59] The main goal of English security was ultimately achieved, but only (as we shall see) after it was vigorously contested by mostly Scottish Jacobites, and only with the creation of a British state that – in spite of its best efforts – could never entirely ignore its Scottish subjects.

It should be clear at the end of this broad overview that the impact of the revolution settlement on the state was dramatic but by no means immediately obvious. The transfer of the throne to William and Mary was not a bold statement of parliamentary supremacy but an awkward operation whose immediate constitutional implications were less clear than whiggish accounts of it have traditionally suggested. It was William's reliance on parliament for wartime revenue that enhanced its executive powers. Chronic warfare led to the growth of a much larger state that took away far more from its subjects in the shape of taxes than the 'absolutist' Stuart monarchs had ever dreamt of appropriating. Thus, while the need to obtain parliamentary consent curbed the prerogative power of the crown, it paved the way for the dramatic expansion of a fiscal–military state that dominated the political controversies of the eighteenth century, much as the proper limits of the royal prerogative had dominated those of the seventeenth.

2

The Fiscal–Military State and its Discontents

1715–1815

The surface appearance of the British state after the battle of Waterloo was much the same as it had been at the end of the War of the Spanish Succession. The waging of war and the protection of property remained the dominant functions of the central government all the way through the eighteenth and well into the nineteenth century. But the immense growth in the scope and cost of warfare and the increasingly complex ways in which the state sought to protect and facilitate property rights made it a very perceptible presence in the lives of Britons. The ways in which it carried out these responsibilities also inspired bitter political controversy, both at home and in the growing empire.

Five issues deserve especially close attention here. The first is the growth of parliamentary supremacy within the 'balanced constitution'. Perhaps the most dramatic sign of parliament's newly established authority over the instruments of government was the Hanoverian succession itself. While the Jacobites posed a vigorous challenge to parliament's self-appointed authority to name the monarch, they were finally suppressed in 1745. Meanwhile, a fairly smooth working relationship had been established between parliament and the Hanoverian kings, who were usually (but not always) reluctant to use the prerogative powers that they still enjoyed. At the same time, the just limits of the 'influence of the crown' remained a matter of serious controversy, especially since the wartime growth of patronage seemed to provide the king and his ministers with ever more opportunities to entice MPs into voting their way on important issues. Nevertheless, it became increasingly clear that parliament was the senior partner in its working relationship with the monarchy.

The second issue is the remarkable growth of the British war machine. Parliamentary supremacy provided the bedrock for a government borrowing system of matchless efficiency which in turn fostered Britain's spectacular military success and hence the growth of its empire. Servicing the national debt generated by this funding system became an immense burden to Britons, who by the end of the Napoleonic Wars were the most heavily taxed people in Europe. Meanwhile, the wartime state assumed vast powers over the lives and liberties of a rapidly growing number of men-at-arms.

The third issue is the widespread political discontent inspired by the growing wartime state. Its perceived excesses spawned vigorous protest movements that made the last three decades the most tumultuous of the century. It was above all the taxation issue in the wake of the Seven Years War (1756–63) that prompted the American colonists to challenge parliamentary sovereignty. The American example inspired a similar protest movement in Ireland that was only temporarily stifled by the grant of internal sovereignty. In England, the ostensible corruption of the wartime state provoked the first formidable parliamentary reform agitation of the century. While the radical protests of the 1790s were chiefly inspired by the French revolutionary promise of universal rights (for men, at least), as time passed they became increasingly preoccupied with the allegedly corrupt and oppressive power of a British state that used its quarrel with revolutionary France as a pretext for suspending the liberties of its subjects whilst loading them with an intolerable burden of debt and taxes.

The fourth issue is the formidable strength of the Georgian state as a guardian and facilitator of property rights. In a society that made a fetish of private property, the state's customary responsibility to protect it assumed broad dimensions. Indeed, at first glance the eighteenth-century state looks like a legislative dictatorship designed not merely to protect the property of the haves, but to enable them to amass more and more of it at the expense of the have-nots. The criminal code dictated that the down-and-out could be and sometimes were hanged for the theft of goods of only paltry value. The propertied gentlemen who dominated parliament gave their statutory approval to the erosion of several paternalist customs which in the past had helped to ease the plight of humbler folk, but which most MPs now viewed as impediments to the growth of capital. Nevertheless, it would be too crude to damn the Georgian state's penal and regulatory practices as so many variations on the theme of class oppression. The criminal law was not as ferocious in practice as it looked on paper, and the poor encountered it as plaintiffs as well as defendants. Moreover, the phenomenal growth of parliamentary legislation in this era reveals that the state aided a wide variety of propertied interests, and the social benefits to be derived from many of them (turnpike trusts and lighting commissions, for instance) were broadly shared.

The fifth and last major issue is the supremacy of local administration in the Georgian era. The widespread assumption that centralization almost inevitably led to tyranny guaranteed that the chief responsibility for virtually all of the (still relatively few) legitimate functions of government other than war-making was vested in local authorities. Custom as well as statute gave justices of the peace the power to intervene in practically every aspect of parish life. Parliament left entirely to local initiative the provision of basic amenities such as the paving, cleaning, lighting, and policing of streets. While initiative was conspicuous in some places, it was conspicuously lacking in others. But the multiplication of local improvement commissions suggests that the general standard rose considerably. By the end of the century, most propertied Britons were paying substantial local rates in addition to centrally imposed taxes, most notably in support of the poor law that granted relief to many of the underprivileged.

'Providence has so arranged the world that very little governance is necessary', the Earl of Shelburne declared in a quintessentially Georgian view of the limited role of the state.[1] But while eighteenth-century Britons were indeed dramatically less 'governed' than their progeny in the modern era, these five themes also make it clear that they were far from being ungoverned. The central authorities sent hundreds of thousands of them to war, levied taxes on all of them, and presided over a complicated framework of local government that touched their daily lives at a number of points.

Parliamentary supremacy in practice: the Georgian constitution

With the great constitutional battles of the seventeenth century now behind them, the Hanoverian monarchy and the legislature settled into a fairly comfortable working relationship. The crown's prerogative powers had already been formally trimmed and considerably eroded in practice even before the accession of George I, which was of course itself dictated by parliamentary statute. Generally speaking, George and his successors were not inclined to jeopardize the delicate balance of the constitution on which their very crowns rested. But it is important not to paint too whiggish a picture of constitutional relations in the Georgian era, because they were fiercely contested from without and occasionally strained from within. In 1715 and again in 1745 the Jacobites took up arms against a dynastic settlement that they considered illegitimate precisely because it had sought to establish parliamentary supremacy over the terms of succession. The 'influence of the crown', moreover, remained a vital political issue throughout the century, not least because George III did not hesitate to risk political crises by defending what he deemed to be his rightful prerogative. Still, the mutual interest in upholding the social hierarchy that the first three Georges shared with a narrow political elite helped to preserve a constitutional balance in which parliament had come to bear most of the weight.

As the historian Paul Monod has pointed out, 'the eighteenth-century state was never fully successful in finding a secure form of legitimation for itself'.[2] This was because there was no strong retort to be made in response to the argument that parliament had diminished the power of the monarchy by violating the hereditary succession on which its legitimacy had supposedly rested. This argument, commonly made by Jacobites and non-jurors alike, was a painfully long time dying.[3] Some of its proponents took the argument to the point of rebellion against the Hanoverian regime in 1715 and once again in 1745. The popularity of the first Jacobite rebellion in Scotland made obvious the widespread disappointment with the immediate fruits of the Union. Some 20,000 Scots took up arms on behalf of the 'Old Pretender', encompassing 8 per cent of the adult male population, as against the mere 2.5 per cent who turned out in support of George I.[4] The 'loyalists' ultimately prevailed, thanks in large part to James Edward's indecisiveness and to the absence of the French military support he had expected to receive. Thirty years later, his son, Charles Edward, managed to raise a small army in Scotland and advance as far south as Derby before being forced into the long retreat that ended in slaughter at Culloden. It was deeply embarrassing that the British army had shown itself so ill-prepared to encounter Bonny Prince Charlie's makeshift force. The government sought to recover some of its lost pride by executing about 120 Jacobite officers and transporting many ordinary clan soldiers, by vastly extending the military roads that had first been constructed in the Highlands in the wake of the Fifteen, by passing a Disarming Act that forbade the possession of arms, the wearing of tartans, and even the playing of pipes, and by striking at the roots of social organization in the Highlands through the abolition of military land tenures and the heritable jurisdictions that had served as the basis for the rebel chieftains' power.[5]

Thus, the suppression of Jacobitism showed that the Hanoverian state was willing to flex its formidable coercive muscle when it was threatened with dissolution. This had been no less true in 1715 than it was thirty years later. The Fifteen marked the establishment of a virtual Whig monopoly of office, for it enabled the Whigs to paint their opponents as traitors after some of the leading men in the Tory party decided to cast their lot with the Pretender. The new Whig regime consolidated its hold on power by clamping down on popular opposition through the Riot Act, which made it a capital offence for anyone within a crowd of twelve or more people to fail to disperse within an hour of being told to do so by a magistrate. It initiated a long series of prosecutions for seditious libel, suspended habeas corpus, and passed a series of measures – the Registration, Constructive Recusancy, Smuggling, and Black Acts – that were at least partly intended to wipe out any residual traces of Jacobite treason. Finally, it passed a Septennial Act (1716) that discouraged popular political activity by reducing the frequency of parliamentary elections. Thus the Whigs, such hearty advocates of libertarianism in 1688–9, had turned into strict disciplinarians, not least because the Jacobite threat had made them deeply mistrustful of political clamour.[6] In the process, they had shown that the new Hanoverian state was not afraid to bolster its dubious legitimacy through the use of force.

With the dynastic struggle finally settled once and for all, Hanoverian monarchs and their parliaments quickly accustomed themselves to cooperating with each other. It helped that the first two Georges were relatively unambitious kings and that the party rivalry at Westminster had all but fizzled out. There was generally a strong congruence of interest between these monarchs and their Whig ministers. Still, it would be a mistake to assume that George I and George II were mere figureheads. Contrary to popular belief, they did not spend all – although they certainly spent a lot – of their time gourmandizing and womanizing. Both of them often used their formidable influence over the framing of British foreign policy to ensure that it would not neglect the defence needs of vulnerable Hanover. Indeed, the Hanoverian strategic connection was the source of intermittent controversy in the Commons, where many MPs insisted it was subordinating British interests to German ones.[7] The first two Georges' powers of assertion were as nothing, however, compared to those of the third. When the young George III acceded to the throne in 1760, he sought to transcend factional bickering by inviting the hitherto proscribed Tories back to court and appointing his own trusted advisors to positions of influence. His ambitions provoked a major crisis when in 1762 he appointed as First Lord of the Treasury his old tutor, the Earl of Bute, and then presided over a systematic purge of the Whig Old Guard from the political offices that they had grown accustomed to thinking were theirs by right. George's insistence that Bute had the power to govern without the Whigs was quickly proved wrong, and what followed was a long series of revolving-door ministries that alternately failed to maintain the support of the king or of the Commons majority. George III and the Whig factions whom he detested both insisted that they were struggling to preserve the balance of the constitution – the Whigs from monarchical tyranny, the king from aristocratic dictation.[8] The outcome of this struggle was an uneasy compromise, in which nobody challenged the king's prerogative to name his own ministers while it became obvious that any such ministers who could not muster a reliable majority in the Commons would ultimately be compelled to resign.

This compromise famously broke down in 1784, when George III went to extraordinary lengths to bring down the Fox–North coalition government. After instructing the Lords to vote down Charles James Fox's India Bill, which he feared would keep the Whigs in office forever by putting a huge mass of Indian patronage into their hands, he installed the younger William Pitt as First Lord of the Treasury, dissolved parliament, and then threw all of the crown's patronage powers behind an electoral effort to oust as many coalition MPs as possible from the next House of Commons. The strong majority that Pitt enjoyed in the new House showed that the king's constitutional influence was still formidable.[9] It also convinced Fox and virtually all other Whigs that the 'influence of the crown' in the Commons was still 'great and extensive', and that it continually sought to subvert the balance of the constitution.[10] Whig fears of the parliamentary 'influence' that the crown enjoyed through its patronage powers were exaggerated. George III's chief source of patronage, for instance, the Civil List, greatly deteriorated in value over the course of his reign, and when it came under parliamentary regulation in 1782 the last vestige of the crown's independent financial power was eliminated.[11] Still, the Whigs had good reason to lament the king's power to name his ministers, for it helped to consign them to the political wilderness for well over forty years.[12]

Despite George III's occasionally vigorous assertion of his remaining prerogatives, however, there was a fundamental unity of purpose between king and parliament that prevented a recurrence of the violent crises that had dominated the seventeenth century. For he and his immediate predecessors were predisposed to cooperate with MPs in what they perceived to be their chief domestic responsibility: the protection of private property. One reason why the Stuarts had been booted out was because they were deemed to pose a threat to it, but their Hanoverian successors were widely seen as its chief upholders, mainly because they respected parliament's hard-won supremacy in the making of laws and the raising of taxes. It was indisputable that parliament now governed alongside the monarch, and parliamentary government throughout the eighteenth century was government of and by a fairly narrow propertied elite, if not exactly government for their behalf alone.

Propertied domination of the House of Commons stemmed from the disproportionate influence of large property owners within an ancient and maddeningly complicated electoral system. The terms of the franchise that determined the election of the 558 MPs who sat in the Commons varied greatly from place to place.[13] While the counties returned two members each on a uniform forty-shilling franchise, the borough vote stemmed from an ancient hotch-potch of customs and privileges so obscure as to guarantee that after every general election there would be a good many disputed returns that would have to be adjudicated in parliamentary committee. There were four main types of borough franchise, but endless variation in practice within each type: the freeman boroughs, which returned nearly half of all English borough representatives; the inhabitant householder boroughs; the burgage boroughs, where the right to vote was attached to ownership of specific properties; and finally the corporation boroughs, in which the franchise was vested in a self-perpetuating oligarchy. There was huge variation in the size of electorates. Several thousand men were eligible to vote in most counties, where long-term inflation had created a great many forty-shilling freeholders, as well as in more populous householder boroughs such as Westminster. On the other hand, the electorates of such infamous boroughs as Dunwich – most of which was now submerged in the North Sea – and Old Sarum – an overgrown pasture – scarcely outnumbered the MPs returned from them.

Those men who were entitled to vote, moreover, generally had very few opportunities to do so. The establishment of a Whig oligarchy in the wake of the Fifteen led to a narrowing of the electorate and a steep drop in contested elections. The Commons committee that sat in judgement on election petitions was blatantly biased, not only routinely seating Whigs over Tories but also doing what it could to narrow the size of the electorate in question.[14] Most parliaments, moreover, ran close to the seven-year limit that had been dictated by the Septennial Act, and there were few electoral contests, mainly because the longevity of parliaments had the effect of making contests enormously expensive for the candidates who fought them. Whereas 65 per cent of the counties went to the poll in 1705, only 7.5 per cent did in 1747. In 1806, the Shropshire electorate enjoyed its first opportunity to vote since 1722.[15]

The narrow terms of the electorate and the paucity of electoral contests combined to reduce the accountability of the House of Commons and to guarantee that it was dominated by gentlemen of substantial property. Indeed, many aristocratic families firmly controlled smaller boroughs, where patronage and deference combined to give their candidates safe passage into the Commons. Aristocratic influence over MPs grew considerably over the course of the century. Peers at least partially controlled 105 seats in 1715, over 200 in 1784, and 236 in 1807.[16] Still, the electoral system was not as narrow and corrupt as at first glance it appears to have been. The 250,000–300,000 electors were not easily manipulated. While voters expected candidates to treat them to beef, ale, and other favours at election time, few of them simply gave their vote to the highest bidder. Relatively few seats were absolutely 'safe' for borough patrons. Candidates who enjoyed the support of a local magnate and/or the government were expected to be attentive to issues of local concern, and were occasionally ousted by the voters when it appeared that they had put the interests of their patron ahead of those of the local community. The unenfranchised, moreover, frequently played important incidental roles in electoral contests, heckling and huzzaing at the hustings and joining in on the treating, sometimes protesting their marginal status by staging their own mock elections.[17]

While the electorate declined over the course of the 'long' eighteenth century, moreover, the decline was not as precipitous as was once supposed. The best estimate thus far is that in England and Wales it fell from 23.9 per cent of adult males in 1715 to 14.4 per cent in 1831. The Reform Act of 1832 only brought the total back up to 18.4 per cent, so for a long stretch of the eighteenth century the electorate was actually larger than it was in the 'decade of reform', when popular politics is sometimes alleged to have come into its own for the first time.[18] Finally, one of the greatest scandals of the Georgian electoral system may not have been all that scandalous after all. Some of the largest cities in the nation, most notably Birmingham, Manchester, Leeds, Halifax, Stockport, and Wolverhampton, were not entitled to return MPs, because they lay outside the ancient borough boundaries. But a good many MPs held property or transacted business in or near cities such as these, and those who did so could be relied on to promote local interests.[19] In short, it is a mistake to dismiss the Georgian electoral system as a sick joke that the ultra-privileged played on the mass of the population. Most Georgian Britons felt that one of the chief duties of a representative assembly was to protect property from the potentially arbitrary power of the monarch. Many of them assumed that the MPs returned by a narrow electorate performed this task reasonably well, chiefly because these MPs were large property holders in their own right.

The golden age of the fiscal–military state

Warfare remained the chief function of the state from the beginning to the end of the eighteenth and indeed well into the nineteenth century. Parliamentary supremacy within the constitutional framework, itself largely a product of the chronic warfare of the 1690s and beyond, helped to make the British state the most efficient war machine in Europe. It provided the financial support necessary to wage war on an ever more massive scale through its unrivalled ability to keep itself creditworthy by allocating fresh taxes to the prompt payment of interest on its war debts. It was parliamentary finance as much as any other factor that accounts for the contrast between the English humiliation of 1667, when a Dutch fleet managed to sail to Chatham, burn several warships, and tow away the magnificent *Royal Charles*, and the glory of 1763, when in acknowledgement of Britain's military supremacy the Peace of Paris ceded it the dominant position in North America, India, West Africa, and the West Indies.[20]

The great wars of the turn of the seventeenth century marked simply the first phase of what turned out to be a very long contest for military supremacy between Britain and France (occasionally in alliance with Spain) that only ended at Waterloo. Britain and France were directly at war with each other almost literally half of the time between 1689 and 1815. Two sources of conflict were especially prominent: French territorial ambitions on the Continent and global trade rivalry. The British were most likely to attempt to check what they deemed to be French aggression when it appeared to threaten Hanover and/ or open navigation through the Scheldt estuary, Britain's main trade route into western Europe. In an age when overseas trade was seen as a zero-sum game, the British were also very aggressive in trying to take away colonies, chiefly from their French and Spanish rivals, and they were spectacularly successful in doing so. Table 2.1 highlights Britain's military achievements during the 'long' eighteenth century, when its only major setback came in the American War of Independence. Strategically speaking, there is no question that Britain won this second hundred years' war. France remained a formidable nation throughout the nineteenth century, but it was Britain that emerged as the world's greatest naval, commercial, financial, industrial, and imperial power.[21]

While the mobilization effort required to wage the Nine Years War had seemed unsurpassable to contemporaries, it was dwarfed by those necessitated by each subsequent conflict. The average annual number of men under British arms grew enormously from one war to the

Table 2.1 Britain's major wars and their outcomes, 1689–1815

War	Main belligerents	British gains and losses
Nine Years War (1689–97)	England, Spain, Austria, and Dutch republic vs. France	*Gains*: French recognition of William III as king of England; *status quo ante* on Continent
War of the Spanish Succession (1702–13)	Britain, Holy Roman Empire, and Dutch republic vs. France and Spain	*Gains*: Gibraltar and Minorca; guaranteed separation of French and Spanish thrones
War of Jenkins's Ear/War of Austrian Succession (1739–48)	Britain, Dutch republic, and Habsburg Empire vs. France and Spain	*Gains*: *status quo ante*, including non-partition of Habsburg Empire
Seven Years War (1756–63)	Britain and Prussia vs. France and Spain	*Gains*: Senegal, Grenada, St Vincent, Dominica, Canada, and all other territory east of Mississippi; commercial supremacy in India from France; French evacuation of German states; Florida from Spain
American War of Independence (1775–83)	Britain vs. the thirteen colonies, France, Spain, and Dutch republic	*Losses*: the thirteen colonies, Senegal, Goree, Tobago, St Lucia
French Revolutionary War (1793–1801)	Britain in various alliances with Russia, Austria, Prussia, and Spain vs. France	*Gains*: Trinidad (from Spain), Ceylon (from Holland) *Losses*: French domination of Europe continues
Napoleonic War (1803–15)	Britain again in various alliances with Russia, Austria, Prussia, and Spain vs. France	*Gains*: France returned to its 1792 boundaries; free navigation of the Scheldt; Tobago, St Lucia, British Guiana, Demerara, Essequibo, Berbice, Malta, and Heligoland; British Protectorate over Ionian Islands

Sources: Geoffrey Holmes and Daniel Szechi, *The Age of Oligarchy: Pre-Industrial Britain, 1722–1783* (Longman, London, 1993), pp. 410–11; Paul Langford, *A Polite and Commercial People: England 1727–1783* (Oxford University Press, Oxford, 1989), p. 350; Eric J. Evans, *The Forging of the Modern State: Early Industrial Britain 1783–1870* (Longman, London, 1983), pp. 413–14

next – reaching almost 200,000 during the American war, and close to 400,000 at the height of the Napoleonic War, along with another 500,000 or so volunteers who were charged with home defence duties.[22] It required a prodigious effort to build up and maintain what quickly became Britain's chief military glory, the navy.[23] To provision its shipboard population in 1760, the Navy Board had to purchase almost 11 million lb of beef, 4.7 million lb of biscuits, over 3.6 million lb of pork and flour, 2.5 million lb of cheese, and over a million lb of butter. The naval dockyards were perhaps the biggest industrial operation in the country, employing over 8,000 workmen each by the 1770s. By 1800, the public capital invested in the British fleet was over five times the total private capital invested in the West Riding woollen industry.[24]

Given the immense scale of military operations on sea and on land, it is small wonder that warfare remained the dominant item of state expenditure. Taken on average, military and naval spending and the payments for debt service that were almost solely necessitated by wartime borrowing never accounted for less than 85 per cent of net public expenditure during every interval of war between 1700 and 1815. During the particularly expensive last three wars of this era, they rose to well over 90 per cent of total spending.[25] Even when peace broke out, civil expenditure rarely accounted for more than a fifth of all public spending.[26] This was mainly because servicing the debt contracted in wartime became the chief fiscal duty of the peacetime state, accounting for 44 per cent of all public spending for 1721–35 and 59 per cent of the total for 1822–31. Spending on non-military services rose 350 per cent between the 1720s and the 1820s, but military spending rose 450 per cent and debt service 750 per cent over the same period.[27] In sum, between 1689 and 1815 well over 80 per cent of all public money spent by the British state on goods and services can be classified as military in origin and purpose. On a per capita basis, Britons spent more on warfare than any of their continental counterparts in this period. At the height of what was by far Britain's biggest war in this era, the war against Napoleon, state spending accounted for perhaps a full quarter of the gross national product, a considerably higher percentage than in any previous conflict, and four times higher than the 6 per cent of GNP consumed by the government on the eve of the war.[28] In short, the Georgian state was largely, and at times almost exclusively, a war machine that gobbled up an ever more prodigious quantity of the nation's resources.

What made it possible for the state to pay for this massive military commitment? First and foremost, its ability to borrow ever greater sums of money at low rates of interest. The funding system that was already well established during the War of the Spanish Succession came into its own by the middle of the century.[29] Britain's extensive and efficient network of financial institutions, rivalled on the Continent only by the Dutch, included a number of agencies that dealt in public securities – the Bank of England as well as other banks in the City and in the provinces, the stock exchange, merchants, brokers, and insurance companies. Government stock became attractive to investors small as well as large, because parliament guaranteed a safe return by earmarking specific taxes to the payment of interest on specific stock issues. As it became obvious to investors that parliament could be trusted to honour its credit obligations, the rate of interest on the funded debt declined. The conversion of the vast majority of the government's liabilities into low-interest stock meant that the cost to the government of borrowing fell dramatically even as its debts mounted. While the national debt grew from under 5 to over 10 per cent of GNP between the Glorious Revolution and Waterloo, the average rate of interest on government loans fell from 9 per cent to under 5 per cent.[30] Parliamentary appropriation of taxes to debt service enabled the government to borrow on considerably more advantageous terms than those available to its French counterpart. In the late 1780s, for example, the French national debt was roughly comparable in size to Britain's, but the yearly interest payments on the French debt were nearly double those on the British. This was because the Bourbon kings were considered a relatively bad credit risk, for, unlike Britain, there was no permanent legislature in France that could exert fiscal discipline over them and ensure that sufficient taxes would be raised to service the debt on a predictable basis.[31] The British state's relative creditworthiness gave it an immense war-making advantage over its chief rival in an era when the vast expense of warfare made public credit one of the state's most formidable weapons.

Debt service depended on tax collection, and the Georgian state managed to extract more in taxes from its subjects than any of its continental rivals. Contemporaries were painfully aware of the parliamentary regime's tax-making power. Shortly after Waterloo, the Edinburgh Reviewer Sydney Smith famously explained how a Briton could look forward to paying

TAXES upon every article which enters the mouth, or covers the back, or is placed under the foot – taxes upon everything which it is pleasant to see, hear, feel, smell, or taste – taxes upon warmth, light, and locomotion – taxes on everything on earth, and the waters under the earth – on every thing that comes from abroad, or is grown at home – taxes on the raw material – taxes on every fresh value that is added to it by the industry of man – taxes on the sauce which pampers man's appetite, and the drug that restores him to health – on the ermine which decorates the judge, and the rope which hangs the criminal – on the poor man's salt, and the rich man's spice – on the brass nails of the coffin, and the ribands of the bride – at bed or board, couchant or levant, we must pay: – The schoolboy whips his taxed top – the beardless youth manages his taxed horse with a taxed bridle on a taxed road: – and the dying Englishman pouring his medicine, which has paid seven per cent. – flings himself back upon his chintz-bed which has paid twenty-two per cent. – makes his will on an eight pound stamp, and expires in the arms of an apothecary who has paid a license of an hundred pounds for the privilege of putting him to death. His whole property is then immediately taxed from two to ten per cent. Besides the probate, large fees are demanded for burying him in the chancel; his virtues are handed down to posterity on taxed marble; and he is then gathered to his fathers, – to be taxed no more.[32]

Smith was not taking all that much creative licence with his subject. At the time he wrote, British taxes had risen to a scarcely conceivable level. In real terms, the per capita tax burden rose by a factor of *eighteen* between 1660 and 1815. It rose 80 per cent during the French Revolutionary and Napoleonic Wars alone, as against 30 per cent in France. At some point during these wars Britain surpassed the United Provinces as the most heavily taxed nation in Europe. In historical terms, these were prodigious feats: English government revenues had been virtually flat for three hundred years before the accession of Charles I. Of course, a growing economy was helping to bring in tax receipts over the course of the eighteenth century, but while real national income grew by a factor of three or so between 1670 and 1810, tax receipts grew by a factor of about sixteen.[33] Thus by the Napoleonic era British taxpayers had good reason to feel as harassed as Sydney Smith made them out to be.

The excise accounted for the lion's share of this enormous increase in tax revenue, growing from 29 per cent of government revenue in 1710 to 52 per cent by 1795. By the latter date the yield from the excise greatly exceeded that from customs duties (18 per cent) and the land tax (15 per cent).[34] Observers continued to assail excise taxes as an infringement on liberty and an unfair burden on domestic trade that ostensibly led to higher workers' wages.[35] But they paid up nevertheless. So long as excise duties were laid on piecemeal, they met with little resistance, mainly because they were well concealed in the retail prices of excisable goods. Britons generally felt that it was only fair to the poor that excise duties fell chiefly on luxury items. Hence the heavy taxes imposed on carriages, hair powder, cards, and dice during the

American and French Revolutionary Wars. But the tax receipts to be had from such trifles were as nothing compared with those obtainable from articles of mass consumption, so the poor were obliged to foot much of the excise bill. Indeed, by 1792–3 the combined receipts from several duties on items of mass consumption – sugar, tea, tobacco, salt, beer, malt, hops, candles, soap, wine, and spirits – amounted to more than half of total net revenue, as against a mere 16.5 per cent from *all* direct-tax receipts.[36] There is no way accurately to measure the social incidence of eighteenth-century taxation. But it seems fair to conclude that the simultaneous rise of indirect and decline of direct taxes meant that the 'middling sort' (who felt the sting from many 'luxury' taxes as well as taxes on 'necessaries') and the labouring classes were bearing a disproportionate share of the tax burden by the last decades of the century. The regressive trend was only briefly reversed after 1799, when the younger Pitt's government collected Britain's first income tax after concluding that in order to save public credit it had no choice but to raise more tax revenue on a yearly basis. The propertied classes acquiesced in this wartime necessity, but they despised as a grievous invasion of privacy a levy that obliged them to reveal to tax collectors the sources and extent of their wealth. Parliament repealed the tax shortly after Waterloo, and took the extraordinary step of ordering that the income-tax records be destroyed.[37] Thus, while the government was able to target the affluent when it needed to do so, both the landed and the moneyed interests got off relatively lightly.

What is certainly true is that *all* ranks of Britons were burdened with far higher tax payments than their French counterparts. Through much of the century the French tax burden did not increase in per capita terms, and by the end of the century the French tax regime was almost certainly less regressive than the British.[38] Yet it was the French one, not the British one, that was widely seen as oppressive, inspired widespread protest, and helped to trigger revolution. What accounts for the British state's ability to raise far more taxes with far less political friction? First, Britain's relatively large urban population, well-developed internal markets, and high per capita income, all of which facilitated a high level of indirect taxation, just as they did in the Dutch republic.[39] Secondly, the structure and assessment of direct and indirect taxes in Britain, which made them relatively 'invisible' to taxpayers. Direct taxes on land were collected by local amateurs, and often 'invisibly' passed on to tenant farmers as part of their rent, while such a broad range of goods were exciseable that it was difficult for consumers to focus their protests on any one duty. In France, on the other hand, both direct and indirect taxes were comparatively 'visible', for peasant-proprietors were obliged to pay the *Taille* directly to central officers, and excise duties fell on a far narrower range of goods, some of them 'necessaries' such as salt. Finally, parliamentary authority in the raising of taxes gave it a legitimacy in the minds of most Britons that the French tax structure did not enjoy. There was equality under the tax laws, whereas in France many regions and social groups enjoyed controversial exemptions. It was particularly difficult for the Bourbon kings to breach the ancient tax privileges of the French nobility, and ultimately it was Louis XVI's effort to do so that triggered the political quarrel of 1789 that led to revolution.[40]

The supremacy of the British tax structure made possible the great military victories of the 'long' eighteenth century. Georgian parliaments were generally very indulgent towards the army and the navy. They had neither the accounting ability nor the inclination to impose frugality upon the service departments.[41] Parliament was especially keen to provide the navy with the funds it needed if it was to rule the waves. The spending ratio between army and navy always favoured the latter in every major conflict prior to the Napoleonic War, when a huge commitment of troops to the Continent was necessary to stymie the French emperor.[42]

It was what historians call 'blue-water' strategic thinking that accounted for this naval predominance. It was already a well-established truism before 1700 that the 'wooden walls' of British sea power were the first defence against foreign invasion. Thus the first priority of Britain's 'blue-water' policy was naval command of the English Channel and the North Sea. But it was just as widely accepted that the navy should be an instrument of commercial warfare. Hence, the second priority of 'blue-water' policy was the promotion of trade and shipping. The 'mercantilist' assumptions around which naval policy revolved were not seriously questioned before the American war: that a dominant share of the world carrying trade and an extensive network of colonial markets would be great advantages to the British economy; that securing both would bring more bullion into the country and stimulate domestic industry; and that the quest for commercial supremacy was a zero-sum game that could only be won through naval mastery.[43]

The final priority of 'blue-water' policy was to make only a very limited commitment of troops to continental warfare. The point was to rule the waves while fighting a defensive war in Europe, using Britain's superior financial resources to bankroll an allied effort to contain France. British operations in Europe thus depended on taking foreign troops into British pay and on subsidizing allied armies.[44] If the European theatre was a secondary concern for the British, it was nevertheless critically important in overextending the French. Of the seven

Anglo-French wars that were fought between 1689 and 1815, the only one that Britain lost was the American war, in which there was no fighting in Europe.[45]

In retrospect, it is clear that 'blue-water' policy made good economic sense. The 'wooden walls' of the navy helped to guarantee that foreign troops would never ravage the mainland, while the commitment to large-scale operations in colonial theatres reaped huge commercial dividends. It is true that the vast extent of that commitment during the French Revolutionary War meant that thousands of British soldiers died of disease in the West Indies while their French counterparts were overrunning much of western Europe. But there is no question that Britain's focus on colonial warfare helped to furnish it with by far the world's largest empire at the Congress of Vienna.[46] The results at the peace-table bore out Henry Dundas's judgement in 1801 that 'the present strength and pre-eminence of this country is owing to the extent of its resources arising from its commerce and its naval power which are inseparable'. As the historian Patrick O'Brien has argued, the obsession with the 'costs' of wartime loans and taxes shared by nineteenth-century liberals and modern economists has obscured Dundas's point. But it was plain enough to his contemporaries, who had good reason to conclude that the nation reaped considerable economic benefits from 'blue-water' warfare.[47] Those benefits in turn stemmed from the state's unrivalled financial power.

If the fiscal–military state assumed vast powers over British taxpayers, it of course assumed the ultimate power of life and death over its soldiers and sailors. The state's militarization of society reached far higher levels than it had ever done before during the Napoleonic War, at the height of which at least 10 per cent of the male population of military age served in one branch or another of the armed forces.[48] It is true that the British government managed to avoid resorting to a levy en masse, even though its French revolutionary opponents had relied on conscription from a very early stage in the fighting. Indeed, the idea of giving the state power over the lives of literally all of its able-bodied male subjects was so abhorrent to Britons that it was only resorted to in the middle of World War I, long after the other major belligerents had committed to it. Still, while there was no general conscription, there was nevertheless a strong element of state compulsion in the Napoleonic recruitment effort. It was certainly present in the terms of militia service, for instance, by which a man who was balloted was obliged to serve for five years within the British Isles unless he could pay for a substitute or pay the fines for non-compliance. The Militia Act that had established this principle of compulsion provoked nationwide rioting when it was introduced in 1757, as did the supplementary militia acts of 1796 through which the militia trebled in size. Cavalry units killed more people in an anti-militia riot in Tranent in August 1796 than were killed in the infamous Peterloo Massacre of 1819.[49]

Other forms of military compulsion, while limited, were common-place in both branches of the armed forces during most major eighteenth-century wars.[50] Naval impressment, for instance, was a serious breach of civil liberty and an unpleasant fact of wartime life. It was skilled seamen who were most likely to be seized by the press-gang. This was a rude intrusion of state power into their lives that was necessitated by the lack of state intrusion into the labour market. Even at the height of war, there was an unregulated competition between the navy, merchants, and privateers for the services of skilled seamen. Merchants refused to accept any comprehensive scheme of naval con-scription or registration, while parliament, generally so obliging when it came to the wartime needs of the armed services, refused to sanction competitive rates of pay for naval crews. Thus the only means of ensur-ing that naval vessels were properly manned in wartime was to seize sailors from ports or on the high seas. Probably at least a third of the navy's wartime sailors were procured in this way.

While at first glance impressment seems like a naked act of state aggression, in practice it was circumscribed. Victims of the press-gang often went to the law and occasionally won their freedom on appeal. Some press rioters literally got away with murder when juries con-cluded that the fatal resistance they had offered to the press-gang was a legitimate act of self-defence. Impressment on land, moreover, required the compliance of constables and magistrates, who were often very reluctant to be seen to facilitate such an unpopular business.[51] Still, the experience of John Nicol, a sailor who was discharged after the Treaty of Amiens in 1801, makes it clear that impressment was a pow-erful tool of coercion. When war with France broke out again a year and a half later, Nicol, now a cooper in Edinburgh, felt like a hunted man. '[M]y wife was like a distracted woman, and gave me no rest until I sold off my stock in trade and the greater part of my furniture, and retired into the country. Even until I got this accomplished I dared not to sleep in my own house, as I had more than one call from the [press] gang.' Finding no work as a cooper well inland where it was safe, Nicol went off to work in the lime quarries near Cranston.[52] Thus he felt obliged to give up his home, his trade, and virtually his entire identity to avoid the long arm of the wartime state.

Press crews were not the only noticeable military units in Georgian society. While civilian control of the armed forces was well established and took a variety of forms, including the billeting and the movement of troops within the British Isles, the military presence was very real. The absence of trained police forces meant that local magistrates routinely relied on army units 'in aid of the civil power' to suppress the riots that were endemic in Georgian Britain.[53] This was a violent society, and the local and central authorities did not hesitate to use the instruments available to them to keep it under some semblance of control. There were about 160 recorded disturbances in England alone between 1740 and 1775. Some of them were extensive, and the suppression of them bloody. Confrontations between soldiers and angry crowds during the widespread bread riots of 1757 claimed thirteen lives, eight of them in an affray at Kidderminster. It took 12,000 soldiers to put down the infamous Gordon riots in London in 1780, which left perhaps 300 dead and countless wounded.[54] Army units were just as likely to be called in to fight pitched battles against well-organized gangs of smugglers as they were to crack rioters' heads. Indeed, one reason why large British armies generally fared poorly in the early phases of major land campaigns was because in peacetime they had been too widely dispersed in small riot-control and anti-smuggling units to enable them to engage in significant large-scale manoeuvres.[55]

By the height of the Napoleonic War, the army was a ubiquitous presence at home, and a vivid reminder of the state's formidable repressive powers. Ireland had long since been an armed camp. In per capita terms, for much of the century there were two British soldiers stationed in Ireland for every one stationed in England. The Luddite disturbances led to a comparable militarization of the English heartland. By the summer of 1812 there were 12,000 soldiers stationed between Leicester and York, a larger army than Wellington had taken to Portugal in 1808 and the largest domestic military force in English history up to that time.[56] Thus, the fiscal–military state did not merely project its power outward. It did not hesitate to use force and the threat of force to preserve stability at home.

The fiscal–military state and its discontents

British subjects did not simply acquiesce in the growing intrusiveness of the fiscal–military state. Its size, its scope, and its very sovereignty became matters of serious controversy in the last quarter of the century. It was first and foremost the growth of taxation and of the British military presence in North America that led to conflict with the thirteen colonies. Rebellion in America very nearly led to rebellion in Ireland. Frustration in England with the conduct and the outcome of the

American war inspired a widespread critique of government extravagance and corruption that in turn inspired a formidable parliamentary reform movement. Both the reform agitation and the critique of the state that inspired it dwindled away in the peace and quiet of the 1780s, but they became louder than ever during the great wars with France at the end of the century. By 1815, it had become the conventional wisdom within a formidable radical reform movement that the fiscal–military state was the root of all evil.

The first major challenge to the sovereignty of the fiscal–military state took place in the American colonies. Of course, the American rebellion was a deeply complicated matter. But one of the most rancorous issues was parliament's authority to impose revenue duties on the colonies, such as the Sugar Act (1764) and Stamp Act (1765), without the approval of the colonial assemblies. The issue of parliament's right to tax in America remained at the forefront of the sovereignty debate for a full decade before war broke out, and there were good reasons why the colonists felt that justice was on their side. For many decades the British government had done little to assert its authority over the colonial legislatures.[57] In the absence of any clear delineation of legislative responsibilities between the colonies and the metropole, the two sides in the constitutional dispute arrived at opposite conclusions. MPs assumed that the parliamentary supremacy which now prevailed in Britain extended into the colonies, and that they thus had no less a right to raise taxes on residents of Boston or Philadelphia than they did on residents of Leeds or Glasgow. This assumption was based on no clearly established American precedents, but it nevertheless appeared to be a truism for MPs who had learnt to take parliamentary sovereignty for granted. The colonists, for their part, felt that parliament, in trying to levy taxes on America, was violating a longstanding custom of non-interference whose longevity carried with it the force of law. The quarrel quickly turned dangerous because both sides felt the justice of their arguments to be patently obvious, and hence the intransigence of their opponents unfathomable. George III and MPs across the political spectrum simply could not understand American arguments that seemed to vest sovereignty jointly in the colonial assemblies and the parliamentary monarchy, for in their minds sovereignty was by its nature indivisible.[58]

The sheer physical distance between Britain and America probably contributed to the mutual incomprehension, and it certainly contributed to Britain's military defeat. In hindsight, the now traditional 'blue-water' strategy was doomed to fail in America, because the burden of waging a large-scale land campaign from 3,000 miles away without the benefit of any continental diversions was too much even for the British war machine. The French and the Spanish jumped into the fray as soon as it became obvious that the rebels were able to hold their own. The Dutch joined them shortly thereafter, and this infusion of European sea power proved to be enough to tilt the balance against the British. Even the abundant resources of the British navy could not be stretched far enough to wage war against so many formidable opponents over such vast stretches of sea.[59]

The American challenge to the sovereignty of the British state provoked a similar challenge to it in Ireland, but in this case bloodshed was avoided, or at least deferred until the uprising of 1798. The Westminster parliament's right to legislate for Ireland, particularly on issues of trade and finance, was frequently proclaimed during the first three quarters of the century, and while MPs in Dublin were loath to acknowledge this right, it was rarely challenged in any direct way until the emergence of the Volunteer movement during the American war. When the British moved most of their forces in Ireland to America, the Irish filled the gap with a Volunteer force of some 25,000 men whose main purpose was to defend the country from the threat of French invasion. But a number of issues politicized the Volunteer movement and turned it into a real threat to British sovereignty. The most significant of them was the Irish commercial slump wrought by the wartime disruption of the American trade. This slump drew hostile attention to the restrictions through which the Westminster parliament had long sought to shackle Irish commerce, and in tandem with the constitutional quarrel over America it in turn drew hostile attention to British sovereignty itself. Faced with the growing possibility of armed rebellion in Ireland just as they were losing their grip on America, MPs at Westminster passed the Renunciation Act (1783), by which they explicitly surrendered Britain's claim to legislate for Ireland. The British executive government remained at Dublin Castle, but the Dublin parliament was given full legislative initiative. Thus the Irish received the internal autonomy that many American colonists professed they would have been satisfied with, and bloodshed was avoided.[60]

It was only avoided for fifteen years, however. It is important to stress that the rising of 1798 that claimed some 30,000 lives was perhaps even more a sectarian bloodbath than it was a challenge to British sovereignty. The United Irishmen who had been radicalized by the French Revolutionary example as well as by British efforts to suppress them sought first and foremost to achieve independence. But they and their loyalist Orange counterparts had let loose popular religious forces beyond their control, and the consequence was a civil war and a holy war wrapped into one. The British army was also deeply implicated in the bloodshed, however, chiefly because it feared that Irish disaffection paved the way for a French invasion. A French fleet carrying 15,000 troops had just missed landing at Bantry Bay in 1796, and a smaller French flotilla carrying the United Irish leader Theobald Wolfe Tone was intercepted off Donegal shortly after the 1798 rising had been suppressed. From the British perspective, a hopelessly divided Ireland would continue to prove an irresistible stepping-stone to the French. Pitt's government assumed that British security required not simply the abrogation of the Renunciation Act, but the annexation of Ireland. The Act of Union of 1800 abolished the Dublin parliament while it strengthened the British administration by denying the principle of devolution for purely Irish affairs, furnished the Protestant Ascendancy with a hundred seats in the House of Commons and thirty-two in the Lords, and lifted tariffs on most Irish goods bound for the British market. The promise of economic advantage and a vast infusion of British patronage was enough to coax the Dublin parliament to approve its own abolition. Pro-Unionists on both sides of the Irish Sea hoped that the Act would not only enhance Britain's security, but stimulate Irish trade and British investment, and stifle religious tensions by backing up the Protestant Ascendancy with British arms and at least the possibility of piecemeal concessions to the Catholic majority. As it turned out, the Act stimulated insurgency by denying even a shred of political autonomy to Ireland, while it implicated the British even more deeply in the endemic sectarian strife. Henceforward, the union itself would be the chief bone of contention between Catholic nationalists and Protestant loyalists. Thus, while the Act of Union marked a dramatic extension of the sovereignty of the British state, it also guaranteed that that sovereignty would be perpetually contested within Ireland.[61]

It was not only in America and in Ireland that the legitimacy of the British state was subject to vigorous challenge in the last third of the century. As the American conflict came to a boil, metropolitan radicals focused their attention on parliamentary reform as the proper means of broadening the government's accountability. They protested against not only what they perceived to be the injustice of the American war, but also the immense burden to taxpayers that stemmed from its allegedly systematic mishandling. The parliamentary managers of the state, they insisted, would become trustworthy managers of the people's taxes only when they owed their seats to a much greater number of taxpayers. Thus 'no taxation without representation' became a radical slogan in Middlesex as well as in Massachusetts.[62] By the early 1780s, the metropolitan radical reform programme had expanded to include universal male suffrage, the exclusion of all placemen, annual parliaments, single-member constituencies, abolition of the property qualification to sit in the Commons, and the secret ballot. This programme had deep roots in a radical tradition that had been nourished by many sources, including natural rights theory and a conviction that the 'ancient constitution' of the Anglo-Saxons served as a democratic precedent. But it was also predicated on the belief that ministers who controlled the instruments of state had corrupted MPs through the extensive application of wartime patronage and now sought to enslave Britons through the sheer volume of taxes that they consumed in a war against American liberties.[63]

The alleged extravagance of the wartime state also inspired the more 'respectable' outdoor reform campaign of the Association movement, which was active in twenty-five counties and eight boroughs at the height of the American war. The country gentlemen and middling townsmen who dominated the Association insisted that the wartime growth of the state had put far too much of the taxpayers' money in the hands of the ministers of the crown, who were squandering much of it on a hapless war effort and putting a good deal of the rest of it into the pockets of placemen. They launched an ambitious petitioning campaign designed to persuade MPs to curb public spending and to enforce frugality and disinterestedness on the executive government through the abolition of the Septennial Act and of fifty proprietary boroughs, along with the addition of a hundred county MPs.[64]

These extra-parliamentary or 'outdoor' reform movements scarcely survived the war that had given birth to them. The ostensible nepotism and extravagance of the British state were no longer burning issues during the decade of peace and prosperity between the end of the American war and the beginning of the French Revolutionary War. Still, the long-term growth of the central bureaucracy and the perpetuation of controversial patronage offices within it helped to ensure that the ostensible waste and corruption of the state would once again become focal points for political protest when Britain returned to war against France. The number of central government officers grew over 66 per cent between 1797 and 1815, from 16,200 to 24,500.[65] The bureaucracy remained what it had been throughout the eighteenth century, an 'extraordinary patch-work'[66] of efficiency and frugality here, torpor and waste there. Thus, for instance, while the Excise administration was a model of 'rational' management,[67] many older departments were riddled with archaic and increasingly expensive administrative practices. One such practice was the grant of sinecures, outmoded offices with little or no work but large emoluments attached to them that were habitually awarded to political insiders as a form of patronage. A closely related practice was the grant of reversions, which enabled the well-connected to bequeath their offices, usually sinecures, to their

close relatives as a form of freehold. Another such practice was re-
muneration by fees, by which public officers were compensated for
specific services rendered rather than by a closely regulated salary.[68]
The cost to taxpayers of these archaisms grew with each new war
and reached large proportions during the French Revolutionary and
Napoleonic Wars. Lord Arden, for instance, holder of the sinecure Reg-
istrarship of the High Court of Admiralty, made a fortune of £19,000 in
1797 alone from the percentage he received on all the naval prizes that
were registered in the court.[69]

These obsolete central offices and practices became a major political
issue in Britain during the French Revolutionary and Napoleonic Wars
because those wars were so vastly expensive to taxpayers, and because
the well-established obsession with corruption and extravagance
meant that the proliferation of wartime offices would be widely
seen as an alarming extension of the government's patronage power.
Indeed, the radical journalist William Cobbett famously characterized
the Napoleonic-era state as 'Old Corruption', and what he and his
fellow radicals meant by it was a vast parasitical system through which
the political elite gorged itself at taxpayers' expense. Sinecures and
reversions, they insisted, robbed the productive classes to pay the well-
connected. Wartime contracts, pensions, and church patronage, they
alleged, were dispensed by the ministers of the crown as rewards to
their cronies or bribes to compromise the independence of politically
influential men. The vast accumulation of the wartime national debt,
they argued, led to a massive transfer of money from the pockets of the
people to the government's fat-cat creditors in the City. The oppressive
tax system, they alleged, fell very heavily on the politically unrepre-
sented, while the wealthy got off lightly. Radicals concluded that an
extremely narrow electorate was the keystone of corruption. Only root-
and-branch parliamentary reform would eradicate state parasitism by
making MPs corruption-proof, answerable to a large electorate that
would either force them to reduce taxes and nepotism or else dismiss
them at the next election.[70]

The size, scope, and unjust practices of the British government and
the putative selfishness of the parliamentary elite that presided over
it were hardly the only matters that exercised American colonists,
Irish Volunteers, and English radicals. These protest movements
were complex and discrete, and sought political reform as a matter
of abstract justice and not simply as a counterweight to an intolerably
expensive government. Still, each of them focused considerable hostility on the alleged excesses of the wartime state, particularly on its
excessive taxation demands. Thus, while the British war machine was
an ever more potent extractor of taxes, its very potency helped to

arouse formidable protest movements and, as we shall see, led to its virtual dismantling in the early nineteenth century.

The Georgian state and the propertied Englishman

Radicals had good reason to characterize the Georgian state as 'Old Corruption'. At first glance, its chief function after the waging of war, and one that was closely related to the waging of war, seems to have been the diverting of large sums of public money into the pockets of the politically well-connected. Thus, according to E. P. Thompson, political life during the period of Whig hegemony

> had something of the sick quality of a 'banana republic'. This is a recognized phase of commercial capitalism when predators fight for the spoils of power and have not yet agreed to submit to rational or bureaucratic rules and forms. Each politician, by nepotism, interest and purchase, gathered around him a following of loyal dependants. The aim was to reward them by giving them some post in which they could milk some part of the public profit.[71]

There is much truth in this assessment. The pursuit of public money was undeniably one of the favourite pastimes of the Whig oligarchs who dominated political life for much of the century. It was with good reason that the grandest oligarch of all, the long-serving prime minister Sir Robert Walpole, was widely caricatured by the Tory wits of his day as the emblem of a thoroughly corrupt age. The 'Great Man' enjoyed the plunder as well as the power of office, and knew how to accumulate great quantities of both. Walpole amassed a fortune big enough to turn his family estate in Norfolk, Houghton, into a veritable palace, to assemble one of the finest picture collections in Britain, and routinely to entertain on a royal scale. His annual outlay on wine alone – over 6,500 bottles a year – cost enough to support the lifestyle of a well-heeled country gentleman. He got good value for money, however, since much of his wine was smuggled. Walpole loaded his family and even his mistress with sinecures and pensions. After he secured the lucrative (and useless) office of Ranger of Richmond Park for his son in 1726, he made himself Deputy Ranger and ran through the princely sum of £14,000 in refurbishing the Park's Old Lodge. Here was a formidable politician who had no qualms about making the system pay off for himself in every conceivable way.[72] Walpole's era is commonly, and probably correctly, seen as the apex of nepotism. But at the end of the century there were still plenty of opportunities for insiders to profit at public expense. As late as 1810, sinecures still cost taxpayers about £300,000 a year, and reversions (i.e. offices bequeathed to their current holders by their predecessors) another £150,000. According to Lord Chancellor Eldon, 'the true rule' for making a successful political career was 'to get what you can and keep what you have'. He left £1.3 million at his death and while living had procured for his son four sinecures and the reversions to two more.[73]

It would nevertheless be a mistake to judge Hanoverian 'corruption' by today's standards.[74] The notion that public office was a public trust did not fully emerge until the Victorian era. There is little doubt that Walpole and Eldon thought of their fortunes from office as just rewards for assiduous toil on behalf of the nation, and few of their personal acquaintances would have disagreed. Moreover, in an age when there were no strong parties to impose voting discipline on MPs, the king's ministers had to rely on the 'influence of the crown' embodied in the patronage network in order to preserve a healthy working majority. Political stability necessitated a good deal of jobbery, and even then there was little assurance that the recipients of jobs would always dance to the government's tune. Even 'loyal' placemen occasionally voted against ministers, particularly on issues of national importance. Finally, even if every placeman *had* been utterly reliable, there were never enough of them to ensure a government majority on a close vote in a full House of Commons. This was even true in 1760, when the number of placemen and pensioners in the House probably reached its all-time high.[75] In short, while profit clearly figured prominently in the minds of many eighteenth-century politicians, high politics was never solely, or even chiefly, about profit.

It was, however, to a great degree about the protection and facilitation of private property. Few things in life were more important to Georgian Britons than their property, and it went without saying among them that the chief duty of the state was to protect it. Indeed, it was a routine practice among eighteenth-century political thinkers to make property chronologically prior to the state, and to argue that it was the pre-existence of the former that necessitated the creation of the latter.[76] Thus in times of peril the state authorities were quite willing to subordinate that other eighteenth-century fetish, the liberty of the subject, to the protection of property. Nowhere was this more evident than during and immediately after the great wars in defence of property that the British fought against the French revolutionary regimes. It was in order to combat putative 'jacobinical levellers' at home that the younger Pitt's ministry and its successors suspended habeas corpus (in peace as well as wartime), sharply curtailed freedom of speech through the Two Acts, Six Acts, and Combination Acts, passed additional measures to prevent seduction from duty and administering of unlawful oaths, initiated a great many prosecutions for seditious libel and blasphemy, and even used *agents provocateurs* in an effort to provoke domestic radicals into treason. Admittedly, the Georgian state was more tolerant of dissent than many of its continental counterparts. But it did not hesitate to back its guardianship of property with considerable force.

That force was most dramatically displayed at the gallows. The government heavily relied on the exemplary power of capital punishment as a means of reducing crime in a society that thought of a centralized police force as an unacceptable threat to liberty. Thus the Georgian state exercised its power to take human life thousands of times, in highly ritualized displays of graphic violence designed to provoke terror in the large crowds of bystanders that typically witnessed them. By the early nineteenth century the execution rate in Britain was far higher than it was in many more 'authoritarian' European countries, and hangings were much more frequent than they had been a century before. Some 7,000 people were executed in England and Wales between 1770 and 1830.[77] Most of them had been convicted of crimes against property, not against persons. The number of capital offences grew from around fifty in 1688 to over 200 in 1820, and the vast majority of the newer capital statutes concerned property crimes.[78] The 'Bloody Code' dictated, for instance, that one could be hanged for the theft of merely five shillings' worth of goods from a shop. Over 84 per cent of those executed in Surrey between 1663 and 1802 had been found guilty of one or several of these many property crimes, while only 8 per cent had been found guilty of murder.[79] Here was vivid testimony indeed to the seriousness with which the Georgian state took its duty to protect property.

The criminal law was undoubtedly ferocious by modern standards, but there were limits to its ferocity. The growth of the 'Bloody Code' was more apparent than real, because capital statutes were not rigidly classified and thus many of them were redundant. The legal system, moreover, relied on exemplary but by no means uniform punishment. Both judges and jurors enjoyed discretionary power to mitigate punishments, and they habitually used it. The arbitrariness of the system was intended to enhance its deterrent force, and while it may or may not have had this effect, it certainly enabled the large majority of capital felons to escape the noose. While a great many of them – some 50,000 over the course of the century[80] – were made to suffer the new and admittedly very harsh 'secondary punishment' of transportation, others received lesser sentences.[81] Ultimately, the discretion at the heart of Georgian law enforcement helped to ensure that the legal system would not simply be used as an instrument of class oppression. Criminal prosecutions were brought by private citizens, not by the state itself, and victims who took their cases to court were often drawn from the same class as defendants. In short, 'the law was not the absolute property of the patricians, but a limited multi-use right'[82] that was available to a wide variety of Britons, although admittedly for many reasons much less available to the very poor (as it is today) than it was to their social 'betters'. Certainly the criminal code served the interests of the propertied MPs who legislated it. Clearly, it was only the owners of trees and not the poor who benefited from the statute of 1766 that made the gathering of wood on someone else's property a crime that was punishable by seven years' transportation for a third offence.[83] But in practice it served the interests of a broad enough number of property holders, small as well as large, to demonstrate that the whiggish claim of the impartiality of the law was not a total sham.

While the severity of the Georgian criminal law was thus often mitigated in practice, it is obvious that the state that presided over it was deadly serious in its efforts to defend private property. As the century progressed, the state's commitment to facilitating the accumulation of private property at the expense of the poor became almost as obvious. It rose from the growing conviction among the propertied that it was the free play of economic forces and not the fulfilment of paternalist obligations that would promote individual responsibility and steer the nation on a providential path towards greater affluence and stability.[84] There are many indications that the eighteenth century witnessed the gradual erosion of the notion that the wealthy had a personal obligation to cultivate ties of fellow-feeling by participating in the lives and protecting the livelihoods of their social inferiors: the decline of the living-in of servants; the remodelling of country houses and their grounds to shield their inhabitants better from the prying eyes of humbler neighbours; the occasional displacement of entire villages for the aesthetic benefit of their landlords; even the receding of rural labourers into the background of landscape paintings.[85] The propertied gentlemen who sat in the two houses of parliament were deeply implicated in this process of erosion, through both what they sanctioned and what they chose not to sanction.

This was a ruling elite that was reaping the benefits of buoyant agricultural prices and diversifying their assets by investing in government securities and a wide variety of enterprises.[86] Profit maximizers themselves, they frequently intervened to protect the profits of masters from their workmen. As Patrick O'Brien has pointed out, the Georgian labour market was anything but free, and MPs generally sought to bolster an ' "authoritarian" framework of law' that shackled many labourers for the ostensible benefit of their masters and of society as a whole. A broad range of employers had long been vested with quasi-judicial authority over their workers through a hotch-potch of statutes that were intended to regulate apprenticeship, poor relief, vagrancy, and delinquency. Parliament did what it could to uphold this hierar-chical labour regime: by turning the traditional perquisites attached to certain types of job into acts of embezzlement, for instance; by enact-ing no fewer than forty statutes that prohibited the formation of trade unions in certain crafts and at certain locations, before it passed the Combination Act of 1800 that sought to prohibit collective bargaining altogether;[87] and by adding a series of penal clauses to the Elizabethan Statute of Artificers that mandated prison terms for labourers who left their work unfinished or who left their masters before their contracts had expired.[88] In Staffordshire alone between 1780 and 1800, there were over 900 prosecutions for violations of the master and servant laws. While the Combination Act proved much more difficult to enforce, it was just one in a long series of measures designed to discipline the work force.[89]

Historians Douglas Hay and Nicholas Rogers have made it clear that MPs sought to do away with certain forms of custom that had hitherto helped to ease the plight of the poor but were now seen as impedi-ments to capital formation, even while they sought to preserve some authoritarian labour practices. From about 1750 to the end of the Napoleonic Wars, they argue, the state presided over 'a massive delegitimation of the claims of popular custom'.[90] Both MPs and magistrates increasingly neglected the enforcement of the wage-fixing clauses of the Statute of Artificers (1563). While as late as the 1770s well-organized trades like the London silk-weavers could secure for them-selves statutory wage-fixing and stringent apprenticeship clauses, the trend was very much in the opposite direction. In that same decade, for instance, woollen workers, hatters, framework-knitters, and dyers all saw their apprenticeship requirements repealed. Parliament abol-ished all such requirements in 1814, just as workers were desperately trying to defend their wages from the hordes of unskilled labourers that demobilization was turning loose on the domestic economy. The Tudor marketing laws against forestallers and engrossers met the same fate as apprenticeship. Exemplary prosecutions of middlemen who sought to raise the price of foodstuffs through such artificial means waned in the last decades of the eighteenth century.[91]

The most dramatic parliamentary assault on common rights came in the shape of enclosure bills, by which landowners sought to divide wastes and common lands amongst themselves and turn them to profitable uses. About half of the cultivable land in England had already been enclosed prior to 1700. But the rate of enclosure by private act of parliament reached its height during the French Revolutionary and Napoleonic Wars.[92] Apologists for parliamentary enclosure stressed at the time, and still stress now, the ways in which it stimulated agricultural productivity, while insisting that it did not adversely affect small landowners and tenant farmers, whose numbers occasionally even grew in regions experiencing a high rate of enclosure.[93] But the social consequences of enclosure remain hotly contested. Some compelling recent accounts subscribe to the 'catastrophist' interpretation that was first advanced by J. L. and Barbara Hammond in the 1910s.[94] They stress the damage that enclosure inflicted on three groups: small landowners who relied on access to commons and wasteland for grazing and who rarely had the money to participate in enclosure schemes; the cottagers who supplemented their meagre incomes from wage-labour on farms and cottage industries by keeping a few chickens or a cow on the local common; and, finally, the many squatters who were left homeless, evicted from their shacks when the commons or wastes they had lived on were taken over by the enclosure commissioners. For the rural poor, enclosure was thus a sort of state-sponsored confiscation of the ground beneath their feet. It was often resisted, through petitions, legal actions, and riot. While in the long run enclosure certainly enhanced the efficiency of English agriculture, the sense of injustice that it inspired in the common people lingered on in their collective memory. Many of them plainly felt they had been robbed by wealthy men who used their access to the state as an instrument of caste warfare.[95]

There is no doubt that the Georgian state's assault on customary rights facilitated the capitalist transformation of the British economy. But it would be wrong to suggest that its economic policies were either uniform or consistent. Indeed, by modern standards the state took very little responsibility for economic development. There was scarcely such a thing as economic 'policy' in the eighteenth century. MPs never consciously sought to usher in a totally free market, either in labour or in commodity exchange. The assault on apprenticeship, for instance, was sporadic and piecemeal.[96] The 'mercantilist system' of the era, moreover, through which the government ostensibly sought to foster commerce through a coherent framework of protective legislation, is a *post hoc* construction, for the growth of protection was an incidental result of the government's frantic search for money. While, for instance, the general level of import duties roughly quadrupled between 1690 and 1704, this was less because the state sought to protect certain industries from foreign competition than because it desperately needed to secure new sources of revenue in wartime. The enforcement of the 'mercantilistic' Navigation Acts, moreover, was rarely strict. While one of their chief aims appeared to be the exclusion of foreigners from colonial trade, British authorities were nevertheless eager to encourage American colonists to engage in multilateral trade when it seemed profitable to do so.[97] The chief aim of tariff policy throughout the century was to raise revenue, and the rate and incidence of duties stemmed from the clash of lobbying interests and not from some master plan for the economy. Now that the seat of economic power was firmly established in the Palace of Westminster, MPs were habitually set upon by favour-seeking lobbyists, some of whom represented formidably well-organized interest groups.

More than any other factor, it was the relative power of these interests that determined when the state would intervene in the economy, how it would intervene, and on whose behalf.[98] Not surprisingly, it was often the poor, for whom nobody spoke, who suffered the most from the results of this intricate competition for influence. The main reason, for instance, why many of London's poorer parishes were awash in a sea of bad gin between 1730 and 1750 was because a parliament dominated by landed gentlemen was reluctant to take steps to curb plebeian demand for even the most unhealthy of beverages so long as it promoted the nascent distilling trade and provided a lucrative market for surplus cereals.[99] There was virtually no statutory protection for labourers on the job, moreover, because workers in dangerous trades had few powerful advocates. Arguably the most dangerous job of all was that of the chimney sweep. This was a trade dominated by small boys whose bones were routinely broken or contorted on the job and who often developed cancer of the scrotum and diseases of the urinary tract from their perpetual contact with soot. Still, it took a humanitarian crusade to coax parliament to pass a measure regulating their trade in 1788, and this act was but poorly enforced.[100] In short, the Hanoverian state was a reasonably effective arbiter of propertied interests, but it generally left the propertyless to shift for themselves.

While Georgian MPs took a fairly narrow view of their proper regulatory functions, they were nevertheless active legislators. Parliament passed nearly 14,000 acts between 1688 and 1801, over five times the number passed between the accession of Henry VII in 1485 and the flight of James II.[101] They tackled more and more legislation as the 'long' eighteenth century progressed, passing an average of 253 acts per session during George III's reign as against fifty-eight per session under William III.[102] The large majority of the so-called 'public acts' relating to matters of national importance pertained to the raising of taxes and/or the waging of war. But Georgian MPs were not as indifferent to matters of social regulation as they have often been made out to be. A considerable number of public acts had to do with what we would now call 'social policy', such as poor-law regulation or the treatment of vagrants. In an age when the king's ministers were not expected to furnish a legislative programme, most of this social legislation was piecemeal, sponsored by interested independent MPs, sometimes with but often without the active support of the government.[103] Thus, while the ambit of parliamentary authority was far narrower in the eighteenth century than it would later become, parliament could be and often was used as an instrument to effect social change.

Aside from the defence of the realm and the protection of property, however, an eighteenth-century parliament's most important role was as a facilitator and a regulator of a very wide variety of propertied interests. The legislative framework it provided helped to stimulate a great deal of for-profit activity that brought dividends to those who invested in it but that also benefited the broader community by building up the economic infrastructure and making town life more palatable. A brief look at the so-called 'private' legislation sponsored by MPs makes obvious the centrality of parliament's role as a promoter of property rights. The vast majority of Georgian statutes fell under three 'private' categories: personal acts that were initiated by the parties immediately involved in the issue at hand, such as divorce and inheritance; acts that were sponsored for the benefit of a specific group, but which had ramifications for many other people, such as those designed to encourage the trade in colonial sugar; and finally, local 'improvement' acts that facilitated enclosure, the digging of canals, the building of turnpike roads, and many other activities of importance to the localities in which they were undertaken. This last 'private' category was by far the largest one, and many of the 'private' measures subsumed within it touched the lives of thousands of people.[104] Over time, these local acts transformed the physical appearance of the country. Turnpike acts authorized the construction of hundreds of miles of road. Canal acts sanctioned the digging up of vast stretches of land and the diversion of a huge volume of water. Enclosure acts facilitated the fencing off and hedging in of the countryside into large privately owned blocs.

This physical transformation was carried out by groups of private entrepreneurs who sought to profit from their investment in enclosures, toll roads, and canals, and by various branches of local government that collected rates in order to pay for the paving and lighting of streets, the dredging of harbours, and the like. But while parliament did not spend centrally collected tax money to carry out these projects, 'private' acts provided its crucial authorization for the raising of loans and the levying of rates on which these myriad economic activities relied. Building a road often required the expropriation of land in return for compensation, while lighting a street required the rate-payers who would benefit from it to pay for it. It is impossible to imagine either activity going very far without parliamentary autho-rization at a time and in a place where property holders were so jealous of their rights and privileges.[105] Britons' faith in parliament as a pro-tector of property meant that they were willing to trust it, and it alone, to interfere with property rights in innumerable ways for the advance-ment of the (ostensibly) common good.

The centrality of local government

The main reason why the central government was able to devote so much of its attention to military concerns was because it left most other matters of governance in local hands. 'For the first, and perhaps the last time in English History', Sidney and Beatrice Webb long ago affirmed in what remains the best history of Georgian local govern-ment, 'the National Government abstained from intervention in local affairs.'[106] This is an exaggerated conclusion, but it nevertheless rings true. The Tudors, the early Stuarts, Cromwell, and the later Stuarts had all sought to centralize the apparatus of government to varying degrees, and they all encountered bitter resistance from magistrates and other parish officers who sought to preserve the large measure of local autonomy that they thought was theirs by right as well as custom.[107] Historical experience had taught many Georgian Britons to equate centralization with tyranny. Thus while they were deeply worried about what they perceived to be a growth in crime, they dis-missed the idea of a central police force as unacceptably 'French' and 'unconstitutional'. The lack of such a force was most noticeable in London. In what was then far and away Europe's largest city, police work was carried out by amateur volunteers who were divided among the 200-odd parishes. There were eighteen different combinations of nightwatchmen in St Pancras alone. This profoundly fragmentary and localized force was probably well-equipped to handle misdemeanour policing, but its utter lack of coordination meant that it had great dif-ficulty managing more ambitious tasks.[108] Faced with what they per-ceived to be a choice between crime waves and despotism, Georgian Britons did not hesitate to pick the former. Their central government, moreover, was all too happy to leave the local authorities alone.

Those authorities came in a bewildering variety of shapes and sizes. The very idea of 'local government' is anachronistic when applied to the eighteenth century, because it implies a uniform pattern that simply did not exist in a series of administrative arrangements that had evolved over many centuries. The most basic unit of local administration was the parish, but there were over 15,600 of them in England and Wales alone, with populations varying between fifty and 50,000 and irregular boundaries that often cut across county lines. The parish was charged with a wide variety of responsibilities, from road repair to poor relief, and the parish authorities were empowered to levy rates in order to meet them. Service in parish offices was unpaid and compulsory, and while the method of selecting officers varied, the tradition had evolved in many parishes that they were to be filled via strict rotation among the men, and sometimes even the women; eligibility stemmed from widely varying sets of customary requirements. Some parishes also created salaried positions, such as the clerk or workhouse master. In urban areas, the main unit of local government was the parish vestry, either an 'open' vestry in which all rate-paying householders were eligible to participate in the decision-making process, or a 'close' or 'select' vestry in which it had come to be lodged in the hands of a tight oligarchy. In either case, the principal rate-payers enjoyed considerable influence, and several acts of parliament between 1780 and 1820 sought to concentrate more and more power in their hands. Many wealthy townspeople sought and often managed to purchase exemption from the onerous duties of parish office. Plutocratic tendencies were generally stronger in rural parishes, however, where by the end of the eighteenth century a close correlation had emerged between the size of one's contribution to the rates and the extent of one's involvement in parish government.[109]

In the eyes of most Britons, parochial government was more noticeable, if much less expensive, than the central government. The Webbs estimated that by 1835, parochial authorities were spending about one fifth as much per year as the central government.[110] But most of the civil services of government were met by what the contemporary poet John Clare called the 'parish state', whose officers were far more visible than those of the central one. The parish overseer, for instance, was a weekly presence in the lives of the poor. Moreover, the parish elite who appointed that overseer had immense and often unregulated power to levy rates for a wide range of services, from the mending of roads to the building of prisons, that were far more palpable, albeit far less expensive, than the defence of the realm.[111]

The most powerful member of that parish elite was the justice of the peace, who had to own land within the county that was worth at least £100 a year to be eligible to serve. In contrast to the Continent, where monarchs entrusted the main offices of local government to paid servants of the state, JPs were the prime examples of the English tradition of 'self-government at the king's command', by which members of the landed elite were largely permitted to rule in their own communities.[112] The central government relied on the justice to supervise virtually all the affairs of the parish. He was the chief enforcer of the law in the neighbourhood, whose powers of punishment ranged from the levying of small fines to the meting out of long prison sentences or severe corporal punishment. Two or three justices meeting in 'petty sessions' had the power to revoke or renew the licences of public houses, to set the poor rate, to appoint parish officers and audit their accounts, to supervise the collection of the land and window taxes, to commit to trial at county Assizes all those accused of assault and graver offences, to fix wages and prices, and to regulate apprenticeships. The justices of a given county who met in Quarter Sessions enjoyed broad quasi-legislative powers, frequently taking it upon themselves to translate the abstract principles of parliamentary statutes into day-to-day policies. In so doing, they handled much of what today we would call the formulation of 'social policy'. This was particularly noticeable with regard to poor relief, where many eighteenth-century innovations stemmed from the pronouncements of Quarter Sessions.[113]

While magistrates enjoyed immense discretionary power, they were never laws unto themselves. Many of the more significant decisions of Quarter Sessions, for instance, had to be confirmed by the judge at the county Assizes. Moreover, the Home Office issued a steady stream of directives to justices precisely because it had to rely on them to perform a host of civil functions, such as the dispersal of riotous crowds and the suppression of seditious literature. While JPs were never entirely trustworthy servants of the state, they often acted in accordance with its instructions.[114] Some of them were certainly capable of abusing their power – by stopping up footpaths around their estates, for instance. The clerical magistrates who came to prominence late in the eighteenth century, moreover, were sometimes all too happy to police the morals of their social inferiors through close observance of sabbatarian laws and stricter licensing of public houses. Nevertheless, JPs were clearly acting in response to a notion of public service in levying rates for a wide variety of purposes that took large sums out of their own and not just their neighbours' pockets. Indeed, a few of them brought a missionary zeal to public service. Thus, for instance, the great road-making specialist John MacAdam used his influence as a justice to preside over the transformation of the abominable highways of the southwestern counties of England.[115]

Some of Georgian Britain's local governors showed considerable initiative in advancing their conception of the public good. Others, however, showed no initiative at all, and still others appear to have been motivated solely by greed. The Webbs have been rightly criticized for their 'Fabian teleology of reform', by which they equated centralization with administrative efficiency and thus condemned the profoundly decentralized agencies of Hanoverian local government as hopelessly inadequate, absurdly archaic, and appallingly corrupt.[116] But there is plenty of evidence to be found in their magisterial survey to make it clear that some localities were ill governed, indeed. Some of the select vestries were obviously more interested in holding feasts for themselves at public expense than in creating a more salubrious environment for their fellow townspeople. Embezzlement was endemic in a 'system' in which considerable sums of rate money passed through the hands of unpaid officers. The complete absence of central planning condemned the more laxly administered urban districts to a nauseatingly squalid state. What the Webbs called the 'almost universal prevalence' of the 'contract system' in local government might have helped to keep the rates down, but it clearly led to serious abuses.[117] Local authorities routinely farmed out many of their responsibilities to private entrepreneurs, and the pursuit of profit led to considerable human suffering. Eighteenth-century prisons, for instance, were private money-making concerns that afforded the gaoler and his turnkeys the opportunity to extort additional fees from prisoners at virtually every step from admission to discharge. While wealthy inmates could afford to make themselves comfortable, poor ones were often condemned to noisome (and, in the winter, freezing cold) common wards where hardened criminals and impressionable first offenders of both sexes mingled freely with each other. It is true that prison conditions were gradually reformed from the 1770s forward, and the absence of strict supervision meant that prisoners enjoyed considerably more autonomy than their Victorian counterparts did.[118] But there is no question that the contracting-out principle created irresistible opportunities for abuse. Nevertheless, local authorities had little choice but to rely on that principle in their efforts to regulate a society that denounced central bureaucracies as inherently despotic, and in which the notion that public services ought to be performed at public expense was slow to take hold.[119]

It seemed equally reasonable to Georgian Britons to create local statutory bodies on an ad hoc basis, via private act of parliament, in order to provide important services that the established local authorities were either unwilling or unable to deliver. Some 1,800 of these so-called improvement commissions had been created by 1830, and together they provided at least the basic amenities for life in many of the rapidly growing towns, such as sewage disposal, water supply, and street-cleaning, -paving, and -lighting. They were also responsible for the vast extension of Britain's transportation network through the creation of innumerable canals and turnpike roads. By 1835 there were 1,100 turnpike trusts, roughly twice as many as all other improvement commissions combined. Even the Webbs were obliged to admit that the improvement commissions were able to make up for many of the structural deficiencies of the parish vestries and the borough corporations. Since the commissions were spontaneously generated from within rather than imposed from without, some localities clearly benefited from their work much more than others did. Financial mismanagement, moreover, meant that that work was often more expensive to rate-payers than it might have been. But the proliferation of the improvement commissions makes it clear that propertied Georgians were willing and able to tackle most of the necessary local duties that they were unwilling to entrust to the state.[120]

Contemporaries agreed that one of the most important of these duties was the relief of the poor out of the parish rates. In the more bureaucratically centralized states of Europe, alms-giving was left to the church and to private charities. In what was arguably the most decentralized of them all it was an important responsibility of local government, enshrined in the poor law. We should not underestimate the extent of charitable giving and self-help in eighteenth-century Britain, where a sophisticated 'mixed economy of welfare' was well established. Subscription charities proliferated over the course of the century, attracting a good deal of the surplus wealth amassed by an ever more affluent middling sort who were eager to establish their philanthropic credentials. Humbler folk themselves frequently subscribed what they could to the innumerable 'box clubs' or 'friendly societies' that provided them with primitive insurance benefits.[121] Indeed, in Scotland and Ireland, where there was no poor law, philanthropy and self-help were the dominant features of social provision. In England and Wales, however, the poor law ensured that one of the chief responsibilities of the 'parish state' was welfare provision.

Over the course of the sixteenth century, the Tudor state had established the framework for a nationwide parochial relief system. It had mixed motives for doing so: to reduce the number of vagrants, for instance, at a time when the authorities feared vagrancy as a threat to social order, and to standardize local experiments that seemed to be providing real benefits to the halt and the lame. The famous Elizabethan acts of 1598 and 1601 set in place the local structure of poor relief for England and Wales that would remain until the passage of the New Poor Law in 1834. By their provisions, parish churchwardens and overseers were charged with the duties of collecting the poor rate, relieving the impotent poor, setting the able-bodied poor to work, and securing apprenticeships for poor children. By 1680, parochial relief had become universal in England, at least. It was dispensed in a number of ways, but most often in the form of small cash doles, provided to the elderly and disabled on a weekly basis, and casual payments to able-bodied men in times of dearth.[122]

Poor relief was the most onerous responsibility of the parish. The number of churchwardens and overseers who administered the system easily outnumbered the centrally appointed servants of the state. As the eighteenth century progressed, they extracted ever more money from better-off parishioners in the shape of poor rates. While those collected in 1696 accounted for some 0.8 per cent of national income and were used to relieve perhaps 3.6 per cent of the English population, those collected in 1802–3 amounted to 1.9 per cent of national income and were applied to the relief of almost 15 per cent of the people. While the value of poor rates varied greatly from place to place, from a national standpoint it was clearly on the rise over the course of the century, equalling 11 per cent of the central government's revenues from direct and excise taxes in 1700 and 19 per cent by the 1780s.[123] The fiscal–military state was a far greater burden to taxpayers, but both the cost and the social impact of the poor rate were more noticeable to them, simply because these were intensely local. They were of course most noticeable to the humble folk who benefited from them, and these benefits could be substantial. It has been estimated that poor-law support for single-parent families in the first decades of the nineteenth century came to almost 80 per cent of the average income from employment of two-parent families, a far more balanced ratio than we see later in the century, by which point poor relief had greatly stagnated in comparison with the growing real wages of most manual workers.[124]

It is nevertheless easy to exaggerate the generosity of the old poor law. The main reason why relief payments came so close to the living standard of wage-earners was because that standard remained just above subsistence level. There were, moreover, institutional strings attached to a good many relief payments. While the 'workhouse test' was not as common as it would become after 1834, there were already at least 600 workhouses in England by the middle of the eighteenth century, whose inmates were set to a variety of irksome tasks in return for their subsistence.[125] The parochial authorities who relied on them were confident that workhouses could be made to instil work discipline and a respect for the scriptures into paupers while they turned a tidy profit for the entrepreneurs who were contracted to run them. But as it happened, the vast majority of the long-term residents of workhouses were the very young, the elderly, and single mothers, few of whom could be put to profitable uses, and most of whom were consigned to wretchedness in dismal places that were run on a shoe-string.[126]

A more potent factor than the workhouse in the lives of the poor was the Act of Settlement of 1662, which made eligibility for poor relief a difficult thing for many of them to obtain. It gave the parochial authorities forty days to remove new inhabitants of dwellings with a yearly value of under £10 to 'such parish where he or they were last legally settled either as a native, sojourner, householder, apprentice or servant' if they appeared 'likely to be chargeable to the Parish'. Thenceforth, only poor labourers who could obtain a certificate of support and of good character from their legal parish of settlement could move outside that parish without fear of removal. The effects of the law of settlement have been hotly debated among historians. It certainly led to frequent and expensive legal battles between the parish issuing a removal order and the parish to which the person or family in question was removed. Very few parishes were so open-handed as to accept without a fight the arrival of impecunious newcomers. Still, it seems doubtful that the law of settlement seriously diminished labour mobility. Able-bodied male migrants had little reason to fear removal so long as they did not threaten to become a burden on the rates, and there is little doubt that the threat of removal deterred many of those who were in need from applying for relief in the first place.[127]

If the law of settlement did not seriously hamper economically useful migration, however, it furnished the local authorities with an immense power over the lives of the poor that they sometimes cruelly exercised. The elderly and the sick were occasionally carted away from home. Vagrants were frequently shuttled about from one parish to the next. Women and children were removed far more frequently than men, and pregnant women were the chief target for parish authorities because they were potentially very expensive to the parish. Perhaps as many as a third of all the removal orders issued in Cambridgeshire between 1662 and 1834 were directed against pregnant women.[128] The apprenticeship clauses of the Act of Settlement, moreover, frequently consigned pauper children to a grim fate. By stipulating that indentured apprentices were entitled to a settlement in the parish in which they served, they encouraged overseers to ease the burden on the rates by sending children in their care to any master who was willing to take them. These masters could be brutally exploitative, and some of them cast apprentices off as soon as the bounty that came with them was safely in hand.[129] Thus, while the poor law eased the plight of many poor people, the terms of the Act of Settlement gave the 'parish state' the means to make the lives of some of them miserable indeed, and it did not hesitate to do so when doing so saved a few pounds of the rate-payers' money.

The formidable powers to aid and to discipline the poor that the state lodged in the hands of magistrates and overseers illustrate the complexities of governance in the eighteenth century. While the central government itself was remote from the daily lives of most people, the parochial authorities on whom it so heavily relied were always near at hand, and were obviously a potent influence, for good or ill, in the lives of the poor. Georgian Britons were no less governed for being governed by a decentralized regime. As the century progressed, that regime became more and more noticeable, particularly in its demands for ever more from its subjects in the shape of taxes and rates. Indeed, by the end of the Napoleonic War many Britons had concluded that it had become far too complicated and burdensome. As we shall see in the next chapter, the perceived excesses of the fiscal–military state led to its dramatic scaling back in the decades after Waterloo.

3

The Limits of the *Laissez-Faire* State

1815–1880

There is no doubt that the late-Victorian state was a more perceptible force in the lives of Britons than its late-Georgian predecessor had been. While in 1815 the central government still assumed very few responsibilities beyond the defence of the realm, by 1880 it was (among many other things) obliging parents to send their children to primary school, limiting the hours of women and child labourers, and sending inspectors out to monitor working and sanitary conditions. At first glance, this broadening of the responsibilities of the state seems like a logical response to the needs of a rapidly growing, urbanizing, and industrializing population. And so, to a considerable extent, it was. But just as historians now question whether an era marked by uneven and often slow rates of growth and fitful technological innovation deserves to be called an era of 'industrial revolution',[1] so too is it worth questioning the 'revolution' in the scope of the British state. By 1880, Britons entrusted it with more responsibilities than they had ever done before. But they did so haltingly and grudgingly, and could console themselves with the thought that the central government cost them less than it had their grandparents, sent few of them to war, and indeed rarely presented itself to their eyes in any shape other than that of the postman.

There are four points about this broader but still distinctly limited state that deserve close scrutiny here. The first is that it was not the hugely expensive military juggernaut that its Georgian predecessor had been. Indeed, one of the chief preoccupations of British politics in the two decades after Waterloo was the dismantling of the fiscal–military state that had grown by leaps and bounds since the Nine Years War. Postwar retrenchment reversed the long-term trend towards ever higher levels of public expenditure for the purposes of war-making. The British navy retained its mastery of the seas throughout the century, and Victoria's armies fought a long series of 'little wars' of imperial expansion. But peace in Europe, combined with buoyant per capita income growth, meant that the mid-century British state, like most of its continental counterparts, was able to meet its military expenses at a far lower cost to the taxpayer than its late-eighteenth-century predecessor had done.

The second point is that the patrician stewards of the Victorian state strove to legitimate its authority, and their own authority within it, by proving to the enfranchised and unenfranchised alike that it was not a broker of special privileges to themselves and their hangers-on. 'Disinterestedness' was a hallmark of elite governance from the 1820s forward, and disinterestedness generally meant the promotion of a sort of negative social fairness through the reduction of the state's capacity to benefit some sectional interests over others. The politics of disinterestedness sought to create a neutral state that stood above and apart from society and a largely self-acting economy, and whose responsibility for the poor amounted to little more than the lowering of consumer prices and the grudging prevention of destitution. Gradual democratization bolstered parliament's authority as a governing institution, but did little to broaden the narrow social agenda of the state. Most voters remained too wedded to individualism, voluntarism, and the ostensibly providential laws of the market, and too worried about the possible abuse of state power, to entrust the central government with substantially greater authority to intervene in their lives.

The third point is that the state's minimal economic and social agenda did not prevent it from acting as an occasionally stern moral disciplinarian. In fact, it was the Victorian state's very commitment to the *laissez-faire* ideal of a free labour market that prompted it to take harsh disciplinary action against the ostensibly feckless poor through the agency of the New Poor Law. The Poor Law Amendment Act (1834) created by far the largest centrally supervised bureaucracy of the Victorian era, and its chief duty was to see to it that the conditions of rate-aided poor relief were so unattractive as to force the 'able-bodied' poor to embrace self-reliance as an alternative. The state's moral intervention in the lives of the down-and-out extended well beyond the workhouse, moreover. Tighter licensing laws and more authoritarian policing tactics were intended to coerce working-class men into orderliness, while the closer regulation of prostitution compromised the civil liberties of working-class women. More generally, state support for the hierarchical legal codes governing labour relations and marriage subordinated the interests of workmen to their masters', and of wives to their husbands'. In short, the economic 'minimalism' of the Victorian state did not prevent it from throwing its formidable moral weight around in support of a narrow social hierarchy.

The final point is that the Victorian state's very efforts to inflict market discipline on the poor prompted it to make fitful interventions in the market itself in order to make the living and working conditions of the poor more tolerable. There was no doctrinaire line drawn between *laissez-faire* and state intervention, because it quickly became obvious to most Victorians that strict *laissez-faire* was both unjust and unwise. Even the centrally appointed agents of the New Poor Law, the ostensible shock troops of *laissez-faire*, were obliged to admit that wretched living and working conditions were bound to undermine industriousness and self-supporting habits among the poor, and that it was thus a proper responsibility of the state to try to ameliorate them. Nevertheless, the sanitary and factory reforms of the Victorian era were piecemeal and limited, and would have been even more so had it not been for the agitation of plebeian pressure groups, zealous bureaucrats, and evangelical humanitarians. Most Victorians felt they had good reasons to keep state intervention the exception rather than the rule: their loathing of higher taxes; the adverse effect that social reform was bound to have on 'respectable' propertied interests such as factory owners; an abiding fear of central dictation and bureaucratic corruption; and a marked preference for local autonomy. This last sentiment meant that most Victorian-era social legislation was discretionary rather than compulsory, and a great many authorities were reluctant to use their discretionary powers for fear of alienating the rate-payers' democracies that had been established by the reform of local government. In short, there was little sympathy for central- or even local-government activism among the early- and mid-Victorians, most of whom were content with a frugal and disinterested state that left them tolerably alone.

The dismantling of the fiscal–military state

In one respect, the mid-Victorian state was much less perceptible to Britons than its late-Georgian predecessor had been. For while it was still widely believed that the defence of the realm was the most important duty of the central government, it was a far cheaper one during the post-Waterloo era of the 'Pax Britannica' than it had been hitherto. Retrenchment cut public spending by 25 per cent over the two decades after 1815, and relative peace and quiet in Europe, interrupted only by the Crimean War (1854–6), enabled British governments to contain military spending thereafter. The civil costs of central government rose as the state gradually assumed new domestic responsibilities. But in financial terms these duties remained small compared to the traditional ones of maintaining the army and navy and paying the interest on a very large national debt that had grown as a consequence of the chronic war-making of the recent past. Thus, while the mid-Victorian state was beginning to intrude in the lives of its citizens in ways that it had never done before, it required far less of them in the shape of aggregate taxation and military service than the Hanoverian state had done.

More than anything else it was the intense pressure brought to bear on the governments of the post-Waterloo years that cut the fiscal–military state down to size. We have already seen that the putative extravagance and corruption of the war machine was a well-established tenet of British radicalism by the end of the American War. It was an even more single-minded radical fixation in the wake of the Napoleonic Wars, which had more than doubled the rate of per capita public spending. Thus in the late 1810s radical commentators such as William Hazlitt felt that they had even better reasons than their predecessors of the late 1770s to insist that 'all persons maintained by the taxes or employed by those who are maintained by them are a clog, a dead weight upon those who pay them . . . – a dead carcass fastened to a living one, with this difference, that it still devours the food which it does not provide'.[2]

'Respectable' opinion within parliament and without dismissed such allegations of state parasitism as wildly exaggerated, and the radical antidote of wholesale parliamentary reform as unnecessary. Still, the perception that the anti-Napoleonic military machine had become intolerably burdensome to taxpayers was widely shared among the urban middle classes, rural landowners and tenant farmers, and a good many opposition and independent MPs. Most members tolerated ever greater expenditure as a regrettable wartime necessity. But they forced wholesale retrenchment on the administration led by the Earl of Liverpool (1812–27) as soon as the Napoleonic threat had come to an end. The Commons's abolition of the income tax in 1816 marked the onset of an era of retrenchment that, with the help of peace in Europe and economic growth at home, made the mid-Victorian state far cheaper to taxpayers than the late-Georgian one had been, and considerably less burdensome to its subjects than its continental rivals were to theirs. While, thanks to the Napoleonic Wars, central-government spending in real terms had risen from £1.94 per capita in 1791 to £4.51 in 1811, it fell to £2.79 in 1821, and to £1.99 by 1841. By 1851, per capita public spending was still well under half its wartime height, and it only began to rise appreciably in the wake of the Boer War. While the British central government had absorbed almost a quarter of the gross national product in the last years of the Napoleonic Wars, it was absorbing only 8 per cent by the 1870s, as against 13 per cent in France and 12 per cent in the new German empire. While by 1880 French public spending in per capita terms had quadrupled and Austro-Hungarian spending had trebled over immediate post-Waterloo levels (according to the admittedly sketchy fiscal details available), British central spending had risen by only 50 per cent.[3]

There were three main reasons why the mid-Victorian state was comparatively inexpensive. The first was one it shared with its continental counterparts:[4] a lower level of military spending. Preserving the overwhelming superiority of the British navy and extending the empire to include about a quarter of the earth's surface obviously meant that military spending remained the central government's highest priority.[5] British forces were involved in thirteen wars and nearly 150 smaller skirmishes over the period, almost all of them in colonial theatres.[6] But in a number of ways this was an empire on the cheap. As late as the 1880s, for instance, it was managed by fewer than 6,000 officials, while the overwhelming technical superiority of British military forces usually meant that their indigenous foes suffered far higher battlefield casualties than they did.[7] Meanwhile, the decisive diplomatic settlement forged at the Congress of Vienna, as well as the military and economic disarray in which the Napoleonic Wars had left virtually all of Britain's continental rivals, helped to keep the peace in (and British forces out of) Europe until the 1850s. Although the Crimean War was expensive while it lasted, by Georgian standards it ended in a hurry.

The second reason why the mid-Victorian central government remained relatively cheap was the slowness with which it took up additional non-military responsibilities. While it devoted considerably more tax money to education, public health, regulation of workplace conditions, and the like at the end of this period than it had done at the beginning, there was no sudden or dramatic reallocation of the state's spending priorities. Per capita spending on civil government was exactly the same in 1841 as it had been on the eve of the French Revolutionary War fifty years earlier. While civil-government spending as a percentage of total spending grew over the next several decades, it did so at a fairly deliberate pace, from an average of 10 per cent for 1846–50 (still well within Georgian-era parameters), to 17 per cent for 1861–5, to 22 per cent for 1876–80. As late as 1880, military spending and the debt service for which it was largely responsible still accounted for 65 per cent of central expenditure.[8] Thus, in fiscal terms, the mid-Victorian shift in the state's priorities was gradual and limited. Taxpayers who were now paying substantially less for the defence of the realm did not suddenly find themselves spending a vast amount more on social services.

The third reason why the mid-Victorian state was relatively light on its subjects' pockets was that there was considerably more money in most of them than there had ever been before. Britain was the world's undisputed industrial, financial, and commercial champion in the mid-nineteenth century. While the roughly 10 per cent of Europe's population that lived within the British Isles at mid-century were still heavily taxed in comparison with their neighbours on the Continent, Britons' control of 60 per cent of Europe's industrial capacity and their supremacy in trade and finance generated a level of affluence that made their central government comparatively affordable.[9]

The gradual dismantling of the fiscal–military state in the decades after Waterloo was accompanied by an incremental reform of the central bureaucracy that made it more recognizably 'modern' and less obviously 'corrupt' than its Georgian predecessor. By the mid-1830s all sinecures had been slated for abolition, the practice of granting reversions had long since fallen into disuse, and the pension money in the hands of the crown and its ministers had been dramatically reduced and brought under parliamentary supervision. These reforms marked the gradual acceptance of the notion that public office was not the private property of the office-holder, but a public trust that should be carried out in person, compensated by strict salary, and superannuated according to an authorized scale of retirement provisions. By 1850, virtually every centrally appointed office was subject to strict terms of service and payment. The only 'rational' bureaucratic principle that was not yet generally accepted by 1850 was recruitment by competition. While the much-vaunted Northcote–Trevelyan Report of 1853 recommended a limited form of open competition based on examinations that privileged the best and brightest from the elite public schools, it took several more decades for uniform standards of competitive recruitment to be established throughout the Civil Service.[10] But even though nepotism in appointments remained a noticeable feature of the Victorian administrative system,[11] that system was much more closely bound by strict rules of service and of compensation, and thus much better insulated against charges of 'extravagance' and 'corruption', than its Georgian predecessor had been.[12]

Like retrenchment, administrative reform was an issue on which the postwar governments were willing to yield to 'respectable' pressure, because they themselves could recognize that more frugal and less obviously nepotistic governance helped to legitimate the authority of what was still a narrow governing class. They took a much less indulgent view of the massive plebeian agitation for root-and-branch parliamentary reform in the wake of Waterloo, however. In fact, the most immediately noticeable feature of the British state in the late 1810s was its repressiveness. The Liverpool administration suspended habeas corpus in peacetime, prosecuted many leaders of the outdoor reform movement, initiated dozens of actions for blasphemy and seditious libel against radical pressmen, imposed strict limits on freedom of assembly, and sought (with much success) to price the plebeian press out of business through the notorious Six Acts passed in the wake of the Peterloo massacre in 1819.[13] By early 1820, the government had turned the tumultuous north of England into an armed camp that was garrisoned by a full third of the soldiers available for home service.[14] It should be added that there were limits beyond which the Liverpool ministry did not permit itself to go. It did not censor the press, for instance, or restrict the rights of juries in libel trials. Still, it did not hesitate to take strong measures to protect what it deemed to be the divinely ordained authority of the propertied classes from the ostensibly 'levelling' demands of radicals for a more broadly representative government.

This Tory fixation on law and order stemmed in part from a belief that there were few positive measures that a government could take to ameliorate suffering in bad economic times. Throughout the postwar Slump, Liverpool and his colleagues insisted that interventionist economic measures were only likely to make a bad situation worse. Thus the prime minister told the House of Lords shortly after Peterloo that

> on enquiry, it would be found that by far the greater part of the miseries of which human nature complained were in all times and in all countries beyond the control of human legislation.
> 'How small, of all the ills that men endure,
> The part which kings or states can cause or cure.'[15]

This was by no means a dogmatic statement of faith in the blessings of *laissez-faire*. Tory non-intervention was not predicated on Ricardian optimism about the transformative dynamism of the unregulated economy. It rested, rather, on two quite different assumptions that stemmed in part from evangelicalism and the gloomy predictions of Malthus: that there was almost nothing that could be done to alter the fickle course of a cyclical economy; and that, left to its own devices, the unprogressive, self-acting economy would reflect God's incomprehensible wisdom, which it was manifestly unwise to question.[16]

This economic fatalism suggested that the government had a duty to remove itself as far as possible from the providential workings of the economy, and that is exactly what the Tories sought to do in the first fifteen years after the war. Thus the tariff reforms of the 1820s sought to restore the 'natural' balance of the economic system by cutting down to size the very high excise duties of wartime.[17] This economic minimalism had the salutary effect of defending the elite stewards of the state against the charge that they had overburdened the people during the war, for tariff reforms began to ease the weight of indirect taxes on the shoulders of the humbler classes. Excise duties fell from 41 per cent of all tax receipts in 1816–20 to only 27 per cent in 1841–5, while the customs duties that fell heavily on the well-to-do rose from 21 to 43 per cent over the same period.[18] Thus the Tory ministries were able to advertise economic minimalism as an act of justice to modest consumers.

The age of disinterestedness: elite stewardship of the minimal state

Through these piecemeal tariff reforms, elite politicians were already beginning to promote minimal government as a mark of their disinterested governance. 'Disinterestedness' was perhaps the most highly prized public virtue within elite political circles by the middle decades of the century. Generally speaking, it meant the promotion of social fairness through negative means, by the stripping away of taxes and state-sponsored privileges that were seen to benefit some groups but to hurt others, such as the Corn Laws and other protective duties, or some of the constitutional privileges of the Anglican Church. But disinterested governance could also mean, and often did mean, the promotion of more positive reforms that were designed to promote social fairness by extending established privileges, most notably the franchise, to a broader number of people.

From the 1820s to the 1880s, the promotion of greater social fairness was a preoccupation of Tory and Whig governments and of their Conservative and Liberal successors. All of them valued it for pragmatic reasons, as an effective means of legitimating what was still a fairly narrow social and political hierarchy. But most of them also valued it for moral reasons, as a means of fulfilling what they perceived to be their Christian duty to promote the best interests of the nation as a whole. There were important party-political differences in the patrician approach to social fairness. Most notably, the Whig governments of the 'decade' of reform (1830–41) were more inclined than their Tory and Conservative opponents or their Liberal descendants to extend the powers of the state as a means of actively promoting social fairness. The Whigs were just as firmly committed to 'cheap government' as their Conservative opponents. In fact, per capita public spending reached its lowest point in the century during their period in office. But the Whig variant of the politics of disinterestedness also included a more positive conception of the proper role of the state.

Their boldest effort to promote social fairness took the shape of the extension of citizenship rights through the Reform Act of 1832. Recently, scholars have sought to play down the significance of the act, arguing that it increased the electorate only from 14 to 18 per cent of adult men; that it more closely connected the right to vote with the possession of property; that it actually reduced the size of the electorate in many of the more populous English boroughs; and that in a number of ways it marked the decline of the Georgian notion of electioneering as an activity in which the unenfranchised could participate in meaningful ways.[19] Others have emphasized the structural continuities between the pre- and post-1832 electoral system, noting that patronage remained an important means of winning votes in many constituencies, and that the new party-political apparatus was remarkably like the old one.[20]

There is much truth in these revisionist verdicts, but one can go along with most of them and still acknowledge that the act was a remarkable constitutional reform that shocked even many of the government's own supporters when its details were announced. More dramatic than its extension of the electorate was its redistributional impact. Its partial or total disfranchisement of burgage-tenure and corporation boroughs made 144 seats in the House of Commons available for redistribution, sixty-four of which were assigned to new constituencies that gave residents of large cities such as Manchester, Birmingham, Sheffield, and Leeds their first opportunity ever to return MPs to the Commons. The act also inspired a dramatic rise in the number of contested elections, giving voters of the post-Reform era far more frequent opportunities to vote than their predecessors had enjoyed.[21] The English and Welsh electorate, moreover, grew by a very substantial 62 per cent between 1832 and 1866, as demographic changes gradually qualified more and more men for the £10 householder franchise that had been established in 1832.[22] In short, the Reform Act was a constitutional innovation that the Tories had never dreamt of making. It evinced a positive conception of the state's duty to promote social fairness, depriving many borough proprietors of much of their glaringly disproportionate influence within the electoral system while acknowledging a much broader range of legitimate interests within that system, most notably the interests of middling property owners in hitherto unenfranchised towns.[23]

The Whig governments also promoted a broader notion of social fairness through their religious policies, which substantially eroded the state-sponsored privileges of the Anglican Church. The church's special relationship with the state had already been undermined by the repeal of the Test and Corporation Acts in 1828, which formally removed all the political disqualifications that had been inflicted on the Dissenting sects in the late seventeenth century, and by Catholic emancipation a year later, which permitted Catholics to sit in parliament and opened to Catholics all Irish offices of state other than those of viceroy and chancellor. These measures were arguably as significant as the Reform Act itself, because they marked the beginning of the end of the 'confessional state' which for the previous 150 years had always sought to restrict and occasionally to exclude from political life the putative enemies of Anglicanism.[24] They also marked a dramatic shift away from the notion that the British state was based on a specific set of religious principles and 'towards officially sanctioned pluralism – and hence towards a state system effectively governed by principles of indifferentism and secularism'.[25] But it was the formidable lobbying efforts of the Dissenters and the threat of civil war in Ireland that prompted the Tory ministry of the Duke of Wellington (1828–30) to carry out these reforms, and not because they were ideologically committed to cutting down on state-sponsored Anglican privileges. By contrast, the Whig–Liberal coalition ministries chipped away at those privileges with gusto. Thus, for instance, they eased the burden on tithe payers by commuting tithes into cash payments that varied according to the prevailing price of corn; licensed Dissenting chapels for matrimonial ceremonies; transferred the registration of births, marriages, and deaths from the church to the state, thus legally recognizing the existence of non-Anglicans for the first time; and placated the Catholic majority in Ireland by abolishing mandatory payment of cess (i.e. tithe) to the established Irish Church.[26]

The Whig conception of fairness tended to be more expansive than the Conservative one with respect to social as well as religious issues. The paternalist sense of *noblesse oblige* among the ultra-privileged Whig aristocracy helps to explain why two of the more significant of the early factory and public-health measures were passed while they were in office: the 1833 Factory Act and the 1848 Public Health Act. Whig indifference to the principles of political economy or disciplinary evangelicalism meant that they were willing to look into the questions of factory, sanitary, and educational reform, and to encourage the notion that it was reasonable for social reformers to expect the state to take positive action in these areas. The Conservatives, by contrast, were still doing their best to avoid such inquiries well into the 1840s, fearing that they would only excite unreasonable expectations of what the central government could do to cure the evils of a rapidly industrializing society.[27]

The more activist style of the Whig ministries encouraged the notion that it was fit and proper for the central government to make social inquiries and to initiate social legislation. Before the Reform Act, the proper functions of the government were mainly seen to be executive – the defence of the realm, the conduct of foreign policy, and the like. Most bills dealing with social policy were initiated by backbenchers. After 1832, there was a rapidly growing expectation that governments would assume responsibility for such legislation, and the Whigs did everything to encourage it. Thus the percentage of divisions in the House of Commons involving government bills rose from 20 per cent of the total in 1832 to over 50 per cent by 1840, and continued to rise thereafter.[28] While Whig governments acted on a wider variety of issues, the broader political public that the Reform Act had brought into being indicated that it expected them to act on even more. Hence the volume of petitions to the House of Commons rose enormously over the course of the decade, from 23,000 for 1828–32 to 70,000 for 1838–42.[29]

Cabinet members were obviously answerable to a broader political nation in the wake of the Reform Act. At the same time, they were less beholden to the wishes of the crown. The Reform Act did away with most of the electoral patronage that the crown still possessed, and shortly thereafter it became obvious that the choice of prime minister now depended not on the will of the king, but on that of the Commons majority. While in 1834 William IV replaced the Whigs with a minority Conservative government led by Sir Robert Peel that was more to William's taste, Peel was forced to resign within six weeks for lack of adequate support in the Commons. The king had no choice but to call back the Whigs. Peel's return to the premiership after the general election of 1841 provided final confirmation that the crown's prerogative power to name its own ministers was effectively null and void. The Conservatives' decisive election victory compelled Victoria to ask Peel to form a government, even though she would much rather have kept the Whigs in office. Thus the one significant prerogative power that monarchs had still routinely used at the beginning of the nineteenth century had been rendered useless by the middle of it.[30]

Victoria was not content to acquiesce in an entirely ceremonial role. She and Prince Albert grew to recognize the importance of seeming to be above the political fray, but they insisted that ministers respect Victoria's formal right to be consulted on any and all matters of government business, and she frequently expressed her opinions on policy. Ministers were by no means obliged to follow Victoria's advice, and her Liberal ministers mostly honoured it in the breach, because from middle age onward she was a Conservative partisan.[31] But while in private Victoria often acted as though she did not recognize that ministries were responsible to the electorate rather than to herself, her popularity stemmed chiefly from her lack of real political authority. By the end of her reign, the prestige of the British monarchy rested on its symbolic power: as an emblem of imperial grandeur, and of the very parliamentary liberalism that prevented her from being the politically powerful sovereign that she often wished to be. Thus, as Vernon Bogdanor has put it, 'modern constitutional monarchy came about much against the will of the queen who was Britain's first constitutional monarch'.[32]

While the monarchy had settled into a largely ceremonial status by 1880, the House of Lords continued to make occasionally controversial use of its amending and veto powers over Commons legislation. Its refusal to pass the Reform Bill provoked serious riots in 1831, and ultimately it required William IV's famous threat to create a sufficient number of pro-reform peers to ensure passage of the bill to persuade the Lords to acquiesce in it. The strong Conservative majority in the Lords remained a thorn in the Whig coalition's side thereafter, particularly on religious issues. But after the 'decade' of reform had drawn to a close, the Lords showed considerably more restraint in their use of the veto. Such restraint helped to ensure that the Lords would carry into the twentieth century their unlimited right to veto legislation.[33] Aristocratic domination of cabinet offices also indicates that peers remained a formidable bloc within the political elite right through the century. The Marquess of Salisbury's Conservative cabinets at the end of it were scarcely less blue-blooded than the younger Pitt's cabinet had been at its beginning. The aristocracy's kinship ties to the House of Commons were still extensive in the middle of the century; in 1841, a full quarter of all MPs were the direct descendants of peers. More generally, the landed classes enjoyed a wildly disproportionate influence within the Commons throughout the century. Over 80 per cent of the MPs in the 1841 House had close family ties to broad acres, while as late as 1895, 60 per cent of MPs were gentlemen of leisure, most of whom derived a significant portion of their incomes from land.[34]

The persistence of landed domination within both houses of parliament is remarkable, but its importance is easily exaggerated. Commercial and financial wealth was already well represented in the Georgian-era Commons, and even the industrialists who remained under-represented there 'saw nothing much wrong in leaving the details of government in aristocratic hands, provided that the government created a suitable framework for the promotion of economic growth and pursued congenial economic policies'.[35] By mid-century, there were few measures raised in either house that starkly opposed the interests of one group of property holders to the interests of others. 'Respectable' opinion felt that all of them were pretty well represented at Westminster, and that the influence of the Lords helped to ensure that parliament would continue to fulfil its functions in a cautious and dignified manner. The passage of legislation was only one of those functions, as the journalist Walter Bagehot and many other commentators pointed out; its deliberative proceedings were also designed simultaneously to express the considered opinions of and to provide learned instruction to the nation.[36] The nation, in turn, paid remarkably close attention to those proceedings. During the parliamentary session, debates in the Commons and the Lords dominated the pages of virtually every newspaper. In sum, parliament, which now convened in Charles Barry's magnificent Palace of Westminster, with its famous clock tower and its 940-foot expanse along the Thames, was probably held in broader esteem by the mid-Victorian generation than by any other one before or since.[37]

One of the chief reasons why this was so was that the politicians who sat there shared with most of their constituents the belief that the central government's main obligation was to permit people to look after themselves. Statesmen sought 'to create a neutral, passive, almost apolitical state, standing above and apart from the fast-moving, chaotic, and open-ended evolution of mid-Victorian society'.[38] Most of the reforming legislation of this era sought to convince an ever more diverse body of social interests that the state was no longer in the business of privileging some of them at the expense of others. As we have seen, even the relatively activist Whig coalition governments of the 1830s were strongly interested in the promotion of a negative social fairness that sought to remove the state from social disputes by cutting down on contentious political privileges – those of borough patrons, for instance. But at the same time, their constitutional reforms encouraged underprivileged groups – Catholics, Dissenters, and the plebeian radicals of the enormous Chartist movement – to call upon the state to play a more active role in the amelioration of their grievances. 'Respectable' opinion ultimately concluded that Whig activism, rather than legitimating the patrician state, had only exposed it to dangerous popular clamour. Thus in 1841 the Conservatives, under the leadership of Sir Robert Peel, won a landslide parliamentary victory, and for the next forty years it was the chief aim of virtually all governments, regardless of their party complexion, to cultivate the neutrality of the state – and public trust in its motives – by ostentatiously dissociating it from social disputes.

Conservative and Liberal governments sought to secure the neutrality of the state through the same repertoire of means. One of them was adherence to public service. Even if mid-Victorian politicians had wanted to gorge themselves on the fruits of office in the manner of Walpole, the decline of patronage gave them few chances to do so. But few of them would have wanted to, anyway. For over the first several decades of the nineteenth century, most politicians had come to believe that it was their responsibility to pay closer attention to the duties than to the emoluments of office. There are several explanations for the development of this self-denying notion of public service, and the growth of evangelical religion and the exacting standard of Victorian 'respectability' that partly stemmed from it are prominent among them. But it also stemmed in part from the conviction that one means of demonstrating the political elite's fitness to govern was to show that it did not subordinate public interest to private profit.

A second means of securing the neutrality of the state was to absolve it of virtually all responsibility for the direction of the economy. Mid-Victorian governments accepted cycles of boom and bust as inevitable facts of life, and did almost nothing to mitigate their impact. The state, moreover, almost completely removed itself from the monetary system through the Bank Charter Act (1844), which strictly linked bank-note issues to the gold supply. From then on, it only occasionally intervened in monetary arrangements in order to help smooth over major liquidity crises. If the gilt-edged security of sterling benefited the exporters of financial services more than it did anybody else, none of the major players in the booming mid-century economy felt that it was doing them serious harm.

Much the same can be said of Free Trade, which by the 1860s was an even more popular shibboleth than Sound Currency. Rhetorically speaking, free trade had started life as a critique of the allegedly unfair protection that the government had granted to the landed interest by means of the protective corn laws of 1815. Northern manufacturers came to see them as a blatant piece of agricultural favouritism, and united under the banner of one of the most formidable extra-parliamentary pressure groups of the century, the Anti-Corn Law League, to do away with the so-called 'bread tax'. Shortly thereafter, Peel took office, and pledged his ministry to a policy of fiscal fairness that hinged on three things: further reduction of indirect taxes in order to lower prices, especially for humbler consumers; the shifting of a considerable part of the tax burden away from those same humbler consumers and onto the backs of more affluent ones through the (remarkably uncontroversial) resurrection of income tax in 1842; and repeal of the corn laws. In 1846, Peel split with the protectionist majority in his party and thus sacrificed his own political career in order to do away with them. He did so for several reasons, but prominent among them was his belief that one of the most effective ways for the ruling elite to legitimate its power was 'by encouraging the idea amongst the great body of the people that we, the rich and the powerful, are willing to take a more than ordinary share of the public burdens, and to remove those burdens from the people as far as it is possible'.[39] There can be little doubt that free trade was immensely popular,[40] and that it did indeed become the potent legitimating device that Peel had envisioned. It helped to turn Peel himself into an almost legendary popular hero after his premature death in 1850, and it helps to account for the virtual hegemony of the Liberal party in the 1850s and 1860s as the party of fiscal fairness, as against the protectionist Conservatives, who were widely stigmatized as the party of landed monopoly.[41]

The minimalist neutrality of the state became an especially prominent political theme during this era of Liberal hegemony, and it was a Peelite, Gladstone, who virtually came to personify it as chancellor of the Exchequer and later as prime minister. While he was by no means a dogmatic adherent of *laissez-faire*, the influence of his policies helped to ensure that with the notable exception of Gilded-Age America, 'no industrial economy can have existed in which the State played a smaller role than that of the United Kingdom in the 1860s'. By the end of that decade, it had rid itself of all protective tariffs; its direct involvement in labour relations was restricted to management of the royal dockyards and the inspection of factories; its responsibility for education extended merely to the rather modest subsidies which it gave to the denominational schools; and its very limited intervention in the areas of public health and the poor laws left a great deal of discretionary power in local hands.[42]

With the minimalist framework now well established, Gladstone perceived it to be one of the chief fiscal duties of the state to ease the burden on the taxpayer to the greatest possible extent, thus permitting money to 'fructify in the pockets of the people'. He paid scrupulous attention to the balance between indirect and direct taxes as a means of doing fiscal justice to the working classes. Thanks in large part to his efforts at the Exchequer, the percentage of central-government revenue taken in the shape of direct taxes (income tax, death duties, and the like) rose from about 30 per cent in the late 1840s to 40 per cent by the early 1880s. Over the same period, indirect-tax revenue, most of it collected on articles of mass consumption, fell from about 70 per cent to 60 per cent of the total. If these reforms were modest in their redistributive tendencies, that is because they were intended to be. Gladstone stressed that the point behind them was to promote fiscal justice between classes, not to reward one at the expense of others. Fair play was just as prominent a theme of Gladstonian religious as it was of Gladstonian financial policy. From beginning to end, his public career was shaped by the moral imperatives of a devout Anglicanism. But he had no compunctions about doing away with some of the less defensible of the church's remaining privileges in his efforts to lift the state out of social controversies. Thus his first ministry (1868–74) arranged for the disestablishment of the Irish Church and enabled Dissenters to take degrees from Oxford and Cambridge.[43]

While Benjamin Disraeli was as flamboyant and pragmatic as Gladstone was sober-sided and moralistic, these adversaries in the great two-party rivalry shared the same predisposition for a minimalist state that generally let society take care of itself. Despite his reputation as an ardent imperialist, Disraeli was never inclined to be a big spender. Unlike Gladstone, he did not seek economy for its own sake. But he appreciated the political utility of state frugality, and thus was never inclined to try to raise taxes substantially above Gladstonian limits.[44] Nor did the much-vaunted Disraelian 'paternalism' entail a much more noticeably interventionist role for the state. Indeed, the most significant legislation pushed through by his 1874–80 government was an act of disengagement. The reform of trade-union law, by protecting unions' right to engage in peaceful picketing, turned the state's role in labour relations into that of a strictly neutral referee.[45] Thus, however wide the personal and tactical differences between their two great leaders may have been, neither the Liberal nor the Conservative parties envisioned an expansive role for the state at the height of the Victorian era.

Nor was there any longer significant 'pressure from below' to enhance the powers of the central government as a means of redressing social grievances. Such pressure had been powerful indeed in the 1830s and 1840s, when the widespread plebeian anger provoked by the limited extension of the franchise in 1832, by the disciplinary rigour of the New Poor Law, and by the narrow limits of factory reform gave birth to Chartism, the most formidable working-class political movement in British history. Chartism was an enormous and sprawling phenomenon that signified many different things to many different people.

But it is accurate to say that most Chartists sought radical parliamentary reform at least partly as a means of placing the state at the service of the 'productive' classes in their struggle against exploitative capitalists. Thus a good number of them sought not only an end to 'Old Corruption', but its replacement by a state that would actively seek to promote social justice through a number of interventionist means, such as compulsory education and the enforcement of higher wages and better working and housing conditions.[46]

While the activism of the Whig governments of the 1830s had encouraged this massive and complex radical movement, the Whigs ultimately relied on a more repressive sort of activism to contain it. For plebeian unrest encouraged them to sponsor enabling legislation for the introduction of borough police forces in 1835 and county police forces in 1839, and a good many localities took advantage of it.[47] Thus while the Whigs were willing to admit that the state had some responsibility to curb social evils, they flatly rejected the solution proffered by the Chartists, radical parliamentary reform, and did not hesitate to use the repressive instruments of the state to keep the movement under control. As the threat of Chartist violence grew in the troubled economic climate of the early 1840s, Peel and the Conservatives took an even sterner approach to its suppression.

Ultimately, there were several reasons why the Chartist movement went into precipitous decline after the House of Commons rejected the third and final Chartist petition on 10 April 1848: the efficacy of the forces of law and order; leadership clashes and the fragmentation of goals within the movement itself; the improvement of the business cycle; and the extensive network of trade unions and friendly societies that were already providing industrial workers with a modicum of protection from the worst forms of exploitation.[48] Some of the credit for the waning of Chartism properly belongs to the relative neutrality of the state, as well. Free trade, the reduction of indirect taxes, the early factory and public-health legislation (which we will examine in more detail later in this chapter) – all of these measures helped to signal that the political elite was perhaps not as *utterly* corrupt as the radicals of the Napoleonic era had assumed it was.[49] Criticism of elite parasitism remained a prominent radical theme throughout the mid-Victorian era.[50] Nevertheless, after 1848 there developed among many radicals a conviction that it was now possible to work within the political system to enforce economy and to promote greater religious liberty. Indeed, now some of the more potent critiques of 'Old Corruption' were being voiced by independent radical MPs who saw the reformed Commons as a potent instrument for the promotion of fiscal justice.[51]

Gladstone's immense popularity among the 'subaltern classes' in the 1860s is a testament not only to their preoccupation with cheap government, but to their belief that at least some elite politicians could be entrusted to preside over it.[52]

Gladstone and other elite politicians, for their part, were more inclined than their predecessors to entrust at least the upper ranks of the working classes with the vote. The Reform Act of 1867 was partly the result of a series of impressive demonstrations on behalf of the right to vote that had been sponsored by the Reform League and other working-class organizations. But it was at least as much a product of elite conviction that it was now safe and prudent to broaden the franchise.[53] Thanks to a bidding war between party leaders, the act more than doubled the number of eligible voters to some 54 per cent of adult men, and established household suffrage on a one-year residency requirement as the borough norm.[54] The second Reform Act was an elite declaration of faith that the 'respectable' artisans at the top of the working-class hierarchy would not use their votes to try to force the state into interventionist adventures. As it happened, their faith was well founded. In the short term, at least, new voters showed little interest in broadening the social agenda of the state, which most of them, like their 'betters', preferred to keep as inexpensive and unobtrusive as possible.

The Victorian state as social disciplinarian

It is possible to exaggerate that unobtrusiveness, however. For despite its minimal framework, the Victorian state could be quite intrusive in its attempts to regulate the behaviour of its most impoverished subjects. The point behind this intrusiveness was to discipline the down-and-out into a standard of personal conduct that was in line with the cherished social virtues of the day: self-reliance, sobriety, orderliness, and sexual decency. Admittedly, there were distinct limits to the disciplinary activities of the Victorian state, because it lacked the administrative resources to engage in anything like a systematic policing of public morals, and because civil libertarianism remained a deeply entrenched social value. But it had no qualms about regulating the behaviour of marginal but numerically substantial groups of poor people, most notably paupers and prostitutes.

The Poor Law Amendment Act of 1834 provides by far the most important case in point. It was the result of a decades-long debate about the ostensible shortcomings of parochial welfare arrangements. The most widely perceived of these shortcomings was the growing expense of the poor law to rate-payers. We saw in chapter 2 that poor-law expenditure grew very considerably over the first ninety years of the eighteenth century; it skyrocketed during the French Revolutionary and Napoleonic Wars. While the level of poor-law spending had stabilized somewhat by the early 1820s, it remained almost double its prewar value in real terms, and began to rise again in the second half of the decade. Rate-payers in rural districts were hit particularly hard by the rising cost of poor relief, as agricultural prices fell whilst unemployment and birth rates rose.[55] The main reason why rural poor relief had become so much more expensive was because it had become so much more widespread. By the turn of the century, it was obvious that the poor law as it was applied in many rural districts had broadened far beyond the limited role as a supplemental aid to the disabled and infirm that had been envisioned for it in the Elizabethan legislation of 1601. In Oxfordshire, for instance, by 1801 the majority of those receiving assistance from the rates were able-bodied adults.[56]

This long-term extension of rural poor relief suggested to many observers that the poor law suffered from a second shortcoming: that it encouraged artificially low wages and rural overpopulation. The chief culprits here, critics argued, were the supplemental forms of relief in aid of wages that had become common in southern and eastern England. Thus they insisted that bread scales (such as the famous 'Speenhamland' scale of 1795 set by Berkshire magistrates in the village of that name) and allowances that provided variable amounts of relief according to the size of a labourer's family did infinitely more harm than good. What incentive did farmers have to pay their workers decent wages when they knew that their fellow rate-payers would subsidize low wages up to subsistence level? What incentive did labourers have to work hard and to exercise 'prudential restraint' in their sexual activity when they knew that the parish would grant them a subsistence whether they were idle or industrious, abstemious or promiscuous? The answers to these questions were not as obvious as critics made them out to be. They tended to mistake the old poor law and the allowance system for the cause rather than the consequence of the structural economic problems of the southern arable districts. It made sense for farmers there to support allowance systems, because these made it more affordable for them to make year-round provision to a seasonal labour force that was chronically underemployed during the difficult postwar years. Moreover, while overpopulation was a serious problem in many southern rural areas, there is no definitive proof that child allowances exacerbated it. Indeed, in the 1820s birth rates sometimes rose in parishes that had recently *abolished* child allowances.[57] But critics of the relief system, increasingly well-versed in Malthusian population theory and political economy, were adamant in their insistence that it was creating a rural population crisis and undercutting labourers' wages.

Pamphleteers on the poor law question continually insisted that the relief system had helped to make the rural poor lazy and improvident, and that they would need to be taught to rely on themselves and stop taking parochial assistance for granted.[58] The notion that recipients of poor relief were improvident loafers who deserved to be stigmatized became widespread. Indeed, this stigma was enshrined in the 1832 Reform Act, which debarred anyone from voting in a general election who had received parish relief at any time during the previous year.[59] For several reasons, the Whig coalition government which sponsored that act felt that the time was also ripe for a root-and-branch reform of the poor laws: because rates were once again on the rise; because it was an activist government that did not shy away from meddling with the parishes; because the riots that had engulfed much of the rural south during the depression of 1830 convinced the Whigs that social relations in the countryside had eroded to an alarming degree; and because even this ostensibly paternalistic government included a number of economic liberals who were eager to cut the Gordian knot of the poor laws.

The Royal Commission on the Poor Laws that the government appointed to prepare the way for legislation was dominated by advocates of *laissez-faire* political economy who were predisposed to 'liberate' rate-payers and paupers from what they perceived to be the demoralizing provisions of the established system. Its report concluded that the old poor law itself was the main cause of rural poverty, and that the allowance system was the chief culprit within it. The most effective means of reducing the poor rates, the report argued, was by making application for relief by able-bodied males a much less attractive option. The way to make it less attractive, or 'less eligible', was to oblige able-bodied applicants to enter a workhouse, in which they would only obtain relief in return for their performance of a variety of irksome tasks. By this means, the commissioners argued, rate-aided poor relief would become so repellent an option for the able-bodied poor that they would be bound to embrace self-reliance as the alternative.

The report suggested the abolition of *all* 'outdoor' relief, recommending the creation of separate workhouses for the aged and infirm, for children, and for able-bodied women as well as men. In order to see that the new workhouse system was properly implemented and enforced, the commissioners suggested the consolidation of parishes into new poor law unions, each with its own workhouse; the elimination of the discretionary power of magistrates through the election of union Boards of Guardians (on which JPs were eligible to sit *ex officio*) who were empowered to set terms of relief and to hire the union officers who would administer the new system; and the creation of a central poor law authority to supervise that system, vested with the powers to appoint assistant commissioners to inspect local arrangements and to dismiss union officers whom they deemed incompetent. In short, the report recommended a dramatic extension of the centralizing principle as a means of forcing the able-bodied paupers to throw themselves on the mercy of the labour market. It embodied a potent blend of evangelical retribution and *laissez-faire* optimism, which assumed that there was a hard core of feckless labourers who needed to be disciplined into self-reliance, and that the free labour market at all times generated enough employment to permit them to *be* self-reliant.[60] This last was a hopelessly naïve assumption, when applied either to the stagnant economy of the rural south, or to the buoyant economy of the industrial north, in which irregular cycles of boom and bust led to radical fluctuations in the demand for labour.[61] Yet the market logic behind it proved to be compelling to large majorities in both houses of parliament, who passed by wide margins a bill that enshrined all of the report's main recommendations.

As it turned out, the new poor law was considerably more revolutionary on paper than it was in practice. The forms and the amount of poor relief continued to vary considerably from union to union, since guardians retained their discretionary power over both. 'Indoor' paupers, for their part, were rarely lodged in separate workhouses according to their gender, age, and state of health (as stipulated by the act), but rather segregated within a single 'mixed' union workhouse. In a number of urban districts, particularly in the north, the threat of fierce local resistance prevented the guardians from even building a workhouse for years on end.[62] More importantly, the large majority of paupers – whether able-bodied or not – continued to receive their relief outside the doors of the workhouse, not least because seasonal and cyclical fluctuations in the demand for labour made it impossible for guardians to effect an absolute divorce between wages and poor relief.[63] Thus in many respects 1834 did not mark a radical turning-point in the administration of poor relief.

In other respects, however, it clearly did. Firstly, there seems little doubt that the new poor law led to a dramatic reduction in the number of able-bodied men in receipt of outdoor relief. By the mid-1850s, that number was comparatively very small indeed – only a few thousand.

Since at that time adult men made up only 5–7 per cent of the workhouse population, the logical conclusion is that most guardians were virtually excluding male breadwinners from relief.[64] Secondly, it is clear that the total cost of poor relief did indeed fall considerably in the decades after 1834. The rough estimates available suggest that national poor relief expenditure dropped from £7 million in 1831 to £4.6 million in 1840, and hovered between £5 and £6 million between 1840 and 1865. As late as the 1870s, Britain had not yet returned to Napoleonic-era levels of poor relief expenditure in *absolute* terms, even without taking into account the buoyant population growth of the intervening decades.[65] One of the first tasks of the Local Government Board that supervised the administration of the poor law was to contain the cost of relief. Established in 1871, the board presided over a 30 per cent nationwide reduction in the number of paupers given outdoor relief over the next seven years. This was a painful squeeze, even though relief rates soon started creeping up again. Considering that the number of able-bodied male recipients of outdoor relief had already been drastically scaled back by the early 1870s, there is little doubt that many women, children, and elderly 'outdoor' beneficiaries suffered from a reduction in aid during the retrenchment campaign.[66] Even before the launching of that campaign, the scale of outdoor relief had been far from generous. Indeed, many boards of guardians had concluded that it was cheaper to the rate-payers to try to sustain paupers on paltry levels of outdoor relief than to put them in the workhouse.

The ultimate point of the workhouse itself was to stigmatize the receipt of relief as something so humiliating that the poor would avoid applying for it. Workhouse conditions varied greatly. Occasionally they were scandalous, as at Andover in Hampshire, where in 1845 it was discovered that starving paupers were sucking the marrow from the bones that they had been made to crush. Even workhouses where decent conditions prevailed were dreaded by the poor as penal institutions that obliged them to give up their freedom and their individuality in exchange for relief. Thus upon entry paupers had all their personal belongings taken from them, were strictly segregated according to sex and age, were 'disinfected', given standard haircuts, and obliged to exchange their own clothing for dingy and ill-fitting uniforms, some of which had the letter 'P' stitched on them as a constant reminder of the wearer's degraded status. Families were broken up in order to promote a Malthusian sort of population control. Paupers were set to humiliating tasks, often of little economic value, such as the picking of oakum from old ropes, the grinding of corn, and the digging of ditches, along with the aforementioned bone-crushing. A strict uniformity was imposed on their diet as well as their hours of work and sleep. In the early years of the workhouse system, at least, meals had to be taken in silence, free time was confined to a single hour a day, and no reading matter was furnished to inmates, not even the Bible. Guardians devised elaborate penalties for those who swore, refused to work, or 'malingered'.[67]

It is possible to exaggerate the repressiveness of the workhouse system. Most workhouses were anything but 'total institutions' because guardians were unwilling or unable to hire enough competent workhouse officers to police the activities of the paupers. Certainly, many of the wilder rumours concerning the workhouse 'bastilles' were entirely false: that workhouse bread was deliberately poisoned, for instance, or that paupers' corpses were used to manure fields, or that workhouse children were killed and then ground into pie filling.[68] The workhouse system was not intended to kill paupers. But it certainly was intended to shame them into independence.

The evidence suggests that the 'honest poor' needed no such shaming, however, for they generally did what they could to avoid the workhouse. Contrary to the assumptions of the poor-law authorities, self-reliance was probably an even more deeply cherished virtue in working-class neighbourhoods than it was in more affluent ones. While there is no way to measure what was undoubtedly the most common form of self-help – small gifts and loans from friends and relatives – the level of more formal types of plebeian mutual aid rose astronomically over the period. Thus membership in friendly societies, which provided short-term sick pay as well as burial payments to humble subscribers, grew from perhaps 700,000 in 1801 to 2.2 million (a full third of the adult male population) by 1880. The number of depositors to savings banks likewise rose, reaching a million by mid-century. Even the poorest of the poor strove to contribute to informal 'penny banks'.[69] There can be no doubt that the vast majority of the humbler classes valued independence, and they strove mightily to avoid pauperdom. That much said, it was nevertheless true that the urban working classes, at least, took a fairly cynical and utilitarian view of the workhouse, and indeed felt little shame in falling back on it when they felt they were left with no choice but to do so. Only late in the century did pauperism become stigmatized in urban working-class neighbourhoods, when spreading prosperity made it easier for the 'respectable' poor to avoid the workhouse altogether.[70]

Avoiding the house was made easier by the flow of charity from wealthier neighbourhoods into poorer ones. The Victorian privileged classes valued private philanthropy both as a Christian responsibility and as a means of limiting the state's intervention in social life, and they gave away prodigious sums of money. By the 1850s, annual charitable receipts in London alone probably exceeded the total annual expenditure on the poor laws for all of England and Wales. In 1885 *The Times* boasted that the annual income generated by London charities was over twice that of the Swiss government.[71] While there is no accurate means of measuring the impact of this vast flow of philanthropy, it is reasonable to assume that it helped to keep a good many people off the poor rolls. Indeed, advocates of stricter charitable policies, most notably the Charity Organisation Society, feared that it was leading to a great deal of 'indiscriminate alms-giving' and thus threatening to undermine the disciplinary rigour of the poor law. In any case, that very rigour taught the poor to identify the Victorian state that supervised the workhouse system as first and foremost a disciplinary agent that sought to humiliate them into self-sufficiency, even at times when the vagaries of the market system made self-sufficiency an unattainable goal for a good many of them.

The down-and-out who managed to avoid the workhouse, moreover, stood a growing chance of encountering some other disciplinary agency of the state beyond its walls. The most formidable of them was the police. Reform of the criminal law did away with the 'Bloody Code', so that after 1838 nobody was hanged save for murder or (until 1861) attempted murder. But the protection of property was simultaneously bolstered by the gradual introduction of police forces. The Metropolitan police force was created by the then home secretary Robert Peel in 1829, while the Municipal Reform Act (1835) required 178 incorporated boroughs to set up police forces under the control of local watch committees, and the County Police Act (1839) granted permissive powers for the establishment of county police forces. It was not until the 1850s that police forces were made compulsory in all boroughs and counties, and as late as 1881 there were thirty-one such 'forces' composed of fewer than six men. Still, the 32,000 policemen employed in England and Wales in that year constituted a far more formidable law-enforcement mechanism than the watchmen and parish constables of the late-Georgian era. While it is always necessary to treat crime statistics with a healthy scepticism, it seems that the annual rate of total indictable offences was on the decline from the 1840s until the turn of the century. While this trend was attributable to a broad range of causes, the extension of police forces was no doubt one of them.[72] The growth of the police marked a dramatic (albeit a gradual) change in the privileged classes' perception of state authority: from something of which one needed to be perpetually wary to something which could be relied on to protect property and preserve order.[73]

Preserving order often meant harassing the down-and-out. The rise of the police reflected and reinforced a decline in social permissiveness.

The new police forces spent much of their energy meddling with the traditional amusements of the common people. Thus in the West Riding of Yorkshire, for instance, the new county constabulary imposed a close supervision on working-class pubs and beerhouses and did what they could to suppress cock-fighting (made illegal in 1849) and foot-racing. Not surprisingly, plebeian communities resented these novel sorts of intervention, which turned their routine amusements into objects of police surveillance. By the last quarter of the century, it was far more likely than hitherto that vagrants, drunkards, and prostitutes would be arrested and sentenced to short terms in gaol. This new moral authoritarianism was vividly illustrated by the penal reforms of Gladstone's first ministry. At a time when the crime rate was seen to be declining, a government that in other spheres was notable for its tolerance granted to magistrates more extensive powers to commit adult vagrants and juveniles to prison; tightened up licensing-renewal procedures for publicans and narrowed pub opening times; and initiated a large rise in the number of prosecutions for public drunkenness. It even pushed through a Habitual Criminals Act that empowered the police to detain repeat offenders *on suspicion* of intent to commit crime, whether or not there was evidence of such intent.[74] Such measures did nothing to endear the police to the plebs; it is small wonder that physical assaults on the 'blue locusts' remained commonplace in many working-class districts right into the twentieth century.[75]

The corollary to the growth of police forces in this era was a growth in the prison population. There is no greater testament to the moral authoritarianism of the Victorian state than the increasingly centralized prison system over which it presided, which sought simultaneously to discipline and to redeem the convict through an increasingly elaborate set of punishments directed more at the mind than at the body. Through much of the eighteenth century, authorities mainly sought to deter crime through physical punishment – by branding offenders, or putting them in the stocks, or making bloody examples of them at the whipping-post and the gallows. But the repertoire of methods championed by evangelical and utilitarian reformers at the end of the century – solitary confinement, cell labour, and religious exhortation – sought to save the souls of convicts whilst ensuring greater uniformity, predictability, and severity in the application of punishments.[76] By the 1830s, strict silence among prisoners was being enforced in many county prisons, and even many petty offenders were obliged to spend up to ten hours a day on the treadwheel, which one JP called 'the most tiresome, distressing, exemplary punishment that has ever been contrived by human ingenuity'.[77]

'Separate confinement' and the 'silent system' were taken to extremes in the centrally administered Pentonville prison that opened in 1842 as a sort of national monument to the new carceral regime. Pentonville inmates were entirely cut off from one another in order to prevent moral contamination from spreading amongst them. Forbidden to speak to each other, they were obliged to wear masks in all common areas in order to prevent them from even recognizing each other. Within a few years the Pentonville authorities were obliged to cut in half the standard eighteen-month sentence because so many inmates were developing symptoms of madness.[78] Admittedly, few other early-Victorian gaols were as rigorous as Pentonville, not least because few of them could afford to hire enough guards to enforce such comprehensive penal measures.[79] The separate and silent systems, moreover, were gradually supplanted by the so-called 'stages system', by which prisoners could expect to receive a growing variety of privileges according to their good behaviour.[80] But the prison system, finally centralized under the Home Office in 1877, was still predicated on a harsh 'reformatory' regimen that provided vivid testimony to the moral and physical force with which the ostensibly minimal Victorian state could intrude in the lives of its most wayward subjects.

That state's most notorious attempt at moral regulation outside the walls of the penitentiary took shape in the Contagious Diseases Acts of the 1860s, which plain-clothes Metropolitan policemen sought to enforce in eighteen ports and garrison towns. The point behind the CD acts was to reduce the incidence of venereal disease among soldiers and naval ratings, and the acts sought to do so in the most intrusive way imaginable. Under the terms of the acts, suspected prostitutes could be forced to submit to repeated vaginal examinations. Those found to be suffering from either syphilis or gonorrhea could be interned in venereal wards of certified 'lock hospitals' for up to nine months at a time. As a consequence of the acts, many working-class women (by no means all of them prostitutes) were subjected to an extremely humiliating form of state compulsion, and those who were consigned to venereal wards were thus incarcerated not for any crime they had committed, but because of their physical state. The acts were vigorously resisted by a number of pressure groups, most notably the Ladies' National Association under the leadership of Josephine Butler, which drew particular attention to the way in which the CD acts reinforced the sexual double standard by stigmatizing prostitutes but leaving their male clients unmolested.[81] While such groups managed to get the acts repealed in 1886, their appearance on the statute books and sporadic enforcement over the course of two decades provide especially vivid testimony to the moral interventionism of the Victorian state.

The CD acts provide simply the most glaring example of the legal double standard that it was the state's responsibility to enforce. Under the common law, it had long been assumed that the family was a single legal entity, that the husband headed it, and that all of its assets and income belonged to him – even those that had been brought into the marriage or subsequently earned by his wife. This principle of 'coverture' was mitigated by the passage of the Married Women's Property Act (1870), which acknowledged a wife's legal right to keep her earnings. But the act perpetuated the double standard by limiting a married woman's ability to control the assets that she brought into her marriage to 200 guineas' worth of real estate and 200 guineas' worth of liquid assets. That double standard was also enshrined in divorce law. Before passage of the Matrimonial Causes Act (1857), virtually the only means of obtaining legal separation was by divorce granted through private act of parliament, the expense of which made it a viable alternative only for the very wealthy. By making divorce obtainable through a civil court, the act made it considerably less expensive and thus a feasible option for many more couples. But the grounds for divorce prescribed by the act were inequitable: while husbands could obtain one on the grounds of simple adultery, wives could obtain one only if they could prove additional aggravation, such as physical cruelty. Moreover, if a wife left her husband without obtaining a divorce, she was considered to be guilty of desertion and forfeited all claim to the custody of her children or any share in her husband's property.[82]

It is true that the legal bias against women was more obvious on paper than in practice. Wives' legal disability to contract and to litigate debts, for instance, was frequently ignored or mitigated in practice,[83] and women did meet with some success in obtaining judicial separations and protection orders from the divorce courts.[84] The double standard was nevertheless glaringly obvious. Masculinity remained the fundamental basis of national citizenship until 1918, when women were given the right to vote in parliamentary elections – on terms which discriminated against them on the basis of age. The mid-Victorian 'protective' measures that reduced the hours of factory work, moreover, helped to construct a 'male breadwinner' ideology of labour, because they were predicated on two interrelated patriarchal assumptions: that working-class men were free agents whose conditions of employment should not be tampered with, and that women's conditions of employment could be tampered with because they were *not* free agents. The notion that men were solely responsible for the economic well-being of their families was deeply embedded in Victorian social policy. It helped not only to deny wages to women, but to complicate their ability to obtain poor relief under the terms of the new poor law, which was so preoccupied with able-bodied males that it scarcely took the needs of women into account.[85]

The assumption that working-class men were economic free agents, however, did not prevent the state from imposing constraints on their ability to gain workplace concessions through collective action. For it presided over a framework of labour law that in many ways favoured employers over their workers. The repeal of the (virtually unenforceable) Combination Laws in 1825 meant that trade unions now enjoyed a legal right to exist and to exert pressure for the raising of wages and the reduction of working hours. But it remained difficult to conduct a strike successfully without being made liable for 'intimidation'; a striker could be imprisoned not only for committing any of a number of specific acts against employers or strike-breakers, but for merely conspiring to commit such acts.

Meanwhile, other forms of anti-union legislation remained on the statute book. Thus six would-be trade unionists in rural Dorsetshire became the 'Tolpuddle martyrs' in 1834, when they were transported to Australia under an act of 1797 that forbade the taking of oaths of labour solidarity. Many more workers suffered milder forms of repression under the master and servant laws, which defined the legal relationship between employers and workers until 1875. These laws were deeply biased in favour of the former, stipulating, for instance, that a workman found in breach of contract could be liable to up to three months' imprisonment, while an employer found in breach of contract could only be sued in a civil action. The law of liability was similarly biased, so that a worker who was injured on the job had virtually no legal remedy.[86] Finally, legal judgments posed serious obstacles to trade unions until well into the 1870s. *Hornby* v. *Close* (1867) stipulated that unions could not secure legal protection for their funds, because their tendency to act 'in restraint of trade' made them technically illegal organizations. Gladstone's first ministry provided statutory protection for union funds, but it also sponsored legislation that made picketing illegal. Hence unions lost their most effective tactical weapon just as they won legal protection for the dues paid by their members. It took four years of intensive lobbying by the Trades Union Congress before the Disraeli administration sponsored the Conspiracy and Protection of Property Act (1875), which finally gave unions the right to engage in free collective bargaining by legalizing peaceful picketing, restricting the legal definition of 'conspiracy', and abolishing imprisonment for breach of contract.[87] In sum, trade unionists had good reason to mistrust the state in this era. They had had to fight hard simply to win its neutrality in industrial disputes, and they were not inclined to think that a central government that had so long begrudged them the opportunity to compete on anything like even terms with their employers could be relied on to intervene in their behalf.[88]

The limits of *laissez-faire*

The Victorian state occasionally *did* intrude in the lives of its humbler subjects in more positive ways, however. While most Victorians felt that the state's intervention in social and economic relationships should be strictly limited, virtually none of them was so convinced of the transcendent virtues of *laissez-faire* as to believe that the state had no proper regulatory role to play. The urban squalor, disease, and overcrowding that had resulted from rapid industrialization obliged virtually every observer to admit that the central government had *some* responsibility to curb these worst excesses, not least because the 'Great Unwashed' might otherwise rise up in revolt. As Karl Polanyi long ago pointed out, the 'great transformation' from heavily regulated to self-regulating markets towards the end of the eighteenth century that christened *laissez-faire* as the great organizing principle of economic life inevitably led to repeated violations of that very principle, because untrammelled *laissez-faire* would have quickly 'destroyed the very organization of production that the market had called into being'.[89] Thus, when confronted with compelling evidence of the relationship between overcrowded slums and a high incidence of certain diseases, even Nassau Senior, the doctrinaire political economist who championed the freedom of the labour market in his co-authorship of the infamous Royal Commission Report on the Poor Laws, was obliged to admit that 'with all reverence for the principle of non-interference, we cannot doubt that in this matter it has been pushed too far'. He concluded that the state should compel landlords and speculative builders 'to take measures which shall prevent the towns which they create from being the centres of disease'.[90] There was thus no strict line drawn between *laissez-faire* and state intervention in Victorian public opinion, and sectional interests that clamoured for the state to adhere to the former on one issue were likely to endorse the latter with regard to some other one.[91]

The inquiries of the central officers of the New Poor Law quickly made it obvious that the physical conditions in which the urban poor found themselves made it virtually impossible for them to pull themselves up by their own bootstraps. A series of investigations culminating in the famous *Sanitary Report* of 1842 by the secretary to the Poor Law Commission, Edwin Chadwick, did much to legitimate the notion that the state could help to promote working-class self-reliance by taking measures to improve public health in the disease-ridden urban slums. The *Report* made a strong and well-publicized case for a correlation between insanitary living and working conditions and high rates of disease and mortality. It suggested that the central government should take steps to combat the main causes of ill health in the slums: inadequate water supply, poor drainage, overcrowded housing, overflowing burial grounds, and the proliferation of 'public nuisances' such as manure-heaps and slaughter-houses.[92] Chadwick's *Report* was hardly a work of humanitarian empathy. It was riddled with middle-class value-judgements about the putative moral turpitude of slum-dwellers, and it advocated public health partly as a practical means of protecting the established political order against plebeian violence.[93] But it was also an important admission that, contrary to the assumptions of the Poor Law Report (which Chadwick himself had co-written with Senior), poor people were by no means entirely responsible for their unhealthy physical surroundings.

Certainly, few of them could be deemed responsible for their own sickness, and the Poor Law Medical Service grew by leaps and bounds over the middle decades of the century as it became obvious that voluntary hospitals could not begin to keep up with the demand for medical treatment among the poor. By the 1860s, over 80 per cent of the hospital beds in England and Wales were to be found in workhouse sick wards.[94] If sick paupers were not responsible for their own poverty, then neither were child paupers. Hence the Poor Law Amendment Act stipulated that a rudimentary education be provided them within the workhouse, and by 1847 enough boards of guardians were seeking to furnish one to merit the appointment of five inspectors of workhouse schools. Eight years later, enabling legislation permitted guardians to pay the school fees of children on outdoor relief. More often than not, guardians sought to keep these educational expenses to a minimum. But the fact that some of them were recommended by the central authorities serves as one more proof that a modicum of positive state intervention stemmed directly from that greatest of all legislative monuments to *laissez-faire*, the new poor law.[95]

Nevertheless, it would be shortsighted to suggest that such intervention arose as an *inevitable* response to the social problems arising from the urban explosion of the first half of the century. Contrary to what some historians have suggested, social reform was not always prompted by a widespread humanitarian notion that a particular evil had simply become generally recognized *as* an evil and deemed 'intolerable'.[96] Reform itself, moreover, by no means always took the commonsensical form of a series of rational bureaucratic measures that gradually closed the loopholes to be found in pioneering legislation. Many of the social debates of the early- and mid-Victorian decades were highly contentious and sometimes highly principled, pitting powerful interests and ideologies against each other. Much of the legislation that stemmed from them remained ineffective for long periods of time, because opponents tried to neuter it and because the state lacked the means and sometimes the will to enforce it. Reformers themselves were inspired by a broad range of motives, and benevolence was not always prominent among them.[97] In short, the process of social reform was disputatious, halting, and distinctly limited by the well-nigh universal perception of 'cheap government' as a social good, and of centralization as an evil to be avoided whenever possible. With these caveats in mind, we can proceed to a brief review of the more conspicuous causes of social reform, and of some of the more important extensions of state intervention for which they were responsible.

One of the most widely cited agents of the factory legislation of the 1830s and 1840s was Tory paternalism, which ostensibly motivated evangelical social conservatives to endorse state intervention as a means of fulfilling their Christian responsibility to protect defenceless women and children. By far the most influential Tory paternalist was Lord Ashley (later 7th Earl of Shaftesbury), who played a major role in the 1842 Mines Act that prohibited women and boys under the age of ten from working underground. Ashley had pressed for a Royal Commission to investigate alleged abuses in the mines, and when it issued a damning report he drew attention to its most scandalous details in order to persuade MPs to vote in favour of a regulatory measure. Thus he cited the report's tales of half-naked women being forced to work as many as sixteen hours a day hauling heavy carts filled with coal through oppressively hot tunnels that were sometimes under four feet high, and the diseases, deformities, and early deaths that resulted from these wretched working conditions. Ashley's courageous efforts did much to secure passage of the bill, and he went on to distinguish himself as a champion of factory education, better working-class housing, and reform of the lunacy laws.[98] But few Tories were willing to go as far as Ashley did in embracing state intervention. For most of them saw it as a potential threat to two of their most cherished ideals: the sanctity of private property and the primacy of local government. Indeed, while Ashley professed himself a staunch Conservative, he felt himself 'sadly alone' in his sponsorship of the mines bill, because the devotion of Peel's Conservative ministry to the providential mechanisms of the market prevented it from helping the measure along.[99] In short, Ashley was one of precious few Conservatives whose humanitarian sense of *noblesse oblige* prompted him to welcome the imposition of legal restrictions on the free market in labour.

Two more were Richard Oastler and Michael Sadler, who were outspoken leaders of the factory-reform and anti-poor-law movements in Yorkshire and Lancashire in the 1830s. Sadler's famous 1830 letter to the *Leeds Mercury* on 'Yorkshire slavery' likened the condition of child labourers in textile mills to that of colonial slaves, and provided some of the moral impetus for the establishment of short-time committees among northern operatives and tradesmen. Shortly thereafter, Sadler, MP for Aldburgh, procured the appointment of a select committee on the factory issue that later published a damning report highlighting the widespread exploitation to be found in the northern textile mills.[100] But Sadler's fellow evangelicals were by no means united on the issue of factory regulation. Indeed, most of them endorsed a brand of Christian political economy that inspired them passively to accept factory abuses, and indeed inspired some of them to oppose legislative efforts to reduce such abuses.[101] Oastler's and Sadler's efforts would probably have got nowhere without the formidable grass-roots support of the short-time committees, whose organizational success owed far more to the likes of the radical cotton-spinner John Doherty and the dissident mill-owner John Fielden than it did to Tory evangelicals.[102]

As it was, the reduction of the working hours of women and children in textile mills was a fitful development that was repeatedly stymied by parliamentary advocates of an unrestricted labour market on the one hand, and by inadequate enforcement on the other. The 1833 Factory Act marked a vast improvement over earlier legislation, because it provided for the establishment of four inspectors to enforce its provisions: the banishment of children under age nine from most textile mills, and maxima of eight hours a day for children under thirteen and twelve hours a day for thirteen- to eighteen-year-olds. But this landmark act was strictly limited, none the less. It was a government compromise measure that undermined parliamentary support for the main goal of the short-time movement, a ten-hour bill on behalf of *all* factory labourers that had been drawn up by Sadler and sponsored by Ashley.[103]

When the 1847 Factory Act finally established a maximum ten hours a day or fifty-eight hours a week for women and thirteen- to eighteen-year-olds, it marked a great victory for the short-time committees. But it took an additional three years of struggle before the cotton-masters and their friends in the Commons accepted the closure of loopholes in the act, leading to a *de facto* compromise of ten-and-a-half hours for all women and children.[104] A series of subsequent measures over the next twenty years extended the principles of 1847 to non-textile factories and workshops. By 1870, legislation barred children under eight from all factories and workshops; reduced the hours of older children to six-and-a-half per day; provided minimum educational requirements for all child labourers; and established a *de facto* sixty-hour week for all adult workers. Still, there was as yet no legal acknowledgement that the state had a right to interfere with the hours of adult male workers. Their working week had been reduced in practice only because factory owners found it impracticable to oblige them to work longer hours than their female counterparts.[105] In short, factory reform was a long-drawn-out, piecemeal, and deeply contentious business.

Two of the most important weapons brought to bear in the battle for reform were parliamentary inquiries and paid inspectorates. It is worth briefly discussing each of them to show just how limited state intervention in the workplace remained throughout this period. The two chief means by which parliament sought to inquire into social issues in the nineteenth century were through select committees and royal commissions. The former were composed exclusively of members of the two houses and empowered to send for papers and to examine witnesses under oath. The latter were composed of government appointees, typically included outside experts as well as politicians, and often sent investigating commissioners around the country in search of evidence. The greater flexibility of royal commissions made them the favoured instruments of social inquiry, and the blue books that they issued constitute the most exhaustive sources of official knowledge on a great variety of subjects. By no means all of that knowledge was compiled with a view to state intervention, however. We have already seen that the main goal of the Royal Commission on the Poor Laws was to pave the way for legislation that would disengage local poor-law authorities from the labour market. Similarly, one of the obvious (and successful) aims of the Royal Commission on the Employment of Children (1833) was to focus parliamentary attention on child labour in the factories in order to divert it from the more controversial issue of the working hours of adults.[106]

Inspectorates were not the double-edged swords that royal commissions could be. Still, it is easy to exaggerate their powers. Admittedly, the growth of central regulatory agencies in general and of inspectorates in particular between 1830 and 1860 is a testament to the state's willingness to intervene in many new branches of national life: railways, charities, mines, lighthouses, merchant ships, lodging houses, and the like. By the early 1870s, factory inspectors had access to 110,000 workplaces, comprising virtually all non-domestic industrial establishments.[107] But while at first glance this regulatory cadre seems impressive, in reality its powers were distinctly limited. Inspectors generally lacked effective means of compelling widespread compliance with the law. Their chief weapons were petty fines, which were easily paid, and lengthy and expensive legal actions that by no means ensured victory for the agents of the government.[108] In any case, most infractions went unnoticed, because there were simply not enough inspectors to detect them. In 1850, a single mines inspector was charged with the physically impossible task of supervising each and every mine in Durham, Northumberland, Cumberland, and Scotland.[109] Twenty years later, each of the twenty-six mines inspectors was still being charged with the regular inspection of an average of 192 mines, when an exceptionally diligent inspector would have had a hard time visiting even seventy mines a year.[110] Not all inspectors *were* exceptionally diligent, and indeed a number of them were deeply sympathetic to management. It is true that the activities of inspectors often led to the development of a sort of interventionist feedback mechanism, through which their recommendations prompted the drafting of more effective legislation, which in turn granted them more extensive powers of inspection.[111] It is also true that Britain was more amply endowed with inspectorates than the major continental states, which were only just beginning to appoint them at mid-century.[112] But the point here is simply that the growth of effective mechanisms of enforcement was a slow and painstaking process.

Of course, that process would have been even slower had it not been for the activist civil servants who took advantage of the principles of official inquiry and inspection to influence the development of poor-law, police, factory, and public-health reform. A good deal of historical scholarship has sought to weigh the extent to which these professional administrators were influenced by the utilitarian doctrines of Jeremy Bentham.[113] Certainly, many of these administrators were self-conscious Benthamites, most notably Edwin Chadwick, who for a time had been Bentham's personal secretary, the educational reformer Sir James Kay-Shuttleworth, the sanitary investigator Dr Southwood Smith, the factory inspector Leonard Horner, the mines inspector H. S. Tremenheere, and William Farr, whose statistical inquiries in the registrar-general's office into comparative mortality rates provided valuable evidence for sanitary reformers.[114] There is no sense here in trying to ascertain how well these men knew Bentham's writings on government. The important point is that they all subscribed to the notion that a good government was one that sought to fulfil Bentham's utility principle – to secure the greatest happiness for the greatest number of people – and that the effort to secure it sometimes justified closer government intervention in the workings of society and economy.[115] Just as often, however, they felt that the utility principle justified government efforts to withdraw itself from the market. Thus the most influential administrative Benthamite of them all, Chadwick, conceived of the new poor law that he had helped to mastermind as a means of helping the poor to help themselves by weaning them from their dependence on parochial relief, and he persisted in conceiving it that way. Like most of his contemporaries, whether Benthamite or not, he saw no inherent conflict of interest between the principles of *laissez-faire* and of state intervention, both of which could be invoked, often at the same time, to advance a particular notion of the public good.[116]

Chadwick and other Benthamite administrators were adept at getting themselves appointed to royal commissions and inspectorates, and at using their official positions to inquire into a broad range of social issues and then promoting and influencing public debate through the advertisement of their findings.[117] Chadwick's aforementioned *Sanitary Report* provides a good example. He used his authority as secretary to the Poor Law Commission to conduct a widespread investigation into the conditions of slum life, publicized those conditions in copious detail, and saw to it that 10,000 copies of the *Report* were distributed gratis. The *Report* sparked a broad public discussion that led to the appointment of a Royal Commission on the Health of Towns, to the creation of the Health of Towns Association, a formidable lobbying group on behalf of sanitary reform, and to passage of a landmark Public Health Act in 1848.

The Public Health Act was arguably the most significant interventionist measure of the mid-Victorian era. It empowered local authorities to establish boards of health on petition of at least 10 per cent of the rate-payers, and granted those local boards the power to manage sewers and drains, water supplies, and gas works, to regulate 'offensive' trades such as tanneries, to remove 'nuisances', to condemn houses that it deemed unfit for human habitation, and to furnish burial grounds, parks, and public baths to the locality. All of these powers were supported by the right to levy rates and to purchase land. The main task of the central Board of Health established by the act was to advise the local boards, but the Board was also given compulsory power to establish local boards in places where the death rate exceeded twenty-three per 1,000. Here, on the face of it, was a bold measure to promote the public good through interventionist means, and Chadwick's efforts had done much to bring it to life. Chadwick himself was appointed as one of the central board's commissioners. But it needs to be stressed that the Public Health Act was as much a testament to Whig as it was to Benthamite interventionism. The Whig grandees had helped̀ to promote public agitation for sanitary reform through the Health of Towns Association, and it was one of them, Viscount Morpeth, who brought in the public health bill, with the support of his colleagues in Lord John Russell's government (1846–52). Chadwick's efforts would have got nowhere without the encouragement of an aristocratic faction that once again showed its willingness to extend the powers of government in order to curb a social ill.[118]

As it happened, however, sanitary reform ended up being just as contentious and almost as gradual a process as factory reform. First of all, amendments turned the Public Health Act into a largely permissive one, and rate-payers who feared the expense of sanitary reform were slow to petition for the establishment of local boards. Thus, a decade after the act went onto the statute book, fewer than a sixth of the residents of industrial Lancashire lived in areas that were under the jurisdiction of a local board. Where local boards *were* established, moreover, there was no guarantee that they would take advantage of their potentially very costly compulsory powers.[119] Meanwhile, Chadwick had been widely vilified for his truculent (and futile) effort to strip the London vestries and private water companies of their powers and put the metropolis under a single sanitary authority, and more justly assailed by the civil engineers for his narrow-minded obsession with water-flushed pipe sewerage.[120] The entire central board was forced to resign in 1854 after bitter parliamentary criticism of their ostensible high-handedness, and the board itself was disbanded four years later.

The ensuing 'era of localism' slowed the pace of sanitary reform. Admittedly, these years witnessed the dramatic growth of some forms of medical intervention. Smallpox vaccination, made compulsory for infants in the mid-1850s, was practically universal twenty years later.[121] Here, as in its strict efforts to quarantine cholera victims, the British state was actually more coercive than many of its continental counterparts. Only after widespread and persistent protests against compulsory vaccination did the government make it easier for conscientious objectors to obtain exemptions for their children. When it came to sanitary reform, however, the central government was content to rely on cajolery to prompt usually reluctant local authorities to take advantage of the permissive powers granted to them to improve public health. Thanks in part to the investigative and promotional work of Sir John Simon at the Privy Council's Medical Department, the 'sanitary idea' managed to live on. While Simon was not the doctrinaire advocate of centralization that Chadwick had been, by 1865 he had concluded that 'the time has now arrived when it ought not any longer to be discretional in a place whether that place shall be kept filthy or not'.[122] A decade later, it was indeed no longer 'discretional', for the cumulative result of a series of new statutes was the establishment of compulsory sanitary machinery for the entire country and the codification of the (now fairly extensive) powers of local public-health authorities.

There were four main reasons why sanitary reform was such a halting and fractious process.[123] The first one was technical controversy and ignorance. Most notably, the proper method of sewage disposal was a matter of fierce debate among civil engineers, and it took many years for most of them to accept as the most efficient method John Roe's system of water disposal through glazed-brick pipelines connected to a central sewer system.[124] A second reason was financial. The installation of sewers was an expensive and unglamorous business, and rate-payers across the political spectrum were often loath to pay for it.[125] A third reason was political. The creation of a local sanitary authority financed through the rates and backed by legal statute posed a grave threat to a number of formidable propertied interests. Among them were the managers of and investors in private water companies and cemeteries, the owners of tenements, and the improvement commissions, highway boards, vestries, and town councils whose powers were likely to be curtailed by the local boards.[126]

A final and particularly important reason for resistance to the 'sanitary idea' was ideological. There was a widespread conviction that it was unjust to force rate-payers to foot the bill for sanitary improvements that would chiefly benefit poor people who were usually exempt from the payment of rates. Small landlords tended to be particularly resentful of local sanitary measures, for these people paid a disproportionate share of the rates and feared that local boards of health would condemn their slum properties. They and many of their fellow rate-payers, moreover, suspected that local sanitary regulation was simply the first step on a path to centralization, and a great many Britons shared the attitude that Dickens famously satirized in the shape of Mr Podsnap of *Our Mutual Friend*: 'Centralization. No. Never with my consent. Not English.' Many advocates of local autonomy, whether Conservative or radical, truly believed that the interventionist schemes of Whig–Liberal governments and their Benthamite associates were but so many attempts to amass patronage whilst destroying local self-government.[127]

Technical disagreements, fear of higher rates, the well-entrenched resistance of propertied interests, deep and widespread mistrust of centralization: all of these factors ensured that sanitary reform would proceed at only a fitful pace. They also ensured that as late as 1880, there was only the faintest notion of an interventionist solution to perhaps the biggest sanitary problem of all, urban overcrowding. Here was a difficulty that was easy enough to discern, particularly in London, the behemoth of the western world, whose population had doubled to 4.8 million over the previous three decades. It was well known that the crude death rate was closely related to population density, and yet there was very little done to try to thin out particularly crowded working-class districts. The pioneering housing legislation of the mid-Victorian decades did indeed provide a legal foundation for some important interventionist principles, including the right of municipal governments to cleanse and demolish buildings perceived to be dangerous to the public health.[128] But in the short term, this legislation only worsened the overcrowding problem, because it encouraged local authorities to pull down insalubrious housing without giving them strong incentives to rehouse the slum-dwellers who were thus displaced.[129] One of the chief aims of the pioneer housing acts of the 1860s was to facilitate the sale of inner-city land that had been recently cleared of slums to the private model-dwelling companies, which offered their investors 'philanthropy and 5 per cent'. But the rehousing efforts of Octavia Hill and the other leaders of the model-dwellings movement did not even come close to making up the deficit in working-class housing that slum clearance was creating.[130] The gap would only start to narrow after the turn of the century, when in a different ideological climate municipal authorities were given central encouragement to become major builders and landlords and not simply destroyers of working-class dwellings.

At least the promotion of public health and the limitation of working hours had become broadly accepted duties of government by 1880. The regulation of wages was another matter. Many of the same activist civil servants who pushed for sanitary improvements insisted that low wages, technological unemployment, and skill redundancy were not fit subjects for social reform, but industrial 'problems' that could only be solved by the laws of the market.[131] Indeed, it was Benthamite officials at the Board of Trade who helped to stymie a minimum wage bill that John Fielden had introduced in 1835 as a means of protecting tens of thousands of handloom weavers whose livelihoods were imperilled by technological deskilling. Fielden's bill failed and the weavers went to the wall.[132] It would be another seventy-five years before 'respectable' opinion would even begin to accept the notion that government had the slightest role to play in regulating chronically low wages.

Finally, it is worth stressing that in those spheres in which the role of the government *was* expanding in this era, much of the expansion was still taking place at the local level. Abiding fears that an over-mighty state would multiply the patronage at its disposal and abruptly do away with the English tradition of local self-government helped to contain central-government growth. Thus, while per capita public spending grew at a deliberate pace, the number of office-holders appointed by the central government scarcely grew at all. In 1846 it was estimated that 16,353 people were central-government employees, over 80 per cent of whom held jobs in four departments that served well-established roles: the post office, customs, excise, and coast guard. A second estimate undertaken twenty-three years later put the total number of public employees at 16,701.[133] In terms of personnel, local government was far bigger. In 1854, for instance, some 80,000 different agencies handled the wide variety of governing responsibilities that remained in local hands.[134] Estimates, admittedly very rough, suggest that local spending as a proportion of total government spending in the United Kingdom rose from 21 per cent in 1840 to 41 per cent in 1890.[135] The large majority of government spending for non-military purposes took place at the local level. By 1886, local authorities in England and Wales spent well over twice as much as the central government did on civil services – £44 million as against £19 million.[136] Thus, if there was a Victorian 'revolution in government' it took place at the local level.

While civil government was still an overwhelmingly local affair in the 1870s, the functions of civil government had broadened over the preceding century to include newer ones such as education, professional police forces, and water supply along with more traditional ones such as poor relief, and the cost of civil government had grown a great deal in consequence. Admittedly, the localities were no longer the laws unto themselves that they had been in the Georgian era. In rural areas, for instance, a series of centralizing measures, many of them initiated by the Whig governments during the 1830s, substantially eroded the powers of magistrates.[137] The immemorial jurisdiction of the parish itself, moreover, was undermined by a series of reforms between the late 1810s and the mid-1830s. Their boundaries were ignored in the organization of poor law unions, highway boards, and town councils.[138] While the 'decade' of reform left most of the functions of civil government (both old and new) in local hands, by rearranging those functions to the detriment of the parish and the magistracy it divested these traditional institutions of much of their power as symbols of local autonomy.[139] The Whigs' lack of respect for local tradition was a good thing for many towns, however. For in too many cases, the traditional unit of town government, the borough corporation, was a self-selected group of oligarchs who were more interested in doling out local patronage than in improving local amenities. The Municipal Corporations Act (1835) sought to turn the borough corporations into less openly partisan and potentially more useful institutions that would attract the services of respectable men of property from across the confessional and party divides. By its terms, 178 'close' boroughs were replaced by town councillors to be elected to three-year terms by rate-paying householders.[140] The Whig government envisioned the Municipal Corporations Act as a democratizing measure, and not a boon to bigger government at the town level. But in permitting the new corporations a power that was not permitted to any other local authorities – the power to levy an unlimited rate for general purposes – the act facilitated the long-term growth of municipal spending on a broader array of services.[141]

Broadening the scope of government was as piecemeal and contentious a process at the local as it was at the national level. Virtually all of the new rating powers granted to local government by parliament in this era were permissive rather than compulsory. Take, for instance, the landmark Education Act of 1870, by which the state sanctioned the immediate establishment of some 2,000 elected school boards in order to furnish a sound, non-denominational drilling in the three Rs to the million-plus working-class children who had not been provided for by the voluntary (mostly Anglican or Nonconformist) schools. There is no question that this act marked a dramatic extension of government involvement in the lives of a great many of the common people. But it left the setting of rates and school fees entirely to the discretion of the new school boards that were elected by the rate-payers. Until 1880, it was also up to the boards to decide whether or not to adopt by-laws making attendance compulsory between the recommended ages of five and thirteen. Thus in the short term, at least, the localities enjoyed immense discretionary power in the performance of their new role of schoolmaster.[142] While some of them took to the task with zeal, others showed themselves more interested in saving the rate-payers' money than in providing decent facilities and instruction to their pupils.

Education was by no means the only sphere in which local discretion guaranteed uneven improvement. The growth of the municipal electorate, for instance, was just as much a bane as it was a boon to the accumulation of broader and more expensive borough responsibilities. We have already seen that petty tradesmen and small landlords were well aware that they bore a disproportionate share of the burden of local rates, and were often loath to see them grow heavier. It is thus no coincidence that formidable rate-payers' associations mobilized on behalf of cheap local government in many towns in the 1850s, just as the corporations were beginning to assume responsibility for expensive public-health improvements.[143] Rate-payer resistance was one of the chief reasons why these improvements were often only very slowly carried out. But while it would be a mistake to assume that humble 'rateocrats' always stood in the way of urban improvements, so too would it be to assume that the more well-to-do businessmen who sometimes dominated town councils always sought to facilitate them. The same northern textile masters who looked upon the building of monumental town halls as a rate-worthy badge of civic honour some-times put off the laying of sewers as a costly and unglamorous enter-prise.[144] Big-business councillors, moreover, could be just as obstinate as their humbler counterparts when it came to protecting their vested interests. Thus Bradford industrialists habitually blocked even minimal efforts to reduce air pollution in perhaps the smoggiest city in England because they deemed them an unacceptable infringement of their prop-erty rights.[145] Their counterparts in Birmingham were far more aggres-sive in the promotion of public health and the provision of services. But it was only in the 1870s, during Joseph Chamberlain's famous may-oralty, that 'gas-and-water socialism' was brought into being there, with the municipalization of the gas and water supplies and the instal-lation of a new sanitary regime. The vaunted 'civic gospel' of Bir-mingham, moreover, owed much to the exceptional sense of civic duty of that city's powerful Dissenting sects.[146]

Chamberlain and company had few imitators before the 1880s.[147] Only then did many prominent local politicians, like their national counterparts, start to conclude that broader government intervention was the proper response to the 'social question' with which they were increasingly preoccupied. We shall address that question and the various answers to it in the next chapter. The point here is that until the 1880s, 'cheap government' and *laissez-faire* were still ruling princi-ples, even if they were frequently honoured in the breach. Most mid-Victorians, while willing to admit that urban and industrial expansion required new forms of intervention, still wished to preserve a govern-ing structure that left them to shift more or less for themselves. Gen-erally speaking, they got what they wanted.

4

The Making of the
Social-Service State

1880–1939

As late as 1880, the British state was chiefly notable for its virtual absence from broad areas of social and economic life. Over the next six decades, its presence became readily discernible in almost all of them. At the beginning of this period the accepted social responsibilities of the central and local authorities barely extended beyond keeping the peace, preventing utter destitution through the poor law, promoting public health, and furnishing children who had not already enrolled in the voluntary schools with a rudimentary education. By the end of it, they had grown to include the provision of old-age pensions, health and unemployment insurance, and public housing. In 1880 the state's economic regulation scarcely went beyond the limitation of the hours of factory labour for women and children and the enforcement of minimum safety standards. By 1939 it included the setting of wages in certain industries, the provision of labour exchanges for unemployed workers, rent control, and industrial arbitration. In short, it had become commonplace for the central and local authorities to intervene in the daily lives of a great many Britons in ways that most mid-Victorians would have found virtually inconceivable.

This chapter will explore four themes that help to account for this transformation. The first is the growth of an environmentalist critique of poverty between 1880 and 1914. A number of factors combined in these years to bring about a halting recognition that much poverty stemmed from environmental influences beyond the control of the poor themselves, and thus suggested that the state had a duty to take more active steps to fight it. Investigative reports of how the very poor lived; the recognition of casual employment as a structural economic problem; growing fears of the adverse effect of the 'degenerate' classes on national efficiency; the emergence of a truly independent working-class political movement: such factors drew attention to the 'social question' of poverty, and suggested a variety of interventionist responses to it – some of them altruistic, some of them moralistic, some of them imperialistic, many of them all three at the same time.

The second theme is the response to the social question enshrined in the Liberal legislation of 1906–14. The much-vaunted welfare reforms of this era, most notably the provision of old-age pensions and health and unemployment insurance, were indeed path-breaking. But they were limited in practice, confined to certain strictly defined categories of recipient. Most of them were also contributory, making them exercises not so much in social solidarity as in the spreading of risk along strict actuarial lines. A variety of motives prompted the Liberal government to pass these measures. National efficiency in an age of imperial competition ranked high among them. In fact, it was greater military spending even more than greater social spending that led to a 'fiscal crisis of the state' in the years leading up to 1914. The Liberals used progressive taxation to facilitate both expenditures simultaneously.

The third theme is the dramatic growth of state intervention in virtually all spheres of life during World War I. Up until 1914, most Britons continued to view centralization as only an occasional and regrettable necessity. The Great War changed all that. Military conscription, censorship and a vigorous programme of state-sponsored propaganda, the capping of workers' wages and manufacturers' profits, rent control, rationing, the outlawing of strikes, government management of essential industries, the imposition of protective duties, the growth of government spending from 12 to 52 per cent of national income, enormous increases in income tax: such measures were unheard of before 1914. It was only the perceived requirements of total warfare that brought them into being.

Most of these measures came to an end with the war itself. But the interwar state was nevertheless a far more noticeable (and expensive) fact of life than its late-Victorian predecessor had been. The fourth and last theme that we shall be exploring here is the prominence of welfare provision as a function of that state. Admittedly, it did not find creative solutions to the economic crises of this era, because the politicians and civil servants who presided over it were generally committed to waiting them out whilst keeping sterling strong, public spending down, and the budget balanced. The prevailing deflationary ideology helped to push up unemployment levels in the staple sectors of the economy in the first half of the 1920s, and did nothing to push them down thereafter. One result was a confrontation between management and labour that implicated the state on behalf of the former against the latter. But class conflict did not lead to the collapse of the

British state, in contrast to many of its continental counterparts, in the interwar years. There are many reasons for Britain's relative stability in this nightmare era. One of the most important was the rapid growth of unemployment insurance. This was a grudging and often humiliating sort of welfare provision. It was the product of a social-service state, which gave its citizens limited, means-tested access to a growing variety of non-pauperizing social services, and not of a welfare state that guaranteed a minimum standard to its citizens *as of right*. Nevertheless, the fact that social-service spending exceeded military spending until the rearmament drive of the late 1930s indicates just how far the priorities of the state had shifted since the late-Victorian era.

The origins of the social-service state, 1880–1914

Few mid-Victorians were likely to have dealt with any central or local officials other than postmen, policemen, and poor-law guardians. By 1914, the ranks of noticeable officialdom had grown to include school-attendance officers, 'foster-parents', probation officers, labour-exchange agents, and health visitors. One can exaggerate the scope of this more broad-ranging state, as well as Britons' awareness of it. As late as 1905, for example, the central government was spending no more on all forms of higher education than it spent to meet the operating costs of a single naval frigate. Nor as yet was there great support for the idea that the state should be taking on a dramatically larger role. Certainly there was very little of the sort of glorification of the state as the embodiment of the nation that was common in Wilhelmine Germany.[1] Indeed, while commentators on government were far more likely to refer to 'the state' at the end of the century than they had been in the middle of it, they often referred to it pejoratively, as an entity that might threaten private initiative and civil liberties.[2] Whether they welcomed it or dreaded it, however, observers were virtually unanimous by the 1880s that the era of the 'nightwatchman' state was over, and that a new era of 'collectivism' or 'socialism' had begun in which the state was bound to amass ever greater responsibilities. Thus in 1888 the Liberal politician W. V. Harcourt could famously declare that 'we are all Socialists now'.[3]

What Harcourt and most Britons meant by 'socialism' was a commitment not to Marxist anti-capitalism, but to the notion that it was a legitimate role of the state not simply to protect private property, but to combat extreme poverty and actively to promote prosperity. We have seen that the principle of state intervention was already well established by the mid-Victorian decades. But it had been acknowledged grudgingly, as the exception that proved the minimalist rule. By 1914, in contrast, state intervention was a principle that was almost universally accepted, and one that was seen to be advancing along a broad front.

What accounts for this shift in perception? A number of factors, most of which encouraged the belief that the poorest of the poor could not pull themselves up by their own bootstraps no matter how hard they tried. This belief helped to legitimate a growing role for the state in the regulation of social and economic life. For if chronic poverty was attributable to environmental and not just to moral shortcomings, then it followed that the central and local authorities had an obligation to try to help the poor to help themselves by improving their physical conditions.[4] The emerging environmental critique of poverty arose first of all from an awareness that chronic poverty remained a stubborn fact of life in what was still the world's wealthiest nation. The well-publicized social surveys of Charles Booth and Benjamin Seebohm Rowntree drew attention to this troubling fact. In *Life and Labour of the People in London* (1893–1901) Booth introduced the now familiar concept of the 'poverty line', a minimum income level below which it was impossible to attain even the nutritional standard necessary to remain in good physical health. By this standard, he concluded, 30 per cent of all Londoners were occasionally 'in poverty or want', with 'no surplus' beyond the bare essentials, while another 8.4 per cent were chronically impoverished – 'at all times more or less in want'. The figures he compiled for the slums of the East End were especially disturbing: 35 per cent on the margin of poverty and 13 per cent engulfed in it.[5] Seebohm Rowntree reached similar conclusions in his survey of York, *Poverty; A Study of Town Life* (1901). Using a statistically more elaborate poverty line, he calculated that 10 per cent of the population lived in 'primary poverty', unable to reach the minimum nutritional standard necessary for healthy existence, while another 17.9 per cent lived in 'secondary poverty', i.e. 'in obvious want and squalor'. Booth and Seebohm Rowntree attributed some of this poverty to alcoholism and other personal deficiencies. But they made it clear that a great deal of it stemmed from the vagaries of the life and economic cycles that were beyond the control of the poor themselves. Thus Seebohm Rowntree's survey established that poverty was to a large degree age-specific, an inevitable affliction for many young families and elderly people in poorer districts, while Booth's made it equally obvious that the single greatest cause of poverty in London was unemployment and under-employment.[6]

Already in the early 1880s, a series of journalistic exposés had given even broader publicity to the living conditions in the urban slums than Booth and Seebohm Rowntree would later draw to age-specific and cyclical poverty. George Sims's series of articles on 'How the Poor Live' in the *Pictorial World* (1883), the Reverend Andrew Mearns's *The Bitter Cry of Outcast London* (1883), another collection of articles in W. T. Stead's *Pall Mall Gazette* (1884–5): these and other newspaper reports and pamphlets drew attention to the squalor and misery of the inner city. This was sensationalistic journalism that often portrayed the urban poor as morally degraded creatures who routinely indulged themselves in drunkenness and even incest. But it also attributed much of this (often unsubstantiated) degradation to the structural problem of overcrowding in the slums. These reports encouraged the appointment of a Royal Commission on the Housing of the Working Classes in 1885 which concluded that overcrowding stemmed not from any obvious personal shortcomings of slum-dwellers, but from the interrelationship of high population densities, low wages, and high rents.[7]

This emerging environmental critique of poverty was also given support from within the universities. At Cambridge, the economist Alfred Marshall studied short-term fluctuations in the trade cycle and concluded that a good deal of unemployment was explicable solely in structural terms. In doing so, he rejected the classical 'wages-fund' theory which held that the aggregate fund for wages was inelastic, and thus that workers who found themselves unemployed did so chiefly if not solely because they sought to sell their labour at too high a price.[8] Meanwhile, at Balliol College, Oxford, the idealist philosopher T. H. Green championed a system of ethics which emphasized that property ownership carried with it certain responsibilities to the community, and thus that property rights were not absolute. When those rights came into conflict with the greater good of the community, the state should limit them. Through the writings of Green and other idealists, academic philosophy was beginning to put the duty of the state to protect the weak on an equal footing with its duty to uphold freedom of contract.[9]

A good many Oxonians who had imbibed the ethic of social responsibility from Green and his Balliol colleague Arnold Toynbee participated in the settlement-house movement, which sought to develop within them a sense of common purpose with the poor. The first such house, Toynbee Hall, was established by Canon Samuel Barnett in Whitechapel in 1884. By the turn of the century it had spawned some thirty imitators, almost half of them in provincial cities. Their novelty lay in the ways in which they sought to pursue the 'common good' under one roof through the joint participation of privileged undergraduates and their working-class neighbours in social work, concerts, university extension programmes, and the like.[10] This closer intimacy with the poor helped to instil in the more affluent residents of the settlement houses the notion that poverty was not only or even chiefly the result of moral weakness.

By the last quarter of the century, the decline of the moralistic conception of poverty was even noticeable within the workhouse system. Guardians throughout England and Wales were at least tacitly admitting that the stigmatizing poor law was too rigid and unjust a system of poor relief, for they were providing ever higher levels of relief through its agency, on increasingly generous terms. Sustained efforts to deter the able-bodied meant that most recipients of outdoor as well as indoor relief were now either very young, very old, or physically disabled in some other way. The workhouse system was in part a welfare system, simply because there was no other institutional provision available for these large categories of disadvantaged people. As the welfare services offered to them grew, so did the cost of the poor law – by almost 20 per cent between 1871 and 1893, during a period of substantial deflation. This rising cost stemmed chiefly from the growth of institutional services provided to indoor paupers – infirmaries, dispensaries, schools, 'cottage homes' in which pauper children received better care and instruction, and the like. As the therapeutic regime of the poor law grew more extensive, workhouses themselves started to look less like prisons and more like clusters of large homes that provided different services to different classes of paupers. The growth of this 'pavilion system' facilitated the gradual loosening up of disciplinary regimens for most inmates who were not classified as vagrants. Medical attention under the poor law became officially nonstigmatizing in 1885, when receipt of it no longer disenfranchised the applicant. The Poor Law Medical Service grew apace, so that by the first decade of the twentieth century it was employing 3,000 district medical officers and 6,000 nurses.[11] In short, the structure of the poor law itself was gradually accommodating the notion that poverty was not simply a moral defect that was to be punished.

In spite of all this evidence, however, there was not a seamless transition from a predominantly moral to a predominantly environmental critique of poverty in the last quarter of the century. Most guardians continued to set poor relief at very meagre rates. There were still examples to be found of paupers who starved to death on outdoor relief because local guardians wrongly assumed that they could supplement their paltry allowances with other sources of income.[12] The large majority of elderly poor were still making do with no public support at all; only 6 per cent of men and 3 per cent of women aged sixty-five to seventy-four received indoor relief in 1901.[13] Many advocates of reform who attributed a good deal of poverty to environmental factors, moreover, were inclined to be very harsh indeed to the 'undeserving' poor. Thus while the majority and minority reports of the landmark 1909 Royal Commission on the Poor Laws both recommended the liberalization of poor relief, they also agreed that habitual 'loafers' should be sent to penal colonies. So too did Charles Booth, Canon Barnett, and Alfred Marshall.[14]

These disciplinary prescriptions for the feckless poor point to a much less altruistic motive that underpinned much of the support for interventionist measures to fight poverty between 1880 and 1914: the need to promote 'national efficiency'. This phrase meant a number of things in this anxious era: a more vigorous set of policies to compete in a more competitive global economic environment and to reverse the (widespread if exaggerated) perception of terminal industrial decline; a tightening up of imperial connections; protectionism; compulsory military service; even state policing of the gene pool, as suggested by the popular science of eugenics.[15] Advocates of state-sponsored national efficiency often held up German models for imitation. But it was the growing possibility of military conflict with Germany that convinced many observers of the need for the state to take a more active role in securing more able-bodied men for the defence of the empire. The physical 'degeneration' of the poor became a national obsession after it took the British three years and £250 million to defeat the ostensibly hapless Boers in southern Africa. Many of the men who had sought to enlist in the army during the Boer War, including the majority from Manchester, had been deemed physically unfit to serve.[16] The doubts thus cast on Britain's ability to defend itself and its empire led to the influential Report of the Interdepartmental Committee on Physical Deterioration (1904). Many of its recommendations for enhancing physical fitness were enshrined in law by 1914, such as the provision of school meals for poor children, and routine school medical inspections and physical education for both sexes. The report included the ominously vague caveat that 'it may be necessary . . . for the State . . . to take charge of the lives of those who, from whatever causes, are incapable of independent existence up to the standard of decency which it imposes'.[17]

Fortunately, the state never resorted to extensive coercion in order to promote national efficiency. Vagrants were never deposited in forced-labour camps, nor were the physically or mentally 'unfit' ever legally sterilized as a means of protecting the gene pool, as many were in California and other American states. But it is a vivid testament to the attractive force of what we would now consider the dark side of national efficiency that Herbert Asquith's Liberal government (1908–16), the sponsor of a number of pioneering social-welfare measures, could also give its support to an act of 1913 which provided for the detention of 'mental defectives' in asylums in order to keep them from reproducing.[18]

It was the same fear of the urban 'residuum' at the root of so many national-efficiency proposals that helps to explain the more aggressive policing of 'deviant' behaviour at the turn of the century. A broad range of legislation, often championed by formidable moral pressure groups, helped to narrow the definition of permissible behaviour in this era and led to the criminalization of drunkenness, soliciting for or into prostitution, cruelty to animals, cruelty to children, failure to send one's children to school, and even 'failing to maintain one's family'.[19] Other new statutes substantially narrowed the limits of appropriate sexual conduct, raising the age of consent for girls to sixteen and turning all forms of male homosexual activity into misdemeanours that were punishable by up to two years' hard labour.[20] 'Habitual' criminals were also singled out for harsher treatment, with the 1908 Prevention of Crime Act going so far as to recommend preventive detention for certain classes of repeat offenders.[21] At the same time, petty offenders were being incarcerated in droves. A quarter of all young men between sixteen and twenty-one who were imprisoned in metropolitan London in 1912–13 served seven-day sentences for offences such as public drunkenness, obscene language, gaming, sleeping rough, or 'playing games in the street'.[22] Small wonder, then, that the police were still widely detested in working-class neighbourhoods, and that an average of one out of every four Metropolitan policemen was being physically assaulted *every year* at about this time.[23]

This moral intrusiveness helps to explain why in the short run the new mass electorate did *not* demand a dramatic increase in state intervention. A series of electoral reforms in the last three decades of the century provided the working classes with unprecedented access to the political system. The Reform Act of 1884 increased the parliamentary electorate by some 76 per cent, extending the franchise to about 60 per cent of adult men. The creation of single-seat parliamentary constituencies in the 1885 Redistribution Act facilitated the election of working-class representatives in several new urban districts that were now dominated by upper-working-class neighbourhoods. Meanwhile, the local franchise was broadened even more dramatically. In 1869, parliament gave unmarried female rate-payers the right to vote in local-government elections, thus adding about a million women voters to the county, borough, and poor-law electoral registers. Twenty-five years later, the creation of a 'lodger' franchise for poor-law elections helped to install working-class men on boards of guardians in the poorer unions.[24] On the eve of World War I, Britain was by no means a democracy. At least a third of the adult male population remained ineligible to vote in parliamentary elections, as were all women. Still, there was a truly mass electorate by the 1890s, and at the time many observers agreed that newly enfranchised workers would immediately press for interventionist legislation as a means of promoting their class interests.

They did not, however, for two reasons.[25] The first was the slowness with which workers as a class were able to gain an effective voice for themselves within the party system. Before the turn of the century the Liberal party was widely regarded as that of the organized working class, and yet its obsessions at the time were those of middle-class Dissent: church disestablishment in Scotland and Wales, local option, Home Rule for Ireland, and the like.[26] A truly interventionist agenda was championed in the 1880s by the fractious intellectuals who dominated the Social Democratic Federation and the Fabian Society. In fact, it was the Fabians who coined the idea of a 'national minimum' in the 1890s, by which they meant (among other things) a minimum wage, anti-sweating legislation, compulsory arbitration, the eight-hour day, the extension of workmen's compensation, old-age pensions, root-and-branch reform of the poor law, and extension of secondary education to the working classes. But while Fabians such as Sidney and Beatrice Webb played an important role in London municipal politics, their success in 'permeating' the major political parties was distinctly limited. They were mainly important for the ideas they introduced into the political arena, and it would take many years before other hands brought them to fruition.[27] With the creation of the Independent Labour Party (ILP) in 1893, we see the emergence of a truly working-class party that was devoted to a series of interventionist measures: the eight-hour day, abolition of overtime and piecework, old-age pensions, health insurance, collective ownership, universal secondary education, home colonies for unemployed workers, abolition of indirect taxation, and a graduated income tax.[28] But it was the ILP's affiliation with the Trades Union Congress in 1900 that led to the formation of the Labour party. That party became formidable because of its very large and growing union constituency, but for the time being that constituency was dedicated less to state intervention than to state neutrality in labour relations.

Ensuring neutrality was the Labour party's highest priority, because a series of anti-union court decisions had done away with it. The judicial assault on the unions culminated in the Taff Vale decision (1901), which undermined the right to strike by permitting employers to sue unions for damages resulting from union-sanctioned strikes. Reversing Taff Vale became the chief goal of the Labour party. It promoted more interventionist measures, as well, most notably the right to work bill of 1907, which would have placed on local government a responsibility to provide work or maintenance to the unemployed.[29] But Labour had little power to influence either minimalist or interventionist legislation before World War I, because its cadre in the House of Commons was still very small, and because as yet it commanded the allegiance of probably no more than 20 per cent of the male work force.[30]

The obsession with Taff Vale points to the second reason for the time-lag between the creation of a mass electorate and the creation of a mass constituency for state intervention: working-class suspicion of a central government that had long gone out of its way to discipline the 'rough' and to deny the interests of the 'respectable' through the enforcement of biased laws. This suspicion encouraged the unions to look to parliament not for ambitious social legislation, but simply for 'fair play' – the separation of economics from politics through free trade, low indirect taxes, and the ability to engage in unfettered collective bargaining.[31] Central to this belief in 'fair play' was the widespread working-class faith in the value of independence. Working people had long been accustomed to look to themselves for social provision, not least because that provided by the state carried the stigma of pauperism until the abolition of the poor law in 1929. Friendly societies, which provided insurance against sickness and old age as well as burial benefits, were by far the largest working-class institutions at the turn of the century.[32] The very comprehensiveness of working-class self-help combined with hatred of the poor law to limit the popular demand for state-sponsored forms of social provision.

Many working-class people, moreover, had good reason to think that established forms of state intervention militated against their best interests. For example, the establishment of compulsory primary education in 1880 reduced many working-class family incomes by taking children out of the work-force and obliging many of their parents to pay school fees until these were abolished in the 1890s. Most of the slum clearance projects of the last three decades of the nineteenth century, moreover, demolished people's homes without furnishing them with new ones.[33] Considering these sorts of imposition, it is small wonder that in the early twentieth century both enfranchised and unenfranchised workers were reluctant to endorse national welfare measures. Few of them had reason to believe that the state could be trusted to do right by them.[34]

Thus, working-class votes were not a potent factor in the gradual expansion of state intervention before 1914. But politicians' *assumption* that such votes would be used for the promotion of 'class legislation' prompted many of them to focus more attention on social issues than they otherwise would have done. It would be short-sighted to attribute the limited social legislation of the 1880s and 1890s *solely* to 'respectable' fears of the mass electorate. But it is reasonable to conclude that they were partly intended as a means of legitimating the capitalist order to the masses.[35] As the Conservative statesman Arthur Balfour put it in 1895, 'social legislation, as I conceive it, is not merely distinguished from Socialist legislation, but is its most direct opposite and its most effective antidote'.[36] It seems clear enough that several of the modest interventionist reforms that made their way onto the statute book during the Conservative premierships of Balfour himself (1902–5) and of his uncle Lord Salisbury (1885–6, 1886–92, 1895–1902) stemmed at least in part from Tory assumptions about the minimum steps necessary to placate the working classes. Salisbury assumed that class struggle was now the great underlying reality of politics,[37] and he did what he could to keep it beneath the surface – through the promotion of humble reform measures such as the 1885 Housing Act, for example, which facilitated Treasury loans for local-government housing schemes, as well as a (distinctly limited) Workmen's Compensation Act (1897) that made it somewhat easier for injured workers to sue their employer for damages.[38]

These were very modest measures. But more ambitious ones that could be expected to take more than trifling sums out of taxpayers' pockets were not likely to be popular with the new electorate, many of whom were still wedded to Gladstonian notions of cheap government and free trade. Indeed, the most obvious political bidding war of the era, which pitted Liberalism and free trade against Conservative tariff reform and closer imperial union in the 1906 general election, ended in a resounding victory for the former, mainly because most humbler voters had no wish to pay for social reform with the higher indirect taxes that Joseph Chamberlain's tariff reform programme would have necessitated.[39] By that time it had become obvious that social policy was integral to high politics in a way that it had not been in the heyday of the new poor law.[40] But most Britons, including most new voters, still expected the central government to manage tax money responsibly and frugally, to intervene in social life only on a carefully limited basis, and to leave most of the workaday business of government to the local authorities.[41]

Indeed, as in the past, it was mainly at the local level that government growth was most noticeable in the decades prior to the Great War. Here, the creation of a mass electorate probably did help to broaden the sphere of governance. Democratic local government finally became a reality in the counties and the metropolis, when the 1888 Local Government Act created county councils to be elected on a house-holder franchise. The year 1894 saw the creation of lower-tier urban and district councils, and most of the local-authority responsibilities outside of the poor law were gradually concentrated in their hands. Five years later, second-tier borough authorities with similar powers were created for London. By the late 1890s, membership of these local authorities was open to all householders, meaning that for the first time significant numbers of women and working men were eligible to serve.[42] In sum, local government reform gradually transferred large areas of responsibility from oligarchical control, divesting magistrates of most of their traditional regulatory responsibilities and throwing them into the hands of representative authorities elected on a very broad franchise.[43]

In the towns, those authorities were extending the range of their activities. Gradually, more and more borough corporations adopted the Birmingham model of development, whereby the corporation acquired control of the local gas works and water supply (and later electricity and public transport) in order to generate revenue. The income drawn from these municipalized services could then be used either to relieve the rates or to provide more amenities. As the historian P. J. Waller has pointed out, this was municipal capitalism rather than municipal socialism. It made good economic sense for towns to provide 'natural monopoly' services more efficiently and at lower cost to the consumer than private companies could hope to achieve.[44] Pragmatic as it was, municipalization was an important means of enhancing the provision of local services. The profits it generated helped to finance many of the activities that one turn-of-the-century local historian noted in his paean to the modest sort of cradle-to-grave social provision that the Liverpool Corporation provided to the local populace:

> It offers to see that the child is brought safely into the world . . . It gives him playgrounds to amuse himself and baths to swim in . . . It sees that the citizen's house is properly built and sometimes even builds it for him. It brings into his rooms an unfailing supply of pure water from the remote hills. It guards his food and tries to secure that it is not danger-ously adulterated. It sweeps the street for him and disposes of the refuse of his house. It carries him swiftly to and from his work . . . If he is sick it nurses him; if he is penniless it houses him; and when he dies, if none other will, it buries him.[45]

Still, the extent of such provisions had much to do with the balance of political power in a given locality, and that balance differed considerably from place to place. In some of the larger cities, and most notably London, it shifted decisively towards the lavish end of the spectrum. The broadening of the metropolitan electorate secured a Lib–Lab majority in the London County Council (LCC) that engaged in a number of small-scale unemployment relief schemes and public health and educational initiatives and carried out the country's most ambitious experiment in slum clearance and council-housing construction.[46] This sort of local interventionism was indeed facilitated by working-class voters and councillors, a good many of them Labour party members, who placed a high value on local self-government. They were predisposed to entrust more responsibilities to the council than to a national government that they continued to mistrust, and on which they could not as yet hope to exert much influence.[47]

It cost a great deal of money to translate dreams of expansive local provision into reality, however, and by no means all of that money came from the profits of municipalization. The lion's share still came from local rates, and local rates were skyrocketing in this era. Between 1875 and 1900, while the population of England and Wales increased by 37 per cent and the rateable value of property by 61 per cent, the revenue generated from rates grew by 141 per cent.[48] Rate relief became a highly contentious issue at the national as well as the local level, but the sheer complexity of the rates, which affected such a wide variety of propertied interests, made them all but impervious to reform in the short term. Hard-pressed rate-payers began to baulk at the expense. Indeed, it was a rate-payers' revolt at the LCC election of 1907 that marked the demise of the progressive coalition and the beginning of an almost thirty-year span of Conservative rule and relatively cheap local government.[49]

By 1905 local authorities were responsible for over half of all government expenditure, and the vast majority of spending on its civil functions.[50] But the fast pace of local-government expansion provoked a fiscal crisis, and the failure of local-finance reform forced the Exchequer to intervene in order to defuse it. Fiscal centralization became more noticeable as the percentage of local-government revenue from Exchequer grants continued to climb. By the first decade of the new century, the income accruing to local authorities from Exchequer grants and loans was exceeding the income generated from rates.[51] Efforts to preserve local autonomy within a broadening framework of social services were being stymied by fiscal problems that could only be overcome by the central government.

The crisis in local finance combined with a spectacular rise in military spending at the turn of the century to undermine the Gladstonian measures that had largely kept budgets and taxation out of the theatre of high politics in the previous era. We have seen that mid-Victorian 'cheap' government relied on the 'Pax Britannica' that had helped to contain military spending over many decades. But in the final years of the century the 'Pax Britannica' gave way to an era of dangerous imperial rivalry and militaristic competition. The costs of formal empire and a naval race with Germany grew precipitously from the 1890s forward. By 1900, the British empire was the biggest that the world had ever seen, embracing some twelve million square miles.[52] Maintaining and expanding it were becoming onerous burdens to British taxpayers, who paid most of the bill for imperial defence.[53] At the same time, the Admiralty, challenged by Germany's hugely ambitious naval-construction drive, was struggling mightily to preserve a 'two-power standard' that committed it to maintaining a fleet that surpassed the combined tonnage of its two largest rivals. Naval expenses grew by a factor of five over the thirty years prior to the Great War.[54] During this period the defence costs borne by British taxpayers were almost twice those borne by their French and German counterparts. Relatively high per capita income levels helped to ease some of the burden on British taxpayers. But they were almost certainly paying more for defence in per capita terms than taxpayers anywhere else in the world.[55] As the military build-up intensified, so too did the Exchequer's efforts to ease the intolerable burden of rates; the immense cost of the Boer War combined with rising local subsidies to *double* central expenditure between 1894 and 1902. How simultaneously to pay for the seemingly irreducible costs of defence and of growing social services became the great question in national politics.[56]

The foundations of the social-service state: Liberal reform, 1906–1914

The Liberal governments of 1906–14 provided an answer that sought to preserve free trade and commit the state to a mild form of wealth redistribution through progressive taxation. At the pivotal 1906 general election, both the Conservatives and the Liberals pledged themselves to the maintenance of high levels of military and social spending. The Tories endorsed Chamberlain's tariff-reform programme, which aimed to promote military preparedness, add new measures of social welfare, revitalize the ailing staple industries, and tie the empire closer together through a neo-mercantilist protective framework.[57] The Liberals countered that protectionism would raise consumer prices, depress real wages, reduce employment opportunities in the export trades, and endanger Britain's position as the world's leading provider of mercantile and financial services. Military and social spending were worthy pursuits, the Liberals emphasized, but they should be financed through a graduated structure of direct taxation, and not a system of protective duties that hit the common people harder than it did the privileged classes.[58] The landslide Liberal victory furnished decisive proof that the mass electorate strongly supported free trade, but was also committed to the notion that social fairness in an age of broader government responsibilities required adherence to the progressive principle in taxation.

That principle had already been established in the 1894 budget, when W. V. Harcourt, then Liberal chancellor of the Exchequer, included a graduated tax of 1 to 8 per cent on the value of inherited estates. Harcourt's death duties marked a crucial break with the past. From that point on, the state has viewed inherited property not as an untouchable hereditary right, but as a source of income that ought to be taxed for the broader good of the nation.[59] With the principle of progressive taxation now established, the prewar Liberal government proceeded to broaden it, most notably through David Lloyd George's 'People's Budget' of 1909, which imposed a 'super-tax' on incomes over £3,000 a year, substantially raised death duties on large estates, and imposed a capital gains tax on the 'unearned increment' on rising land values.[60] The 'People's Budget' did much to resolve the fiscal crisis of the state. There were no major tax additions until 1914, when Lloyd George increased the rate of death duties once again, lowered the 'super-tax' threshold, and introduced a graduated scale of tax on high incomes of £1,000 and more. Thanks to such measures, the share of government income generated from direct taxes rose to an unprecedented 60 per cent.[61]

While Liberal finance helped to shift part of the fiscal burden from indirect to direct taxation, the weight of indirect taxes still fell disproportionately hard on the poorest sections of the working class. It was probably middle-class payers of income tax who benefited most of all from the Liberal tax reforms; the large majority of them were paying less in 1914 than they had done when the Liberals took office, mainly thanks to children's deductions.[62] While the very wealthy were paying considerably more, most of them could easily enough afford to do so, considering that as late as 1906 Britons who were worth over £1,000 a year were paying a mere 8 per cent of their incomes to the state.[63] Still, many owners of broad acres took the new taxes on land as a declaration of war. The Tory majority in the House of Lords responded by vetoing the 'People's Budget', thus violating the two-centuries'-old tradition by which the peers had acquiesced in a government's annual fiscal measures. It took two general elections and George V's hesitant threat of a mass creation of Liberal peers to end the constitutional crisis in August 1911, when a majority in the Lords sullenly acquiesced in the passage of a Parliament Act that limited their veto power over any piece of legislation to three sessions and stripped them of the power to meddle with finance bills. A great many peers concluded that the act had emasculated their chamber, and after its passage they stayed away in droves. To many observers, the Parliament Act, in tandem with the Liberal fiscal measures that had precipitated it, appeared to symbolize the terminal decline of aristocratic political power. As it turned out, the prestige of the aristocracy was a painfully long time dying. Whether measured in terms of wealth, social cachet, or representation in cabinets, for instance, aristocrats continued to exercise disproportionate influence through much of the twentieth century.[64] But in constitutional terms the Parliament Act merely belaboured what had long been obvious: that the House of Commons was the pre-eminent branch of the central government, and that the party which enjoyed majority support within it enjoyed formidable power to translate its legislative goals into reality.

The Liberals' welfare goals were ambitious, and their welfare legislation implicated the state in social and economic relationships in ways that would have been unthinkable only a few decades earlier. Thus the 1908 Pensions Act immediately provided almost half a million of the aged poor with a measure of weekly support from the Exchequer. These pensions were very small (no more than 5 shillings a week), and applied only to the very old (those over seventy), the very poor, and the demonstrably 'respectable': applicants who had had a brush with the law within the last decade or who were deemed to be 'habitual loafers' were turned down. Still, this was a landmark act which acknowledged that the 'respectable' elderly could be poor through no fault of their own, and that they were thus entitled to state support as a right of citizenship that was free from the stigma of the poor law.[65]

The same acknowledgement was enshrined in the most ambitious welfare measure of the prewar era, the National Insurance Act. The health insurance scheme embedded in the controversial part one of the act helped to provide some fourteen million Britons with basic medical care and short-term family income support when wage-earners fell sick. Once again, there were strict limits to the measure. Only adult workers earning less than £160 a year were eligible, and their dependants were not covered. The intensive lobbying of powerful vested interests – the industrial insurance companies, the medical profession, the friendly societies, and the trade unions – helped to limit the terms of the scheme and to ensure that its administration would chiefly be assigned to them. The 'approved societies' had the right to disqualify workers whom they deemed to be 'bad risks'. The act did virtually nothing to promote preventive medicine, or to facilitate access to doctors. Since it was a contributory scheme, it was limited in its redistributive effects, and employees paid in the lion's share of the contributions.[66] Still, it set an important precedent for state intervention in a new sphere by allocating tax money to the provision of non-stigmatizing health insurance and basic medical care for a good many working-class Britons.

The same can be said for the unemployment insurance provisions enshrined in part two of the act, by which the central government for the first time acknowledged that the Exchequer had a responsibility to assist able-bodied workmen who lost their jobs through no fault of their own. Part two established compulsory unemployment insurance for workers in the shipbuilding, engineering, and construction industries, who were susceptible to seasonal and cyclical unemployment and most of whom were not covered by established union schemes. Like part one, it was contributory, its payouts were limited (to fifteen weeks a year at a maximum of 7 shillings a week), and it was restricted to a handful of trades. Nevertheless, it allocated a considerable amount of central tax money to the provision of yet another form of non-stigmatizing welfare benefit that would have been unthinkable a couple of decades earlier, and by 1914 it covered 2.3 million workers.[67]

The Liberal governments likewise took unprecedented steps to promote the well-being of children. Thus the Education (Provision of Meals) Act of 1906 permitted Local Educational Authorities (LEAs) to provide school meals to needy children, at no charge and with no poor-law disabilities attached. LEAs were slow to provide such meals, but another act of 1914 made it compulsory for them to do so. Likewise, the Education (Administrative Provisions) Act of 1907 required LEAs to carry out medical inspections of schoolchildren. Finally, the Children Act of 1908 liberalized the penal treatment of minors by establishing separate juvenile courts and prohibiting children under sixteen from being sentenced to adult prisons. It also sought to enforce parental responsibility for children by imposing penalties for parental negligence.[68] Through such measures the state undertook to promote the welfare of children not only in school but in the home, and in the process it narrowed the hitherto very broad range of legally acceptable parental conduct.

The Liberal governments also took some of the first interventionist steps in another area of private life that had been virtually off limits to the Victorian state: workplace relationships, hitherto regulated only by the factory acts. First of all, the Trades Disputes Act (1906) reversed the

Taff Vale decision by granting trade unions immunity from civil actions. The Trades Unions Act (1913) similarly reversed the Osborne Judgment of 1909, which had effectively prohibited unions from imposing on their members a political levy in support of the Labour party. Individual trade unionists retained the right to opt out of political levies, and these still had to be endorsed by majority vote of a union's members. But the act helped to secure a solid base of financial support for the Labour party.[69]

While the Liberals acknowledged the right to strike, they did not hesitate to use force against strikers who were deemed to pose a serious threat to public order. In Britain as elsewhere, the prewar era was a period of massive labour unrest. A 50 per cent rise in union membership combined with relatively low levels of unemployment, lagging wages, intransigent management, and growing industrial militancy to trigger an unprecedented wave of strikes, peaking in 1912 with over forty million lost working days.[70] Large-scale strikes of railwaymen, dockers, and transport workers led to serious economic disruptions, while the forging of a Triple Alliance among them provoked fears of a general strike that would bring the government to its knees. The Liberals responded with force. Troops were called into the Rhondda valley after a fracas at Tonypandy that pitted striking miners against Glamorgan constables reinforced by flying detachments of the Metropolitan police. Soldiers shot dead two men at Llanelli during the national rail strike of 1911. Troops were likewise sent to Merseyside during the industrial disturbances there in the summer of 1911 that left two dead and scores injured. Here was a remarkable resurrection of the seemingly defunct practice of using troops 'in aid of the civil power', even if the Liberal governments showed more restraint than their continental counterparts in the policing of industrial disputes in this tumultuous era.[71]

While the Liberal governments did not hesitate to use the coercive powers of the state to contain industrial disputes, they often sought to try to arbitrate them. The Conciliation Act of 1896 charged the Board of Trade with the task of looking into the causes of industrial quarrels and offering mediation to the disputants. Thus for the first time ever, a branch of the central government was involved in the continuous monitoring of industrial relations. The Liberal ministries not only made active use of the Board of Trade for this purpose, but also experimented with other methods of intervention. Through such means the state involved itself in a series of triangular relationships with labour and management in an effort to keep the industrial peace. The government arbitrated on a strictly voluntary basis. There was no statutory framework for negotiations, and no coherent 'labour policy'. The large majority of disputants still preferred to sort things out amongst themselves.[72] But the very fact that the central government offered to mediate furnished additional proof that it was now willing to intervene in economic relations in ways that would have been unacceptable a few decades earlier.

So too did the Trade Boards Act (1909), which set up statutory bodies to regulate wages in the sweated tailoring, shirt-making, and confectionery trades. At first, the act only affected some 100,000 workers. But it was nevertheless a path-breaking measure, for it marked the return of the state to the business of the setting of wages, from which it had withdrawn with the repeal of the Elizabethan statute of labour in 1814. Finally, the Liberal government reluctantly committed itself to the principle of a minimum wage for miners via the Coal Mines (Minimum Wage) Act (1912), which established a network of district boards charged with the task of setting minimum wages on a regional basis. The Liberals were very reluctant to interfere with the fixing of wage rates in such a large labour market, and it was only the need to end a national miners' strike that prompted them to act in this case. Even so, they staunchly refused the miners' demand for a 'national minimum', and declined to suggest wage scales to the district boards, who were thus given a free hand to perpetuate the traditional wage anomalies in the coal industry.[73] Nevertheless, the government's acknowledgement of the principle of a minimum wage marked a sharp break from the Victorian past, when the state had steadfastly refused to meddle with the laws of supply and demand in the labour market. So, finally, did the Labour Exchanges Act (1909), which established a national network of registries where the unemployed could be brought together with prospective employers. By 1914, there were over 400 exchanges scattered throughout the United Kingdom, and they were registering over two million workers a year. Many unionists shunned the exchanges early on because they feared that employers might use them to hire strike-breakers.[74] But their establishment offered further proof that it was now a governing assumption that able-bodied workers could find themselves unemployed through no fault of their own, and that it was a proper duty of the state not only to provide them with financial support when they had been done out of their jobs, but to help them find new ones.

In sum, the Liberal reform measures enrolled the state in a wide variety of activities from which it had hitherto almost completely excused itself, most notably the provision of unemployment and health insurance, child welfare, industrial arbitration, job-hunting, and wage-setting. The motives for these measures were decidedly mixed. Some of them can be traced to the shifting intellectual milieu of the turn of the century, which acknowledged that there were environmental sources of poverty, and that the state had a duty to address them in ways that would advance the good of the nation. That milieu was partly shaped by the 'new Liberal' thought of intellectuals such as J. A. Hobson and L. T. Hobhouse, who argued that the state had a responsibility to help create an environment in which all individuals could realize their full potential. Hobson in particular championed the notion of a state-enforced 'minimum' standard of life as a means of doing so, and the idea of a 'minimum' or 'safety net' was in turn articulated by a few of the younger Liberal politicians who had casual contact with new Liberal intellectuals.[75]

The organicist altruism of new Liberal thought was only one of many factors that influenced the Liberal welfare legislation, however. More obvious was the perception that welfare reform provided a means of stabilizing the industrial order at a time of labour unrest. The Liberal legislation sought to achieve other goals, as well. School physical examinations and health insurance helped to ensure a less sickly population at a time when imperial competition was widely perceived as a struggle between peoples in which the stronger races would prevail. Progressive tax reform provided a means of financing broader social reforms, but it was chiefly attractive as a way to pay for guns and battleships at a time when it was widely assumed that a major European war was imminent.

Just as several factors prompted the Liberals to legislate, so did several factors influence the shape of that legislation. Pressure groups were already accepted as a fact of life at Westminster and Whitehall, and several of them, such as the British Medical Association and the industrial insurance companies, played major roles in the drafting of specific welfare measures. In many cases, the Liberals drew on international models, as well. While, for instance, the National Insurance Act was not as authoritarian in intent as Bismarck's welfare legislation, its administrative details were worked out with the German precedents very much in mind. Such overseas examples were ready to hand, because Britain was by no means alone in experimenting with new forms of state-sponsored welfare in this era. Thus, for instance, the Liberal prime minister H. H. Asquith could single out New Zealand as 'a laboratory in which political and social experiments' such as compulsory industrial arbitration, reform of the sweated trades, and family allowances 'are every day made for the information and instruction of the older communities of the world'.[76]

In the end, it is important to stress the limitations of these 'experiments' as applied to Britain prior to World War I. They marked an important departure from the poor-law principle by establishing minimal non-pauperizing standards of assistance in certain areas, but the poor law remained the basis of social security. It was not abolished until 1929, because neither the Liberal governments nor their immediate successors could reach consensus as to what should replace it, or how to reform local rates in such a way as to promote greater uniformity of relief.[77] A good many very poor families still relied on the poor law, because the Liberal measures did little to help them. None of those measures addressed the issue of chronic underemployment among the 'residuum' of unskilled workers, even though this was widely recognized as a leading cause of poverty. The restrictions placed on unemployment insurance meant that it was chiefly available to the well-organized skilled workers who were least in need of it. In practice, labour exchanges were little more than places to read about vacancies and to collect unemployment payments. In spite of the new health insurance, poor people in need of hospitalization still usually had to rely on the poor law. Old-age pensions, the only non-contributory benefit of the era, were not generous enough to cover the barest subsistence, nor were they intended to be. Still, they cost the Treasury enough to persuade it that future benefits would have to be based on contributory schemes. The most disadvantaged members of the risk pools thus created were further disadvantaged by the apportionment of risk within them, because they were the ones who could least afford to make compulsory flat-rate contributions.[78] Meanwhile, the prevailing negative conception of social fairness in the sphere of production made the Liberals extremely hesitant to interfere with workplace relations beyond the enforcement of free wage bargaining.[79]

It is doubtful that the Liberal welfare reforms held much appeal for the workers whom they were partly intended to fob off. If the British working classes did not seriously challenge the existing social and political order in the years before World War I, this was not because social legislation had appeased them, but because, generally speaking, they were just as committed as their 'betters' to voluntarism, self-help, and distinctly limited state intervention.[80] In fact, many workers perceived certain aspects of the new legislation as unwelcome intrusions in their lives. First of all, the nascent welfare system seriously intruded on their cherished right to privacy. Before the National Insurance Act the state kept no long-term records of Britons who were exempt from payment of income tax; by the early 1920s, a record office at Kew contained files on the working histories of twelve million manual labourers.[81] Skilled workers, moreover, tended to resent unemployment and health insurance because these were largely paid for out of their own pockets. Trade unionists, moreover, most strongly advocated 'bread-and-butter' measures such as the eight-hour day and the 'right to work', which Liberals dismissed as 'sectional' and disruptive. The government's refusal to take them seriously helped to exacerbate the widespread labour unrest.[82] Working-class women had even less to gain from the new legislation than their male counterparts. The unemployment provisions of 1911, for instance, discriminated against women in many ways, excluding married women out-workers on the faulty logic that their incomes were strictly secondary to those of their husbands, for instance, and obliging women who had made unemployment contributions whilst they were single to forfeit all claim to them upon marriage.[83] Working-class mothers were intruded upon in a variety of ways by the infant-welfare movement that culminated in the passage of the Children Act. They were now periodically harassed by school doctors, health visitors, and representatives of the local School Care Committees, who insisted that mothers had an ethical responsibility to promote their children's health even though substandard living conditions that they were powerless to change often made this a hopeless task. Much of this (usually unsolicited) advice was dispensed with a view to lowering infant mortality as a means of enhancing national efficiency, and did little to address mothers' chief concerns: poor diet, chronic non-fatal illness, and birth control.[84]

In short, while the Liberal reforms marked a significant extension of the state's social responsibilities, they were strictly limited, and at the same time were resented as overly intrusive by a good many of the working-class people whom they had ostensibly been intended to help. Moreover, the slow and deliberate extension of the reforms thereafter did little to foster a sense that the state was now actively seeking to advance a more capacious notion of the public good or the rights of citizenship. More generally, while the boundaries and the sheer expense of the state had grown very considerably between 1880 and 1914, it was still assumed that the proper role of the national government was simply to establish a general framework that would enable economy and society to regulate themselves.[85] It would take the massive disruption of World War I to shatter that framework and turn the state into a truly formidable presence in the lives of all Britons.

War interventionism I: 1914–1918

We have seen that many Victorian assumptions about the properly limited relationship between state and society had already been eroded by the eve of the Great War. But it was only during the war itself that those assumptions were swept aside, and only because the needs of all-out warfare required Britons to abide a continuous state intervention in virtually every aspect of their lives which under any other circumstances they would have found intolerable. Of course, the British state was by no means exceptional in its wartime authoritarianism. This was a war in which the nation-states of Europe demanded unparalleled sacrifices of their populations. The most obvious sacrifice was that of a generation of young men. Some 745,000 British soldiers were killed during the war, and another 1.6 million wounded. These casualty rates were actually relatively light – only about half the German and Turkish rates. One in every ten Frenchmen and one in every four Serb men of fighting age were killed in combat.[86] The most obvious points to make about the Great War are that it was to date the most technologically sophisticated and sustained blood-letting in history, and that it was the total mobilization of the belligerent states that made it possible.

Obviously, waging war on such a scale required the enormous growth of the state's traditional responsibilities in the sphere of military logistics. The wartime expansion of the British Expeditionary Force that was stationed on the Western Front provides us with a good idea of the effort involved. The BEF started the war with 120,000 men, 40,000 animals, 334 lorries, 133 cars, 166 motorcycles, 300 guns, and sixty-three aircraft, and ended it with 2.36 million men, 404,000 animals, 31,770 lorries, 7,694 cars, 3,532 ambulances, 14,464 motorcycles, 6,437 guns, and 1,782 aircraft. Providing technical support for such an immense military operation was a Transport Directorate that controlled over 4,000 miles of road, a Medical Service that maintained 95,000 hospital beds, a light railway that carried 175,000 tons of provisions a week, and a Signal Service that despatched 40,000 telegrams and connected 80,000 telephone calls a day. The BEF was only the largest of Britain's many wartime military units; armies numbering over 100,000 soldiers were also to be found in Salonika, Egypt, and Mesopotamia, for instance.[87]

The Victorian principle of 'cheap government', already compromised by the prewar military build-up and expansion of civil services, was rendered obsolete by the fiscal requirements of total war. Britain relied just as much on its superior financial resources during the Great War as it had during the Napoleonic War, and British taxpayers were burdened with a comparably heavy load of debt and taxes. Altogether, total British war expenditure came close to equalling that of all the Central Powers combined.[88] Government spending amounted to 12 per cent of national income in 1913; it equalled 52 per cent by 1918. It fell thereafter, but stabilized at roughly 25 per cent, double the prewar standard, until rearmament started to drive it up again in the mid-1930s.[89] Thus the Great War transformed Britons' perception of what constituted acceptable levels of government spending, making tolerable even after the war levels of taxation that would have been inconceivably high before it began. But the fact that state growth was so 'accidental', so closely connected to the dictates of war, meant that there was precious little discussion of its implications for British citizens.

One of the most obvious implications was that paying taxes was all of a sudden a much more onerous business. The government sought to distribute the wartime tax burden even-handedly. Affluent people were hit by the Treasury as never before. Death duties rose very considerably, the yield from super-tax grew ten-fold, excess profits taxes were ratcheted up to 80 per cent, the standard rate of income tax grew more than five-fold from 1 s 2 d to 6 s in the pound, and income-tax rates were more steeply graduated, reaching 43 per cent on earned incomes of £10,000 or more. Ballooning taxes on 'unearned' incomes played a considerable role in persuading a great many gentry families to sell off part or all of their landholdings.[90] At the same time, however, the wartime lowering of the income-tax ceiling combined with rising incomes to roughly treble the number of income-tax payers, so that payment of income tax was no longer reserved for the affluent. Meanwhile, the working classes shouldered a disproportionate share of the mounting wartime excise taxes, which fell hardest on items of mass consumption, most notably alcohol and tobacco. It is fair to conclude that the wartime tax trend was modestly progressive.[91] But all classes obviously felt the weight of a much heavier burden of taxes.

Inevitably, the British state assumed vast new powers over the subject in order to meet the insatiable demands of war. Dedication to the Victorian ideal of voluntarism made the government very reluctant to introduce military conscription, even though the other major belligerents had done so long before the outbreak of war. But it felt compelled to do so by January 1916, and while at first conscription was limited to single men, it was extended to husbands shortly thereafter. For the first time, all able-bodied adult men who did not gain an exemption were statutorily obliged to take up arms and, if necessary, lay down their lives for the good of the nation. The 16,000 or so conscientious objectors who refused to submit to the draft were harshly dealt with. All of them were obliged to perform war-related services such as ambulance work, over 6,000 of them spent time in prison, 1,500 of them more than once, and a good many were sentenced to hard labour.[92] Thus the wartime state seriously compromised the traditional civil liberties of able-bodied adult men in its effort to stock and restock the armed forces.

In Ireland, of course, the British authorities had relied on the curtailment of civil liberties as an instrument of control ever since the Act of Union. A brief overview of modern British state formation is no place to attempt a detailed examination of nineteenth-century Irish history. Suffice it to say that Ireland, while an integral part of the United Kingdom, was governed like an imperial possession in which the authority of a privileged caste – the Protestant Ascendancy – was reinforced by a British army of occupation. The growing political force of Irish nationalism thrust Home Rule onto the political agenda in the 1880s, but Home Rule was bitterly opposed by the Protestant majority in the northeastern counties of Ireland and by Conservative MPs at Westminster, whose commitment to British sovereignty in Ireland was so strong that they took to calling themselves Unionists. Ireland's political fate was thus an open question when World War I broke out, but the ruthlessness with which the British authorities put down the nationalist rising of Easter 1916, their efforts to suppress the Sinn Fein party and other militant nationalist organizations thereafter, and their decision to apply conscription to Ireland in April 1918 combined to undermine British sovereignty rather than bolstering it.

Burgeoning Catholic resentment made Sinn Fein the most popular political party in the southern twenty-six counties at the 1918 general election, and rather than taking their seats at Westminster the Sinn Fein representatives declared a separatist Irish Parliament in Dublin. This act of defiance touched off a brutal war that pitted nationalist paramilitaries against the Protestant-dominated Royal Irish Constabulary and 'irregular' military units recruited in England, the so-called Black and Tans and Auxiliary forces. The street fights, ambushes, assassinations, tortures, and reprisals that marked the conflict only came to an end in July 1921, when the threat of an intensified British military effort prompted a nationalist delegation to accept the partition of Ireland through the establishment of a separate Home Rule parliament in six counties of Ulster, and dominion status – i.e. self-rule with allegiance to the British Crown and membership in the Commonwealth – for the twenty-six southern counties. Partition immediately triggered a vicious civil war, this time between the pro-treaty forces of the new Irish Free State and the anti-treaty forces that fought for a single Irish republic and claimed for themselves the title of the Irish Republican Army. By May 1923 the Free Staters had gained the upper hand. But while their opponents put down their guns they continued to insist that the only legitimate sovereign power in Ireland would be a united republican government that ruled over every inch of Irish soil. Meanwhile, in the North, the Protestant-dominated Home Rule parliament took a series of measures that virtually excluded the Catholic minority from political life and discriminated against them in the provision of social services such as housing and education. Having thus 'domesticated' Ireland's intractable political differences through main force, the British state and its stewards in Westminster and Whitehall had no desire to interfere once again in order to protect the rights of a Catholic minority.[93]

The wartime state's formidable coercive powers were most dramatically and controversially put to use in the disastrous effort to quell Irish nationalism. But they were noticeable elsewhere, as well, particularly in the Defence of the Realm Acts (DORA), which limited freedom of speech in the interest of national security, granting powers of censorship over domestic news to the military and to the government. These powers were never systematically used. It remained commonplace for newspapers to publish casualty lists, for instance, and even particulars of troop positions, at least in the early stages of the war. Still, anti-war commentary was sometimes vigorously suppressed, and the government initiated a good many press prosecutions under the terms of DORA. It also sought to sustain civilian morale through a continuous (if fairly modest) propaganda operation that culminated in the creation of a Ministry of Information headed by the press tycoon Lord Beaverbrook. Thus, like its counterparts at the time, the wartime government did not hesitate to filter the truth and to broadcast half-truths and lies in an effort to shape public opinion. Nor did it hesitate to curtail the liberties of the subject in a number of other ways that it deemed necessary for the national good. DORA empowered local authorities to impose stiff fines on citizens who failed to observe strict black-out rules; to restrict pub opening hours (to the benefit of public health, as alcohol-consumption rates declined accordingly); and even to prohibit whistling for cabs. It also mandated trial by court martial rather than by jury for citizens charged with committing certain types of crime that were deemed to jeopardize the war effort, and authorized the death penalty for offences committed 'with the intention of assisting the enemy'. The wartime state even tampered with the hours of the day, introducing Daylight Savings Time in 1916 in order to save electricity and enhance industrial productivity.

The central framework of government was radically restructured while the central bureaucracy grew by leaps and bounds in an effort to facilitate war-making. A party truce was declared, a coalition government was formed, and a small war cabinet abruptly replaced the traditional cabinet of senior ministers that had been evolving over the past two centuries. When Lloyd George succeeded Asquith as prime minister in 1916, he brought with him a more 'presidential' style of political management, concentrating a great deal of decision-making power in his own hands, most notably through the creation of his own personal secretariat of policy advisors, the so-called 'Garden Suburb'. The number of civilians employed by the central government more than doubled between the beginning and the end of the war, to over 850,000.[94] New departments mushroomed in Whitehall in response to the vast flow of new business, such as the Ministries of Labour, Shipping, Pensions, and Health, and the gargantuan Ministry of Munitions. A good many private businessmen were recruited into their upper echelons, as the government sought to promote managerial efficiency in the civil service.[95]

Even the prewar Liberal governments had been very hesitant to intervene in the workings of the economy. But the effort of the wartime coalitions to harness that economy to meet the needs of total war led to a massive extension of state interference in every sphere of economic life. By the time of the Armistice, the central government was presiding over the registration and direction of labour, the control of rents, wages, and prices, food rationing, the compulsory purchase and requisitioning of essential materials, and the management of war-related industries. It assumed overall control of land and sea transport, and it massively intervened in agriculture, determining land use, organizing distribution, fixing prices, and greatly influencing the market as a buyer and seller of foodstuffs. The Ministry of Munitions, whose office staff grew to over 65,000 employees, assumed ownership of over 250 factories, mines, and quarries, superintended the operations of some 20,000 workplace facilities, and either directly or indirectly employed some two million munitions workers. The Munitions of War Act (1915) granted it the power to take over factories for the duration of the war, to oblige manufacturers to take on government work, and to transfer machinery and skilled workers from private to state-managed factories. Perhaps most importantly, the act gave legal force to the provisions of a previously negotiated 'Treasury Agreement' that prohibited strikes and lock-outs in all factories engaged in production that was 'required for a satisfactory completion of the war'; forced compulsory arbitration on labour and management; permitted the 'dilution' of tasks that were traditionally reserved for skilled union workers via the employment of semi-skilled female as well as male workers; established a system of 'leaving certificates' that limited workers' power to change jobs without their employers' consent; suspended a range of restrictive workplace practices; and permitted the government to control profits in certain war-related industries.[96]

The Munitions of War Act thus vastly magnified the role of the state in the industrial world, and workers who were still very much committed to the hard-won principles of free collective bargaining and the right to seek the highest possible wages often resented the intrusion. The unions had agreed to make the sacrifices entailed in the act because they had received guarantees that its terms would only be in effect for the duration of the war, and that the pay and position of union workers would not suffer as a result. Their cooperation netted them some important wartime advantages. The Ministry of Munitions gave union officials and shop stewards a consultative role in the productive process that few of them had enjoyed in the past, and included them on tribunals that supervised workplace conditions and penalized not only workers but also employers for infringements of the ministry's regulatory codes. For much of the war, moreover, the unions were given a good deal of authority over the process by which skilled workers deemed essential to domestic production were exempted from military conscription. The gradual erosion of that authority combined with government efforts to extend the principle of 'dilution' to work not covered by the Munitions Acts inspired some of the most serious wildcat strikes of the war in 1917. But the strength of the unions, whose membership doubled during the wartime period of full employment, helped to ensure that full-blown industrial conscription was never introduced in Britain.[97]

Still, there is little question that the wartime state ensured that workers would make a disproportionate sacrifice on the home front. The British government did a better job than most other belligerents of apportioning the domestic sacrifices of the war years, because it was willing to abide by at least a modicum of profit restriction. But while employers were permitted to take profits up to 20 per cent greater than those that had prevailed in 1914, a good business year, workers bore the brunt of spiralling inflation, food rationing, and housing shortages.[98] In some respects, however, workers undoubtedly did well for themselves out of the war. 'Dilution' by no means led to rampant deskilling throughout the industrial economy. It was mitigated by the complicated and localized negotiating process between labour and management, and by unions' willingness to permit lower-skilled workers into some branches while excluding them from others. The insatiable demand for labour meant that virtually all workers, many of them for the first time in their lives, could assume that their jobs would still be there for them a month into the future, and at least for the duration of the war. It also meant that wages in some trades managed to outpace high levels of inflation at least modestly. Finally, the doubling of trade union membership solidified the Labour party's base of support, while Labour's participation in the wartime coalition helped to legitimize it as a viable party of government.[99]

That coalition, moreover, presided over a series of important extensions of social insurance. Thus it provided war pensions on increasingly generous terms to the dependants of all those who were killed or seriously wounded in battle. It agreed to the provision of non-contributory 'out-of-work' pensions up to a maximum of twenty weeks for demobilized servicemen, at 24 shillings in addition to child supplement.[100] It granted separation allowances to the families of soldiers, a generous (albeit a patriarchal) non-contributory benefit whose cash value was enhanced over the course of the war.[101] Finally, the government presided over the 1918 Representation of the People Act, which created universal male suffrage by detaching all property qualifications from a man's right to vote, while it simultaneously created over eight million women voters by granting the franchise to women over thirty years of age. Thus the size of the electorate was roughly trebled overnight, mainly because the majority in parliament sought to reward unenfranchised men as well as a good many women for their wartime services, and because, in the case of women, politicians wanted to avoid a recurrence of the sex war over the question of the suffrage that had embarrassed the prewar Liberal governments. The sexual double standard remained until 1928, when women were finally granted the right to vote on the same basis as men. A series of acts passed in the interim gave them the right to stand for parliament as well as access to the legal profession and the civil service, and eliminated the double standard in the laws governing divorce. Women's organizations played an important role in getting all of these measures onto the statute book. But the innumerable ways in which women had contributed to the war effort clearly helped to make the measures possible by persuading a considerable body of 'respectable' male opinion to relent in its dogged resistance to the extension of women's rights.[102]

Thus the need to wage war on a hitherto inconceivable scale fostered the massive growth of the state, prompted it to intervene in virtually every aspect of social and economic life, and made it answerable for the first time (in theory, at least) to a truly democratic electorate. It needs to be stressed that there was nothing inevitable about these dramatic changes, for they stemmed from a war effort whose vast dimensions nobody had foretold. Wartime intervention was a thoroughly improvised affair in Britain, just as it was everywhere else. The British state proceeded haltingly, balancing the need to respect the interests of capital, labour, and the private citizen against the need to mobilize the country's resources as efficiently as possible.[103] There was clearly no mandate for authoritarian intervention in a country whose political leadership could bring itself to introduce military conscription only in the middle of the war, and to introduce full-scale food rationing only in the summer of 1918, despite Britain's susceptibility to blockade. Such reluctance makes clear that, as the historian J. M. Bourne has pointed out, 'state control was not an idea whose time had come, but an exceptional measure for exceptional circumstances, to be abandoned when the world came to its senses'.[104]

The limits of 'normality', 1919–1939

The world finally came to its senses in November 1918, and a great many of the British state's wartime controls were jettisoned. Shortly thereafter, the postwar industrial Slump set in, and the international financial crisis at the end of the 1920s made a bad economic situation worse. In retrospect, there is little doubt that the disengagement of the state from the economy – embodied in a strong pound, balanced budgets, and fiscal austerity measures – contributed to massive unemployment in the traditional smokestack industries, and no doubt that the state sided with management in the wave of industrial unrest that stemmed directly from the Slump. Still, the most obvious point to make about the class conflict of the interwar period that led to such disastrous results in many European countries is that it did not seriously threaten the legitimacy of the British state, much less bring it down.

One might have expected that Britain's pronounced social stratification, large manufacturing sector, and formidable trade unions would have enhanced the possibility of violent upheaval there in this tumultuous era. There are several reasons why this never happened.[105] One was the regional and sectoral variations in the economy, which were creating many jobs in light industry and the retail trades in the South and the Midlands just as they were taking heavy industrial jobs away in the North, Scotland, and South Wales. Another was the social cohesion that was manifest in many ways, such as low crime rates and broad participation in voluntary institutions. A third was the longstanding tradition of self-reliance and political scepticism, most noticeable among the working classes, which assumed that there was little that government could do to change the world. But another important reason was that the prevailing deflationary ideology did not bring about a complete return to prewar 'normality'. Public expenditure levels remained considerably higher than they had been before the war, and spending on welfare services was particularly buoyant. This was still a distinctly limited and often niggardly social-service state that stigmatized poverty in a variety of ways. But its welfare provisions were an important social stabilizer that helped to make mass unemployment bearable and thus, for better or worse, politically tolerable.

There was no immediately obvious disengagement of the state from economy and society after the Armistice. But the Lloyd George coalition government's ambitious social programme was thwarted by the severe budget cuts of the early 1920s.[106] There were several related reasons for the economy drive. One of them was the collapse of the postwar economic boom by 1921, as governments throughout Europe were faced with slackening demand and excess industrial capacity. The British government, like many of its European counterparts, tightened its belt as it waited out the Slump. Another reason for postwar retrenchment was anxiety about the vast size of the national debt and the growing cost of servicing it; by 1920, a full 40 per cent of central expenditure was allocated to debt service.[107] A third reason was the strong commitment to a return to limited government that was entrenched within powerful institutions such as the City and the Treasury, whose permanent secretary, Sir Warren Fisher, was recognized as head of the civil service and given considerable influence over senior appointments in other departments. The vast panoply of wartime economic controls was almost entirely dismantled within three years of the Armistice, because relatively few individuals who were vested with real decision-making power wished to preserve them.[108]

This same commitment to limited government was entrenched within the mass electorate. It is true that the Treasury was a bastion of fiscal conservatism with strong motives and formidable powers for obstructing innovation.[109] But if it was devoted to retrenchment, balanced budgets, deflation, and the dismantling of economic controls, so too, evidently, were a great many voters. For these policies were closely associated with the Conservative party, and more people voted for the Conservative party than any other one at every single election in the interwar era.[110] What explains the Tories' hegemony in the first decades of British democracy? Not simply their formidable electioneering apparatus, but their skill in crafting an anti-materialist and explicitly anti-'socialist' message that simultaneously sought to incite fears of class warfare and to extol the virtues of restraint, individual responsibility, free enterprise, and a patient determination to wait out economic hard times.[111]

Conservative rhetoric played an important role in securing acquiescence in the prevailing 'Treasury view', which suggested that the best means of generating economic growth in the postwar climate was to keep the budget in balance through spending cuts; to avoid public borrowing for social services; and to curb inflation and preserve the attractiveness of sterling as an international currency through the setting of high interest rates and the return to the gold standard at its prewar parity of $4.86 to the pound. The return to gold, it was argued, would bolster Britain's weakened status as a world leader in financial services and bring about an adjustment of interest rates that in the long run would maximize production and stimulate employment. This argument reflected the orthodox economic assumption that the free market system was ultimately self-regulating, and that the proper role of the government was thus to avoid interfering with the 'natural' rates of interest, prices, and wages. But when the Conservative government returned to the prewar parity in 1925, it simply exacerbated the Slump that had first hit the smokestack industries in 1921, when the severe contraction of postwar demand first became obvious. For the commitment to 'dear' money meant that employers would have to cut jobs and wages if they were to keep their products price-competitive abroad. Thus the implementation of the 'Treasury view' helped to set the stage for the industrial confrontations of the early 1920s, as union workers fought to save their jobs and their wages in the face of a deflationary regime. But at the time, it was widely supported by 'respectable' opinion, even by a good many industrialists, as the only obvious alternative to rampant inflation, the destruction of savings, a general collapse of trade, and repudiation of the government's debts.[112]

The political economy of deflation was supported by classical economy theory, but it was also supported by fear of Communism, which had triumphed in Russia, and which had only been suppressed through violence in Hungary, Germany, and Italy. Even vaguely socialistic state policies were enough to alarm most propertied interests at the height of the red scare in the first half of the 1920s. Perhaps even more significant in Britain, however, was fear of the organized working classes. It was easy for the burgeoning professional and commercial middle classes that held the key to the Conservative party's electoral fortunes to accept retrenchment, 'dear' money, and high unemployment as integral to the postwar structural adjustment, because the first two protected their savings deposits and investments while the last one chiefly affected manual workers.[113]

A series of postwar governments went along with middle opinion in equating union efforts to preserve or improve upon wartime gains with selfish 'sectionalism', and sought to stifle these efforts. Employers in the industrial sector sought layoffs and wage cuts while workers sought to consolidate their wartime gains, and the result was a series of bitter strikes that cost an unprecedented eighty-five million working days in 1921. The most serious confrontation was in the coal industry, where miners who sought a 30 per cent wage hike, a six-hour day, and nationalization clashed with owners who sought pit closures. A lock-out prompted the Miners' Federation to request sympathetic action from their partners in the 'Triple Alliance', the dockers and railwaymen. The Lloyd George coalition managed to fob off with concessions the more moderate leadership of these latter unions, however, and on 'Black Friday', 15 April 1921, they pulled out of joint action with the miners. The government's efforts to weaken trans-union solidarity paid off, for 'Black Friday' marked the beginning of a major employers' counter-attack. Key sections of the union movement went down to defeat in a series of confrontations, while others accepted layoffs and wage cuts without a fight. By 1924 money wages had fallen by as much as a third in some industrial sectors, and union membership had plunged by almost a third from its peak of 8 million at war's end.[114]

When the Trades Union Congress reluctantly called a general strike in 1926 in the wake of another miners' lock-out, Stanley Baldwin's Conservative government was well prepared to break it. Contingency plans had long since been worked out, and military, naval, and police detachments aided by a vast cadre of mostly middle-class volunteers saw to it that most essential services were carried out with minimal disruption. The TUC quickly backed down, and the miners were ultimately forced to swallow more wage cuts and redundancies. The government added insult to injury with the Industrial Disputes Act (1927), which among other things placed legal impediments on the right to picket and to strike, forbade civil-service unions to affiliate to the TUC or the Labour party, and sought to reduce that party's treasure chest by substituting contracting-in for contracting-out in union balloting on political levies. The Labour party's income from union contributions fell by more than a quarter over the next couple of years, union membership continued to decline, and the Conservative stabilization of postwar industrial relations was complete.[115]

The postwar governments did not try to crush the union movement altogether, but rather to tame industrial militancy through a combination of statutory controls and strategic compromises with moderate union leaders, often at the expense of their more militant rank-and-file. Union membership and the Labour party vote slowly recovered in the late 1920s, and representatives of the TUC and employers' organizations at least showed a willingness to communicate with each other, although little of substance emerged from their discussions. The government encouraged such dialogue, and often consulted representatives of labour and management on matters of policy. But it was happy to permit free collective bargaining to run its course, especially now that industrial militancy had been tamed through a combination of measured repression, deflation, and high unemployment.

The world-wide trade contraction that followed the Wall Street stock market crash in 1929 prompted the government to take a number of interventionist steps that it had long sought to avoid. Devaluation of sterling in 1931 helped to enhance the competitiveness of British goods and paved the way for lower interest rates. Free trade became a thing of the past in 1932, when the government imposed duties on a wide variety of imports in order to prevent Britain becoming a dumping-ground for foreign manufactures.[116] The government also sponsored several rationalization schemes designed to reduce excess capacity in the shipbuilding, textile, and mining industries, while it set up an elaborate system of quotas and price supports for domestic agriculture. Finally, it made fitful efforts to attract new investment to depressed regions, mainly through tax concessions.[117] Thus the Depression forced the state to preside over the demise of free trade and the gold standard and to take a more active role in steering the economy.

None of these measures, however, had much impact on the most formidable problem of the era: mass unemployment. Between 1921 and 1939, there were never fewer than a million people (i.e. 10 per cent of the insured work force) unemployed. At the nadir of depression in the winter of 1932–3, almost three million people were out of work.[118] Well-publicized hunger marches of unemployed workers from the shipbuilding town of Jarrow and other 'pockets of poverty' drew attention to the problem of chronic unemployment, but no ambitious government efforts to tackle it were forthcoming. There remained little support for interventionist measures to create jobs. John Maynard Keynes was beginning to develop his notion that insufficient demand was at the root of the Slump, and that the government had a useful role to play in stimulating it by enhancing consumption or investment or both. The Liberal party enshrined Keynesian logic in its 1929 manifesto, *We Can Conquer Unemployment*, which sought to prime the pump by means of a £650 million road- and house-construction package. But most economic historians agree that this project would hardly have been enough in and of itself to stimulate a major recovery. Moreover, Keynes's thinking on the subject of countercyclical spending was as yet unrefined. Only in 1936 would it mature into the *General Theory of Employment, Interest and Money*.[119]

Even if Keynesian theory had come together at an earlier date, it would have had no support among the economic traditionalists who managed the fiscal and monetary policies of the Conservative, Labour, and 'National' coalition governments of this era. They continued to insist that 'pump-priming' expenditure would simply divert the limited supply of capital from its normal channels. The Liberals had been wracked by schism during the war, and could not muster enough seats in the Commons to make an impact thereafter. The dominant Conservative party was still wedded to the deflationary ideology that it had advocated since the end of the war. While the Labour party clearly benefited from the introduction of universal male suffrage, it was an uneasy coalition, representing trade unionists on the one hand who were more interested in the defence of free collective bargaining than they were in social legislation or even job-creation schemes, and a formidable socialist constituency on the other that was pledged to a broad measure of intervention. It was only in the late 1930s that Labour rallied behind the principle of macroeconomic intervention. At the beginning of the decade, it had no plan at all for stimulating employment. Philip Snowden, who served as chancellor of the Exchequer in Ramsay MacDonald's Labour government of 1929–31, was utterly committed to deflation, balanced budgets, and free trade. At the nadir of the Slump, all that party leaders could promise was enhanced unemployment benefits.[120]

Labour and the Conservatives were by no means alone in their adherence to deflation. Few European countries were experimenting with reflationary policies at this time. Even if more of them had sought to do so, it is debatable that they would have made much progress, because national budgets were not yet big enough to provide states with much leverage to influence the shape of the economy. Finally, the economic scenario of the mid-1930s seemed to provide a measure of support for traditional cyclical theory, because recovery was becoming noticeable in a number of countries, some of which had adopted interventionist fiscal policies, but some of which had not. Britain had not, yet its 4 per cent annual growth rate from 1932 through to 1937 was exceeded only by Nazi Germany's. High rates of long-term unemployment persisted, however, as did resistance to loan-financed public spending, until the rearmament drive of the late 1930s eroded both of them.[121]

In the meantime, the two major parties relied on the piecemeal growth of social services to limit the damage inflicted on the unemployed. The most important exercise in damage-limitation was the vast extension of unemployment insurance. Some policy-makers took part in it from an ideological commitment to the idea of a 'national minimum', but perhaps most of them out of fear that civil disorder would escalate if the unemployed were not fobbed off. But all of them focused on insurance because they could think of no way of putting people back to work. It all started with the Unemployment Insurance Act of 1920, which passed into law with little comment at a time when the jobless rate was still low. The act extended the landmark 1911 scheme to all manual workers as well as to most non-manual workers earning less than £250 a year, granting 15 s. a week for up to fifteen weeks to men, 12 s. to women, and half-rates for workers under age eighteen. This was a measure that adhered to the principles of 1911: that a person's entitlement to benefit should be closely linked to past contributions; that benefits were to be paid for a strictly limited period; and that payment would have to be preceded by some test of one's willingness to work. As the historian Jose Harris has observed, the ad hoc growth of unemployment insurance in the 1920s 'consisted of a series of futile attempts to adapt these cautious principles to the pro-crustean bed of chronic depression'.[122] A series of struggles ensued that pitted unemployed protesters against the government, and the notion of relief as a social right against the notion of relief as a form of private insurance on strict actuarial lines.

These battles ended in a series of grudging compromises. In 1921, 'uncovenanted benefit' was introduced for those who had exhausted their formal entitlement to insurance payment, but at first it was discretionary and limited. Three years later it became non-discretionary and unlimited in duration. Unemployment benefit levels gradually rose, until they became considerably more generous than sickness benefits. Allowances for dependants were introduced. The formal connection between contributions and eligibility for benefit was done away with in 1927, when a system of 'transitional' benefits was introduced for those who had been unable to make contributions for the minimum fifteen weeks in the previous year. Meanwhile, the real value of unemployment benefit skyrocketed thanks to a combination of deflation and voted increases. For a man with a dependent wife and two children it was 240 per cent higher by 1931 than it had been a decade earlier; for a single man, it was 92 per cent higher. Over the same period, the total state contribution to unemployment insurance rose from £3 million to £37 million, and from 3 to 23 per cent of total social-service spending.[123]

By the 1930s, the British unemployed worker was protected by the most comprehensive scheme of centrally coordinated unemployment benefits in the world.[124] But benefits did not yet amount to a uni-versal right. They were still carefully limited, selectively granted on the basis of character judgements. While they rose appreciably, benefits were always set at levels significantly below the average wages of manual labourers in full-time work. Applicants for 'uncovenanted' benefit had to pass a 'genuinely seeking work test', by which they were obliged to stand before a Local Employment Committee and show it a list of firms they had recently visited in search of a job. They also had to exhibit a 'state of mind' indicating that they preferred working for wages to living on state handouts. Some three million claimants were refused benefit on the basis of this test before pressure from backbenchers prompted the Labour government to abolish it in

1930; 'at no time' during the preceding interval '. . . did any prominent politician or government official seriously suggest that the work they were supposed to be seeking actually existed'.[125] Means tests were also impose for most of the period between 1922 and 1928 in an effort to reduce the cost of uncovenanted benefit. Claimants could be disqualified if it was discovered that they had been dismissed for 'misconduct', a deliberately vague category that included strike activity and 'insolence' as well as drunkenness. Thus the rules sought to draw a line between 'deserving' and 'undeserving' poverty, and the only recourse for claimants who were placed in the latter category was the poor law.

Unemployment expenditure continued to soar despite means testing, and helped to provoke a political crisis in August 1931, when the May Committee recommended a 20 per cent reduction in benefit among other retrenchment measures. The Labour government broke up over this issue, paving the way for the Tory-dominated 'national' coalition in which MacDonald stayed on as prime minister and Snowden as chancellor. As it happened, the new government reduced benefits by only 10 per cent. But it also limited the period for which benefit could automatically be drawn to twenty-six weeks. All those not entitled to benefit under these terms were required to subject themselves to a means test carried out by the new local poor-law authorities, the Public Assistance Committees (PACs). Mass protests organized by the National Unemployed Workers' Movement against the means test did not prevent it from being fully implemented. By early 1932 nearly a million people were applying to the PACs for 'transitional' benefit. Most of them were thus obliged to stand before the poor-law authorities for the first time in their lives, and it was profoundly humiliating for them to be treated as paupers. Some PACs set 'transitional' scales that were substantially lower than the comparable scales for standard benefit, so that many of the long-term unemployed were forced to make do with substantially less than their newly redundant counterparts. The Unemployment Insurance Act of 1934 that replaced the means test on individual incomes with a test on household income provoked enormous hostility among working-class people. While the act spared claimants from the stigma of the poor law by assigning the adjudication of benefits to separate Unemployment Assistance Boards, it licensed these boards to snoop into the intimate details of family life, and enabled them to disqualify or reduce the benefits of claimants whose parents received old-age pensions or whose children were working in dead-end jobs. Families sometimes broke up in order to avoid these sorts of means-tested deduction.[126] The household means test inspired massive street protests when it was introduced and bitter memories thereafter, as children recalled how their fathers' war pensions had been set against their claims to benefit.[127]

Thus the overwhelmingly working-class claimants of extended unemployment benefit were subjected to a series of petty indignities before they actually received it. Those who did receive it were made to feel like scroungers by middle-class commentators who all too often equated the unemployed with the work-shy.[128] Statistically speaking, women always stood a much higher chance than men of having their claims to 'transitional' benefit reduced or rejected. This sort of gender discrimination stemmed from the widely accepted primacy of the male breadwinner, which also helps to explain why, for example, the TUC and the Labour party resisted welfare measures such as family allowances that might potentially pose a threat to male wages.[129]

The carefully limited and deliberately humiliating dole was not the sort of social provision that was likely to endear working people to a state that most of them still instinctively mistrusted. Still, it helps to explain why by the mid-1920s, for the first time ever, working-class people were receiving more in social services than they were paying in taxes, and why by 1937 the provision of social services was raising working-class incomes by an estimated 8 to 14 per cent.[130] Probably only a little of this modest redistribution stemmed from progressive tax reform. The very rich could easily afford to pay the much higher taxes that were being levied on them after the war, and in relative terms the working classes were still paying considerably more in tax than their middling counterparts.[131] More important than progressive taxation to the interwar growth of social services was a pronounced shift in budgetary priorities away from military and towards civil expenditure. In 1890 military spending came to 2.4 per cent of GNP while spending on social services only amounted to 1.9 per cent. In 1932 the relative proportions were 2.8 per cent and 12.9 per cent, respectively. While retrenchment had hit the social services fairly hard in the early 1920s, it hit the service departments much harder; the defence budget was trimmed a full 40 per cent between 1921 and 1923.[132] By 1934, gross public expenditure on civil purposes more than trebled defence spending, and for the first time ever claimed a higher share of total expenditure than military spending and debt service combined.[133] Rearmament had increased the military's share of GNP to 8.9 per cent by 1938, but social services still outpaced it at 11.3 per cent.[134] The percentage of national income spent by central and local government on social services rose from 5.5 per cent in 1913 to 13 per cent in 1938.[135] Total government expenditure as a percentage of GNP grew appreciably – from 26 per cent in 1920 to 35 per cent in 1939 – so that social services constituted a bigger slice from a bigger pie.[136]

Unemployment relief accounted for most of the growth in social spending, but education, old-age pensions, and housing accounted for some of it. There was nothing revolutionary in the interwar growth of these other social services. Most of them were simply ad hoc, piecemeal extensions to the modest 'safety net' furnished by the Liberals before the war. While they added up to an unprecedented measure of welfare provision, they by no means added up to a comprehensive welfare state. On the eve of World War II, there was as yet no such thing as universal coverage or provision of comprehensive services in health or education on a nationwide basis. Most benefits that were not given to individuals in return for their contributions to national insurance schemes were means-tested in one way or another. There was no dramatic break-up of the poor law, or of its stigmatizing principles of relief. It is true that the Local Government Act of 1929 did away with the administrative framework of the poor law by disbanding the unions and boards of guardians and dispersing care for non-able-bodied paupers to a variety of other agencies, whilst assigning provision for the able-bodied to the new Public Assistance Committees. But PACs, appointed rather than elected local bodies, often set more frugal relief scales than boards of guardians had done, particularly in urban districts, where in the recent past Labour guardians had set very generous rates indeed as a form of unemployment relief. Manual workers, moreover, had to rely on a patchwork of compulsory and voluntary insurance, free and paid doctors, and means-testing and charity to see them through illness. Most of the long-term ill ultimately had little choice but to go to the PAC for assistance, a humiliating alternative that encouraged many to avoid treatment for as long as possible. In short, the failure to establish uniform national standards for the provision of medical care and unemployment relief meant that assistance was patchy and meagre, and that a good many of the principles of the poor law lingered on. It was not truly abolished until 1948, when parliament established a universal framework for public assistance.[137]

The same failure to establish uniform standards was obvious in the educational system. H. A. L. Fisher's Education Act of 1918 raised the school-leaving age to fourteen and established a system of part-time continuation schools that were supposed to provide more working-class teenagers with at least a modicum of secondary education. Educational provision continued to vary widely, however, and remained thin at the secondary level, because the local educational authorities retained broad discretionary powers and because the postwar budget cuts all but wiped out central support for the continuation schools. Public spending on education actually declined in terms of net national income between 1922 and 1939. As late as 1938, only about 13 per cent of the relevant age-group were attending grant-aided secondary schools. The only viable route to a university education was through the grammar schools, and free places there for working-class students were very hard to come by. One survey determined that while the percentage of working-class children attaining a secondary education had almost trebled between 1900 and 1940, a middle-class boy was still over four times as likely to attend grammar school as a boy from a skilled working-class family, and over five times as likely as a boy from a semi-skilled or unskilled background. The state had begun to channel very considerable sums of public money to the universities through the University Grants Committee (established in 1919), but for the time being these remained bastions of privilege. By 1940, boys from the professional classes were thirteen times more likely to attend university than their working-class counterparts, while a middle-class girl was sixty times more likely to do so than a working-class girl.[138]

The state's role in the provision of pensions for the elderly was no less carefully circumscribed than its role in the provision of education for the young. While old-age pensions were greatly extended in the 1920s, they remained very small, and the adoption of the contributory principle in paying for them limited their redistributive impact. While the Liberal pension plan of 1908 had been extremely modest, limited only to very poor people over seventy, it had been an exercise in social solidarity and deliberate redistribution, in the sense that the pensions were granted on the basis of need rather than contribution. An act of 1925 greatly expanded the pool of eligible pensioners to all those who contributed to national health insurance, and enabled recipients to begin collecting their pensions at age sixty-five. But this was a strictly contributory scheme that was supposed to cost the Exchequer no additional money once it had been set up. The elderly poor were now obliged to finance their own pensions,[139] and these were not enough to live on. In the late 1930s, Seebohm Rowntree estimated that a full third of York's old-age pensioners were living below his own strict poverty line.[140]

The central role of the contributory principle in the funding of old-age pensions between the wars makes it clear that this era witnessed no easy transition from private to public welfare provision, from 'individualism' to 'collectivism'. In the management of social risks, working-class Britons still relied very heavily on their own savings, on friendly societies and trade unions, and on charitable support. Most forms of working-class 'self-help', moreover, were more solidaristic and directly redistributive in intent than all forms of state provision, whether a friendly-society contribution that helped to pay for a co-worker's funeral or a gift of food or money to a hard-pressed neighbour. The proliferation of contributory schemes makes it clear that the state sought to enforce and supplement self-help rather than replace it. Finally, while organized charities were not as prominent in the provision of social services as they had been at the turn of the century, the so-called 'new philanthropy' of the interwar years still relied heavily on private charitable agencies, even if these tended to be more closely linked to central and local government than they had been in the past.[141]

Central and local initiative, however, did help to ensure that many slum-dwellers were rehoused between the wars. Local authorities greatly enhanced their slum-clearance efforts, and for the first time became major providers of low-cost housing. By 1939 some 245,000 of an estimated 470,000 slum dwellings had been demolished or condemned, while local authorities had built 1.1 million new dwellings and provided subsidies in connection with roughly 15 per cent of the 2.9 million privately built homes put up during the interwar years.[142] Still, retrenchment and high interest rates helped to limit the ambitious housing acts of the 1920s, thus ensuring that the urban overcrowding that had drawn so much attention during the war remained a serious problem long after the war had ended. Most of the new dwellings built in this era were owner-occupied houses, and these were beyond the means of the vast majority of working-class people, who owned even less of the housing stock in 1939 than they had done in 1915.[143] The poorest members of the working class, moreover, could ill afford even the strictly controlled rents of the new council-housing estates built on the outskirts of many large cities. Those who could afford to live in big suburban estates, such as those built by the London County Council at Becontree and Dagenham, spent a good deal of their free time travelling to and from work, and many of them missed the closer family life and easy sociability of their old inner-city neighbourhoods. Finally, fiscal austerity meant a long-term decline in council-housing standards, so that the slum-clearance replacement housing of the mid-1930s was not nearly as attractive or commodious as the 'garden-city' housing of the early 1920s.[144]

The new arrangements for unemployment, medical care, education, and housing make obvious one last feature of the interwar expansion of social services: the continued primacy of local government in providing them. Local authorities probably enjoyed broader discretionary powers over a broader range of civil functions in this era than at any time before or since. Admittedly, Whitehall played a crucial role in some of the new social programmes, most notably old-age pensions and national insurance. Hence, while rate income more than doubled the income generated from central grants and loans in 1889–90, by

1938–9 it had fallen to only 28 per cent of local income, as against the 40 per cent generated by grants and loans.[145] This growing reliance on central financing, moreover, gave Whitehall a great deal of power over local authorities in the shape of audits, the right to veto loans, and a constant stream of circulars and advisory letters. At the same time, the breadth and complexity of parliamentary statutes gave to central agencies very considerable powers to revise local by-laws, to inspect and amend local administrative schemes, and to take legal action against defaulting councils.[146] Nevertheless, the local authorities had by no means been swallowed by their central counterparts. They still enjoyed considerable discretionary power over the allocation of the 51 per cent of all social-service spending that passed through their hands.[147] This was one of the main reasons why Labour constituencies fought hard to win control of municipal boroughs in this era. They met with some notable successes, particularly in the metropolis, where the party won control of the London County Council. Local electoral success enabled grass-roots supporters to extend local welfare arrangements in ways that made a palpable difference in their daily lives.[148] But it must be stressed that local autonomy was often, perhaps more often than not, a boon to municipal austerity rather than 'collectivism'. In the many places where local welfare activism was less pronounced, economy-minded LEAs were likely to hold the line against educational expansion, while stingy PACs trimmed public assistance to the bone. Not only raising but simply defining a national standard of social provision was an impossible task so long as local agencies retained so much discretionary power. It would take the experience of yet another total war to centralize the framework of social services and to convince voters, politicians, and bureaucrats alike that the establishment of a universal, non-pauperizing welfare system was a proper task for the state.

5

Total War and Cradle-to-Grave Welfare

1939–1979

By the late 1930s, the social services provided by central and local government in Britain were arguably more extensive than they were anywhere else in the world.[1] But they were not nearly as extensive as they would become in the decades after World War II, and as yet they did not constitute a welfare state. In Asa Briggs's useful definition, the welfare state

> is a state in which organised power is deliberately used (through politics and administration) in an effort to modify the play of market forces in at least three directions – first, by guaranteeing individuals and families a minimum income irrespective of the market value of their work or their property; second, by narrowing the extent of insecurity by enabling individuals and families to meet certain social contingencies (for example, sickness, old age and unemployment) which would otherwise lead to individual and family crises; and third, by ensuring that all citizens . . . are offered the best standards available in relation to a certain agreed range of social services.[2]

By 1939, the state came reasonably close to meeting the first two of these goals. But it made no effort to address the third one. That goal was a product of World War II, when the notion first came into vogue that it was the central government's responsibility to see to it that *all* of its citizens enjoyed a high standard of social security *as of right*. Indeed, the very phrase 'welfare state' was first popularized during the war, when it was used to distinguish the British state's commitment to the well-being of its citizens from the servile treatment that its authoritarian foes meted out to their subjects. That commitment was even more extensive than Briggs's definition makes it out to be.[3] For over the next thirty years, both of the major political parties pledged themselves not only to uphold an extensive system of social security, but routinely to use the instruments of state to foster economic growth and full employment.

This chapter will focus on three points about the welfare state. The first is that it chiefly stemmed from the need to wage yet another global war, which turned the British state into a highly centralized one and inspired rising expectations of social provision. This time around, there was a more decisive commitment to total war that led to even more extensive (and efficient) government intervention than the Great War had brought about. Wartime plans for postwar reconstruction came to focus on the 'cradle-to-grave' notion of social security enshrined in the Beveridge Report, which called for full employment, a free national health service, family allowances, and the abolition of poverty through comprehensive social insurance, with benefits to be paid as a statutory right.

The second point is that while the welfare state assumed a much greater role for itself than the prewar state had done, it did not fundamentally reshape Britain's steep social hierarchy. A massive extension of social-security benefits on the principle of universality; the creation of the National Health Service; bringing 20 per cent of the national economy into public management: these were remarkable achievements that Attlee's Labour governments (1945–51) carried out at a time of grave economic uncertainty. They would have been unthinkable before World War II greatly enhanced the state's capacities and made continuous intervention much more broadly acceptable than it had ever been before. The unprecedented economic expansion of the next twenty years encouraged consensus between the major political parties about the central government's ambitious new priorities. But this revolution in the scope of the state did not bring about a social revolution. Nationalization did not lead to anything remotely resembling worker control. Regional and class disparities in access to health care remained. The commitment to universal benefits arguably channelled a disproportionate share of 'free' social services to middle-income groups at the expense of those below them on the social scale. The postwar welfare state sought to enhance, and did enhance, the quality of its citizens' lives in many ways that would have been unheard of at the beginning of the twentieth century. But state intervention did not create an egalitarian society.

The third and last point is that dissatisfaction with the postwar state seemed to grow in more or less direct proportion to its commitments. By the 1960s, it was becoming common on the political left to fault the welfare state for its seeming failure to eliminate poverty, and equally common on the right to attack it for wasting taxpayers' money.

Meanwhile, the state's sponsorship of economic growth left it vulnerable to criticism as growth rates lagged well behind those of many of Britain's European counterparts, and as macroeconomic policies failed to strike a long-term balance between full employment and low inflation. The state's authority seemed to dwindle as its role as an interest broker expanded. Incessant bargaining with powerful interest groups made it difficult to control spending, and made the government overly dependent on the long-term cooperation of big business and the trade unions.

By the 1970s, a number of powerful forces were challenging the sacrosanct notions of democratic accountability and parliamentary sovereignty: a Whitehall bureaucracy whose discretionary powers seemed to be growing at the expense of cabinet ministers and local councillors; a European Community bureaucracy whose constitutional relationship with the British government was unclear; a resurgent nationalism in Scotland and Wales that raised the thorny issue of devolution; and, most violently, the factional strife in Northern Ireland, in which the British state was deeply implicated, especially after the imposition of direct rule in 1972. Ultimately, however, it was not the issue of sovereignty but the state's apparent failure to contain inflation and unemployment during the economic crisis of the 1970s that prompted many Britons to conclude that it had taken on too many responsibilities at too great a cost, and that it was time to curb its 'excesses'.

War interventionism II: 1939–1945

The British state's need to carry out its traditional war-making function on an unparalleled scale once again prompted it to intervene in virtually every aspect of social life between 1939 and 1945. But while that intervention had been fitful and reluctant in the early stages of World War I, it was much more resolute in the early stages of World War II. It was readily accepted that the defeat of the Axis powers required an extension of state authority that went well beyond the precedents established during the Great War. Once again, the government obliged its citizens to make endless sacrifices for the good of the nation, and far more civilians paid the ultimate sacrifice of their lives than in any war before or since. While British battlefield casualties were only half those of 1914–18 (amounting to about 350,000), long-range aerial bombardment killed 100,000 non-combatants. British civilian casualties were actually comparatively light. Altogether, perhaps forty million people died as a direct result of the war, and most of them were not soldiers. So the first point to make about World War II is the utter lack of respect for the value of human life with which the belligerent nation-states fought it.[4]

This time round, there was no trace of the hesitation to compel men into the armed forces that had marked the Liberal government's approach to war-making in 1914. Despite its posthumous reputation for weakness and vacillation, Neville Chamberlain's National Government adopted conscription in August 1939, *before* Britain's declaration of war against Germany. It also instituted a rationing system only a few months into the war,[5] and presided over the creation of several new ministries of state in an effort to coordinate production on the home front. A general framework for mobilization was thus already in place when Churchill's all-party coalition came into office in the spring of 1940. Caught up in a fight for national survival, the coalition devoted virtually all of the country's human resources to the struggle. By the end of the war there were over five million Britons enlisted in the armed forces.[6] The age limit for compulsory service for able-bodied men was ultimately raised to fifty, and Churchill's coalition government even reluctantly agreed to the conscription of women into the Auxiliary Services and Civil Defence, and into industrial work under the direction of the Ministry of Labour. While the only women actually called up were nineteen- to twenty-four-year-olds who were neither married nor the mothers of young children, their conscription marked a dramatic extension of women's participation in a public sphere from which the state had traditionally sought to exclude them.[7]

Mobilizing the domestic work force for full-scale war production proved to be an even more onerous task for the state than inducting a quarter of that work force into the military. The threat of chronic labour shortages forced the government to assume command over the allocation of labour through a series of 'manpower budgets'. With the indomitable Ernest Bevin at its head, the new Ministry of Labour presided over an enormous expansion and redistribution of the working population in order to maximize the efficiency of the war economy.[8] The allocation of workers was simply the most important of a broad array of physical controls by which the government sought to coordinate the war effort at home. Under the supervision of the new Ministry of Production, various departments of state assumed the role of 'production authorities', charged with the tasks of licensing firms, setting production quotas, and allocating supplies. By 1943, the peak year of war mobilization, virtually every sector of agriculture, manufacturing, mining, and the distributive trades had been brought within this system of central supervision. A quasi-corporatist structure rapidly developed on a regional basis, in which industrialists, trade unionists, and state officials negotiated questions of production, working conditions, and work discipline. By 1944, over 4,500 Joint Production Committees had been set up to deal with such matters. This dense consultative network helped to create a considerably more amiable climate of wartime labour relations than that which had prevailed during the Great War.[9]

So too did the restraint with which the wartime government exercised its coercive powers over the workplace. These powers were even greater than they had been during the Great War, and included a ban on strikes and lock-outs (not lifted until 1951), strict penalties for unofficial strikers, and compulsory arbitration. The trade unions readily acquiesced in them, mainly because they were confident that Bevin, former head of the Transport and General Workers Union, could be trusted to use them even-handedly. Indeed, he made remarkably little use of his statutory powers, preferring to maintain the peacetime system of collective bargaining as far as possible. This flexible attitude paid off. Even though wage rates were buoyant throughout the war, neither inflation nor the level of strike activity spiralled out of control. When the Ministry of Labour did intervene, it was usually to improve working conditions by setting up canteens and medical services, imposing stricter safety regulations, and establishing nearly fifty new boards to raise wages in chronically low-paid sectors of the economy.[10] It is true that wartime industrial methods in Britain were antiquated by American standards, and that the failure to update plant and techniques during and immediately after the war was probably a significant factor in Britain's relative industrial decline thereafter.[11] But the point of economic mobilization was not to modernize the physical plant but to defeat Hitler, and most scholars now agree that Britain's industrial output was considerably higher than Germany's during the war itself. Aircraft production rose from 8,000 in 1939 to 26,000 in 1943. There was a four-fold increase in tank production in the first two full years of war. In short, the wartime state, caught up as it was in a desperate struggle, squeezed remarkable productivity gains out of the domestic work force.[12]

It also squeezed out of its citizens an unprecedented amount in taxes. Both direct and indirect tax receipts roughly trebled over the course of the war. Income tax was the keystone of war finance, just as it had been during the Great War. While rates on lower incomes were much lower than they would become by the 1960s, war finance obliged a great many wage-earners to pay income tax for the first time. Manual workers also felt the pinch of wartime taxation through the much higher indirect taxes they were obliged to pay on items of mass consumption such as beer and tobacco. In relative terms, however, the middle classes were probably hit even harder by the wartime tax reforms, and the very well off were hit hardest of all. In 1937–8 one would have needed a gross income of about £12,000 to arrive at a post-tax income of about £7,000; by 1941–2 one would have needed to gross about £150,000 in order to net £7,000 after taxes. Taken together, the wartime tax reforms were progressive. They are one reason why the real value of purchasing power in the hands of the top sixth of all British income earners fell roughly 30 per cent between 1938 and 1948, whilst that of the bottom five-sixths rose about 25 per cent. But the point to stress about war taxes is that they hit all classes much harder than any of them had been hit before the war.[13] While at the height of World War I government expenditure amounted to just over half of GNP, at the height of World War II it came close to three-quarters of GNP. Spending levels declined after the war came to an end, but remained considerably higher than they had been before the fighting broke out, just as they had done after the Armistice. In 1955, public expenditure still amounted to 37 per cent of GDP, compared with 26 per cent of GDP in 1937.[14] In other words, postwar retrenchment did not even come close to stripping the state of its greatly enhanced wartime spending capacity. Tax receipts remained very high after the war, and, as we shall see, the postwar Labour government devoted them to the construction of the welfare state.

Of course, the main point of this greatly increased tax burden was to finance the war effort without running up crippling levels of debt. But another one was to keep inflation under control by reducing consumer demand. Indeed, it was chiefly the Churchill coalition's commitment to fighting inflation that encouraged it to pioneer the Keynesian strategy of using the national budget to try to regulate levels of consumption and investment. In this sense, the first 'Keynesian' budget was the one presented by Kingsley Wood in 1941, which sought to close an estimated £500-million gap between revenue and expenditure and to dampen consumer demand through a combination of higher taxes and compulsory savings. In seeking to manage the general level of demand in the economy through use of the budget, the state assumed for itself a much bigger responsibility for the direction of the economy than it had been willing to take on before the war.

The wartime enthusiasm for planning extended well beyond demand management. From the collective sacrifice of the fight against Nazism grew a widespread belief that it was possible and proper for a democratic society to attempt to enhance the quality of its citizens' lives through the agencies of a more powerful state. There was broad interest in reconstruction planning, in Whitehall, the universities, the trade unions, and even in the business circles that had hitherto eschewed planning as a bane to market freedom. As early as 1941, all three of the major political parties had formed reconstruction committees, and professional groups such as the British Medical Association came up with their own schemes. In short, 'for perhaps the first time in the history of British government, the onus of proof lay on the proponents of muddling through'.[15] Consensus by no means emerged as to the proper scope of the postwar state. But the impact of the Blitz combined with bitter memories of the Slump to convince many observers that social ills needed to be fought, that the state should use its formidable powers to fight them, and that in using these powers the state need not jeopardize personal freedom.[16]

This wartime faith in the social possibilities of planning helps to explain the popularity of the report on *Social Insurance and Allied Services* (1942), universally known as the Beveridge Report because of the dominant role played by the committee's chairman, Sir William Beveridge, in researching and writing it. The Beveridge Report was the most influential bluebook of all time, selling over 100,000 copies within a month of its publication. It was discussed at public meetings all over the country, and a special cheap edition had to be published for the troops. Beveridge's suggestions focused the vague discussions of postwar reconstruction on a specific agenda that envisioned a greatly expanded role for the central government as a provider of social security. His chief recommendations were the establishment of a national health service; 'avoidance of mass unemployment'; and the abolition of poverty through a comprehensive system of contributory social insurance, with subsistence-level benefits (based on contemporary notions of adequacy rather than the minimum necessary for survival) that would be universal in scope and payable to citizens as a statutory right. Thus he envisioned a far more uniform and comprehensive system of social security than the interwar patchwork had provided.[17]

For all their popularity, there was no wartime guarantee that Beveridge's proposals would be implemented once the war was over. First of all, most historians now agree that early analysis of the growing wartime interest in expanded welfare provision, most notably the pioneering work of Richard Titmuss, exaggerated the 'Dunkirk spirit' of social solidarity that ostensibly emerged from the shared sacrifices that the Blitz imposed on the British people.[18] The widespread efforts to sidestep wartime rationing restrictions, growing popular resentment of bureaucratic interference in daily life, the gradual rise in the frequency of unofficial strikes, surging resentment within the military of the growing pay differentials between civilians and members of the armed services – these all suggested that plenty of people were getting fed up with the imposed sacrifices of wartime, and were not inclined to put up with them indefinitely for the advancement of a nebulous conception of the 'public good'. Finally, while wartime social surveys found that many blue-collar Britons were dissatisfied with the patchy health care and widespread commercial insurance of the interwar years, there was 'no evidence to suggest that grass-roots opinion was harbouring any wider vision of more far-reaching social revolution'.[19]

Moreover, while most influential politicians and civil servants accepted the key principle of universal contributory social insurance outlined by Beveridge, virtually none of them felt that it should be pursued until the war was over, and few of them believed that it could be established thereafter anything like as cheaply or as swiftly as Beveridge had suggested.[20] Certainly there was no consensus within the wartime coalition government that a welfare state constructed along Beveridgean lines would be an *inevitable* corollary to the defeat of Hitler. Churchill himself was loath to endorse any blueprint for postwar social reform, and the Conservatives more generally were inclined to think that Beveridge's proposals would be unaffordable in the atmosphere of fiscal uncertainty that was bound to prevail after the war.[21] What the 1945 election campaign and Labour's surprisingly lopsided victory did suggest, however, was that there was much less support for a return to 'business as usual' than there had been at the end of World War I.[22]

Both the Labour and Conservative election manifestos were committed to the maintenance of full employment, the establishment of a national health service, and the creation of a more comprehensive social-security system. Where they chiefly differed was on the issues of nationalization and the preservation of wartime physical controls, and here they differed vociferously. The Tories ran a self-consciously libertarian campaign, with Churchill notoriously declaring that the implementation of 'socialism' in Britain by a Labour government would require some form of Gestapo, 'no doubt very humanely directed in the first instance'.[23] Labour won a landslide victory despite, and perhaps partly because of, such predictions. There were many reasons for the party's success: superior campaign organization; the wartime doubling of union membership; the assertiveness of a more self-confident working class; Labour's skilful management of the domestic war effort (with Bevin serving as minister of labour, Herbert Morrison as home secretary, and Clement Attlee as deputy prime minister); and a widespread perception that the Conservatives were the 'guilty men' who had presided over the appeasement and economic stagnation of the 1930s, a perception that trumped Churchill's personal popularity. In this last respect, the state activism of the war years was crucial to Labour's electoral success. It had helped to turn 'business as usual' into a term of opprobrium,[24] and to provide Labour with an opportunity to commit the state's expanded capacity to the provision of a much broader range of social services.

The classic welfare state, 1945–1965

The Labour governments of 1945–51 took advantage of this historic conjuncture to push through the most ambitious interventionist programme in British history. Their most significant contribution was the establishment of a truly comprehensive scheme of social insurance for sickness, unemployment, and old age. The National Insurance Act (1946) followed most of Beveridge's prescriptions. It provided a flat-rate, contributory scheme for basic sickness benefit, with additional benefits for families of male members of the work force who became ill; it paid contributory unemployment benefits for twenty-six weeks and extended further benefits to the long-term unemployed on the basis of credits; it provided modest maternity and widows' benefits and family allowances; and it raised the level of benefit to old-age pensioners. The act, together with the introduction of a very modest family allowance, finally came close to guaranteeing the 'national minimum standard' that had been the goal of welfare reformers since the first decade of the century. Like its more limited predecessors, it was a contributory scheme; employers and employees would have to pay into the system simply to make it affordable. But unlike its predecessors, it was a universal scheme, because Labour accepted the crucial Beveridgean principle that British citizens should be entitled to social insurance *as of right*, regardless of their financial circumstances. The alternative would have been a return to the extensive means-testing of the 1930s, which Labour rejected as too demeaning. Indeed, to signal that the old regime of conditional, grudging, and niggardly poor relief had finally come to an end, the 1948 National Assistance Act triumphantly announced that 'the existing Poor Law shall cease to have effect'. Variants on the interwar means test and 'genuinely seeking work test' survived for those who applied for assistance beyond the statutory limits. But it was felt at the time that the establishment of a universal right to benefits would keep the number of such applicants within manageable limits.[25]

With the creation of the National Health Service in 1948, the Labour government also established a universal right to tax-supported medical services. Even before the war, dissatisfaction with the patchwork quality of health care had generated considerable interest in the creation of a 'socialized' medical service that would be heavily subsidized by the Exchequer. But the Attlee ministry's plan for a national service nevertheless met potent resistance from the British Medical Association, which feared that doctors would lose their professional autonomy and suffer salary reductions if they became state employees. Aneurin Bevan, Labour's formidable minister of health, was able to strike a compromise that conceded much to the BMA on the question of pay scales and methods of payment, and ensured that doctors would be well represented at all administrative levels of the new service. But the government got most of what it wanted in the NHS: a contributory scheme in which the Exchequer played a major role, the nationalization of hospitals, the creation of regional boards and councils, and new municipally run health centres. The creation of the world's most comprehensive health service, and the *only* one expressly committed to achieving equality in the distribution and use of health care, marked a dramatic broadening of the British state's role in the lives of its citizens, which those citizens enthusiastically welcomed. Well over 90 per cent of the population enrolled in the NHS almost immediately.

The Health Service was the most popular and widely admired of the Attlee government's social achievements. Like the other pillar of the postwar welfare state, the National Insurance Act, the NHS was predicated on universality and a flat-rate contributory formula. The goal of universality stemmed from the government's conviction that the poor could get the best services available only if they shared them with the better-off, and that the receipt of social services was a right of citizenship and not a stigma reserved for the poor. Labour saw similar benefits in the related principle of contributory insurance: egalitarianism, freedom from bureaucratic snooping into one's personal behaviour, the preservation of incentives to work and save, and, last but not least, a solvent Treasury, which could not reasonably be expected to foot the whole bill for the welfare state.[26] As we shall see, both the universal and contributory principles ultimately benefited well-to-do Britons even more than poor ones. But the important point here is that the Labour government's commitment to them led to a much wider provision of social services to all Britons than the state had made available to them in the past.

Similarly, Labour's commitment to the growth of public housing helped to ensure that local authorities, armed with large Exchequer subsidies, would become a bigger provider of housing than they had been between the wars. At the Ministry of Health, Bevan presided over the most ambitious housing scheme since the middle of the 1920s. Chronic labour and material shortages, bad weather, and a credit squeeze limited the local-government housing campaign to 800,000 dwellings by 1951, far short of what Bevan had envisioned, and humble indeed compared to the goal of 300,000 dwellings a year made good by Bevan's Conservative successor in the early 1950s, Harold Macmillan. Still, by dedicating the central and local governments to an ambitious housing plan in a grim fiscal climate, the Labour government provided the first push in what would turn out to be a persistent effort to enhance Britons' quality of life by increasing and improving the nation's housing stock.[27]

At the same time, the Attlee ministry's nationalization of the Bank of England, cable and wireless, civil aviation, coal, electricity, road and rail transport, gas, and iron and steel committed the state to the management of about a fifth of the national economy. There were several reasons why nationalization had been a longstanding goal of the Labour party: the improvement of labour relations in industrial sectors where traditionally they had been rancorous; state sponsorship of large-scale capital investment; the more efficient management of 'natural' monopolies; and the containment of consumer prices. With the exception of iron and steel, which the Tories defended as relatively efficient private enterprises, Labour's plans met with little resistance. First of all, this was because most of the proclaimed reasons for nationalization were more pragmatic than 'socialistic'. Second, there were already well-established precedents for public management, such as the British Broadcasting Corporation and the London Passenger Transport Board. Third, the board members of the new public corporations were given a relatively free managerial hand. Finally, the boards themselves were largely composed of the same business executives who had managed the industries in question before nationalization. Thus, while private ownership of some key sectors of the economy came to an end, 'public' ownership did little to change the process of executive decision-making.

Short-term results seemed to indicate that nationalization was paying considerable dividends. The National Coal Board, for instance, enhanced the productivity and profitability of a chronically troubled industry, while at the same time it managed to keep the peace with miners, whose working conditions were made far better than they had been in the 1930s. More importantly, a shared commitment to nationalization helped the Labour government to persuade the trade unions to agree to voluntary wage restraint during the difficult transition from war to peace. The unions were willing to make short-term sacrifices on behalf of a government that was committed to full employment and to regular consultation with themselves. While the unions finally rejected wage restraint in 1950, the preceding period of wage containment had helped the government to withstand a series of economic crises, and the industrial peace that extended into the late 1950s provided ample justification for Labour's consultative approach to industrial relations.[28]

The establishment of a truly comprehensive system of social security; the creation of the world's most ambitious system of national health care; at least partial fulfilment of bold plans for the growth of public housing and industrial harmony: these were impressive achievements, made all the more remarkable by the fact that the Labour governments managed to carry them out at a time of deep financial insecurity. The enormous costs of waging the war left the Treasury facing a 'financial Dunkirk', with accumulated foreign debts of over £4,000 million, greatly reduced foreign assets, an export level that had shrunk to a mere 40 per cent of its 1939 value, and serious shortages of raw materials. To weather the storm, the government ultimately had to rely on a combination of American loans, balanced budgets, export drives, and intensive capital reinvestment. It abandoned most of the physical controls of the war years in its effort to manoeuvre its way through the postwar crises, mainly relying on the management of demand through the annual budget to control inflation and promote employment. But if Labour's economic policies were less 'interventionist' than those of the wartime state, few Britons noticed, because among the measures of fiscal austerity that the 'iron' chancellor Sir Stafford Cripps relied on at the Exchequer were an extension of rationing and a voluntary wage freeze.[29] Strict containment of the consumer-goods sector of the economy helped to lay the basis for economic recovery, but it cost Labour at the polls. The government's own efforts to measure public opinion made it clear that most Britons were less interested in building a New Jerusalem than enhancing their domestic comforts. Despite its legislative and rhetorical efforts, Labour in power was unable to mould the electorate into community-spirited citizens who were willing to tolerate long-term discomfort for the sake of a rather vague notion of the public good.[30] Perhaps the chief reason why Churchill and the Conservatives returned to office in 1951 was that they crafted a libertarian electoral campaign that capitalized on the mounting frustrations of consumers who had had enough after a full decade of state-imposed austerity.[31]

A good many Britons grew weary of Labour's incessant calls for economic self-sacrifice to promote the national good. But the government's commitment to 'fair shares' at least meant that it had sought to impose the greatest sacrifices on those who could most afford to make them.

In order to keep down inflation and to pay for the state's new welfare commitments, the Attlee ministry kept direct taxation at wartime levels. The share of national income taken by the government, a whopping 38 per cent in 1946, had fallen only 3 per cent by 1951. But Labour's modest progressive reform of the direct-tax structure brought a measure of tax relief to most manual workers and some of the humbler middle classes at the expense of the well-to-do. At the same time, the government helped to spur economic development in less prosperous regions such as Scotland and the Northeast by making vigorous use of the Distribution of Industry Act (1945), which gave it considerable authority to coerce firms into siting new plants in such regions whilst providing them with financial incentives to do so.[32] Such measures indicated that Labour was committed to making good on its promise to create jobs throughout the United Kingdom. Full employment did indeed arrive in the wake of the war, with the jobless rate falling to under 2 per cent of the insured work force by 1948. Admittedly, postwar job creation owed much to external forces, most notably the timely insertion of Marshall and other types of American aid and the sheer breadth of the American-led postwar economic boom, in which the western European economies all shared. But Labour signalled its eagerness to take advantage of these favourable conditions to promote employment through its regional development schemes and its export campaign.

Thus the postwar Labour governments took advantage of the greatly enlarged scope of the wartime state to extend the range of the state's peacetime commitments. The important point to make about the Conservatives' return to office is that despite their rhetoric, they did little to reduce those commitments thereafter. It still makes good sense to label the period between the early 1950s and the early 1970s an era of 'consensus politics', even though the descriptive accuracy of this term is no longer as broadly accepted among historians as it once was. For the two major parties were both committed to preserving the broader capacity of the postwar state, even while they frequently disagreed about the details of taxation and economic management. Broadly speaking, there was as much of an inter-party commitment to 'big government' in these years as there had been to minimal government a century earlier.

That commitment took a number of forms. One of the most noticeable was the assumption that it was the government's duty to try to foster and control economic growth. As we have seen, before World War II it was still widely assumed that the economy was largely at the mercy of market forces. But as the Labour intellectual Anthony Crosland noted in the 1950s, the doctrine of the 'invisible hand' was killed off by the Depression, and after the war 'even Conservatives and businessmen . . . subscribe[d] to the doctrine of collective government responsibility for the state of the economy'.[33] The unprecedented economic boom of the postwar era inspired confidence in the state's ability to 'steer' the economy. This was a golden age of expansion, with world income growing at a rate of 3.7 per cent and world trade at 6.5 per cent a year between 1953 and 1963; over the next ten years they grew at an average of 5.2 per cent and 8.9 per cent a year, respectively. Even though Britain's share in this growth was relatively low by western standards, the era saw huge increases in domestic savings and consumption, particularly on such big-ticket items as homes and cars. In this rosy climate, both Labour and the Conservatives identified economic growth as a top priority of the state. Thus in 1954, the Tory chancellor R. A. Butler hopefully spoke of doubling the national standard of living over the next quarter-century.[34]

One of the chief economic goals of both Labour and Conservative administrations in the postwar decades was the maintenance of full employment. The unemployment level in Britain never exceeded 3 per cent at any point between 1948 and 1970. This was chiefly thanks to a long expansionary trend that had more to do with international trading conditions than with national economic policies. Still, politicians relied on demand management in an effort to make a good employment situation even better. When production started to sag or unemployment started to rise, the government sought to stimulate demand through a combination of tax cuts, lower interest rates, and the easing of import restrictions. When, on the other hand, the economy appeared to be overheating, with inflation creeping up and a rising level of imports generating balance-of-payments deficits, it sought to reduce demand through a combination of tax increases, higher interest rates, and the tightening of import restrictions. This alternating cycle of 'stop' and 'go' was the principal means by which successive governments sought to fine-tune the economy.

Minor differences of approach remained between the two parties. Generally speaking, Labour favoured higher taxes and heavier public investment, while the Conservatives favoured periodic doses of tax relief and relied more heavily on the manipulation of the terms of private credit than on public investment. Neither party showed much interest in French-style 'indicative planning', i.e. the setting of long-term economic goals over several budgets. Planning became more fashionable in the 1960s, when the Conservatives created a National Economic Development Council (NEDC), and Harold Wilson's Labour governments (1964–70) sought to implement a National Plan. But the NEDC's planning efforts were strictly limited, and the Wilson ministry's more ambitious planning goals were invariably sacrificed to short-term considerations, most notably the need to uphold the value of sterling in the face of serious balance-of-payments deficits. Short-run demand management was thus the main weapon wielded by both parties in their efforts to create jobs and to foster growth.

Another 'consensus' feature that broadened the role of the state in the economy was regular consultation with trade unions and employers' organizations. There was plenty of this sort of tripartite negotiation going on by the 1930s, but it became far more noticeable during the war, when the imperatives of economic coordination prompted the government to take a much more active role in preserving industrial peace. After the war was over, the Trades Union Congress and the Confederation of British Industry retained their access to Whitehall and Downing Street, with potential disputes occasionally being settled over 'beer and sandwiches at number ten'. Conservative governments cultivated almost as cosy a relationship with the unions as did their Labour counterparts, mainly because they felt they had no choice but to cooperate with a union movement that had almost doubled its membership between 1938 and 1951 (from 4.8 to 9.5 million), and because they assumed, rightly or wrongly, that their electoral success depended on some measure of working-class appeasement.[35] Both parties thus concluded that a healthy economy required not only routine fine-tuning, but routine negotiation with powerful producer interests. While before the 1890s the state had steadfastly sought to avoid economic interest brokerage, by the 1950s it was relying heavily on it as a means of sustaining growth.

Another element of political consensus was a cross-party commitment to the enhancement of social security. With only minor exceptions, successive governments spent ever more money, and devoted ever more of this money to the provision of social services. As elsewhere in western Europe, government spending in Britain accounted for a growing proportion of GDP, from 29 per cent in 1938, to 34 per cent in 1950, to 42 per cent by 1973. Social-security spending accounted for an ever greater portion of the whole. Across western Europe, expenditure on income maintenance, public health, housing, and education rose from about 25 per cent of GNP in 1950 to about 45 per cent by the mid-1970s.[36] Britain's social-expenditure trends put it roughly in the middle of the western league table. There were several reasons for this unprecedented expansion of social spending, such as an increase in the number of old-age pensioners and schoolchildren; a gradual rise in the number of difficult-to-cut social benefits; periodic rises in the value of those benefits; and the growing cost of administering them as they became more complex.[37]

In Britain's case, the growth in social-service spending would have been even more dramatic had successive governments not devoted vast public resources to military purposes in an effort to preserve great-power status. While the Attlee ministry dramatically pulled British forces out of India and Palestine, it had no intention of dismantling the empire, which was probably worth more to the domestic economy than ever before. There were still nearly a million Britons under arms in 1948, over twice as many as there had been in the late 1930s. This was mainly because the Labour government, worried about the possibility of American withdrawal from and further Soviet aggression in Europe, took the unprecedented step of retaining conscription after the war had ended. National Service continued until 1960. Britain's growing reliance on nuclear deterrence in the 1950s, while politically controversial, facilitated substantial cuts in conventional forces. But defence spending still hovered close to 10 per cent of GNP, considerably higher than that of western European countries. The withdrawal of British arms to the west of Suez in the late 1960s led to further cuts in defence spending, but by the late 1980s Britain was still devoting more of its GNP to military spending than any advanced capitalist nation other than the United States.[38]

While the British state's traditional defence role remained a prominent one after World War II, spending on social services nevertheless dramatically outpaced it. Postwar defence expenditure peaked at 29 per cent of total government spending in 1954, and declined thereafter to a mere 10 per cent in 1975. Social spending grew from 44 per cent to 52 per cent of the whole over the same period.[39] Thus the social services grew partly at the expense of the armed services in the postwar era, just as they had done between the wars. If we compare the expenditure breakdowns for 1975 with those of 1875, we see the complete reversal of the state's spending priorities away from the military and debt service towards a growing array of social services. This trend was already well established between the wars, but it greatly accelerated after 1945. Between the late 1940s and the late 1980s, social expenditure in the United Kingdom rose from less than a third to over half of total government spending, and from one-tenth to one-fifth of GNP.[40]

By far the most expensive item in the postwar social-service budget was one that did not even exist before the turn of the century: the payment of social-security benefits, which had grown to well over a third of the total by the late 1970s.[41] The burgeoning cost of this commitment grew as the population aged and as the real value of benefits increased through a series of political decisions. Between 1951 and 1968, the net income of a national-insurance claimant with a wife and two children rose from a little over one-third to almost three-quarters that of an average wage-earner.[42] The second largest item of social spending, on education, had only just begun to be a charge on the Exchequer in the high-Victorian era. In 1944, the Butler Education Act, which raised the school-leaving age to fifteen, kicked off a fitful trend towards educational expansion. Educational spending accounted for almost a quarter of all social spending by the late 1970s. It had already surpassed defence spending a decade earlier, thanks mainly to the rapid growth of the school-age population, extensive school-building and refurbishing efforts, the establishment of about a dozen new universities, and the introduction of polytechnics and industrial training schemes.[43] The third largest item of social spending, on the National Health Service, accounted for about a fifth of the total by the late 1970s. British taxpayers actually spent less for the NHS than most other western Europeans did for their government-financed medical services. But costs rose over the years, as the number of hospitals and specialist services expanded, as the elderly population grew, as technological advances increased the cost of hospital care, and as the number of NHS employees roughly doubled to almost a million. Only slightly less than the cost of the NHS was that of public housing. Over two million Britons were rehoused through local slum clearance programmes in the 1950s and 1960s that were heavily subsidized by the Exchequer. Chronic overcrowding and housing shortage were said to be things of the past by the mid-1970s, when, for the first time ever, authorities were reporting a slight housing surplus. Certainly there was more widely available and more affordable low-end housing than ever before, thanks mainly to council-house building drives and rent controls.[44]

In sponsoring economic growth and greatly expanding access to medical care, old-age pensions, education, and housing, the postwar state assumed responsibility for the establishment of decent minimum standards in areas of social life that it had largely avoided before the turn of the century, and with which it had interfered only fitfully before World War II. But it is important to stress the limits of the welfare state along with its accomplishments. For it did not attempt to reshape the structure of British society on radically egalitarian terms. The Labour governments and their successors greatly shored up the basis of social security, but neither they nor most of their constituents were interested in using the powers of the state to transform what was still a markedly class-conscious and hierarchical society.

First of all, the Attlee ministries, as the historian Ross McKibbin has pointed out, 'operated deeply, but on a narrow front' in their quest for

social fairness.[45] Thus, for instance, they did virtually nothing to antag-
onize such bastions of privilege as the City or the grammar schools.
While Labour imposed a small 'once and for all' capital levy in 1948,
it otherwise spared dividends and undistributed profits. City acceptance of Labour's very modest redistributive goals was plain to see
when share prices actually plummeted and took several months to
recover after Attlee's government fell in October 1951.[46] Moreover,
while the Butler Education Act (1944) did indeed broaden access to
education, it also perpetuated a status hierarchy in which grammar
schools remained the route to university while a disproportionate
share of working-class children received a much less ambitious education in technical or secondary modern schools. Grammar schools
remained the preserve of the well-to-do: in 1953, only 9 per cent of
English grammar school entrants were the children of unskilled
manual workers. A tiny minority of the mere 3.2 per cent of the eligible age-group matriculating at universities in 1954 were children of
unskilled or semi-skilled fathers.[47] Postwar educational expansion
ultimately enhanced opportunity, but mostly on behalf of the middle
rather than the working classes. Of the cohort reaching age twenty for
the period 1933–42, only 1 per cent of working-class and 7 per cent of
middle-class young men entered university; for 1963–72, the corre-
sponding proportions were 3 per cent and 26 per cent, respectively. The
rise of comprehensive schools in the 1960s helped to level the educational playing field a bit, but spending per pupil remained considerably lower for secondary moderns, and the rationing of post-secondary
education on the basis of competitive examinations tended to privilege
more affluent students who had access to the sources of cultural capital
that helped to secure high test scores.[48] Finally, nationalization brought
almost no change to the hierarchy of the workplace. Workers were
given small say in the management of the nationalized industries. For
their part, the unions did little to fight for worker control, because they
were generally content to preserve the familiar system of adversarial
bargaining.

The limits of the welfare state's egalitarian commitments were even
obvious where the breadth of its activity was most noticeable: the provision of social insurance. Wartime anxieties about the cost of a universal system ruled out any serious consideration of Labour's prewar
ideal of a purely tax-financed system with no means tests. The contributory alternative that was adopted rested not on the redistribution
of wealth from class to class, but on the reapportionment of risk
across broad social categories that did not specifically recognize class
distinctions – from young to old, healthy to sick, employed to unem-

ployed. As the burden of taxes and insurance contributions mounted over the years, it became increasingly obvious that working-class people were paying for most of their own social-security benefits, with the state simply obliging them to save for the purpose of self-help. This was not surprising, for the system of flat-rate contributory insurance was never intended to bring about major shifts in the distribution of income. Beveridge and the postwar governments that translated his scheme into reality did not seek to level the social hierarchy, but only to ensure that the conditions of those living towards the bottom of it more or less kept pace with the rising standards of those above them at a time of growing affluence.[49]

Even this modest goal was only partly fulfilled, however, and through means that fell short of Beveridge's recommendations in significant ways. Family allowances were set at a much lower rate than he had suggested, for instance, and while old-age pensions were initially set at a somewhat higher level than he had recommended, there was no plan for bringing them up to subsistence level in the future, as he had envisioned. Eliminating means tests altogether had been a central ambition of the Beveridge Report. But the failure to set contributory benefits at subsistence level all but guaranteed the proliferation of means-testing as time went by. The result has been a subject of endless debate. On one hand, means tests have the potential to channel resources more efficiently to those in need, and seem inherently more just than the distribution of universal benefits to citizens who are affluent enough to do without them. On the other hand, the intrusiveness of means tests was just as bitterly resented by those who were subjected to them in the 1970s as it had been by those who were obliged to submit to them forty years earlier. Means tests were increasingly complicated and expensive to administer, and means-tested benefits were plagued by relatively low rates of 'take-up', as a good many eligible recipients did not apply for them, either through ignorance or because they wished to avoid the shame associated with them. That sense of shame was no doubt sharpened by strenuous efforts to detect welfare fraud, and by the periodic rounds of 'scroungerphobia' inspired by the disproportionate attention that the tabloid press drew to the cases of welfare fraud that it managed to dig up.[50]

Ultimately, means-tested benefits were bound to rise along with the overall expense of social security, because the official definition of what constituted the 'subsistence level' or 'poverty line' was frequently redefined upwards so as to keep the guaranteed minimum in line with rising standards of affluence. These expensive adjustments accorded with the concept of 'relative poverty' that was championed by sociologists such as Peter Townsend and Brian Abel-Smith, which measured the value of benefits not against an absolute physical minimum but against rising average incomes. While it is reasonable for an affluent society to treat poverty in relative terms, doing so means that 'poverty' never disappears, since the poverty line gravitates upwards in step with the overall growth in incomes. By the 1970s the vast majority of Britons were well above the poverty line defined by Beveridge in the mid-1940s; but if one took the number of Britons in receipt of or eligible for means-tested benefits as a measure of the extent of poverty, then more of them were impoverished at the latter than at the former date. The index-linked poverty line generated as much frustration as it did extra revenue for the social services. Critics on the right correctly argued that it set an unattainable goal, while critics on the left correctly argued that it furnished vivid proof that decades of lavish social spending had done virtually nothing to promote greater equality of condition.[51]

Ultimately, the welfare state probably did promote a redistribution of income downwards, but only to a very modest degree. Perhaps the most detailed estimate of the era was that of the Royal Commission on the Distribution of Income and Wealth (1976–9), which concluded that welfare benefits increased the wealth of the poorest 20 per cent of British households from a mere 0.9 per cent of 'original' national income to 9.2 per cent of the 'final' income that took into account the payment of such benefits.[52] Thus social policies were promoting an unprecedented measure of redistribution. But the redistributive trend was short-lived. By 1987, the final income distribution in the United Kingdom was almost exactly the same as it had been in 1949. The slight move towards greater equality up to the mid-1970s was reversed by the higher unemployment levels of the subsequent decade.[53]

Other evidence makes clear just how modest was the redistributive trend up to the mid-1970s. The impact of taxation, for instance, was broadly neutral. While affluent Britons continued to pay far more in direct taxes than they had ever done before the war, so too did humbler ones. It is true that by the mid-1970s the tax structure was clearly more progressive than it had been a century earlier. In 1977, average total taxes came to 38.1 per cent on the top 10 per cent of income levels, 35.6 per cent on the middle 10 per cent, and 20.1 per cent on the lowest 10 per cent.[54] But these aggregate numbers are less telling than the fact that by the 1970s, a good many low-income families found themselves in the grotesque position of being regarded as wealthy enough to be taxed by the Inland Revenue while at the same time being deemed poor enough to qualify for means-tested benefit. The income-tax ceiling had been lowered so far that many poorer households were now stuck in a 'poverty trap', where even a slight increase in pay would simultaneously raise their tax liability and make them ineligible for income support. Here was a built-in disincentive to find more profitable employment that had everything to do with the fiscal demands of the welfare state and nothing to do with the personal character of the welfare recipient.[55]

A final point to stress is the obvious one that low-income Britons were by no means the only ones to profit from welfare benefits. Indeed, it has been a common argument throughout the postwar era that social-service spending disproportionately favours the comfortably well-off. While council housing subsidies, rent rebates, and allowances were 'pro-poor' in their final distribution, spending on primary education was roughly neutral, while the National Health Service, public spending on education over the age of sixteen, public transportation subsidies, and tax breaks for home-ownership and occupational pensions were 'pro-rich' in their distributive effects. The NHS, for instance, while arguably one of the most 'democratic' health-care providers in the world, tended to benefit middle-class Britons more than it did working-class ones, simply because the former were more likely to take advantage of the full range of services it had to offer.[56] Of course, one of the founding beliefs of the welfare state was that citizens were entitled to a broad array of social services as a basic right that had nothing to do with their financial circumstances. A system that set out to funnel benefits solely to the poor would have defeated this principle, would have turned welfare into stigmatizing charity, and would have been politically unacceptable to the more affluent taxpayers to whom it provided no entitlements. But an inevitable consequence of the 'universal' alternative that was established in the late 1940s was to channel a great many tax-supported benefits to people who could have managed well enough without them.

Ultimately, then, the welfare state did little to promote greater equality of outcome in a society that was still notable for its hierarchical structure. But equality of outcome was the stated goal of very few of its advocates. The broadly accepted goal was to establish a decent minimum for all Britons that was more or less in line with the rising standard of living. Generally speaking, the welfare state met that goal, and in doing so provided far more services to far more citizens than the British state had ever done before. But it was the unprecedented economic growth of the postwar era that had made a lavish welfare state politically feasible. When in the early 1970s it seemed that growth was no longer sustainable, the political consensus in support of the welfare state no longer seemed so either.

The welfare state and its discontents, c.1965–1979

By the late 1960s it seemed that discontent with the welfare state was growing in proportion with its responsibilities. Economic stagnation revealed the limits of demand management and led many to conclude that the state was either over-steering the economy or not steering it strongly enough. The central government's authority seemed to erode as it found it increasingly difficult to secure the cooperation of powerful producers' groups. Anti-tax sentiment rose as the tax burden increased at a time of slow growth. Dissatisfaction mounted over the perceived shortcomings and excesses of social security. At the same time, the growth of bureaucratic power in Whitehall, Britain's entry into the European Community, the question of Scottish and Welsh devolution, and the troubles in Northern Ireland all posed challenges to the cherished notions of ministerial accountability and parliamentary sovereignty. As the authority of the state seemed to diminish with its ever-widening commitments, many observers agreed with Margaret Thatcher that those commitments needed to be trimmed back if that authority was to be salvaged.

At the root of much of this dissatisfaction was the perception of relative economic decline. The economy actually experienced historically high rates of growth in the postwar decades: close to 3 per cent of GDP per year between 1951 and 1973. But in the same period the French economy was growing over 5 per cent and the West German economy over 6 per cent a year. While British living standards were rising, those of virtually all other advanced industrial countries were rising considerably faster, and it was this failure to keep pace that provoked widespread criticism of Britain's putative economic shortcomings.[57] The vast literature on Britain's relative economic decline points to a long list of culprits: a shortage or diversion of investment; insufficient or inconsistent demand; poor industrial relations and inflexible labour practices; a rigid and antagonistic class structure; insufficient training; unimaginative managerial techniques and antiquated business structures; and an inbred cultural conservatism that frowned on entrepreneurship.[58] There is no sense here in trying to parcel out shares of the blame. The important point to make is that the postwar state was bound to be implicated in the country's economic woes in multiple ways, simply because the postwar state had assumed such a broad role in trying to foster economic growth.

First of all, the state was blamed for its seeming inability to accelerate growth through investment and planning. During Harold Wilson's administration (1964–70), the central government became more active in its efforts to steer the economy. It injected a great deal of money into regional development schemes. It created a Department of Economic Affairs (DEA) that was assigned the task of developing a National Plan for the enhancement of economic growth. It sought to rejuvenate various declining industries by sponsoring rationalization schemes through an Industrial Reconstruction Corporation (IRC). It established a Ministry of Technology to harness what Wilson called 'the white heat of a second industrial revolution' for the revitalization of British industry. Finally, when Labour returned to power in 1974, once again under Wilson, it created a National Enterprise Board (NEB) that was charged with the task of rationalizing state investment and promoting industrial planning agreements. While these efforts at planning and coordination generated an impressive list of acronyms, they were mostly ad hoc improvisations that did little to invigorate a sluggish economy.[59] Thus the gap between what the government promised and what it was able to deliver in economic terms widened dramatically over the course of the 1960s. Popular confidence in the state's ability to steer the economy waned accordingly.

Dissatisfaction with the fiscal burdens imposed by the state rose simultaneously. Government revenue doubled between 1964 and 1970, at a time when prices rose by a third. Taxes and insurance contributions took nearly 20 per cent of an average worker's earnings by the end of the 1960s, almost two-and-a-half times as much as they had taken at the beginning of the decade. While the government pressed ever harder on taxpayers, it was unable to reward them with economic gains that compensated for their contributions to the Exchequer.[60] This dramatic growth in the level of taxes was related to another perceived shortcoming of the government: its failure to manage demand in a way that would simultaneously promote steady growth, control inflation, and protect the value of sterling. 'Stop-go' management of the economy became ever more precarious, as the government's efforts to stimulate demand quickly led to higher inflation and larger trade deficits; its subsequent deflationary efforts did little to reduce these deficits, whilst they exacerbated the chronic problem of low productivity and saddled Britons with higher taxes. Dramatic oscillations of macroeconomic policy wreaked havoc with long-range forecasting and compromised the Wilson ministry's plans for sustained growth.[61]

The ineffectuality of 'stop-go' was by no means entirely the government's fault. There was only so much that the British or any other state could do to regulate demand in an open international economy, and Britain's economy was more open than most. Reflationary efforts could only be taken so far, because they were likely to produce serious balance-of-payments deficits and a depreciating currency before they could exert much impact on either employment or productivity levels.[62] Deflationary efforts, on the other hand, required a measure of wage and price restraint, which in turn required the cooperation of big business and the trade unions. Securing that cooperation became an increasingly difficult task for the central government. Here was another way in which the managed economy weakened the power of the state rather than enhancing it. For not only did it raise dangerously high expectations of what the state could deliver in economic terms, it also greatly increased the political clout of producer groups. As successive governments intensified their efforts to steer the economy in the 1960s and early 1970s, they were obliged to rely ever more heavily on corporatist compromises with business and the unions. This perpetual bargaining often resulted in short-term agreement on difficult issues such as redundancies and wage or price restraint. But it also implicated the state in a game of interest brokerage, in which business interests expected it to dole out generous subsidies whilst the unions expected it to secure increasingly generous wage agreements. By the 1970s the intensification of interest brokerage had provoked widespread concern about 'government overload' and 'pluralistic stagnation', as academics and journalists expressed their fears that policy-making had become a series of ad hoc arrangements in which the government sought to obtain the consent of groups that were not predisposed to subordinate their own sectional interests to an abstract notion of the public good.[63]

Much of the criticism of the government's role as interest broker focused on its relationship with the trade unions. Assessing the unions' role in the economic stagnation and political crises of the late 1960s and 1970s is a difficult matter. It is fair to say that their wage demands helped to induce inflation and their reliance on high manning levels and restrictive job descriptions had a negative impact on productivity. But so too did many other factors with which organized labour had little or nothing to do. If trade unionists sought to optimize their sectional advantages, this made them no different from any other interest group that sought to influence policy. But union power became an economic 'problem' with important political ramifications at this time because a series of governments had come to rely on the unions' consent to keep inflation under control. Obtaining this consent was never easy, since full employment gave the unions a strong hand in wage bargaining. But it became particularly difficult to obtain by the late 1960s, when more and more workers in low-wage sectors of the economy were organizing and frequently striking to ensure that their meagre pay would at least keep pace with rising prices and taxes.

The Wilson government was concerned about the growing volume of strikes and the inflationary trend of strike settlements. In 1969, the secretary for employment, Barbara Castle, issued a White Paper, *In Place of Strife*, that sought to strengthen the government's hand in its dealings with the unions by giving it the authority to insist on pre-strike ballots, to enforce a 'conciliation pause' before the calling of strikes, and to impose penal sanctions on individual strikers through a new Industrial Relations Court. The TUC damned *In Place of Strife* as an infringement of free collective bargaining, the cabinet and the Labour party split over it, and the result was a humiliating climb-down for the government.[64] Edward Heath's Conservative administration (1970–4) also sought to rein in unofficial strikes and high-wage compromises, but it too was forced to abandon its proposed penal sanctions. Inflationary wage settlements continued, and provoked a crisis in 1973 when the National Union of Miners called a nationwide strike. Heath, now faced with the most serious industrial crisis since 1926, called a general election in his search for a mandate to get tough with the unions. Voters, however, were not prepared to lay the blame for the deteriorating economic situation solely on the unions, and gave Labour a razor-thin victory. After returning to Downing Street, Harold Wilson settled the coal strike on the miners' terms. Thus by the mid-1970s the sectional strength of the trade unions seemed more formidable than ever before. Both Labour and Conservative governments had sought and failed to curb it through authoritarian measures. In attempting to wield the powers of the state against the unions, they had merely compromised the state's authority.

That authority was being challenged much more violently in Northern Ireland. Over the previous forty years, the Irish question had caused relatively few headaches for British politicians. The nationalism of the Irish Free State mostly took peaceful and constitutional forms, and the agreement with Britain that turned the Free State into the independent Republic of Ireland in 1949 was amicably secured. Devolved government in the North had led to open discrimination against the Catholic minority, but there was relatively little violence between Protestants and Catholics.

All of that changed when in 1968–9 Protestant mobs, sometimes aided and abetted by the police, turned on Catholic demonstrators who were seeking equal opportunity under the law. The violence had become so serious by August 1969 that the Wilson government sent in British troops in an effort to restore order. But instead the troops became ever more deeply involved in a guerilla war that pitted Protestant police and paramilitaries against the newly established Provisional IRA, which sought to bring the six counties into the Republic. In its effort to uphold the Stormont regime, the British government gave its support to a policy of internment through which IRA suspects and sympathizers were detained without trial and in some cases even tortured. The Heath administration sought to stabilize the situation in the North by suspending the Stormont government and establishing direct British rule in late 1972, but the violence continued. It seemed obvious enough to most mainland British observers that the key to stability was an arrangement that would guarantee the Catholic minority a permanent voice in the provincial government. But power-sharing efforts were stymied by sectarian violence, and direct rule continued. In 1974 the violence spread to England itself when the IRA detonated a series of pub bombs, the most deadly of which killed twenty-one people in Birmingham. The British state, its image tarnished by the ruthless 'policing' tactics it had endorsed, seemed powerless to end a conflict that pitted militant nationalists who vehemently rejected Britain's right to govern in Ulster against militant loyalists who insisted that their physical safety relied on the indefinite continuation of direct rule.[65]

The troubles in Northern Ireland posed by far the most direct challenge to Westminster sovereignty. But that sovereignty seemed to be eroding in a number of less dramatic ways at the same time. It is true that enormous power was now concentrated in the cabinet, composed as it was of a party leadership that imposed strict voting discipline on MPs and whose extensive manifesto commitments now dominated the legislative agenda. But by the late 1960s it was in part the very scope of the government's commitments that led many observers to conclude that cabinet ministers and the Commons majority answerable to them were ceding too much decision-making power to the civil bureaucracy. While in 1901 under 6 per cent of the working population were public employees, by 1982 the proportion had reached nearly 30 per cent, high even by western European standards. By the late 1970s the National and Local Government Officers' Association (NALGO) boasted well over 400,000 members, making it the largest white-collar union in the western world. A country that was so often noted in the past for its minimal bureaucracy now seemed to be awash with bureaucrats.[66]

The growth of bureaucratic power seemed to be compromising the ideal of democratic accountability in several ways. The broad range of services now administered by central and local government spawned a vast number of quasi-judicial tribunals that gave formidable powers to non-elected officials to influence citizens' lives in ways that had little to do with parliamentary statute.[67] By the early 1980s a broad range of 'quasi-autonomous non-governmental organizations' (quangos) directly appointed by cabinet ministers to deal with a vast range of regulatory issues controlled some £37,000 million of public money.[68] Meanwhile, parliamentary scrutiny of the national budget had fallen into terminal decline. Obsolete estimate procedures turned Commons approval into a rubber stamp for financial commitments that the government had already made. Most budgetary matters were sorted out informally within Whitehall, and a great deal of government expenditure was now predetermined and automatic, making it difficult for MPs either to cut or reallocate it to any significant degree.[69]

While the decision-making authority of the civil service waxed, its reputation waned. It had peaked in the Attlee years, when widespread faith in the powers of government activism prompted many Britons to agree with the Labour intellectual Douglas Jay's well-known dictum that the gentleman from Whitehall knew best. That assessment seemed laughable in the late 1960s, when it became fashionable to deride the civil service for its complacency, its Oxbridge dilettantism, and its obsession with official secrecy. This line of criticism culminated in the final report of the Fulton Commission (1966–8), which emphasized the need to recruit fewer 'amateurs' and more 'professionals' with specialized training into the service. Little came of the Fulton Report, however, and, whether fairly or not, the civil-service 'generalist' went on to become one of the chief scapegoats in the literature of decay that was in vogue in the 1970s.[70]

While Whitehall's reputation declined, its power over local government increased. The Attlee government divested the local authorities of their control over the administration of trunk roads, gas and electricity, and, most notably, the hospitals. Later rounds of centralization deprived them of water provision and the residual health services. While Whitehall relied on the local authorities to deliver a wider variety of public services than ever before, it closely supervised their activities through an endless stream of regulations, circulars, and inspectors' reports. Local government spending skyrocketed in the postwar era, accounting for some 18 per cent of GNP by 1975, six times the proportion it had amounted to a century earlier. But local discretionary spending was at an all-time low. By the mid-1970s, well under a fifth of local-authority income came from the rates; over twice that much came from Exchequer grants. This growing financial dependence on the centre led to a greater equalization of the standard of services across districts, but it also ensured the continued erosion of local autonomy. Voter turnout at local elections declined to around 40 per cent as Britons increasingly associated local government with a remote 'corporate state' that was stationed in Whitehall. Both local autonomy and localist sentiment were much weaker than they had been early in the century, but popular faith in the central government's ability to manage local affairs efficiently and democratically can hardly be said to have grown stronger.[71]

In fact, one important reason for the resurgence of nationalism in Scotland and Wales in the late 1960s and 1970s was the perception that the intensive regional development efforts of the postwar era had transferred too much decision-making power to Westminster and Whitehall and had failed to halt long-term economic decline. Economic frustration was especially noticeable in Scotland, where the Scottish Nationalist Party, a marginal group since its establishment in 1934, came into prominence with a string of municipal and by-election victories. Initially, postwar Welsh nationalism focused more closely on cultural than on economic issues, and the revival of the Welsh language became the rallying cry of the nationalist Plaid Cymru party. But economic resentment became a powerful force in Welsh politics in the mid-1960s, at a time of falling agricultural prices and widespread pit closures. Support for Plaid Cymru became noticeable even in the Labour-dominated southern industrial regions of Wales. While the Union was by no means in jeopardy, the Labour government of 1974–9 sought a safety-valve for nationalist sentiment in Scotland and Wales. Thus it recommended the establishment of a Scottish elected assembly that would have legislative authority over a variety of internal matters but no tax-raising powers. It also proposed a much weaker assembly for Wales, to be charged with executive responsibilities for certain aspects of social policy to be paid for out of a modest block grant. Labour's devolution bills were cumbersome, and their passage through parliament was marked by political manoeuvring that generated confusion about what the government thought it was trying to accomplish. In 1978 the measures were submitted to referenda which required that a minimum of 40 per cent of all eligible voters vote 'yes' in order for devolution to take effect. While the 'yes' vote won by a slim margin in Scotland, low turnout meant that it fell well short of the required 40 per cent. In Wales, the 'no' vote won by a large majority. In the end, the devolution debate probably only inflamed nationalist sentiment in Scotland and Wales by making it feel both insulted and rebuffed: insulted because the devolution bills conceded little authority to the proposed legislatures, and rebuffed because the bills had come to nothing.[72]

If the proper balance of political authority within the United Kingdom was a troublesome question, so too was the proper relationship between the United Kingdom and the European Community, which Britain finally entered in 1973. Before the 1960s, closer western European integration was an ideal that most British politicians had professed to encourage, but only from a distance. The Churchillian notion prevailed that 'we are with Europe, but not of it. We are linked, but not compromised. We are interested and associated, but not absorbed.'[73] Churchill and other Britons had good reasons to feel this way. First, in marked contrast with western Europe, the British experience of World War II had bolstered rather than destroyed faith in the nation-state. Secondly, it was not immediately obvious that Britain was no longer a world power. It retained many of its imperial commitments in the short term, and the sterling area was still a formidable financial and commercial bloc. Stressing Britain's American relationship over its European one seemed logical for a number of reasons, most notably because the USA had the money to help stabilize sterling and the British economy more generally, and because rubbing elbows with a superpower reinforced the comforting notion that Britain remained one itself. Such reasoning prevailed throughout the 1950s, when it was not yet clear that the European Economic Community that was brought into being by the Treaty of Rome (1957) would ever become substantially more than a free-trade zone. Britain finally applied for membership in 1961, however, because the Suez crisis had brought home the fact that Britain had indeed lost much of its world influence, and because it was now obvious that British economic growth was sluggish by western European standards. Ironically, nationalist objections on the Continent delayed British entry into the EEC for over a decade. General de Gaulle vetoed two separate British applications (in 1961 and 1967) mainly because he feared that British membership would weaken French influence in the EEC, and because he did not think that Britain's trading relationship with the Commonwealth could be accommodated within a pragmatic federation of sovereign states in search of mutual economic advantage.

The passage of de Gaulle from the political stage finally cleared the way for British entry in 1973. But the government and the country as a whole took a resigned approach to the EEC. Among the small majority of MPs who voted in favour of membership, the sense prevailed that Britain's painfully obvious economic weakness left it little choice but to join. The unprecedented referendum called on the issue of membership by Wilson's government in 1974 ended in a two-to-one victory for the 'yes' side, but there was little sign that the 'European idea' generated much passion among British voters. Many of those who had misgivings cited the thorny issue of sovereignty. Much of the EEC's decision-making authority was concentrated in the hands of a non-elected executive, the European Commission, that was answerable neither to national assemblies nor to national voters. It was unclear how much influence individual states would be able to exert in the implementation of EEC programmes, the most notable of which at the time was the new Common Agricultural Policy (CAP), an extensive system of food price supports that was heavily subsidized by consumers. Finally, the terms of EEC membership placed an unprecedented limit on parliamentary sovereignty, because they gave to the European Court of Justice the ultimate power of judicial review over conflicts between parliamentary and Community legislation. Thus a handful of judges from member states were vested with considerable powers to rule on matters of national law. The decision-making power of the EEC was hardly a burning political question in Britain in the 1970s. But like so many other issues at the time, British entry suggested that the authority of the central government was not as formidable as it once had been.[74]

Worries about government 'overload' and an over-mighty bureaucracy, trade-union militancy, domestic terrorism, Scottish and Welsh nationalism, the growing prominence of the 'European idea' – these were all symptoms of a broad social and political crisis. As the historian Jose Harris has noted, the 'traditional constitutional view that a variety of norms and national identities could be contained and harmonised within an impartial, secular, instrumental state' was rapidly eroding, and the authority of that state was compromised accordingly.[75] Obliged to play the role of referee to a wide variety of assertive interests, both its impartiality and its efficacy were questioned on all sides. Thus, for instance, libertarians could hail a series of measures over the course of the 1960s that all but removed the state from its traditional role as moral policeman: the decriminalization of adult male homosexuality (1967), the liberalization of divorce law (1969), the suspension of the death penalty (1964) and its ultimate abolition (1969), and the Abortion and Family Planning Acts (1967), which created a role for state agencies in the provision of contraceptives and abortions. But social conservatives assailed these measures as proof that the state was fostering a 'permissive society' that seemed not only to condone but to encourage casual sex, illegal drug use, and rising crime rates. Likewise, Britain's growing immigrant community (over 5 per cent of the population of England and Wales by 1966) could press for and welcome anti-discriminatory legislation while still having good reason to complain about Commonwealth immigration restrictions and police harassment.

At the same time, government efforts to liberalize immigration policy and to promote greater racial equality provoked a racist backlash on the far right. Finally, an assertive women's movement could hail the government's liberal approach towards contraception and abortion and applaud its efforts in the mid-1970s to provide for paid maternity leave as well as penal sanctions against sex discrimination. But feminists could still deplore the state's failure to ensure equal pay for equal work. Single-interest groups of all ideological persuasions assailed the seeming failure of government to respond to the questioning of traditional sources of social authority that accompanied the new 'lifestyle politics'.[76] In short, the state was bound to come in for more than its fair share of abuse in its efforts to regulate an increasingly diverse and restive society.

At the same time, by the 1970s the state was unable to command much popular admiration for what it provided on a more lavish scale than it had ever done before: social security benefits. Certain sectors of the welfare state did seem to instil a sense of corporate solidarity, most notably the NHS, which to most Britons was still a symbol of national pride. But taken as a whole, the welfare state was too vast, too impersonal, too intrusive, and too expensive to inspire much allegiance or affection. Even during the heyday of the Attlee governments, it had been difficult for citizens to summon up a passionate commitment to what for most of them was little more than 'a super-insurance company on a national basis';[77] it became even more difficult thereafter, as the welfare state became more bureaucratized and its ideological underpinnings went almost completely unexamined by intellectuals and politicians alike.[78] In Britain as in other advanced industrial nations, social services had grown up alongside mass democracy. But generally speaking it was the politicians and the government bureaucrats who had built up those services, partly in response to what they *perceived* to be the wishes of a mass electorate. What exactly the electorate did wish for was rarely put to the test, because 'consensus' politics rarely gave them a clear choice of alternatives on the issue of welfare provision. Once the universalist system was established in the late 1940s, it was not so much the voters who shaped its development as a combination of economic growth, administrative inertia, and the political pressures brought to bear by sectional interest groups such as the TUC, the CBI, the BMA, the National Federation of Old Age Pensions Associations, the Child Poverty Action Group, and so on.[79]

Private citizens thus had little reason to feel a sense of democratic ownership in the social security system. Perhaps those with least reason to feel it were those who relied on it most heavily. Recipients of supplementary benefit were still subjected to humiliating means tests, just as they had been forty years earlier. The downward extension of income tax penalized those who were able to find more gainful employment. By the late 1960s many of them were living in the depressing tower-blocks that loomed large on the inner-city skyline. The infamous collapse of the Ronan Point block in Newham, east London, in 1968 merely confirmed the already widespread opinion that such high-rises, while relatively cheap to build, were not really fit for human habitation.[80]

Tower-block housing was widely perceived as simply one of the most glaring flaws of a welfare state that critics from across the political spectrum were assailing for its growing cost (or, alternatively, for its niggardliness), its seeming failure to reduce poverty, its structural rigidity, and its lack of democratic accountability.[81] This mounting dissatisfaction with and alienation from the welfare state was by no means exclusive to Britain. It was noticeable throughout the advanced industrial nations in the early 1970s, when the long postwar economic boom that had made the growth of lavish entitlements relatively painless came to an abrupt end. That dissatisfaction was more intense in Britain chiefly because the British economy was seen to be suffering more than its counterparts. By the mid-1970s, once-mighty Britain had fallen to eighteenth in the international league table in GDP per head. Public spending was careering out of control at close to 60 per cent of GDP. For the first time ever, spending dramatically exceeded revenue, forcing the government to borrow at unprecedented peacetime levels. The balance-of-payments deficit reached record proportions. The pound had lost 30 per cent of its value since the devaluation of 1967, and inflation ran at over 25 per cent. In short, the economy seemed to be in free fall, despite or perhaps because of the government's best efforts to manage it.

In retrospect, it seems reasonable to conclude that the British economy was hit particularly hard during the Slump of the mid-1970s at least partly because its maturity made it more difficult to retool and to channel the flow of investments into high-growth, export-oriented sectors.[82] But the economy's miserable performance turned the search for scapegoats into a national pastime. Most critics pointed their fingers at the state. Those on the Labour left, a formidable force in the constituencies, insisted that it was not doing enough to steer the economy, and advocated a reflationary strategy fortified by strict import controls and withdrawal from the EEC, along with a much more aggressively interventionist industrial policy featuring a thirty-five-hour working week, comprehensive planning agreements, and the extension of public ownership to profitable sectors of the economy.[83] Meanwhile, more and more Conservatives were insisting that the state was already guilty of trying to do far too much.

The replacement of Edward Heath with Margaret Thatcher as Conservative party leader in 1975 was a fillip for the libertarian wing of the party. Its 'new right' critique of the state focused on several related themes: first, that it threw too much of the taxpayers' money in too many directions, largely because postwar economic growth had encouraged a spendthrift mentality in both of the major parties; secondly, that the state's habitual accommodation of powerful sectional interests, most notably the trade unions, had reduced its authority, contributed to inflation, and encouraged those interests to make ever more strident demands; thirdly, that neither taxpayers nor welfare recipients were getting adequate value for money from a bloated social security system; fourthly, that the welfare state, in promising too many things to too many interest groups, had discouraged self-reliance and raised expectations that it could not meet; fifthly, that economic planning was inefficient and politically dangerous, because it weakened parliament by granting too much power to the executive; and sixthly, that Keynesian demand management had been an abject failure, for in its ultimately futile efforts to maintain full employment it had permitted inflation to spiral out of control whilst generating huge budget deficits and tax levels so high as to retard private investment.[84]

The Labour government was by no means prepared to endorse this damning assessment. Facing rampant inflation in 1975, however, it felt it had no choice but to tighten its belt. Denis Healey's April budget was the first of the postwar era that sought to deflate the economy in the face of rising unemployment. A balance-of-payments crisis the following year prompted even sterner measures: large budget cuts, long-term pay restraint, and a commitment to monetary targets in return for an enormous loan from the International Monetary Fund. The IMF agreement and exchange-rate concerns took the reflationary option out of the government's hands, but even before the IMF negotiation the prime minister, James Callaghan, had made it clear in a famous speech to the 1976 Labour Party Conference that his government would no longer attempt to reflate:

> We used to think that you could just spend your way out of recession and increase employment only by cutting taxes and boosting government expenditure . . . [But] it only worked by injecting bigger doses of inflation into the economy followed by a higher level of unemployment at the next step. . . . The option [of spending yourself out of a recession] no longer exists.[85]

Callaghan and company were now prepared to sacrifice jobs in order to bring inflation under control, and thus the unemployment level doubled to over 6 per cent during the lifetime of the 1974–9 Labour government.[86]

According to most indicators, the austerity measures seemed to be promoting recovery. The pound regained a good deal of its value, North Sea oil generated a balance-of-payments surplus, and the inflation rate fell dramatically. But just as it appeared that the economy was on the rebound, the government's efforts to cajole the unions into going along with continued pay restraint failed, and the country was once again thrown into crisis. In July 1978, Callaghan requested that the TUC accept a 5 per cent pay increase norm for the next year, at a time when inflation had fallen to 7.5 per cent. The TUC rejected his offer. Shortly thereafter, striking workers at Ford won a large pay increase for themselves, setting a precedent for public-sector employees. During the ensuing 'Winter of Discontent', NHS workers, ambulance drivers, schoolteachers, dustmen, and even grave-diggers struck for higher pay. Schools closed; rubbish piled up; hospitals were picketed; some burials were delayed. Many of the strikers were chronically low-paid manual workers who had legitimate complaints. But ultimately even the white-collar civil servants whose duty it was to draft the pay codes went off the job, putting in claims that were as high as six times the inflation rate.[87]

Britons watched this sorry spectacle play out every evening on the television news, and public opinion rapidly turned against the government as much as it did against the unions. It appeared that the Labour leadership had lost its ability to command the allegiance of its ostensible allies in the union movement. What was easily forgotten at this time of crisis was that hard-pressed workers had managed to rein in their frustrations for three years while an equally hard-pressed government's dependence on the international financial markets meant that it had nothing to offer them but further self-sacrifice. In the end, it is probably fair to say that the authority of the state was being compromised not so much by the unions as it was by the complexities of an international economic situation that left national governments with a limited ability to 'steer' their economies in ways that could generate benefits all round.

Understandably, however, frustrated British voters were looking for scapegoats closer to home. The 1979 general election was fought over the question of 'Who Governs Britain?' just as much as the 1974 general election had been. This time, the electorate furnished a more decisive answer, handing the Conservatives a forty-four-seat majority in the new parliament. Margaret Thatcher moved into Downing Street vowing that her government would tame not only the unions, but all the other 'excesses' generated by an overgrown welfare state. After thirty years of buoyant growth, it appeared that the capacities of the state were about to be cut back. To what extent, and with what effect, remained to be seen.

6

The Limits of State Power, 1979 to the Present

The Conservatives entered office in 1979 vowing to liberate Britons from an over-mighty yet ineffectual state. Several years would pass before 'consensus' Tories were ousted from the cabinet. But the new government's rhetorical style made it clear from the outset that it was pledged to make war on the 'consensus' assumptions of the postwar era that had (ostensibly) led to the dramatic extension of state influence into spheres of life where it did not belong. Thus Thatcher and her supporters insisted that Keynesian demand management had fuelled inflation; that corporatism had given extortionate influence to producer groups; that a bloated social-security system discouraged private initiative; and that high taxes diverted too much income from consumers who knew how to manage it wisely to a government that manifestly did not. The bold language that many Conservatives habitually used to castigate the welfare state from the mid-1970s strongly suggested that, given the opportunity, they would scale it back.

In fact, the results of the Conservatives' avowedly minimalist project have been considerably less straightforward than their rhetoric. In some respects the central government is noticeably less interventionist than it was in the 1970s. But it is scarcely less expensive, and possesses even greater power over intermediate institutions than the 'classic' welfare state of the immediate postwar decades. The Thatcherite legacy for state formation is an ambiguous one, and the task of this chapter is to come to terms with this ambiguity. It will seek to do so by emphasizing four main points.

The first one is that the Thatcher and Major governments *did* reshape the state in a number of significant ways. Most importantly, they absolved it of the responsibility to promote full employment. Concluding that economic growth depended on low inflation and a strong pound, the Conservative governments were willing to abide high unemployment rates in order to meet these goals. They also absolved the state of the responsibility to appease producer groups through continuous consultation. It soon became obvious that corporatism was a thing of the past, as the Thatcher government not only ignored the demands of trade unions but sought to discipline them through set-piece confrontations and a series of laws that curtailed their ability to strike and even to organize. The Conservatives took the state out of the process of production in yet another conspicuous way: through a series of privatizations that extended from the 'commanding heights' of industry (coal, steel, and the like) to a good many 'natural monopolies' (water, gas, railways) as well. They likewise presided over a dramatic privatization of the housing market, which greatly reduced public authorities' role as builders and managers of dwellings. Finally, the Thatcher and Major governments promoted the contracting out of public services in an effort to enhance the efficiency and reduce the cost of secondary institutions such as the National Health Service. Thus by the end of the twentieth century the British state was playing a conspicuously smaller role in the management of the economy and the provision of services than it had done three-quarters of the way through it.

The second point is that despite all of these market reforms, and the polemical assaults on the welfare state that accompanied them, the overall level of public spending did not fall during the Thatcher–Major era. In fact, social-security expenditure rose substantially, chiefly because chronically high unemployment levels obliged the government to spend unprecedented amounts on public assistance. Meanwhile, the relative popularity of entitlements such as pensions and the NHS protected them from deep cuts. In short, the social-security functions of the postwar state were not significantly reduced. Nor were they significantly enlarged, however, and containing them required strong political will at a time when high unemployment, structural changes in the economy, and an ageing population were all exerting expansionary pressure on the welfare system. While the Conservative governments did not succeed in 'rolling back' the welfare state, moreover, they made it abundantly clear that the state was no longer in the business of promoting greater equality. We have seen that what little redistribution the postwar state achieved had come about through progressive taxation allied with supplementary benefits to low-income families. The Conservatives did away with the former and pared down the latter. The income gap widened between the comfortably well-off and the impoverished, and the government's indifference fostered a climate in which gross inequality seemed more publicly acceptable than at any time since the 1930s.

The third point is that the Conservatives' ostensibly 'minimalist' project actually enhanced the powers of the central government in a number of ways. Subjecting intermediate institutions to fiscal discipline and competitive pressure inevitably required the central government to tighten its influence over them. Thus local government was divested of much of its power over housing and education, and its tax-raising powers were sharply curtailed. Public-sector profession- als who had enjoyed considerable autonomy in the past were subjected to closer scrutiny and financial control by the government. Privatiza- tion created a host of new regulatory agencies that seemed to be accountable chiefly (if not solely) to the ministers who had appointed them. At the same time, the government's efforts to enforce official secrecy, to control the flow of information through the media, and to enhance police powers inspired fears of an over-mighty state that did not respect the importance of dissent to a healthy democracy. In short, this was a profoundly centralizing Conservative regime that was resolute in its efforts to defend and to enhance the sovereign powers of the British state over which it presided. Hence its tortured internal debate on the issue of closer European integration, a trend that made sense as a response to economic globalization, but one that seemed to threaten the centralized national sovereignty that the Thatcherites held dear.

The final point is that, thus far, the return of the Labour party from the political wilderness has done little to change the diminished economic role that the Conservatives gave to the state. But it has insti- gated a series of constitutional reforms that could ultimately bring about a more decentralized polity. Demand management is still out of political favour. The trade unions have not returned to their former status as a virtual estate of the realm. Privatization and the encouragement of internal markets in the provision of public services remain high political priorities. The government continues to extol the virtues of tough policing and welfare-to-work. On the other hand, the commitment that Tony Blair and his colleagues have made to Scottish and Welsh devolution, to a democratically elected local authority for London, to reform of the House of Lords, and to a more welcoming approach to the European Union suggest the makings of a constitutional transformation, in which the dramatically cen- tralized powers of the contemporary British state are to be limited and dispersed. What they do not suggest, however, is the fading away of the powerful national state of the postwar era. At the end of the twentieth century, Britons still expected it to intervene in their lives in ways that their great-grandparents would have found scarcely conceivable.

The Conservative reshaping of the postwar state

Margaret Thatcher and her Conservative colleagues entered office at the end of the 1970s pledging to curb the putative excesses of the welfare state, which they held largely responsible for the loss of confidence in government that was such a marked feature of that decade. What Britons at the time were perhaps least confident about was the state's ability to steer the economy. Low productivity, unprecedented public deficits, record levels of taxation and social-security spending, high inflation, and a rising level of unemployment: all of these trends seemed to indicate that demand management and other forms of government intervention were failing to promote economic stability and growth. There were, of course, many external factors that contributed to the 'stagflation' of the 1970s, most notably the enormous increase in the price of oil. But inevitably, a government that had assumed such a prominent role for itself in the management of the economy was widely blamed for the decade's economic miseries. This was by no means solely the case in Britain. The recession of the 1970s affected virtually all of the world's mature industrial economies, and the perception of 'government failure' led to a political shift to the right not only in Britain but in a good many other countries, such as the USA, Norway, Belgium, and Canada. Fiscal conservatives rode into office on a wave of resentment, as large numbers of lower-middle-class and blue-collar voters looking for tax relief abandoned parties of the centre-left. The most popular nostrum for prosperity was a reduction of the state's capacity to 'interfere' with the economy through tax cuts, spending limits, inflation control, deregulation, and privatization.[1]

It is probably correct to say that at no point during Thatcher's eleven years in office did a majority of Britons subscribe to this Conservative agenda. While the Tories always enjoyed a commanding majority in the House of Commons, their share of the vote for the three general elections with Thatcher at the helm never rose higher than 43 per cent. But the vagaries of the first-past-the-post electoral system combined with radicalization and schism on the political left to secure for the Tories a long period of hegemony in which they were free to do more or less as they pleased with the much-maligned state.[2] It is evident enough in retrospect that the Tories had not concocted a blueprint for a reformed state when they entered office. While there was a consistency in Conservative rhetoric – to take a 'resolute approach' born out of 'conviction politics' that would liberate Britons from the cold embrace of the 'nanny-state' – the means of achieving this 'liberation' were rarely worked out ahead of time in any detail. At the heart of

Thatcherism was a reckless enthusiasm for ad hoc experimentation in pursuit of libertarian ends.

The first such experiment was the pursuit of monetarism and supply-side economics, which divested the state of its customary postwar role as a guarantor of full employment. These were theoretical attacks on Keynesian demand management, principally developed by Milton Friedman and his colleagues in the 'Chicago School' of economics, which briefly came into political vogue in Britain and the USA with the elections of Thatcher and Ronald Reagan. Perhaps the most significant of the theoretical assumptions embraced by the first Thatcher government was that there would always be a trade-off between inflation and unemployment, and that there was a 'natural rate' of employment which at certain points in the economic cycle was bound to fall well below the level of full employment. If at such points a government sought to stimulate demand (through a combination of lower interest rates and higher levels of public spending, for instance) it would only encourage inflation, making a bad situation worse. The logical conclusion was that macroeconomic policy should concentrate on keeping inflation under control to the exclusion of virtually everything else, since, according to monetarist orthodoxy, it could not adequately control the levels of employment or of output within the national economy.[3] Following this logic, the new Tory government pursued an extremely tight fiscal policy in order to squeeze inflation out of the system. As interest rates rose and the money supply tightened, the inflation rate fell from a peak of 22 per cent in early 1980 to about 5 per cent three years later. But unemployment doubled in the first two years of the first Thatcher government, peaking at 12.5 per cent or over three million unemployed in 1983. High interest rates and an overvalued pound wreaked havoc on the industrial sector. Manufacturing output plunged by over 15 per cent, manufacturing capacity dropped by over a quarter, and GDP fell by over 3 per cent, making the recession of the early 1980s considerably worse in Britain than it was elsewhere. Even after the government's abandonment of monetary targets in 1985, unemployment remained stubbornly high. While it fell during the consumer boom of the late 1980s, it was still true that by any reasonably objective measurement the lowest unemployment rate attained in that decade was higher than the highest unemployment rate during the much-lamented 1970s.[4]

Thatcher and her colleagues had assumed that tight monetary policies would have only a small and brief impact on employment levels. But this miscalculation did not cost them their jobs. The Tories won re-election by a landslide in 1983 despite Depression-level unemployment, benefiting greatly from the recent victory over the Argentine military in the Falklands and the disarray of the Labour party. The Conservatives paid no electoral price for joblessness, and for the first time since another highly deflationary era, the early 1920s, mass unemployment was naturalized – widely perceived to be part of the natural order of things, which a government could take on only at the expense of the overall health of the economy.[5] Dole queues once again became part of the fabric of life in traditional manufacturing centres.[6] Now, as in the 1930s, the government had little to offer the long-term unemployed but supplementary benefits and the promise that recovery was just around the corner. The government's responsibility for stimulating employment had apparently come to an end.

So, too, had its responsibility to seek the advice of trade unionists and manufacturers in the management of the economy. Thatcher and her supporters insisted that the chronic efforts to cajole the trade unions into wage restraint in the 1970s had compromised the sovereignty of government, and had too often ended in extortionate wage settlements that hurt British competitiveness.[7] It soon became obvious that the government would no longer even consult, much less negotiate, with the unions. Len Murray, the TUC's general secretary, took early retirement after having crossed the threshold of number ten only three times in the first five years of Thatcher's residence there.[8] There was no longer any question of 'beer and sandwiches'. Manufacturers too were essentially told to go their own way. Many of them went to the wall in the early 1980s while the government refused to loosen its monetary policy. Finally, while Thatcher and company did not entirely abandon industrial policy and 'corporate welfare' schemes, they cut the scale of manufacturing subsidies and insisted on allocating them more selectively.[9]

While industry suffered simply from neglect, however, the trade unions were forced to swallow a series of statutes that limited their freedom to strike. Unballoted and secondary strikes were made actionable. It became illegal for unions to discipline members who refused to participate in authorized strikes. Unions were made legally responsible for unofficial strikes if they refused to disavow them. Employers were granted permission to provide their workers with incentives for decertifying their unions.[10] The Thatcher government also relied on set-piece confrontations with public-sector unions to make clear that there would be no more compromises. By far the most significant clash was the 1984–5 miners' strike. When, under the leadership of the combative Arthur Scargill, the National Union of Miners went out on an unballoted strike to try to prevent massive pit closures, Thatcher denounced the NUM as 'the enemy within'. Her government sanctioned heavy-handed tactics in the policing of a strike that was marked by violence on both sides.[11] Ultimately, the miners were obliged to surrender, the mining industry contracted severely, and NUM membership plummeted.

The NUM story was only the most dramatic example of union decline in the 1980s. Total union membership fell from 55 to 39 per cent of the work force as more and more workers entered the ranks of the lightly unionized service sector while jobs were methodically shed in the heavily unionized industrial sector.[12] Structural changes in the economy were an important factor in the political decline of the union movement. But so too was a Conservative government that was committed to shoring up the state's authority by breaking off its relationship with the unions.

Thatcher and her colleagues were likewise committed to withdrawing the state from the direct management of enterprise. By the 1970s, the nationalized industries were under attack from the political right for their relatively low productivity, their poor financial performance, their lack of public accountability, and the pattern of antagonistic labour relations that had developed within some of them.[13] While by no means all of the enterprises in state ownership were guilty as charged, they offered an obvious target to a government which insisted that privatization would bring efficiency and long-term profitability to enterprises that would now be forced to cope with market competition. Privatization, the Tories argued, would likewise help to create a 'shareholders' democracy', as consumers would take advantage of the low share prices offered by the government to buy stock in newly privatized companies. Perhaps the Conservatives' most obvious motive for privatization was the political advantages to be gained from it: the gratitude of small shareholders and the vast flow of revenue from the sale of stock, which would enable the government to keep taxes down and its borrowing requirement within manageable limits.

For all these reasons, the Thatcher government embarked on a massive round of privatization which has yet to run its course. In 1979, a good many of Britain's most prominent industrial enterprises were under state ownership, such as shipbuilding, coal, steel, gas, telecommunications, and airlines. By the time Thatcher left office in November 1990, the sources of about half the state's productive output had been sold off, and 650,000 workers transferred from public to private employment.[14] The privatizing trend further intensified under the Major government (1990–7), culminating in the sale of massive enterprises such as water supply and the rail network. By 1994–5, the Tory governments had privatized some fifty major enterprises to the tune of £60 billion, and there was plenty more still to come.[15] This enormous sell-off of public-sector assets was only the most prominent feature of the privatization effort. It also included widespread deregulation – the opening up of state activities to competition with the private sector (in transport and telecommunications, for instance) – and the tendering of contracts to private firms for the provision of services such as rubbish collection.[16]

Thus the Conservative governments greatly reduced the impact of the state as a direct provider of goods and services in the British economy. Whether the shrinking of this role has brought all of the promised benefits to the public is debatable. Privatization certainly led to some notable successes, such as British Steel, British Airways, and British Telecom, which quickly emerged as highly efficient and profitable firms. But these gains were partly achieved by ruthless job-shedding, which may have enhanced long-term productivity but obviously caused serious hardship to thousands of laid-off workers and their families. Moreover, the more recent privatization of 'natural monopolies' such as gas, water, and the railways has proved to be deeply unpopular. In the short term, for instance, the privatization of British Rail led to higher fares, hasty downsizing, fewer trains, the further deterioration of antiquated rolling stock, and widespread suspicion that public safety was being compromised in the rush for profits.[17]

Finally, some of the newly privatized enterprises seemed no more accountable to the government than they were to consumers. Despite the surface appearance, privatization has not been a straightforward exercise in state minimalism. For the government still plays an important role in many 'privatized' firms through its licensing activities, through the potent influence it exerts as a purchaser and contractor of services, through the allocation (and ownership) of shares, and through its establishment of a dense network of regulatory agencies (Ofgas, Ofrail, etc.) that are supposed to serve as industry watchdogs. While the members of these agencies are government appointees, neither their regulatory powers nor their accountability to parliament have been clearly defined. The result is that important sectors of the economy are now overseen by a vast 'quangocracy' that is supposed to represent the government and the public interest but is not clearly answerable to either one. In this respect, at least, privatization has not so much reduced the influence of government as obscured how that influence is supposed to operate.[18]

Privatization did mark a deliberate and dramatic contraction of the state's power within the housing market, however. The Thatcher-era housing reforms marked a sharp reversal of the seventy-year trend by which the central and local authorities had gradually enhanced their role as builders and landlords. In 1980, a landmark statute gave council tenants the right to buy their dwellings at a discounted rate and facilitated the rapid withdrawal of local-authority housing subsidies. By the end of the decade, 1.5 million former tenants had purchased their homes, while local authorities were now obliged to charge full market rents, meaning that they had lost their competitive advantage over private landlords. In short, the reforms of the 1980s ushered in a tenurial revolution, by which the number of council tenants precipitously declined, and private landlords were given strong incentives to rent as well as to build.[19] The housing market was one sphere in which the withdrawal of government was as politically astute as it was dramatic. Conservative policies enabled many of the better-off council tenants to become home-owners, who had the government to thank for a substantial increase in mortgage-interest tax relief.[20]

The Thatcher and Major governments also sought to insert market principles into services that remained in the public sector. Thus, for instance, the civil service was forced to behave less like a privileged corporate interest and more like a competitive business. Thatcher herself was convinced that a bloated bureaucracy was at the heart of many of government's woes in the 1970s, and she ruthlessly cut it down to size. Early in her first term, Sir Derek Rayner of Marks & Spencer was brought in to whip the civil service into shape. The efficiency reviews and redundancies that followed in his wake produced perhaps a billion in savings and a staff reduction of 20 per cent by 1987.[21] The government's *Next Steps* report of the following year recommended that the large majority of civil servants be assigned to a series of new executive agencies which would be given control over the grading, pay, and working conditions of their employees. By the mid-1990s, over 70 per cent of civil servants were working under the auspices of such agencies. By that time, a good many erstwhile central responsibilities had either been contracted out or transferred to the private sector, and the government agencies that handled the rest of them were obliged to set efficiency targets and to report on their progress in achieving them. Taken together, these reforms marked a cultural revolution in the civil service through which it was transformed from a coddled estate of the realm into just another business that was charged with the delivery of services.[22]

The third-term Thatcher government likewise sought to instil the consumerist ethos into basic and higher education. The landmark measure here was the 1988 Educational Reform Act. It established a national curriculum as well as nationwide testing of students at ages seven, eleven, and fourteen; transferred the management of school budgets from the Local Education Authorities to school governors; enabled individual schools to opt out of LEA control by applying for grant-maintained status; and gave parents greater freedom to choose which schools their children attended. While Conservatives insisted that the act was meant to encourage healthy competition and value for money, critics feared that it would create a more stratified system in which the schools towards the top of the league tables based on the nationwide tests became more selective, better endowed, and less accessible to students from underprivileged backgrounds, while the schools towards the bottom stagnated.[23]

The Educational Reform Act's provisions for higher education were equally sweeping and controversial. It wrested the polytechnics from the local authorities, ended academic tenure for new instructors, and tightened central control over the allocation of grant money to universities. Once again, the stated goal was to encourage competition. Thus the new Universities Funding Council was charged with the task of promoting value for money and enforcing tighter managerial principles, and given the power to impose contracts on universities in return for grants as a means of ensuring that these goals were met. Shortly thereafter, polytechnics were allowed to give themselves the title of universities, and to compete with their better-established counterparts for students and money through a Higher Education Funding Council. At the same time, the government initiated a dramatic round of higher educational expansion, so that the number of full-time students grew at an unprecedented rate, from 700,000 in 1988 to over a million by 1993. As the student population rose, so too did student–teacher ratios, teaching and research performance assessments, and other types of value-for-money pressures. This was expansion on the cheap, for public expenditure on higher education by no means kept pace with the growth of the student body. One inevitable result was that by the mid-1990s, universities were beginning to charge flat-rate fees to students and parents for the first time. More and more students were obliged to take out state-sponsored loans in order to cover living expenses, as local-authority maintenance grants dwindled and eventually disappeared.[24] In short, the market reforms of higher education have greatly enhanced access to the system, but have obliged students to foot some of the bill for their education and have divested universities and their faculties of much of their decision-making authority.

Value for money was also the driving force behind the market reforms of the National Health Service that were first initiated in 1989. These established a division between the purchasers and providers of public health care, the purchasers being the District Health Authorities and the GPs who opted to be given control over their own budgets, and the providers being the 300 or so Hospital Trusts whose expenses were to be closely monitored by business managers. At the same time, patients were required to pay for eye examinations, dental check-ups, and a higher percentage of escalating prescription charges to help relieve the Exchequer's rapidly growing health-care burden. Still, the NHS was spared the sort of deep cuts that the universities had to endure in the early 1980s, because the NHS remained a popular entitlement. There was considerable fear that the growing emphasis on financial constraints and managerial accountability was but a preliminary to full-blown privatization. But this would have been too politically risky, and in any case it made little sense to trade in a relatively cheap but generally adequate universal public health-care system for something like the American model – a private system that left too many people uninsured while furnishing admittedly first-rate care to the rest, but at vast expense.[25]

In sum, there is no question that the Thatcher and Major governments reshaped the postwar state in significant ways. They divested it of its role as a guarantor of full employment; took it out of its corporatist partnership with the unions and heavy industry; virtually did away with its ownership of the means of production and distribution; and greatly reduced its role as a provider of housing. Elsewhere, the Conservatives sought to enhance the efficiency of public institutions such as the civil service, the educational system, and the NHS by exposing them to competitive pressures. Thus the state was almost completely withdrawn from some spheres of activity in which it had figured prominently before 1979. In other spheres where it continued to make its presence felt, it now acted in accordance with a markedly different set of managerial assumptions.

The survival of the welfare state

It is nevertheless easy to exaggerate the extent of the Thatcherite 'revolution' in the state. For the Tories did not even come close to stripping the state of the extensive social-security responsibilities that had been given to it during the 'consensus' era. Indeed, they failed to reduce aggregate public spending, even though one of the first pronouncements of the Thatcher government in 1979 was that 'public expenditure is at the heart of Britain's present economic difficulties'.[26] It accounted for 43 per cent of GDP in that year, slowly shrank to 39 per cent in 1990, but climbed back up to 44.5 per cent in 1994. Thus, according to this most basic of measurements, the Tories did not succeed in 'rolling back' the state. If one factors out borrowing and the sale of assets, the public sector accounted for roughly 40 per cent of GDP in 1970, in 1980, in 1990, and in 2000, putting Britain halfway up the league table for the advanced industrial countries.[27] In other words, in recent decades aggregate public spending has been all but impervious to ideological shifts from one administration to the next.

The Tory governments, moreover, presided over a dramatic increase in social-security spending, the item of expenditure which they had been most adamant about pruning. In real terms, it grew by over 80 per cent between 1978 and 1996. Burgeoning unemployment benefits accounted for most of this increase, the price that the government was obliged to pay for a high rate of joblessness and part-time work. Social-security spending would have been even greater had the Tories not constantly tinkered with the terms of benefits so as to reduce their real value: making a number of them taxable, for instance; substantially reducing the value of old-age pensions; narrowing eligibility for short-term unemployment benefits; and transferring responsibility for the payment of sickness and maternity benefits from the government to employers.[28]

The Tories frequently justified these cost-containment exercises as means of promoting self-reliance and financial responsibility. Denying income support to 16–18-year-olds and reducing unemployment benefit for 18–25-year-olds, for instance, was intended to provide them with stronger incentives to seek work, and their parents with stronger incentives to support them out of family income. This same effort to encourage family 'responsibility' prompted the government to sponsor the landmark Child Support Act (1990). It sought to lower the rapidly mounting public cost of single parenthood in a society with a dis- turbingly high divorce rate by obliging all single mothers on income support to authorize the government to take legal action to coax maintenance payments out of the absent father.[29] By these and other measures the Tories sought to instil the virtues of self-reliance into a social-security system that had (allegedly) all too often compromised those virtues in the recent past.

Still, for a party whose leader was as outspoken in her condemna- tion of 'permissiveness' as she was in her praise of personal responsi- bility, the Tories did little to enforce a rigid standard of morality upon the governed. Tory right-wingers might have decried the moral revolution of the 1960s by which the Labour government legalized homosexuality and abortion and liberalized divorce, but they did not launch a counter-revolution. With the notable exception of the notori- ous Clause 28 of the 1988 Local Government Act, which prevented the use of public money for the dissemination of information about homosexual lifestyles, there was little effort to roll back the putative excesses of the 1960s and 1970s. Similarly, while the Conservatives' tight immigration controls and emphasis on law and order helped to fuel racial tensions, they made no direct attack on the civil-rights legislation of the 1960s.[30] Finally, in a country where by the early 1990s the divorce rate was seven times what it had been thirty years earlier, there were compelling reasons for lamenting the decline of two-parent families. Yet there was little effort to reverse that decline by legislative means.

Ultimately, there was only limited popular support for moral crusading in what remained a reasonably tolerant society. That sense of tolerance, tinctured by self-interest, proved to be one of social security's most important safeguards. Putting it simply, there was no Tory dismantling of the core services of the welfare state because most people, including a number of prominent Tory moderates, wanted to keep them – from the usual mixture of selfish and altruistic motives. By 1991, 65 per cent of those polled expressed their desire to see the government increase welfare spending even if it meant raising taxes. Not surprisingly, there was widespread public support for the protection of universal entitlements that were seen to provide obvious benefits to most people, such as state pensions and the NHS.[31] The enduring popularity of universal entitlements combined with a widespread conviction that the provision of a 'safety net' remained a crucial state responsibility to protect the Beveridgean system of social insurance. Thus in the early 1990s, through a combination of cash benefits and 'income in kind' (such as schooling for children), the state was still keeping an 'income floor' of £6,000–8,000 a year under the poorest third of the population. This 'floor' was largely paid for by contributions from taxpayers in the top half of the income table.[32]

Still, it is important to stress that while social security survived more or less intact, for the first time in a century the share of public expenditure devoted to it was no longer on the rise.[33] This was an impressive achievement, considering the very large increases in spending needed to pay for rising numbers of unemployment claims and the growing pension and medical costs associated with the greying of the population. Tory apologists could argue, with some justice, that the government had at least begun to exercise the fiscal restraint over welfare spending that would be necessary to avert bankruptcy in confronting social and economic trends over which it had little control: more elderly people, fewer stable families, and less job security in a global labour market.[34] But critics could just as compellingly stress some of the human costs associated with the Tory exercise in welfare containment, such as the growing personal expense of higher education; the great rise in NHS charges for prescription drugs; more extensive means-testing, most notably for long-term elderly care; and a serious decline in the value of state pensions that had been nowhere near subsistence level in the first place.[35]

This cost–benefit analysis of Tory policies can be extended into virtually every sphere of policy-making. Thus, for instance, inflation was brought under control, but unemployment remained stubbornly high. Output per head in manufacturing was substantially higher than it had been in the 1970s, but the flipside of efficiency was massive job-shedding and worker insecurity. Trade union legislation brought much-needed discipline to the labour market, but left many workers feeling defenceless in an era of remorseless downsizing. Average income grew, and with it visible marks of affluence such as overseas holidays. But the number of Britons whose incomes were low enough to make them eligible for income support skyrocketed. A strong pound and the deregulation of financial markets helped the City to thrive, but the high price of sterling hurt British exports. Huge brokers' fees and astronomical levels of executive pay were signs of the enhanced profitability of British firms, but one could easily see them as symbols of a short-sighted 'greed culture' that thrived on redundancies and comparatively low rates of long-term investment. Housing reform created a vast number of owner-occupiers, but rent increases and the shrinkage of council-housing stock doubtless contributed to one of the most striking developments of the era: widespread homelessness. For the first time in living memory, large numbers of young people could be seen sleeping rough in London and other major cities.

This balance-sheet suggests that the Tory governments presided over a society that was becoming increasingly unequal, and income statistics support this verdict. Generally speaking, the trend towards greater income equality established during World War II continued until the mid-1970s, at which point it was reversed. This new trend towards greater inequality accelerated considerably after the Tories entered office in 1979. By 1985, income inequality was greater than it had been at any time since 1949, and the wealthiest fifth of the population took a greater share of total income (over 43 per cent) than at any time since the war. Since then, income inequality has grown at a faster rate than in any other OECD country, with the possible exception of New Zealand, so that the United Kingdom now leads the European Union in this unfortunate category.[36]

A number of factors helped to explain this trend, but prominent among them was the dismissal of greater equality as a state goal. Job-shedding in the manufacturing sector, the growth of part-time work, more precarious conditions of employment for relatively low-skilled workers and the simultaneous acceleration of higher incomes:[37] these trends had much to do with capital flight to cheaper labour markets, corporate pressure to enhance dividends through 'flexible' labour practices, the growing demand for technical expertise, and a host of other factors that stem from economic globalization. But government policies accelerated these trends in important respects – through the abolition of wage councils and the statutory weakening of trade unions, for instance, and even more noticeably through reforms in the structure of taxes and benefits. Income differentials in Britain would have widened considerably over the last twenty years even if the distribution of taxes and benefits had not changed. But enormous cuts in the top rate of income tax and substantial cuts in the standard rate have combined with large increases in indirect tax (most notably VAT) and the gradual elimination of the Treasury's contribution to the National Insurance Fund to widen the income gap that much further. Thus it has been estimated that if the 1978–9 tax and benefit structure had still been in place in 1994–5, the poorest tenth of the population would have been 40 per cent better off in terms of final income than they ended up being. 'Only the richest tenth of the population gained unambiguously from the intervening tax and benefit changes.' The regressive impact of these discretionary changes to the tax and benefit system was partly offset by the movement of many earners into higher income-tax bands at a time when most people in regular employment were enjoying pay increases. But the dramatic shift from direct to indirect taxation limited the effect of this automatically 'progressive' mechanism.[38] In any case, it was abundantly clear after the tax cuts of 1988, from which the top 1 per cent of taxpayers reaped a greater dividend than the bottom 70 per cent combined, that the government had abandoned the notion that the state should make active use of progressive taxation as a means of promoting greater equality.[39] By the end of the decade, it was obvious that the only people who were paying far less in taxes than they had at the beginning of it were the very rich. This marked the decisive reversal of a progressive trend that predated World War I.[40]

Blatantly regressive tax reforms, the tightening up of Income Support at a time of high unemployment, a Salvation Army study which estimated that on one night in 1989 there were 75,000 'overtly homeless' people in London alone (most of them put up in hostels and cheap bed-and-breakfasts, many of them living in squats, and 10 per cent of them sleeping rough):[41] such facts suggested to many observers that the Tories were seeking to use the mechanisms of state to promote market individualism at the expense of social justice. 'You know, there's no such thing as society', Thatcher famously declared. She went on to say that 'it's our duty to look after ourselves and then, also, to look after our neighbour.' But it was telling that she reserved no room for the state within this minimalist framework of social provision.[42] Of course, the state's contribution to social provision was still enormous compared to what it had been in the mid-Victorian era. But in extolling the rugged individualism and entrepreneurial spirit of that era, in their less guarded moments the Thatcherites seemed to be harking back to an age when most 'respectable' people still felt that state-sponsored income redistribution was unproductive and unjust.

Strengthening the centre

The Thatcherites, however, were anything but Victorian in their enthusiasm for concentrating power in the hands of the central government. Indeed, the avowedly libertarian Tory governments of the 1980s and 1990s showed even less respect for the autonomy of secondary institutions than the Labour governments of 1945–51 that established the welfare state.[43] As Andrew Gamble has pointed out, this is less paradoxical than it might seem at first glance. For, according to the Tories, it required a 'strong' central government to attempt to 'free' the economy from the massive programme of state intervention fostered by the centralizing reforms of the Attlee era, and to free the state itself from the endless rounds of sectional interest brokerage that had eroded its authority over the intervening decades.[44] Thus, many of the market-oriented reforms we have already examined involved major transfers of power from periphery to centre. Producers' groups were stripped of much of their political clout. Privatization led to the proliferation of regulatory quangos that were appointed directly by the government. Public-sector professionals in the NHS and the universities were divested of much of their autonomy. Whitehall itself was subjected to 'quasi-market' reforms, efficiency testing, and downsizing. But the secondary institution that suffered the most drastic reduction of power was local government.

We have already noted that the reforms of the 1980s greatly reduced local authorities' role in the provision of housing. We have also seen that the 1988 Education Act imposed more uniform curricula on Local Education Authorities, took the polytechnics out of their hands, and enabled individual schools to opt out of LEA supervision. These measures were simply one part of the Thatcher government's multi-faceted campaign to force local authorities, especially big-spending councils under Labour control, to cut back on their far-flung commitments. Labour had already begun to scale back the level of grant support to local government during the fiscal crisis of the mid-1970s, but their Tory successors greatly accelerated this trend. They quickly pushed through legislation that permitted the central government to curtail grants to any local authority that spent beyond a standardized level. Local spending continued to rise nevertheless, mainly in response to cuts in central subsidies. So the government's next step was to cap the rates of 'spendthrift' councils.

Rate-capping was an unprecedented centralizing measure of great constitutional significance, for local authorities had been free to set their own rates since the sixteenth century. It greatly intensified a feud between the parliamentary majority and Labour-dominated councils that ended in the mid-1980s with the capping of eighteen of them. After winning that argument, the government abolished the local authorities that had given it the most trouble, the Greater London Council and the six other metropolitan counties. Their responsibilities were transferred to lower-tier authorities and to a complex array of government-appointed quangos. The abolition of democratically elected local governments and their replacement by central appointees was a most naked display of parliamentary sovereignty. Whatever the excesses of the municipal 'loony left' that was thus sent packing, opinion polls made it clear that most Britons regarded this as a disturbingly undemocratic manoeuvre.[45]

After its victory in the rate-capping battle, the parliamentary majority moved to replace the rates with the so-called community charge. This was accurately labelled a poll tax by its opponents, for it sought to supplant the rates – progressive taxes on the value of property from which a great many people on low incomes had been exempt – with a new tax on local services to be levied on every adult. The government's main argument on behalf of the poll tax was a communitarian one: that everyone who enjoyed the right to vote in local elections ought to pay for the support of local services. But a great many Britons felt that the tax was an affront to communitarian values, for it obliged people on low incomes to pay the same annual flat rate (estimated at an average of about £350 in 1990) as the affluent people who lived three streets away. The introduction of the poll tax in Scotland in 1989 and in England and Wales the following year inspired widespread civil disobedience; there were street demonstrations all over the country, and many people simply refused to pay. Ultimately, the government had no choice but to abandon it. The most widely unpopular measure of the Thatcher years, the poll tax prompted serious concern about the accelerating pace of centralization, particularly in Scotland, where a government that enjoyed negligible support had foisted it on people who were adamantly opposed to it.[46] But the demise of the poll tax did virtually nothing to swing the pendulum back towards local control. For under the Major administration, local spending caps remained and were made even more uniform. The new council tax, an amalgam of the poll tax and the old rating system that mandated universal contributions but on progressive lines, paid for only a fifth of all local expenditure.[47] Most of the rest was paid by the Treasury, giving it greater financial control over local government than it had ever had in the past. Thus, while the late Victorians had been staunch advocates of local discretion and local finance, their descendants a century later could well wonder what purpose local government served in a system that was dominated by Westminster and Whitehall.

While the Tory governments greatly enhanced the central government's power to discipline recalcitrant local authorities, they also enhanced its power to discipline society through a series of law-and-order measures that sought to fight crime and to promote national security. Widespread fears that the crime rate was spiralling out of control prompted the Tories to spend much more than their predecessors had done on the expansion of police forces, on police pay rises, and on prison construction. At the same time, the police were granted new powers to search for and seize evidence, to arrest, detain, identify, and interrogate suspects, and to control crowds. Serious riots in Brixton and Toxteth in 1981 convinced many Britons of the need for tougher standards of law and order. But they convinced many others that the police were not in the habit of dispensing equal justice to racial minorities, and that for this and other reasons their powers needed to be more strictly monitored and possibly narrowed rather than broadened. But under the Tories, the Home Office was all for broadening them, and the American-style 'zero tolerance' mentality that prevailed there under Major's home secretary, Michael Howard, gave birth to the police bill of 1994, which would have made it unnecessary for police and customs officers to obtain a judge's warrant before entering and secretly bugging premises in their search for evidence related to serious crimes. While prior permission was saved by the amending process, Howard's bill prompted critics from across the political spectrum to express their fears that the government was compromising civil liberties in its zeal to fight crime.[48]

Fears simultaneously grew that its efforts to protect official secrecy were jeopardizing freedom of expression. Citing national security concerns, the Thatcher governments prosecuted eleven civil servants for alleged violations of the terms of the Official Secrets Act (1911), a far higher prosecution rate than any of its recent peacetime predecessors. Its own Official Secrets Act of 1989 was no less sweeping than its notoriously broad predecessor. It excluded the 'public interest' as an admissible defence for public servants who sought to reveal evidence of government malfeasance, and broadened the Security Service's powers to intercept communications – just as the collapse of the Communist bloc was bringing to an end the Cold War era of espionage. Meanwhile, the BBC and ITV were strongly pressured to censor or cancel programmes that were seen to embarrass the service, while the government embarked on an extraordinary legal campaign to suppress published allegations of MI5 dirty-tricks campaigns and a possible 'shoot to kill' policy in Northern Ireland.[49]

The narrowing of civil liberties, the decline of local government, the extension of police powers, the fixation on official secrecy: by the late 1980s, such developments were inspiring serious calls for constitutional reform. New opposition groups such as Charter 88 began to insist that the proper antidote to what they perceived to be the Thatcher government's authoritarian tendencies was a written constitution, a bill of rights that formally defined and defended basic civil liberties, and an electoral reform that would make the Commons majority more responsive to the will of the majority of voters. Few people outside activist circles were as yet willing to contemplate such sweeping changes to the British political tradition. But a good many of them were beginning to feel that the parliamentary sovereignty revered by their ancestors was now deeply problematic. For the combination of strict party discipline, the government's domination of the Westminster agenda, the decline of parliamentary scrutiny, and the unchallengeable status of parliamentary statute had combined to create what in 1976 Lord Hailsham memorably labelled an 'elective dictatorship', in which the sovereignty of parliament really meant the sovereignty of the majority in the House of Commons.[50] Thanks to Britain's first-past-the-post electoral system, that majority was now typically brought to power by a minority of the voting public, and was only directly answerable to that public at the next general election. Hailsham had identified the system's 'central defects' as 'the absolute powers we confer on our sovereign body, and the concentration of those powers in an executive government formed out of one party which may not fairly represent the popular will'.[51] But as lord chancellor in a Tory government that won a commanding majority in the Commons on a mere 43 per cent of the vote and sought to use that majority decisively to change the direction of British politics, he was, as he later said, 'given no remit to carry through constitutional changes of any kind'.[52]

It is perhaps not too outlandish to suggest that during the 1980s the prime minister and the cabinet that directed the Commons majority exercised a sovereignty that was nearly as absolute as that which the monarch had possessed three centuries earlier. The only formal check

on their power was the notion of a government-in-waiting to be furnished from the Commons opposition, but that opposition was now
so weak and divided that it did not present a viable alternative.[53] Of
course, the monarchy and the Lords had long since ceased to exercise
any meaningful influence over the elected government, and that was
the way virtually everybody wanted it. While the peers could still occasionally make significant use of their amending powers, their veto
powers were now minimal, and in any case most peers were political
appointees who had few quarrels with a sitting government. Thanks
to relentless media coverage, the royal family was more conspicuous
to Britons than it had ever been before. But the monarch's political
influence was of course now virtually nil, to everyone's satisfaction.
The House of Windsor still exercised a useful public role as a charitable institution, as an emblem of cultural distinctiveness, and as a
tourist attraction.[54] But the endless accounts of petty jealousy and
marital strife within it made it the most conspicuous dysfunctional
family in Britain, an object of strong but merely prurient interest. The
symbolic significance of the Lords and the monarchy was still capable
of inspiring passionate debate in an old country that was weighing the
prospect of constitutional renewal. But this was a debate about symbolic status, not about real political power, which was now virtually
monopolized by the government of the day.

While that power was as yet scarcely challenged from within, it was
being limited from without by two related factors: the globalization of
the economy and European integration. The Tories unanimously
welcomed the former, but disagreed so bitterly about the latter as to
threaten the party's future viability. Two of the more overworked
truisms in contemporary life are that national economies are ever
more closely interconnected in ever more complicated ways, and that
these interconnections have limited states' ability to control economic
developments within their own borders. A number of factors have
contributed to the decline of economic 'manageability':[55] the ever-rising
volume of international trade; the growth of multinational corporations
that have the power to extract generous concessions from governments
that are trying to attract investment; the expansion of international
credit markets that are not readily influenced by the decisions of central
banks; the revolution in information technology, which has greatly
increased the mobility of capital and facilitated international specula-
tion against national currencies; and the decline of exchange-rate stability, particularly since the weakening of the dollar as an international
reserve currency in the 1970s. All of these trends have encouraged
western governments to shift their emphases from macroeconomic
'controls', the protection of jobs, and the enhancement of entitlement

programmes to the promotion of greater competitiveness through inflation control, privatization, leaner welfare budgets, and the encouragement of more flexible labour markets – all of which are seen as weapons in an intense international competition for inward investment.[56] Thus globalization has seriously reduced states' ability to 'steer' their economies. But this particular loss of state power was one that the Thatcherites actually welcomed. They saw globalization as a means of *restoring* the state's ability to govern, which they felt had been dangerously compromised by the ineffectual economic interest brokerage of the 1960s and 1970s. For the putative logic of globalization – that there was 'no alternative' to fiscal restraint, low inflation, widespread job-shedding, and weakened trade unions – furnished them with a potent economic argument for the retreat of the state from an exposed political position.

The Conservative governments were thus eager to facilitate the decline of the state's power to influence the economy that globalization portended. But they were reluctant to cede even the slightest bit of its power to the European Community, which in 1994 was rechristened the European Union. It was clear from the outset that the Thatcher administration, like its predecessors, viewed EC membership as little more than an unavoidable necessity. Indeed, the new prime minister's most prominent 'European' ambition was to reduce Britain's annual contribution to the EC budget. This was a fight worth making, for the British contribution was disproportionately large, and much of it went to supporting the CAP, which privileged continental farmers at the expense of British consumers. Ultimately, Thatcher won her 'British rebate', but the truculence with which she had conducted her campaign suggested to continental political leaders that she was not about to compromise what she deemed to be Britain's national interests in order to promote closer European integration.[57] Her defiance became abundantly clear in the wake of the Single European Act (1986), through which EC member states committed themselves to the reduction of frontier controls and the virtual elimination of impediments to the free movement of capital and labour within the Community. The Thatcher government readily signed on, but it should have been obvious even at the time that this push towards closer economic integration was bound to affect national policies in a variety of spheres, such as taxation, business practices, and workers' rights.

The 'sovereignty' debate did not intensify until 1988, however, when plans were unveiled for the creation of a European Central Bank and the eventual introduction of a single currency through the agency of the European Monetary System, established in the late 1970s as a means of promoting exchange-rate stability. That same year, EC president

Jacques Delors started to promote the idea of a Social Charter (later renamed a Social Chapter) of minimum workers' and citizens' rights in spheres such as workplace health and safety, environmental protection, and gender equality. Delors publicly predicted that in a decade's time 80 per cent of all economic, financial, and social legislation pertaining to member states was likely to be formulated by the EC itself. In response, Thatcher famously declared that 'we have not successfully rolled back the frontiers of the state in Britain only to see them reimposed at a European level, with a European super-state exercising a new dominance from Brussels'.[58] As time went on, Thatcher's hostility to the idea of closer integration became increasingly outspoken, and her party became seriously divided between 'Eurosceptics' and Tories who felt that closer cooperation made good practical sense. Ultimately, the internal divisions over Europe, combined with the poll-tax controversy and skyrocketing interest rates, led to Thatcher's downfall. The resignation of her foreign secretary, Sir Geoffrey Howe, on the European question triggered a leadership challenge that forced her own resignation in November 1990.[59]

The Tory controversy over Europe only grew more heated after Thatcher's departure, however. Her successor, John Major, strove to find a middle ground that in his words would put 'Britain at the heart of Europe' whilst reassuring the Eurosceptics that he would not move very far in a European direction. In the short term, this strategy seemed to pay off, for Major won plaudits at home when he returned from the Maastricht conference of December 1991 with concessions: an 'opt-out' clause which permitted Britain to make up its own mind at its own pace as to whether or when to commit to the European single currency, scheduled to come into being in 1999; and a similar 'opt-out' on the Social Chapter, which guaranteed certain workers' rights, including a minimum wage. But triumph turned to disaster on 'Black Wednesday', 16 September 1992, when a massive run on sterling led to its *de facto* devaluation by forcing the government to pull Britain out of the Exchange Rate Mechanism (ERM) of the European Monetary System less than two years after it had finally joined. Up to that point, the Major administration had been adamant about the need to preserve the pound's value by keeping it within the established bands of the ERM, even after it had become obvious that these bands significantly overvalued the pound in relation to the Deutschmark. Thus the abandonment of ERM was a spectacular reversal of policy, which quickly led to much higher levels of public borrowing and taxation, tainted the Tories' reputation for sound financial management, compromised Major's leadership credentials, and made the Eurosceptics all the more insistent that economic integration should go no further.[60]

From that point, the Tory crisis over Europe only deepened. The most divisive issue was whether or not Britain should enter into the EU's common currency, the 'Euro'. Its proponents argued that entry would promote investment, enhance consumption, and lead to lower interest rates and consumer prices all round. Critics retorted that the common currency would impose an economic straitjacket on a set of very diverse European economies by divesting them of power to set their own exchange and interest rates; that it would inevitably oblige the British government to raise taxes in order to bring UK tax levels in line with those of other member states; and that it would take the EU one step closer to political federation.[61]

The debate over the common currency was not restricted to the Tory party. It was plain to many observers, for instance, that European Monetary Union (EMU) would require market reforms that were bound to cause serious disruptions in continental countries whose economies had not been 'liberalized' to the same extent as Britain's. There was a real possibility that British taxpayers would have to foot part of the bill for easing high levels of regional unemployment else-where – a sort of insurance premium to be paid in expectation of the widespread economic growth that was supposed to follow from closer integration, but which nobody could guarantee. EMU was thus fraught with uncertainty, and even the Labour party, now avowedly pro-European, was in no hurry to commit to it. There were other good reasons to hesitate on the march towards closer integration as well, most noticeably the conspicuous 'democratic deficit' within the EU. The lion's share of the EU's legislative authority remained concentrated in the hands of the bureaucrats of the European Commission, who never had to face voters. While the Commission is nominally subordinate to the Council of Ministers that is composed of the heads of member governments, and while the democratically elected European Parliament has managed to assume broader authority for itself in recent years, the Commission is still a most formidable but not properly accountable institution.[62]

Within Tory circles, at least, these misgivings were not as prominent as those over the ever more noticeable cession of parliamentary sovereignty that was required to play by the EU's rules. A party whose majority in the Commons had vested the central government with unprecedented powers could not abide the possibility that those powers might be significantly reduced by decisions taken in Brussels (by the European Commission), Strasbourg (by the European Parliament), or The Hague (by the European Court of Justice). 'Sovereignty' remained a fixation with the Tories because many of them simply denied its right to exist anywhere other than Westminster. Thus Howe had to remind his colleagues in his resignation speech that, unlike virginity, sovereignty was not a simple question of 'now you had it, now you did not'.[63] Indeed, one of the stronger arguments to be made on behalf of closer European integration is that it is a means of *preserving* sovereignty, by turning the heart of Europe into a formidable bloc with enhanced power to compete in a global economy that is challenging *national* sovereignty in so many ways. Rather than a portent of the inevitable decline of the nation-state or the germ of a federal super-state, then, it makes sense to see the EU chiefly as a means of shoring up the economic foundations of member states through the pooling of common risks.[64] But building the foundational supports will continue to require a sharing of sovereignty that is antithetical to the British constitutional tradition and to its staunchest guardians in the Conservative party.

New Labour in power

In 1997, while the Conservatives were at odds with themselves on the doctrinal question of sovereignty and much else besides, a Labour party that had stripped itself of its doctrinal baggage handed them their worst electoral defeat since 1832. This last section on 'New' Labour in power is intentionally brief, because Tony Blair's administration is still a work in progress and because an historical overview is not a good place to speculate about the future. But three things seem clear enough at the time of writing. The first is that the Conservatives' reduction of the state's economic commitments and containment of its welfare commitments are not likely to be reversed any time soon. The second is that their centralization of state power may be gradually reversed. The third is that regardless of these recent trends, the British state is still far more centralized and far more extensively involved in the lives of its citizens at the start of the twenty-first century than it was before the outbreak of World War II.

Conservative electoral success led to the 'modernization' of the Labour party by which it committed most of its interventionist tenets to the ideological scrap-heap. It was already obvious by the mid-1980s that the Tories had succeeded in giving interventionism a bad name among the moderate voters who decide the outcome of national elections. As a result, the jettisoning of 'socialist' principles was already well under way when Tony Blair assumed the leadership of the party, although the decisiveness and public-relations savvy with which he set about the task helped to assure Middle England that Labour could once again be entrusted with power. New Labour renounced demand management, corporatism, public ownership, a sociological approach to crime prevention, and higher taxes. They did not take back their words after entering office.

Thus the Blair government continued to insist that demand management had paid too little regard to the damaging consequences of inflation, and that in any case it was ineffective in a global economy in which the movement of capital cannot be controlled by national governments. It also insisted that fiscal discipline and a low-tax regime were essential for long-term growth. Gordon Brown, the chancellor of the Exchequer, granted the Bank of England a sort of quasi-independence in the setting of interest rates, committed the government to a 2.5 per cent inflation target, and promised that in the short term there would be no tax or spending increases. Indeed, he cut the basic rate of income tax to its lowest level in seventy years, whilst government spending as a percentage of GDP was headed for its lowest level in forty.[65] This was obviously a much leaner financial regime than the free-spending one over which Labour had presided in the 1970s, and there was no sign that the Blair administration intended to go on a spending spree in the foreseeable future.

There was likewise no sign of a return to seventies-style corporatism. It is true that the New Labour government sponsored legislation to facilitate trade-union recognition, consolidated into British law the Social Chapter of the EU's Maastricht Treaty that acknowledged basic workers' rights, and established Britain's first statutory minimum wage. This last was an especially important achievement, for it fulfilled a century-old goal of the union movement, and has helped to bring up wages in low-paid sectors of the economy. But these reforms did not herald a return to the cosy partnership of the 1970s. New Labour retained most of the statutory restrictions that their Conservative predecessors had imposed on the unions, acknowledging that these had helped to diminish restrictive labour practices and to shield the government from charges of interest brokerage on the unions' behalf. It also showed no intention of returning any of the privatized industries to public ownership, despite the expressed wishes of union leaders. Indeed, New Labour stressed the benefits of wage restraint, flexible labour markets, the private sector, and the importance of all three in creating jobs. Economic expansion brought unemployment levels to their lowest point in twenty years. But the widespread emphasis on short-term profitability, job-shedding, and just-in-time production prompted considerable insecurity among a wide variety of workers. Many of them organized in response; union membership was on the rise for the first time since Thatcher had taken office. New

Labour's adherence to market principles did little to reassure the unions that the government was squarely on their side. An atmosphere of mutual wariness prevailed, in which both sides began to question the utility of the historic institutional ties between them.

New Labour pledged itself to job creation. But it repeatedly emphasized that in a mature economy facing intense global competition, the best way to add jobs was to create a comparative advantage in high value-added sectors by promoting long-term investment in technology and advanced training. It was not entirely clear how a government that had committed itself to low taxes and financial stringency would be able to meet these goals without resorting to just the sort of 'steering' and big spending that it found so distasteful. What its fiscal austerity meant in the short term, at least, was the abolition of maintenance grants to university students and the charging of tuition fees for the first time ever. Budgetary restraint was also a motive force for welfare reform. Few people argued with New Labour's conviction that the welfare system should be seeking to move people out of idleness and into jobs. Their 'welfare-to-work' initiative, which provided incentives for employers to hire young people off the dole, was a promising start. But critics pointed out that the compulsory nature of 'workfare' marked a significant step away from the notion that it was the state's responsibility to make an effort to provide all of its citizens either with work or with maintenance, and suspected that this responsibility would not easily be restored during the next serious recession, when even energetic job-seekers were likely to have difficulty finding work.

In marked contrast with the Tories, New Labour extolled the virtues of social justice and communitarianism. In pursuit of these ideals, the Blair administration has restored the topping up of low incomes as a policy goal, chiefly through the minimum wage and through the grant of substantial tax credits to poor families. But it was significant that the government played down these measures and continually insisted that it did not seek greater equality of outcome.[66] Worried about tarnishing its neo-liberal credentials, it was loath to admit that its quiet efforts on behalf of low-income support were a significant departure from Tory practice.

New Labour was far more outspoken in its commitment to a series of constitutional reforms which made it clear that they intended to disperse much of the power of the central government that the Tories had so resolutely built up. The Blair administration promised a widespread programme of constitutional reform that was advertised as an antidote to the putative excesses of Thatcherite centralization. Devolution in Northern Ireland, Scotland, and Wales, a more welcoming attitude towards the EU, the restoration of democratic government to London, reform of the House of Lords: all of these measures had the potential to disaggregate power and to diminish the notion of absolute parliamentary sovereignty in ways that would have been inconceivable under the Tories. But what their long-term consequences will be is anyone's guess.

The results of devolution are at once the most difficult to predict and the most likely to be dramatic. Devolutionist sentiment in Scotland and Wales, rebuffed in the referenda of 1978, grew stronger during the 1980s and 1990s. Conservative policies did much to encourage it. A series of liberal market reforms fell with particular force on these regions, which still relied on heavily unionized manufacturing industries. Regional assistance started to dry up just as the manufacturing sector fell into deep recession. Meanwhile, it was widely perceived in Scotland that the British government was not devoting a sufficient amount of North Sea oil revenue to Scottish purposes. The 'democratic deficit' became increasingly noticeable, as Tory governments that enjoyed precious little electoral support either in Scotland or in Wales experimented with the poll tax on the former and foisted many quangos on the latter. As popular sentiment grew ever more hostile to the centralizing ways of Westminster, the Labour party endorsed devolution, which the Scottish Nationalist party and Plaid Cymru welcomed as a step towards independence.

Whether New Labour's measures of devolution will strengthen or weaken the Union is an open question. The ultimate fate of devolution in Northern Ireland is still very much up in the air. A power-sharing arrangement between Protestants and Catholics that finally promised to end thirty years of Troubles and to pave the way for a peaceful resolution of the tortured question of Ulster's political destiny was enshrined in the Good Friday Agreement of 1998. But full implementation of the agreement is predicated on taking the guns out of the hands of the paramilitaries, and power-sharing could come to grief if decommissioning is not carried out in a manner that is acceptable to all parties. The outlook for Scotland and Wales is by no means as dangerously uncertain as it still appears to be for Northern Ireland, but it is just as unpredictable. The powers of the new Scottish parliament and Welsh assembly are carefully limited. Only the former has been given the power to raise taxes, and the Westminster parliament still enjoys primary control in Wales and Scotland over economic policy, social security, employment legislation, defence and foreign affairs, security and border controls. It also retains its formal sovereignty, in the sense that neither of the devolved legislatures have been vested with statutory authority to declare independence. On the other hand, they have both been given considerable discretionary powers over such diverse matters as education, public health, law and order, the environment, local government, and transport. They also enjoy an important measure of control over public spending – both of them through the power to allocate block grants, and the Scottish parliament through its power to impose a 'tartan tax', as well. Devolution is a truly novel exercise in power-sharing, and jurisdictional disputes are bound to arise over a host of issues. Whether the parties involved will be able to settle into a smooth working relationship remains to be seen. If they are, then the United Kingdom will offer compelling proof that the nation-state is compatible with a multi-tiered notion of sovereignty. It undoubtedly helps that New Labour have committed themselves to just such a notion of sovereignty, not only through devolution, but through their efforts to cultivate a more amicable relationship with the European Union, which is probably helping to sustain the United Kingdom by pumping a considerable amount of development money into Scotland and Wales. Thus, power-sharing and 'pooled' sovereignty may well be the order of the day. On the other hand, it may not be. If Westminster and the new legislatures cannot find ways to get along with each other, separatist sentiment is bound to grow, particularly in Scotland, where the SNP has emerged as a formidable party, and the result could be the break-up of Britain.

One of the chief goals of devolution was to make government more accountable to regional voters. This was a goal that New Labour pursued in England, as well. Precisely how it was to be achieved remained to be seen. One option that enjoyed considerable support was the creation of English regional assemblies that would be vested with many of the same responsibilities that have been devolved to Scotland and Wales. Whatever the outcome, it seems clear that New Labour will preside over a significant dispersal of the central government's responsibilities to the English regions. Moreover, it committed itself to reversing the most dramatic centralizing gesture of the Thatcher era, the abolition of the democratically elected Greater London Council. A new Greater London Authority has recently come into being, which is to work in partnership with an elected mayor. Thus, while the central government still possesses immense power over local authorities, the early signs indicate that we may be witnessing the first stage in the reversal of the century-long centralizing trend that has stripped local government of so much of its discretionary authority. Still, there was an increasingly noticeable tension between the Blair government's rhetorical commitment to the disaggregation of political power and its increasingly blatant efforts to retain control of the political agenda. This tension was perhaps most obvious in the extraordinary lengths it went

to in its failed effort to prevent the 'old Labour' dissident Ken Living-
stone from winning London's first mayoral election.

New Labour's ambivalence about the dispersal of power was
scarcely less noticeable in its proposed reform of the House of Lords.
One goal here was to modernize the constitution by taking away the
voting privileges of the hereditary peers. But it is not yet clear whether
the members of the new upper chamber will end up being democratically elected, appointed by the government, or some combination of
the two. An appointed chamber would be a super-quango that would
permit the majority in the Commons to do whatever it pleased, while
an elected chamber would be certain to pose a more formidable obsta-
cle to the Commons majority than the present House of Lords. It is difficult to imagine that any government with a commanding majority in
the Commons would voluntarily create trouble for itself by legislating
a purely elected upper house into existence. Yet it is still possible that
New Labour will ultimately feel compelled to do so in order to live up
to its stated commitment to democratization, just as it may find itself
compelled to endorse some measure of proportional representation. It
seems less likely, however, that New Labour's stated commitment to
constitutional modernization will lead to significantly more 'open' government; its freedom of information legislation seemed destined to
leave the government with a great deal of discretion over the release
of information to the public. Whatever the outcome, however, the
important point is that New Labour showed itself willing to approach
several constitutional issues in ways that at least had the potential to
place significant checks on the central government's 'elective dictatorship'. There were increasingly noticeable limits to New Labour's
commitment to constitutional reform. But that it was even willing to
consider reform set it apart from its predecessors.

Conclusion

Let us conclude with a brief overview of British state development over the last three centuries. The main point is that there has been a dramatic broadening of the state's functions over this long period, and particularly over the past century. As late as the high-Victorian era, Britons entrusted the central and local authorities with only a small handful of responsibilities: defending the realm, preserving the peace, preventing destitution, paving, lighting, and cleaning the streets, providing a bare minimum of workplace and sanitary regulation. Today, Britons pay a far higher volume of taxes in exchange for a far broader range of services, such as universal education, old-age pensions, unemployment insurance, health care, welfare benefits and affordable housing for low-income families, job-training, industrial development, and comprehensive town planning. The reaction against the perceived excesses of the welfare state over the past couple of decades has checked the hitherto dramatic growth in the scope of state services. But that scope remains far broader than it was on the eve of World War II, and demographic trends and the relative popularity of many entitlement programmes suggest that there will be no return to the limited social-service state of the interwar years, much less the 'nightwatchman state' of the mid-Victorian era.

Certainly there will be no return to the conditions of the eighteenth century, when the mounting scope and expense of warfare in an age of imperial rivalry ensured that the traditional military function of the state would dominate all others. We have seen that while public spending grew dramatically between 1688 and 1815, the vast majority of that spending was devoted to military purposes. Army and naval expenditure combined with debt service never accounted for less than 85 per cent of net central government expenditure during any wartime period between 1700 and 1815. Even during intervals of peace, defence spending remained three to four times greater than spending on civil purposes, and it required 45 to 60 per cent of the annual peacetime budget to pay the interest on a national debt that had been bloated by chronic warfare.[1] One need only note the growing cost of the poor law and the proliferation of turnpikes and canals to see that the latter half of the Georgian era saw a dramatic broadening of the functions of local authorities. But these functions were far narrower than they would be a century later, and the cost of providing them was far less than the cost of maintaining the war machine.

That cost was of course a much smaller burden to the mid-Victorians than it had been to their Georgian forebears. The 'Pax Britannica' after 1815, along with Britain's economic supremacy, brought an enormous windfall to British taxpayers, and most of this 'peace dividend' stayed in their pockets. As late as 1890, central government expenditure as a percentage of GNP was only two-thirds what it had been on the eve of the French Revolutionary War.[2] While it is much more difficult to measure, there is no doubt that local-government spending was considerably more buoyant. Still, it can hardly be said that either central or local authorities were in a hurry to transform the traditional framework of governance in response to the social ills inflicted by unprecedented population expansion and urban–industrial development. Poor-law expenditure, for instance, was lower in the 1870s than it had been in the 1810s, even if one does not factor in the buoyant demographic growth of the intervening decades.[3] Factory and sanitary legislation was fiercely contested, often defeated, mostly discretionary, and by no means always enthusiastically taken up at the local level. State intervention remained the exception rather than the rule because most Victorians felt that 'good government' was necessarily cheap, that local autonomy was sacred, that centralization was potentially corrupt, and that social reform was no more important than the protection of legitimate propertied interests.

For a number of reasons, central and local responsibilities finally did broaden dramatically during the thirty years prior to the Great War. The 'discovery' of chronic poverty through social investigation and journalistic exposés; the erosion of a moralistic notion of poverty even within the workhouse system; fear of the 'residuum'; a widespread obsession with the need to promote 'national efficiency'; the (largely inaccurate) elite perception that the new mass electorate expected and would be appeased by a more activist approach to social reform: all of these factors help to explain why by 1914 the authorities were providing public services that had scarcely been dreamt of a generation earlier, such as limited unemployment and health insurance, old-age pensions, public housing, and industrial arbitration. At a time of growing imperial rivalry and unprecedented arms races, these new social responsibilities of the state were inextricably connected with its traditional military ones; the martial reasons for promoting 'public fitness' were no less obvious than the more altruistic reasons for doing so. As the state's responsibilities grew, its cost mounted. Central expenditure doubled between 1894 and 1902, and the end of the Boer War brought little relief to hard-pressed taxpayers, who had to foot the bill for the intensifying naval rivalry with Germany. The looming fiscal crisis of the state prompted the central government to shift the revenue balance towards direct taxation, and also obliged it to assume a growing portion of a burden that the localities could no longer carry on their own. By 1910, local authorities were receiving more of their income from central grants and loans than they were from the rates, and central control of local finances has been tightening ever since.

In Britain, as elsewhere in the West, the first three-quarters of the twentieth century witnessed an unprecedented acceleration in the scope and cost of the state. Public spending as a percentage of GDP grew from 13 per cent in 1900 to 46 per cent by 1979. The standard rate of income tax increased by a factor of ten over the same interval, and the ratio of public-sector receipts to GDP by a factor of four. Even though Britain participated in two world wars during this era, the state's military role had been decisively subordinated to its welfare role by the end of it. While defence spending fell from 46 per cent to 10 per cent of total public expenditure between 1900 and 1979, social spending grew from under 18 per cent to over 52 per cent.[4] By the second half of the century, Britons had good reason to perceive the state as first and foremost a provider of social services, and to assume, for better or worse, that the lion's share of those services were managed by Whitehall rather than the town hall; by the mid-1970s, less than a fifth of local-authority income came from the rates.[5]

What accounted for this remarkable shift in the role and the dimensions of the state? Perhaps the most obvious factor is the ratcheting effect of the two world wars on the cost of government and on Britons' tolerance of state interference in their lives. We have seen that the need to wage total war twice over greatly increased the fiscal capacities of the state, and that those capacities were by no means cut back to prewar levels once hostilities had ended. We have likewise seen that the wartime emergencies gave a legitimacy to forms and degrees of government intervention that were hitherto unacceptable, and encouraged the notion that social security was a right which the state owed to its patriotic and longsuffering citizens. It is nevertheless possible to exaggerate the impact of warfare on the growth of the state's social-service function. The principle of state provision of certain types of social insurance was already well established before 1914, while the growth of social services was at its most buoyant during two intervals of peace, roughly 1920–35 and 1948–68. The broadening of social insurance in the former era owed less to the notion that wartime patriotism ought to be rewarded than it did to the need to take the sting out of mass unemployment. In the latter era, welfare expansion owed more to economic growth and bureaucratic incrementalism than it did to the egalitarian spirit of the Blitz, which was probably neither as strong nor as durable as historians once made it out to be. The redistributive mechanisms of the postwar welfare state saw to it that the standard of living of the poorest more or less kept pace with rising affluence. But the welfare state's attendants neither sought nor inadvertently achieved much in the way of greater 'equality of outcome'.

If it is easy to exaggerate the scope and implicit ambitions of the 'classic' welfare state, it is no less easy to exaggerate the success of the reaction against them. The Conservative governments of the 1980s and 1990s undoubtedly scaled back the state's far-flung commitments through a variety of means: privatization, deregulation, the reduction of public-sector services, the favouring of low inflation over full employment, the abandonment of corporatist negotiation, and the like. There is likewise no real doubt that the Conservatives ended the postwar state's modest commitment to fight *relative* poverty. There are many reasons why the income gap has broadened over the past two decades, but reform of the tax and benefit structure is prominent among them. It is safe to say that the expansiveness of the seventies-era welfare state is now very much a thing of the past. Neither the major parties nor the voters place much confidence in 'statist' solutions to social problems, and public expenditure as a percentage of GDP is no greater today than it was a quarter-century ago. But perhaps the more important point is that it is scarcely any less, either. Despite all the rhetoric, there has been no significant 'rolling back' of the state, chiefly because it has proved to be virtually impossible to achieve real cuts in broadly popular entitlements such as old-age pensions and subsidized medical care, particularly in the face of a noticeably greying population.

In short, perhaps the most that can be said, and it is a significant statement, is that the politics of the past quarter-century has brought to an end a century-long trend of unparalleled government growth. Nevertheless, in concluding this book, it is important to stress the limits of the 'transformation' of the state in the past couple of decades. Since the 1970s, its scope has been significantly diminished in some respects and contained in others. But it remains much more extensive than it was on the eve of World War II. It still disposes of roughly 40 per cent of GDP, far more than it had ever disposed of during any period before that war, chiefly because the tax base that was so greatly enhanced during and after the war has not been scaled back to anything like its prewar dimensions. More of the state's expenditure is devoted to the provision of social services than ever before, and only after 1945 was one of the most expensive of these services, health care, placed on a universal basis. We have seen that the 'safety net' is still in place, even though it looks very different from the one envisioned by Beveridge. Demographic trends suggest that the current emphasis on cost containment within the welfare system is likely to continue. But social-security entitlements are not likely to be drastically reduced so long as a large majority of Britons retain their belief that it is a chief duty of the state to provide them. Meanwhile, the historic trend away from military and towards social spending shows no sign of easing up. Britain's imperial decline, the 'Pax Americana', and the end of the Cold War have greatly reduced the state's military role. By 1990 roughly four times as much money was being spent on health, education, and social security as on defence. Military spending accounted for a mere 4 per cent of GDP in 1990, admittedly more than it did in any other EU country, but considerably less than the 6.6 per cent that it had amounted to in 1950.[6]

Thus the contemporary British state is still very much a welfare state. It is worth pointing out in conclusion that, like other national states, it is likely to retain a good deal of its sovereignty for the foreseeable future. Globalization has undoubtedly weakened its economic power, but it will remain a formidable economic player simply because it raises and spends so much money and because it regulates internal commerce. Closer integration has and will continue to shift decision-making authority from Westminster to the institutions of the European Union. But a truly federal union does not seem a likelihood any time soon, because national consciousness and political tradition militate against it, in Britain and elsewhere. Within Britain itself, decision-making power is being dispersed to the regions, but this dispersal of power need not inevitably lead to the dissolution of the Union; it may actually bolster it by making it more broadly tolerable. Of course, even if territorial sovereignty is ultimately divided up, this implies no diminution of the influence of territorial states themselves. Indeed, political tradition strongly suggests that the central government of an independent Scotland would be more interventionist than its English counterpart. For all of these reasons, it is worth paraphrasing Mark Twain by way of a conclusion: reports of the state's death have been greatly exaggerated.

Notes

Introduction

1 Among the more noteworthy contributions to this literature are Peter B. Evans, Dietrich Rueschemeyer, and Theda Skocpol, eds, *Bringing the State Back In* (Cambridge University Press, Cambridge, 1985); Gianfranco Poggi, *The Development of the Modern State: A Sociological Introduction* (Stanford University Press, Palo Alto, CA, 1978); Charles Tilly, ed., *The Formation of National States in Western Europe* (Princeton University Press, Princeton, NJ, 1975); Charles Tilly, *Coercion, Capital and European States A.D. 990–1990* (Blackwell, Oxford, 1990); S. N. Eisenstadt and Stein Rokkan, eds, *Building States and Nations* (2 vols, Sage, Beverly Hills, 1973); Anthony Giddens, *The Nation-State and Violence* (University of California Press, Berkeley, 1985); Michael Mann, *The Sources of Social Power* (2 vols, Cambridge University Press, Cambridge, 1986, 1993); John A. Hall, *Powers and Liberties: The Causes and Consequences of the Rise of the West* (Blackwell, Oxford, 1985); Brian Downing, *The Military Revolution and Political Change: Origins of Democracy and Autocracy in Early Modern Europe* (Princeton University Press, Princeton, NJ, 1992); Hendrik Spruyt, *The Sovereign State and its Competitors* (Princeton University Press, Princeton, NJ, 1994); Margaret Levi, *Of Rule and Revenue* (University of California Press, Berkeley, 1988); Thomas Ertman, *The Birth of Leviathan: Building States and Regimes in Medieval and Early Modern Europe* (Cambridge University Press, Cambridge, 1997); Felix Gilbert, ed., *The Historical Essays of Otto Hintze* (Oxford University Press, Oxford, 1975); Ronald Batchfelder and Herman Freudenberger, 'On the Rational Origins of the Modern Centralized State', *Explorations in Economic History*, 20 (1983), pp. 1–13.

2 See esp. John Brewer, *The Sinews of Power: War, Money, and the English State 1688–1783* (Century Hutchinson, London, 1988); Lawrence Stone, ed., *An Imperial State at War: Britain from 1689 to 1815* (Routledge, London, 1994); John Brewer and Eckhart Hellmuth, eds, *Rethinking Leviathan: The Eighteenth-Century State in Britain and Germany* (Oxford University Press, Oxford, 1999).

3 John Brewer, 'The Eighteenth-Century British State: Context and Issues', in *An Imperial State at War*, ed. Stone, p. 53.

4 Jan-Erik Lane, David McKay, and Kenneth Newton, *Political Data Handbook: OECD Countries* (Oxford University Press, Oxford, 1997), pp. 100, 105–6;

Peter Flora, Franz Kraus, and Winfried Pfenning, *State, Economy, and Society* (2 vols, Macmillan, London, 1987), vol. 1, pp. 440–3; Mann, *The Sources of Social Power*, vol. 2, pp. 362–3, 806; Philip Harling and Peter Mandler, 'From "Fiscal–Military" State to *Laissez-faire* State, 1760–1850', *Journal of British Studies*, 32 (1993), pp. 44–70, esp. pp. 48–9; W. H. Greenleaf, *The British Political Tradition* (3 vols, Methuen, London, 1983, 1987), vol. 1, p. 33; David Butler and Gareth Butler, *British Political Facts, 1900–1994* (7th edn, St Martin's, New York, 1995), p. 287.

Chapter 1 The Revolution Settlement and the Rise of the Fiscal–Military State, 1688–1715

1 John Brewer, 'The Eighteenth-Century British State: Context and Issues', in *An Imperial State at War: Britain from 1689 to 1815*, ed. Lawrence Stone (Routledge, London, 1994), pp. 54–6.
2 Quoted in *The Eighteenth-Century Constitution*, ed. E. Neville Williams (Cambridge University Press, Cambridge, 1965), pp. 74–5.
3 Lois Schwoerer, 'Introduction', in *The Revolution of 1688–1689: Changing Perspectives*, ed. Lois Schwoerer (Cambridge University Press, Cambridge, 1992), pp. 2–3.
4 Geoffrey Holmes and Daniel Szechi, *The Age of Oligarchy: Pre-Industrial Britain, 1722–1783* (Longman, London, 1993), pp. 220–2, 278; W. A. Speck, *Reluctant Revolutionaries: Englishmen and the Revolution of 1688* (Oxford University Press, Oxford, 1988), p. 165; Jonathan Israel, 'Introduction', in *The Anglo-Dutch Moment*, ed. Jonathan Israel (Cambridge University Press, Cambridge, 1991), p. 10.
5 Tony Claydon, *William III and the Godly Revolution* (Cambridge University Press, Cambridge, 1996), p. 235.
6 Betty Kemp, *King and Commons 1660–1832* (Macmillan, London, 1959), p. 141.
7 Anthony Fletcher, *Reform in the Provinces: The Government of Stuart England* (Yale University Press, New Haven, CT, 1986), pp. 24–5.
8 Lionel Glassey, *Politics and the Appointment of Justices of the Peace 1675–1720* (Oxford University Press, Oxford, 1979), pp. 91–2.
9 Jonathan Israel, 'The Dutch Role', in *The Anglo-Dutch Moment*, ed. Israel, pp. 105–62.
10 J. P. Kenyon, *Revolution Principles: The Politics of Party 1689–1720* (Cambridge University Press, Cambridge, 1977), pp. 32, 45, 200–1.
11 John Morrill, 'The Sensible Revolution', in *The Anglo-Dutch Moment*, ed. Israel, pp. 73–104, esp. p. 103; Howard Nenner, *By Colour of Law: Legal Culture and Constitutional Politics in England, 1660–1689* (University of Chicago Press, Chicago, 1977), pp. 173–5.
12 See esp. Lois Schwoerer, *The Declaration of Rights, 1689* (Johns Hopkins University Press, Baltimore, 1981).
13 Morrill, 'The Sensible Revolution', pp. 88–90; Jennifer Carter, 'The Revolution and the Constitution', in *Britain After the Glorious Revolu-*

tion, ed. G. S. Holmes (Macmillan, London, 1969), pp. 39–58, esp. pp. 42–3; Tim Harris, *Politics under the Later Stuarts: Party Conflict in a Divided Society 1660–1715* (Longman, London, 1993), pp. 132–5; Henry Horwitz, *Parliament, Policy and Politics in the Reign of William III* (Manchester University Press, Manchester, 1977), pp. 13–14; H. T. Dickinson, *Liberty and Property: Political Ideology in Eighteenth-Century Britain* (Holmes & Meier, New York, 1977), pp. 80–1; J. R. Jones, 'The Revolution in Context', in *Liberty Secured? Britain Before and After 1688*, ed. J. R. Jones (Stanford University Press, Stanford, 1992), pp. 11–52, esp. pp. 28–30.

14   Robert Beddard, 'The Unexpected Whig Revolution of 1688', in *The Revolutions of 1688*, ed. Robert Beddard (Oxford University Press, Oxford, 1991), pp. 11–101, esp. p. 94.

15   Gordon Schochet, 'From Persecution to "Toleration" ', in *Liberty Secured?*, ed. Jones, pp. 122–57; Speck, *Reluctant Revolutionaries*, p. 187.

16   G. V. Bennett, 'Conflict in the Church', in *Britain After the Glorious Revolution*, ed. Holmes, pp. 155–75; G. V. Bennett, *The Tory Crisis in Church and State 1688–1730* (Oxford University Press, Oxford, 1975).

17   G. C. Gibbs, 'The Revolution in Foreign Policy', in *Britain After the Glorious Revolution*, ed. Holmes, pp. 59–79, esp. pp. 66–9.

18   Michael J. Braddick, *The Nerves of State: Taxation and the Financing of the English State, 1558–1714* (Manchester University Press, Manchester, 1996), pp. 190–1.

19   Braddick, *The Nerves of State*, pp. 29–30.

20   Martin Van Creveld, *Supplying War: Logistics from Wallerstein to Patton* (Cambridge University Press, Cambridge, 1977), pp. 5–6.

21   Michael J. Braddick, *Parliamentary Taxation in Seventeenth-Century England: Local Administration and Response* (Royal Historical Society, Woodbridge, 1994), pp. 3–13; Marjolein t'Hart, 'The Emergence and Consolidation of the "Tax State": II. The Seventeenth Century', in *The Rise of the Fiscal State in Europe, c.1200–1815*, ed. Richard Bonney (Oxford University Press, Oxford, 1995), pp. 281–94.

22   Patrick O'Brien and Philip A. Hunt, 'The Rise of a Fiscal State in England, 1485–1815', *Historical Research*, 66 (1993), pp. 129–76.

23   J. R. Western, *Monarchy and Revolution: The English State in the 1680s* (Rowman and Littlefield, Totowa, NJ, 1972), pp. 3–4, 395; Horwitz, *Parliament, Policy and Politics*, pp. 30–1, 199–201; Israel, 'Introduction', pp. 17–18.

24   Kemp, *King and Commons*, pp. 72–3; Henry Roseveare, *The Financial Revolution 1660–1760* (Longman, London, 1991), p. 47; Horwitz, *Parliament, Policy and Politics*, pp. 85–7.

25   J. A. Downie, 'The Commission of Public Accounts and the Formation of the Country Party', *English Historical Review*, 91 (1976), pp. 33–51; Jones, 'The Revolution in Context', pp. 37–9; Claydon, *William III and the Godly Revolution*, pp. 206–7.

26   E. A. Reitan, 'From Revenue to Civil List, 1689–1702', *Historical Journal*, 4 (1970), pp. 571–88.

27 Jones, 'The Revolution in Context', pp. 33–4; John Miller, 'Crown, Parliament, and People', in *Liberty Secured?*, ed. Jones, pp. 53–87, esp. pp. 83–5.
28 An expression now commonly used by historians that was coined by John Brewer, *The Sinews of Power: War, Money and the English State 1688–1783* (Century Hutchinson, London, 1988), p. xvii.
29 Brewer, *The Sinews of Power*, pp. 89–91; Peter Mathias and Patrick O'Brien, 'Taxation in Britain and France, 1715–1810', *Journal of European Economic History*, 5 (1976), pp. 601–50, esp. p. 637.
30 J. V. Beckett, 'Land Tax or Excise: The Levying of Taxation in Seventeenth- and Eighteenth-Century England', *English Historical Review*, 100 (1985), pp. 285–308.
31 Patrick O'Brien, 'The Political Economy of British Taxation, 1660–1815', *Economic History Review*, 2nd ser., 41 (1988), pp. 1–32, esp. p. 19.
32 R. A. C. Parker, 'Direct Taxation on the Coke Estates in the Eighteenth Century', *English Historical Review*, 72 (1956), pp. 247–8.
33 Beckett, 'Land Tax or Excise', p. 305; Braddick, *The Nerves of State*, pp. 148–9, 170–1; Roseveare, *The Financial Revolution*, pp. 7–8.
34 O'Brien, 'The Political Economy of British Taxation', p. 4.
35 P. G. M. Dickson, *The Financial Revolution in England* (Macmillan, London, 1967), pp. 47–50.
36 E. L. Hargreaves, *The National Debt* (Edward Arnold, London, 1930), ch. 1; D. W. Jones, *War and Economy in the Age of William III and Marlborough* (Blackwell, Oxford, 1988), pp. 14–15; Roseveare, *The Financial Revolution*, pp. 36–40.
37 G. S. Holmes, *Augustan England: Professions, State and Society, 1680–1730* (George Allen & Unwin, London, 1982), pp. 258–60; Roseveare, *The Financial Revolution*, pp. 48–9.
38 Holmes, *Augustan England*, pp. 257–8.
39 Holmes, *Augustan England*, pp. 246–52, 257–8; Howard Tomlinson, 'Financial and Administrative Developments in England, 1660–88', in *The Restored Monarchy, 1660–1688*, ed. J. R. Jones (Rowman & Littlefield, Lanham, MD, 1979), pp. 94–117, esp. pp. 115–16.
40 Brian W. Hill, *The Early Parties and Politics in Britain, 1688–1832* (St Martin's, New York, 1996), p. 12.
41 Holmes and Szechi, *The Age of Oligarchy*, pp. 329–30; W. A. Speck, 'The Electorate in the First Age of Party', in *Britain in the First Age of Party*, ed. Clyve Jones (Hambledon Press, London, 1987), pp. 45–62; W. A. Speck, 'Whigs and Tories Dim their Glories', in *The Whig Ascendancy: Colloquies on Hanoverian England*, ed. J. A. Cannon (St Martin's, New York, 1981), pp. 51–70, esp. pp. 53–5.
42 Geoffrey S. Holmes, *British Politics in the Age of Anne* (Macmillan, London, 1967), p. 21.
43 Glassey, *Politics and the Appointment of Justices of the Peace*, pp. 16, 262–3; Lionel Glassey, 'Local Government', in *Britain in the First Age of Party*, ed. Jones, pp. 151–72, esp. p. 159; Norma Landau, *The Justices of the Peace,*

1679–1760 (University of California Press, Berkeley, 1984), pp. 84–5; Fletcher, *Reform in the Provinces*, pp. 28–30.

44 Gary DeKrey, *A Fractured Society: The Politics of London in the First Age of Party 1688–1715* (Oxford University Press, Oxford, 1985), esp. pp. 219–20, 252–3.

45 Clayton Roberts, 'Party and Patronage in Later Stuart England', in *England's Rise to Greatness, 1660–1763*, ed. Stephen Baxter (University of California Press, Berkeley, 1983), pp. 185–212, esp. pp. 188–93; Harris, *Politics under the Late Stuarts*, pp. 162–3.

46 Kemp, *King and Commons*, pp. 54–62; Geoffrey S. Holmes, *Politics, Religion and Society in England 1679–1742* (Hambledon Press, London, 1986), pp. 36–7, 55–6.

47 J. G. A. Pocock, *The Machiavellian Moment: Florentine Thought and the Atlantic Republican Tradition* (Princeton University Press, Princeton, NJ, 1975).

48 Quoted in M. J. Daunton, *Progress and Poverty: An Economic and Social History of Britain 1700–1850* (Oxford University Press, Oxford, 1995), p. 513.

49 Brewer, *The Sinews of Power*, pp. 208–9.

50 Holmes, *British Politics in the Age of Anne*, p. 161; Daunton, *Progress and Poverty*, p. 514; Braddick, *The Nerves of State*, p. 194.

51 Brewer, *The Sinews of Power*, pp. 142–3.

52 See e.g. D. W. Hayton, 'The Williamite Revolution in Ireland, 1688–91', in *The Anglo-Dutch Moment*, ed. Israel, pp. 185–214, esp. pp. 185–6; Daniel Szechi and David Hayton, 'John Bull's Other Kingdoms: The Government of Scotland and Ireland', in *Britain in the First Age of Party*, ed. Jones, pp. 241–80, esp. pp. 260–1; Michael Hechter, *Internal Colonialism: The Celtic Fringe in British National Development, 1536–1966* (University of California Press, Berkeley, 1975), pp. 70–3.

53 See esp. J. G. Simms, *The Williamite Confiscation in Ireland 1690–1703* (Faber and Faber, London, 1956); S. J. Connolly, *Religion, Law, and Power: The Making of Protestant Ireland 1660–1760* (Oxford University Press, Oxford, 1992), pp. 264, 309–11; Jones, 'The Revolution in Context', pp. 46–7.

54 Hayton, 'The Williamite Revolution in Ireland', pp. 208–11.

55 Karl Bottigheimer, 'The Glorious Revolution in Ireland', in *The Revolution of 1688–1689*, ed. Schwoerer, pp. 234–43, esp. pp. 242–3.

56 Brian Levack, *The Formation of the British State: England, Scotland, and the Union, 1603–1707* (Oxford University Press, Oxford, 1987), pp. 138–9, 167–8.

57 Vernon Bogdanor, *Devolution* (Oxford University Press, Oxford, 1979), pp. 75–7.

58 Quoted in Levack, *The Formation of the British State*, p. 205.

59 David Daiches, *Scotland and the Union* (John Murray, London, 1977), pp. 165–6; T. C. Smout, 'The Road to Union', in *Britain After the Glorious Revolution*, ed. Holmes, pp. 176–96; P. W. J. Riley, *The Union of England*

and Scotland (Manchester University Press, Manchester, 1978), pp. 313–14.

Chapter 2   The Fiscal–Military State and its Discontents, 1715–1815

1 Quoted in Patrick O'Brien, *Power with Profit: The State and the Economy, 1688–1815* (University of London Press, London, 1991), p. 8.
2 Paul Monod, *Jacobitism and the English People* (Cambridge University Press, Cambridge, 1989), pp. 43–4; Tim Harris, *Politics under the Late Stuarts: Party Conflict in a Divided Society 1660–1715* (Longman, London, 1993), p. 238.
3 J. C. D. Clark, *English Society 1688–1832* (Cambridge University Press, Cambridge, 1985), p. 131; J. A. W. Gunn, *Beyond Liberty and Property* (McGill-Queen's University, Montreal, 1983), pp. 149–51; John Morrill, 'The Sensible Revolution', in *The Anglo-Dutch Moment*, ed. Jonathan Israel (Cambridge University Press, Cambridge, 1996), pp. 92–3.
4 Daniel Szechi, *The Jacobites, Britain, and Europe 1688–1788* (Manchester University Press, Manchester, 1994), pp. 76–7.
5 See esp. Bruce Lenman, *The Jacobite Risings in Britain 1689–1746* (Scottish Cultural Press, Aberdeen, 1995).
6 Nicholas Rogers, *Whigs and Cities: Popular Politics in the Age of Walpole and Pitt* (Oxford University Press, Oxford, 1989), ch. 1; Monod, *Jacobitism and the English People*, pp. 347–8.
7 Jeremy Black, *British Foreign Policy in the Age of Walpole* (John Donald, Edinburgh, 1985), p. 45; Jeremy Black, 'Foreign Policy and the British State 1742–1793', in *British Politics and Society from Walpole to Pitt*, ed. Jeremy Black (St Martin's, New York, 1990), pp. 147–76, esp. pp. 156–9; Daniel A. Baugh, 'Great Britain's "Blue-Water" Policy, 1689–1815', *International History Review*, 10 (1988), pp. 33–58, esp. pp. 42–3.
8 John Brewer, *Party Ideology and Popular Politics at the Accession of George III* (Cambridge University Press, Cambridge, 1976), pp. 115–23; Frank O'Gorman, *The Emergence of the British Two-Party System 1760–1832* (Edward Arnold, London, 1982), pp. 1–3, 28–9, 188, 217; Richard Pares, *King George III and the Politicians* (Oxford University Press, Oxford, 1953).
9 John Cannon, *The Fox–North Coalition* (Cambridge University Press, Cambridge, 1973).
10 Quoted in Arthur Aspinall and E. A. Smith, eds, *English Historical Documents 1783–1832* (Oxford University Press, Oxford, 1959), p. 140.
11 E. A. Reitan, 'The Civil List in Eighteenth-Century British Politics: Parliamentary Supremacy versus the Independence of the Crown', *Historical Journal*, 9 (1966), pp. 318–37, esp. pp. 318–23.
12 Michael Roberts, *The Whig Party 1807–1812* (Macmillan, London, 1939).
13 This paragraph is closely based on John Cannon, *Parliamentary Reform 1640–1832* (Cambridge University Press, Cambridge, 1973), pp. 29–31, 108.

14 Romney Sedgwick, ed., *The House of Commons 1715–1754* (3 vols, Oxford University Press, Oxford, 1970), vol. 1, pp. 14–15; W. A. Speck, '"The Most Corrupt Council in Christendom": Decisions on Controverted Elections, 1702–42', in *Party and Management in Parliament, 1660–1784*, ed. Clyve Jones (Leicester University Press, Leicester, 1984), pp. 107–22, esp. pp. 113–14.

15 Cannon, *Parliamentary Reform*, pp. 36–7.

16 J. V. Beckett, *The Aristocracy in England 1660–1914* (Blackwell, Oxford, 1986), pp. 428–30.

17 Douglas Hay and Nicholas Rogers, *Eighteenth-Century English Society: Shuttles and Swords* (Oxford University Press, Oxford, 1997), pp. 64–5.

18 Frank O'Gorman, *Voters, Patrons, and Parties: The Unreformed Electoral System of Hanoverian England 1734–1832* (Oxford University Press, Oxford, 1989), esp. pp. 1–66, 107–9, 141–59, 170–81.

19 Paul Langford, 'Property and "Virtual Representation" in Eighteenth-Century England', *Historical Journal*, 31 (1988), pp. 83–116; Paul Langford, *A Polite and Commercial People: England 1727–1783* (Oxford University Press, Oxford, 1989), pp. 711–12; Paul Langford, *Public Life and the Propertied Englishman 1689–1798* (Oxford University Press, Oxford, 1991), pp. 196–9.

20 Henry Roseveare, *The Financial Revolution 1660–1760* (Longman, London, 1991), pp. 1–2.

21 C. A. Bayly, *Imperial Meridian: The British Empire and the World, 1780–1830* (Longman, London, 1989), esp. chs 4–6.

22 John Brewer, *The Sinews of Power: War, Money and the English State 1688–1783* (Century Hutchinson, London, 1988), p. 30; Linda Colley, 'The Reach of the State, the Appeal of the Nation: Mass Arming and Political Culture in the Napoleonic Wars', in *An Imperial State at War: Britain from 1689 to 1815*, ed. Lawrence Stone (Routledge, London, 1994), pp. 165–84, esp. p. 167.

23 This paragraph relies on the numerical information provided in Brewer, *The Sinews of Power*, pp. 35–7.

24 Hay and Rogers, *Eighteenth-Century English Society*, pp. 152–3.

25 Philip Harling and Peter Mandler, 'From "Fiscal–Military" State to *Laissez-faire* State, 1760–1850', *Journal of British Studies*, 32 (1993), pp. 44–70, esp. p. 48.

26 Patrick O'Brien, 'Public Finance in the Wars with France 1793–1815', in *Britain and the French Revolution, 1789–1815*, ed. H. T. Dickinson (St Martin's, New York, 1989), pp. 165–88, esp. p. 165.

27 Harling and Mandler, 'From "Fiscal–Military" State to *Laissez-faire* State', pp. 48–9; Michael Mann, *States, War and Capitalism: Studies in Political Sociology* (Blackwell, Oxford, 1988), pp. 107–9.

28 O'Brien, 'Public Finance in the Wars with France', pp. 176–7; Michael Mann, *The Sources of Social Power* (2 vols, Cambridge University Press, Cambridge, 1986, 1993), vol. 2, pp. 214–15.

29 P. G. M. Dickson, *The Financial Revolution in England* (Macmillan, London, 1967), part 2; Brewer, *The Sinews of Power*, pp. 116–26; O'Brien, 'Public Finance in the Wars with France', pp. 172–3.

30 O'Brien, *Power with Profit*, pp. 28–9.

31 Hilton Root, *The Fountain of Privilege: Political Foundations of Markets in Old Regime France and England* (University of California Press, Berkeley, 1994), pp. 163–78; James C. Riley, *The Seven Years' War and the Old Regime in France: The Economic and Financial Toll* (Princeton University Press, Princeton, NJ, 1986); Richard Bonney, 'The Eighteenth Century: II. The Struggle for Great Power Status and the End of the Old Fiscal Regime', in *The Rise of the Fiscal State in Europe, c.1200–1815*, ed. Richard Bonney (Oxford University Press, Oxford, 1995), pp. 315–92, esp. p. 345; Paul Kennedy, *The Rise and Fall of the Great Powers* (Random House, New York, 1987), p. 84.

32 [Smith], 'America', *Edinburgh Review*, 33 (1820), pp. 77–8.

33 Patrick O'Brien, 'The Political Economy of British Taxation, 1660–1815', *Economic History Review*, 2nd ser., 41 (1988), pp. 1–32, esp. pp. 1–2, 4, 6; Peter Mathias and Patrick O'Brien, 'Taxation in Britain and France, 1715–1810', *Journal of European Economic History*, 5 (1976), pp. 601–50, esp. pp. 606–7; Patrick O'Brien and Philip A. Hunt, 'The Rise of a Fiscal State in England, 1485–1815', *Historical Research*, 66 (1993), pp. 129–76, esp. p. 155.

34 Figures derived from B. R. Mitchell, *British Historical Statistics* (Cambridge University Press, Cambridge, 1988), pp. 575–6.

35 William Kennedy, *English Taxation 1640–1799* (George Bell & Sons, London, 1913), pp. 62, 113.

36 J. V. Beckett and Michael Turner, 'Taxation and Economic Growth in Eighteenth-Century England', *Economic History Review*, 2nd ser., 43 (1990), pp. 377–403, esp. pp. 394–5.

37 Arthur Hope-Jones, *Income Tax in the Napoleonic Wars* (Cambridge University Press, Cambridge, 1939); E. R. A. Seligman, *The Income Tax* (2nd edn, Macmillan, New York, 1964), pp. 62–81; Margaret Levi, *Of Rule and Revenue* (University of California Press, Berkeley, 1988), pp. 142–3.

38 Mathias and O'Brien, 'Taxation in Britain and France', esp. pp. 633–5.

39 E. A. Wrigley, 'Society and the Economy', in *An Imperial State at War*, ed. Stone, pp. 72–95, esp. p. 73; Gabriel Ardant, 'Financial Policy and Economic Infrastructure of Modern States and Nations', in *The Formation of National States in Europe*, ed. Charles A. Tilly (Princeton University Press, Princeton, NJ, 1975), pp. 164–242, esp. p. 200.

40 Mathias and O'Brien, 'Taxation in Britain and France', pp. 636–9; Root, *The Fountain of Privilege*, ch. 3; Michael Kwass, 'A Kingdom of Taxpayers: State Formation, Privilege, and Political Culture in Eighteenth-Century France', *Journal of Modern History*, 70 (1998), pp. 295–339.

41 Daniel A. Baugh, *British Naval Administration in the Age of Walpole* (Princeton University Press, Princeton, NJ, 1965), pp. 464–8; Henry Roseveare, *The Treasury 1660–1870* (George Allen & Unwin, London, 1973), pp. 90–3; Immanuel Wallerstein, *The Modern World System* (2 vols, Academic Press, New York, 1980), vol. 2, p. 247.

42 David French, *The British Way in Warfare 1688–2000* (Unwin Hyman, London, 1990), pp. 59, 227.

43   Brewer, *The Sinews of Power*, pp. 11–12, 167–8.

44   Baugh, 'Great Britain's "Blue-Water" Policy', pp. 53–4.

45   Paul Kennedy, *The Rise and Fall of British Naval Mastery* (Allen Lane, London, 1976), pp. 115–16.

46   Piers Mackesy, 'Strategic Problems of the British War Effort', in *Britain and the French Revolution*, ed. Dickinson, pp. 147–64, esp. pp. 149–60; Piers Mackesy, *War Without Victory: The Downfall of Pitt 1799–1802* (Oxford University Press, Oxford, 1984), pp. 225–9; Richard Glover, *Peninsular Preparation: The Reform of the British Army 1795–1809* (Cambridge University Press, Cambridge, 1963), pp. 4–5.

47   O'Brien, *Power with Profit*, esp. pp. 19–22; Dundas, quoted on p. 21.

48   Clive Emsley, 'The Social Impact of the French Wars', in *Britain and the French Revolution*, ed. Dickinson, pp. 211–28, esp. pp. 213–14.

49   J. R. Western, *The English Militia in the Eighteenth Century* (Routledge & Kegan Paul, London, 1965), pp. 290–1; Clive Emsley, *British Society and the French Wars, 1793–1815* (Macmillan, London, 1979), pp. 101–3.

50   Brewer, *The Sinews of Power*, pp. 49–50.

51   N. A. M. Rodger, *The Wooden World: An Anatomy of the Georgian Navy* (Collins, London, 1986), pp. 164–83; Baugh, *British Naval Administration*, pp. 148–62, 492–500; Stone, 'Introduction', in *An Imperial State at War*, ed. Stone, pp. 12–13; Brewer, *The Sinews of Power*, pp. 49–51.

52   Quoted in Emsley, *British Society and the French Wars*, pp. 100–1.

53   Tony Hayter, *The Army and the Crowd in Mid-Georgian England* (Rowman & Littlefield, Totowa, NJ, 1978), p. 186.

54   Stanley Palmer, *Police and Protest in England and Ireland 1780–1850* (Cambridge University Press, Cambridge, 1988), pp. 63–4; J. A. Houlding, *Fit for Service: The Training of the British Army, 1715–1795* (Oxford University Press, Oxford, 1981), p. 60.

55   Houlding, *Fit for Service*, pp. 391–5.

56   Palmer, *Police and Protest*, pp. 61–2, 181–2; Brewer, *The Sinews of Power*, p. 32; Hay and Rogers, *Eighteenth-Century English Society*, p. 133.

57   J. H. Parry, *Trade and Dominion: The European Overseas Empires in the Eighteenth Century* (Weidenfeld & Nicolson, London, 1971), pp. 139–41.

58   Jack P. Greene, *Peripheries and Center: Constitutional Development in the Extended Polities of the British Empire and the United States, 1607–1788* (University of Georgia Press, Athens, 1986), esp. pp. 74–87, 102, 127–8, 145–50.

59   Piers Mackesy, *The War for America, 1775–1783* (Harvard University Press, Cambridge, MA, 1965).

60   See R. B. McDowell, *Ireland in the Age of Imperialism and Revolution 1760–1801* (Oxford University Press, Oxford, 1979), esp. pp. 1–299; Marianne Elliott, *Partners in Revolution: The United Irishmen and France* (Yale University Press, New Haven, CT, 1982), pp. 1–30.

61   Elliott, *Partners in Revolution*; Marianne Elliott, *Wolfe Tone: Prophet of Irish Independence* (Yale University Press, New Haven, CT, 1989); Marianne Elliott, 'Ireland and the French Revolution', in *Britain and the French Revolution*, ed. Dickinson, pp. 83–102.

62   Brewer, *Party Ideology*, pp. 18–20, 206–12.

63 F. D. Cartwright, ed., *Life and Correspondence of Major Cartwright* (2 vols, A. M. Kelley, New York, 1969), vol. 1, pp. 133–4; Philip Harling, *The Waning of 'Old Corruption': The Politics of Economical Reform in Britain, 1779–1846* (Oxford University Press, Oxford, 1996), pp. 35–6.

64 See esp. E. C. Black, *The Association: British Extraparliamentary Political Organization 1769–1793* (Harvard University Press, Cambridge, MA, 1963), chs 2–3.

65 Harling, *The Waning of 'Old Corruption'*, p. 69.

66 G. E. Aylmer, 'From Office-Holding to Civil Service: The Genesis of Modern Bureaucracy', *Transactions of the Royal Historical Society*, 5th ser., 30 (1980), pp. 91–108, esp. p. 106.

67 Brewer, *The Sinews of Power*, pp. 101–14.

68 S. E. Finer, 'Patronage and the Public Service: Jeffersonian Bureaucracy and the British Tradition', *Public Administration*, 30 (1952), pp. 329–60; Harling, *The Waning of 'Old Corruption'*, pp. 22–3; Sir Norman Chester, *The English Administrative System 1780–1870* (Oxford University Press, Oxford, 1981), pp. 18–20.

69 Harling, *The Waning of 'Old Corruption'*, pp. 72–3.

70 Philip Harling, 'Rethinking "Old Corruption"', *Past & Present*, 147 (1995), pp. 127–58, esp. pp. 127–8.

71 E. P. Thompson, *Whigs and Hunters: The Origins of the Black Act* (Pantheon, New York, 1975), p. 197. See also E. P. Thompson, 'The Peculiarities of the English', in *The Poverty of Theory and Other Essays* (Monthly Review Press, New York, 1978), p. 141; Philip Corrigan and Derek Sayer, *The Great Arch: English State Formation as Cultural Revolution* (Blackwell, Oxford, 1985), pp. 88–9.

72 J. H. Plumb, *Sir Robert Walpole: The Making of a Statesman* (Houghton Mifflin, Boston, 1956), pp. 120–1; J. H. Plumb, *Sir Robert Walpole: The King's Minister* (Houghton Mifflin, Boston, 1961), pp. 85, 90–3; J. H. Plumb, *Men and Places* (Pelican, London, 1966), pp. 168, 174.

73 Harling, *The Waning of 'Old Corruption'*, pp. 16–17, 72, 111–14; Harling, 'Rethinking "Old Corruption"', p. 46.

74 Joel Hurstfield, *Freedom, Corruption and Government in Elizabethan England* (Jonathan Cape, London, 1973), pp. 139–41.

75 Sir Lewis Namier and John Brooke, *The House of Commons 1754–1790* (3 vols, Oxford University Press, Oxford, 1964), vol. 1, p. 135; Sir Lewis Namier, *The Structure of Politics at the Accession of George III* (2nd edn, Macmillan, London, 1957), ch. 4; Ian Christie, 'Economical Reform and the "Influence of the Crown", 1780', *Cambridge Historical Journal*, 12 (1956), pp. 144–54, esp. p. 147.

76 Langford, *Public Life and the Propertied Englishman*, pp. 28–9; Patrick Atiyah, *The Rise and Fall of Freedom of Contract* (Oxford University Press, Oxford, 1979), p. 21.

77 V. A. C. Gatrell, *The Hanging Tree: Execution and the English People 1770–1868* (Oxford University Press, Oxford, 1994), pp. 6–9.

78 Douglas Hay, 'Property, Authority and the Criminal Law', in *Albion's Fatal Tree: Crime and Society in Eighteenth-Century England*, eds Douglas Hay,

Peter Linebaugh, and E. P. Thompson (Pantheon, New York, 1975), pp. 1–86, esp. p. 18.

79 J. M. Beattie, *Crime and the Courts in England 1660–1800* (Princeton University Press, Princeton, NJ, 1986), p. 591.

80 A. Roger Ekirch, *Bound for America: The Transportation of British Convicts to the Colonies 1718–1775* (Oxford University Press, Oxford, 1987), p. 1.

81 Beattie, *Crime and the Courts*, ch. 8; Peter King, 'Decision-Makers and Decision-Making in the English Criminal Law', *Historical Journal*, 27 (1984), pp. 25–58; John H. Langbein, 'Albion's Fatal Flaws', *Past & Present*, 98 (1983), pp. 96–120; Joanna Innes and John Styles, 'The Crime Wave: Recent Writing on Crime and Criminal Justice in Eighteenth-Century England', *Journal of British Studies*, 25 (1986), pp. 380–435.

82 John Brewer and John Styles, 'Introduction', in *An Ungovernable People: The English and their Law in the Seventeenth and Eighteenth Centuries* (Rutgers, New Brunswick, NJ, 1980), pp. 11–20, esp. p. 20.

83 Bob Bushaway, *By Rite: Custom, Ceremony and Community in England 1700–1880* (Junction Books, London, 1982), pp. 217–18.

84 John Money, *Identity and Experience: Birmingham and the West Midlands 1760–1800* (McGill-Queen's University, Montreal, 1977), pp. 249–50.

85 K. D. M. Snell, *Annals of the Labouring Poor: Social Change and Agrarian England 1660–1900* (Cambridge University Press, Cambridge, 1985), ch. 2; Langford, *A Polite and Commercial People*, pp. 440–1.

86 Thompson, 'The Peculiarities of the English', esp. pp. 40–7; M. W. McCahill, 'Peers, Patronage and the Industrial Revolution, 1760–1800', *Journal of British Studies*, 16 (1976), pp. 84–107; P. J. Cain and A. G. Hopkins, 'Gentlemanly Capitalism and British Expansion Overseas: I. The Old Colonial System, 1688–1850', *Economic History Review*, 2nd ser., 39 (1986), pp. 501–25.

87 O'Brien, *Power with Profit*, p. 67.

88 Hay and Rogers, *Eighteenth-Century English Society*, p. 132.

89 Henry Pelling, *A History of British Trade Unionism* (Macmillan, London, 1963), pp. 14–18; Hay and Rogers, *Eighteenth-Century English Society*, pp. 198–200.

90 Hay and Rogers, *Eighteenth-Century English Society*, p. 96.

91 Ibid., esp. pp. 84–5, 104–6, 110–13, 141–2.

92 François Crouzet, 'The Impact of the French Wars on the British Economy', in *Britain and the French Revolution*, ed. Dickinson, pp. 189–210, esp. p. 197.

93 See e.g. J. D. Chambers and G. E. Mingay, *The Agricultural Revolution 1750–1880* (Schocken, New York, 1966).

94 J. L. and Barbara Hammond, *The Village Labourer 1760–1832* (Longman, London, 1911), esp. chs 2–4; Snell, *Annals of the Labouring Poor*, ch. 4; J. M. Neeson, *Commoners: Common Right, Enclosure and Social Change in England, 1700–1820* (Cambridge University Press, Cambridge, 1996).

95 See esp. Neeson, *Commoners*, pp. 290–1.

96 Atiyah, *The Rise and Fall of Freedom of Contract*, p. 67; O'Brien, *Power with Profit*, p. 9.

97 D. C. Coleman, 'Mercantilism Revisited', *Historical Journal*, 23 (1980), pp. 773–92; Ralph Davis, 'The Rise of Protection in England, 1689–1786', *Economic History Review*, 2nd ser., 19 (1966), pp. 306–17; M. J. Daunton, *Progress and Poverty: An Economic and Social History of Britain 1700–1850* (Oxford University Press, Oxford, 1995), pp. 536–41; Daniel A. Baugh, 'Maritime Strength and Atlantic Commerce: The Uses of a "Grand Marine Empire"', in *An Imperial State at War*, ed. Stone, pp. 185–223.

98 Brewer, *The Sinews of Power*, ch. 5; John Norris, 'Samuel Garbett and the Early Development of Industrial Lobbying in Great Britain', *Economic History Review*, 2nd ser., 10 (1957–8), pp. 450–60; Tim Keirn, 'Parliament, Legislation, and the Regulation of English Textile Industries, 1689–1714', in *Stilling the Grumbling Hive: The Response to Social and Economic Problems in England, 1689–1750*, eds Lee Davison, Tim Hitchcock, Tim Keirn, and Robert Shoemaker (St Martin's, New York, 1992), pp. 1–24.

99 Lee Davison, 'Experiments in the Social Regulation of Industry: Gin Legislation, 1729–1751', in *Stilling the Grumbling Hive*, eds Davison et al., pp. 25–48.

100 Langford, *A Polite and Commercial People*, pp. 502–3.

101 Julian Hoppit, Joanna Innes, and John Styles, 'Project Report: Towards a History of Parliamentary Legislation, 1660–1800', *Parliamentary History*, 13 (1994), pp. 312–21, esp. pp. 313–14.

102 P. D. G. Thomas, *The House of Commons in the Eighteenth Century* (Oxford University Press, Oxford, 1971), pp. 45–6.

103 Joanna Innes, 'Parliament and the Shaping of Eighteenth-Century English Social Policy', *Transactions of the Royal Historical Society*, 5th ser., 40 (1990), pp. 63–92.

104 David Lieberman, *The Province of Legislation Determined: Legal Theory in Eighteenth-Century Britain* (Cambridge University Press, Cambridge, 1989), pp. 22–3; Sedgwick, *The House of Commons 1715–1754*, vol. 1, pp. 9–10.

105 Langford, *Public Life and the Propertied Englishman*, p. 146.

106 Sidney and Beatrice Webb, *English Local Government* (new edn, 11 vols, Hamden, CN, 1963), vol. 1, p. xviii; Josef Redlich and Francis W. Hirst, *Local Government in England* (2 vols, Macmillan, London, 1903), vol. 1, p. 56.

107 Lionel Glassey, 'Local Government', in *Britain in the First Age of Party*, ed. Clyve Jones (Hambledon Press, London, 1987), pp. 152–3.

108 Palmer, *Police and Protest*, pp. 71–4.

109 The Webbs, *English Local Government*, vol. 1; Bryan Keith-Lucas, *The Unreformed Local Government System* (Croom Helm, London, 1980), ch. 1; David Eastwood, *Government and Community in the English Provinces, 1700–1870* (Macmillan, London, 1997), pp. 34–45.

110 The Webbs, *English Local Government*, vol. 1, pp. 4–5.

111 Eastwood, *Government and Community*, p. 47.

112 Norma Landau, *The Justices of the Peace, 1679–1760* (University of California Press, Berkeley, 1984), pp. 1–2, 362; Esther Moir, *The Justice of the Peace* (Penguin, Harmondsworth, 1969), p. 127.

113 Landau, *The Justices of the Peace*, pp. 23–5, the Webbs, *English Local Government*, vol. 1, pp. 300–1, 390–1, 418–19.

114 Moir, *The Justice of the Peace*, pp. 121–3, 146–7; Joanna Innes, 'Politics and Morals: The Reformation of Manners Movement in Later Eighteenth-Century England', in *The Transformation of Political Culture*, ed. Eckhart Hellmuth (Oxford University Press, Oxford, 1990), pp. 57–118, esp. pp. 67–8.

115 The Webbs, *English Local Government*, vol. 1, pp. 369–70; Eastwood, *Government and Community*, pp. 99, 107–8, 130–1, 244.

116 Eastwood, *Government and Community*, pp. 1–4.

117 The Webbs, *English Local Government*, vol. 1, p. 525.

118 Beattie, *Crime and the Courts*, pp. 306–7; Joanna Innes, 'The King's Bench Prison in the Later Eighteenth Century', in *An Ungovernable People*, eds Brewer and Styles, pp. 250–98.

119 Atiyah, *The Rise and Fall of Freedom of Contract*, pp. 19–21.

120 The Webbs, *English Local Government*, vol. 4, esp. pp. 1–3, 152, 200–1, 348; P. J. Corfield, *The Impact of English Towns 1700–1800* (Oxford University Press, Oxford, 1982), pp. 177–9; Langford, *Public Life and the Propertied Englishman*, pp. 207, 214, 234–6.

121 Joanna Innes, 'The "Mixed Economy of Welfare" in Early Modern England', in *Charity, Self-Interest and Welfare in the English Past 1795–1834*, ed. Martin Daunton (UCL Press, London, 1996), pp. 139–80; Kathleen Wilson, 'Urban Culture and Political Activism: The Example of Voluntary Hospitals', in *The Transformation of Political Culture*, ed. Hellmuth, pp. 165–84.

122 For useful summaries, see J. D. Marshall, *The Old Poor Law 1795–1834* (2nd edn, Macmillan, London, 1985); Paul Slack, *The English Poor Law, 1531–1782* (Cambridge University Press, Cambridge, 1995).

123 Slack, *The English Poor Law*, pp. 22–6.

124 Daunton, *Progress and Poverty*, pp. 449–50.

125 Tim Hitchcock, 'Paupers and Preachers: The SPCK and the Parochial Workhouse Movement', in *Stilling the Grumbling Hive*, eds Davison et al., pp. 145–66, esp. p. 160.

126 The Webbs, *English Local Government*, vol. 4, pp. 114–16; Eastwood, *Government and Community*, p. 130; Lynn Hollen Lees, *The Solidarities of Strangers: The English Poor Laws and the People, 1700–1948* (Cambridge University Press, Cambridge, 1998), p. 71; Slack, *The English Poor Law*, p. 35.

127 See e.g. K. D. M. Snell, 'Pauper Settlement and the Right to Poor Relief in England and Wales', *Continuity and Change*, 6 (1991), pp. 384–99. For a contrasting view, see Norma Landau, 'The Laws of Settlement and the Surveillance of Immigration in Eighteenth-Century Kent', *Continuity and Change*, 3 (1988), pp. 391–420.

128 The Webbs, *English Local Government*, vol. 7, pp. 308–9, 332–4; Lees, *The Solidarities of Strangers*, pp. 28–30; Ursula R. Q. Henriques, *Before the Welfare State: Social Administration in Early Industrial Britain* (Longman, London, 1979), p. 16; Eastwood, *Government and Community*, p. 48.

129 Dorothy Marshall, *The English Poor in the Eighteenth Century* (G. Routledge & Sons, London, 1926), pp. 187–206; the Webbs, *English Local Government*, vol. 7, pp. 198–9.

Chapter 3   The Limits of the *Laissez-Faire* State, 1815–1880

1 For an overview, see David Cannadine, 'The Past and the Present in the English Industrial Revolution 1880–1980', *Past & Present*, 103 (1984), pp. 159–67.

2 William Hazlitt, *Political Essays* (William Hone, London, 1819), pp. 261–2.

3 Philip Harling and Peter Mandler, 'From "Fiscal–Military" State to *Laissez-faire* State, 1760–1850', *Journal of British Studies*, 32 (1993), pp. 44–70, esp. pp. 56–60; Philip Harling, *The Waning of 'Old Corruption': The Politics of Economical Reform in Britain, 1779–1846* (Oxford University Press, Oxford, 1996), p. 178; Michael Mann, *The Sources of Social Power* (2 vols, Cambridge University Press, Cambridge, 1986, 1993), vol. 2, ch. 11.

4 Mann, *The Sources of Social Power*, vol. 2, pp. 370–5.

5 Patrick O'Brien, 'The Impact of the French Revolutionary and Napoleonic Wars, 1793–1815, on the Long-run Growth of the British Economy', *Review* (Fernand Braudel Centre), 12 (1989), pp. 335–96, esp. pp. 373–9.

6 David French, *The British Way in Warfare 1688–2000* (Unwin Hyman, London, 1990), pp. 120–1.

7 Lance Davis and Robert A. Huttenback, *Mammon and the Pursuit of Empire: The Political Economy of British Imperialism, 1860–1912* (Cambridge University Press, Cambridge, 1986), pp. 13–14.

8 B. R. Mitchell, *British Historical Statistics* (Cambridge University Press, Cambridge, 1988), pp. 9–12, 580–7.

9 Norman Gash, ' "Cheap Government", 1815–1874', in his *Pillars of Government and Other Essays on State and Society, c.1770–1880* (Edward Arnold, London, 1986), p. 54; Paul Kennedy, *The Rise and Fall of the Great Powers* (Unwin Hyman, London, 1988), pp. 151–2.

10 Jenifer Hart, 'The Genesis of the Northcote–Trevelyan Report', in *Studies in the Growth of Nineteenth-Century Government*, ed. Gillian Sutherland (Routledge & Kegan Paul, London, 1972), pp. 63–81; Henry Roseveare, *The Treasury 1660–1870* (George Allen & Unwin, London, 1973), pp. 168–70.

11 J. M. Bourne, *Patronage and Society in Nineteenth-Century England* (Edward Arnold, London, 1986).

12 Philip Harling, 'The Politics of Administrative Change', *Jahrbuch für Europäische Verwaltungsgeschichte*, 8 (1996), pp. 191–212.

13 E. P. Thompson, *The Making of the English Working Class* (Vintage edn, New York, 1963), ch. 15.

14 Stanley Palmer, *Police and Protest in England and Ireland 1780–1850* (Cambridge University Press, Cambridge, 1988), p. 190.

15   *Hansard's Parliamentary Debates*, vol. 41, col. 497 (30 Nov. 1819).

16   Boyd Hilton, *The Age of Atonement: The Influence of Evangelicalism on Social and Economic Thought, 1795–1865* (Oxford University Press, Oxford, 1988), pp. 220–6.

17   Boyd Hilton, *Corn, Cash, Commerce: The Economic Policies of the Tory Governments 1815–1830* (Oxford University Press, Oxford, 1977), esp. pp. 176–84.

18   Albert H. Imlah, *Economic Elements of the 'Pax Britannica': Studies in British Foreign Trade in the Nineteenth Century* (Harvard, Cambridge, MA, 1958), p. 122; Harling, *The Waning of 'Old Corruption'*, pp. 182–5.

19   Frank O'Gorman, *Voters, Patrons, and Parties: The Unreformed Electoral System of Hanoverian England 1734–1832* (Oxford University Press, Oxford, 1989); James Vernon, *Politics and the People* (Cambridge University Press, Cambridge, 1993).

20   Norman Gash, *Politics in the Age of Peel* (W. W. Norton, New York, 1953); O'Gorman, *Voters, Patrons, and Parties*, pp. 392–3.

21   D. E. D. Beales, 'The Electorate Before and After 1832: The Right to Vote, and the Opportunity', *Parliamentary History*, 11 (1992), pp. 139–50.

22   Miles Taylor, 'Interests, Parties and the State: The Urban Electorate in England, c.1820–72', in *Party, State and Society: Electoral Behaviour in Britain since 1820*, eds Jon Lawrence and Miles Taylor (Scolar, Aldershot, 1997), pp. 50–78, esp. pp. 54–5.

23   Jonathan Parry, *The Rise and Fall of Liberal Government in Victorian Britain* (Yale University Press, New Haven, CT, 1993), pp. 78–88.

24   J. C. D. Clark, *English Society 1688–1832* (Cambridge University Press, Cambridge, 1985), esp. pp. 408–13.

25   John Walsh and Stephen Taylor, 'Introduction: The Anglican Church in the Eighteenth Century', in *The Church of England, c.1689–c.1833: From Toleration to Tractarianism*, eds John Walsh and Stephen Taylor (Cambridge University Press, Cambridge, 1993), pp. 61–2.

26   See e.g. Richard Brent, *Liberal Anglican Politics: Whiggery, Religion, and Reform 1830–1841* (Oxford University Press, Oxford, 1987); Peter Virgin, *The Church in an Age of Negligence: Ecclesiastical Structure and Problems of Church Reform 1700–1840* (Cambridge University Press, Cambridge, 1989); A. D. Gilbert, *Religion and Society in Industrial England* (Longman, London, 1976), ch. 6.

27   See esp. D. E. D. Beales, 'Peel, Russell, and Reform', *Historical Journal*, 17 (1974), pp. 873–82; Peter Mandler, 'Cain and Abel: Two Aristocrats and the Early Victorian Factory Acts', *Historical Journal*, 27 (1984), pp. 83–109; Peter Mandler, *Aristocratic Government in the Age of Reform: Whigs and Liberals, 1830–1852* (Oxford University Press, Oxford, 1990), esp. pp. 141–50, 182–93, 237–67.

28   T. A. Jenkins, *Parliament, Party and Politics in Victorian Britain* (Manchester University Press, Manchester, 1996), pp. 37–8.

29   Parry, *The Rise and Fall of Liberal Government in Victorian Britain*, p. 141; Colin Leys, 'Petitioning in the Nineteenth and Twentieth Centuries', *Political Studies*, 4 (1956), pp. 45–64, esp. pp. 47, 58–61.

30 Vernon Bogdanor, *The Monarchy and the Constitution* (Oxford University Press, Oxford, 1995), pp. 17–41; Betty Kemp, *King and Commons 1660–1832* (Macmillan, London, 1959), pp. 111–12.

31 G. H. L. Le May, *The Victorian Constitution: Conventions and Contingencies* (Duckworth, London, 1979), p. 24.

32 Bogdanor, *The Monarchy and the Constitution*, p. 40; W. Ivor Jennings, *Cabinet Government* (Cambridge University Press, Cambridge, 1936), pp. 253–81.

33 A. S. Turberville, *The House of Lords in the Age of Reform 1784–1837* (Faber and Faber, London, 1958); E. A. Smith, 'Charles, Second Earl Grey and the House of Lords', in *Lords of Parliament: Studies, 1714–1914*, ed. Richard W. Davis (Stanford University Press, Stanford, 1995), pp. 79–96; Richard W. Davis, 'Introduction', in *Lords of Parliament*, ed. Davis, pp. 1–8; Jenkins, *Parliament, Party and Politics*, pp. 11–12.

34 J. V. Beckett, *The Aristocracy in England* (Blackwell, Oxford, 1986), pp. 432–3.

35 G. R. Searle, *Entrepreneurial Politics in Mid-Victorian Britain* (Oxford University Press, Oxford, 1993), p. 294.

36 Walter Bagehot, *The English Constitution* (1867; Cornell University Press edn, Ithaca, NY, 1993), ch. 4.

37 Parry, *The Rise and Fall of Liberal Government*, pp. 8–9; Jenkins, *Parliament, Party and Politics*, pp. 18–19.

38 Jose Harris, *Private Lives, Public Spirit: Britain 1870–1914* (Penguin, London, 1993), p. 184.

39 Quoted in Harling, *The Waning of 'Old Corruption'*, p. 252.

40 See esp. Anthony Howe, *Free Trade and Liberal England 1846–1946* (Oxford University Press, Oxford, 1997), esp. chs 1, 3, 7–8.

41 Parry, *The Rise and Fall of Liberal Government*, pp. 166–79.

42 H. C. G. Matthew, *Gladstone, 1809–1874* (Oxford University Press, Oxford, 1986), pp. 168–9.

43 J. P. Parry, *Democracy and Religion: Gladstone and the Liberal Party, 1867–1875* (Cambridge University Press, Cambridge, 1986); Boyd Hilton, 'Gladstone's Theological Politics', in *High and Low Politics in Modern Britain*, eds Michael Bentley and John Stevenson (Oxford University Press, Oxford, 1983), pp. 28–57.

44 Peter Ghosh, 'Disraelian Conservatism: A Financial Approach', *English Historical Review*, 99 (1984), pp. 268–96.

45 Paul Smith, *Disraelian Conservatism and Social Reform* (Routledge & Kegan Paul, London, 1967); Boyd Hilton, 'Disraeli, English Culture, and the Decline of the Industrial Spirit', in *A Union of Multiple Identities: The British Isles, c.1750–c.1850*, eds Laurence Brockliss and David Eastwood (Manchester University Press, Manchester, 1997), pp. 44–59.

46 Dorothy Thompson, *The Chartists: Popular Politics in the Industrial Revolution* (Pantheon, New York, 1984); Margot Finn, *After Chartism: Class and Nation in English Radical Politics, 1848–1874* (Cambridge University Press, Cambridge, 1993), pp. 82–103.

47 F. C. Mather, *Public Order in the Age of the Chartists* (Manchester University Press, Manchester, 1959), chs 3–4; Palmer, *Police and Protest*, ch. 5.

48 John Saville, *1848: The British State and the Chartist Movement* (Cambridge University Press, Cambridge, 1987), pp. 205–29.

49 Gareth Stedman Jones, 'Rethinking Chartism', in his *Languages of Class: Studies in English Working-Class History 1832–1982* (Cambridge University Press, Cambridge, 1983), pp. 174–8; Trygve Tholfsen, *Working-Class Radicalism in Mid-Victorian England* (Columbia University Press, New York, 1977); Stewart Weaver, *John Fielden and the Politics of Popular Radicalism 1832–1847* (Oxford University Press, Oxford, 1987), pp. 14–15, 249; John Foster, *Class Struggle and the Industrial Revolution* (Weidenfeld & Nicolson, London, 1974), pp. 206–9.

50 Olive Anderson, *A Liberal State at War: English Politics and Economics during the Crimean War* (Macmillan, London, 1967); Searle, *Entrepreneurial Politics*.

51 Miles Taylor, *The Decline of British Radicalism 1847–1860* (Oxford University Press, Oxford, 1995).

52 Eugenio Biagini, *Liberty, Retrenchment, and Reform: Popular Liberalism in the Age of Gladstone, 1860–1880* (Cambridge University Press, Cambridge, 1992), esp. pp. 84–102; Eugenio Biagini, 'Popular Liberals, Gladstonian Finance, and the Debate on Taxation, 1860–1874', in *Currents of Radicalism*, eds Eugenio Biagini and Alastair Reid (Cambridge University Press, Cambridge, 1991), pp. 134–62.

53 Maurice Cowling, *1867: Disraeli, Gladstone, and Revolution* (Cambridge University Press, Cambridge, 1967).

54 O'Gorman, *Voters, Patrons, and Parties*, p. 182; Parry, *The Rise and Fall of Liberal Government*, pp. 215–17.

55 J. D. Marshall, *The Old Poor Law 1795–1834* (2nd edn, Macmillan, London, 1985), pp. 23–6; David Eastwood, *Governing Rural England: Tradition and Transformation in Local Government 1780–1840* (Oxford University Press, Oxford, 1994), pp. 134–5; Derek Fraser, *The Evolution of the British Welfare State* (Macmillan, London, 1973), p. 38.

56 Eastwood, *Governing Rural England*, pp. 142–3.

57 M. J. Daunton, *Progress and Poverty: An Economic and Social History of Britain 1700–1850* (Oxford University Press, Oxford, 1995), pp. 458–9; Mark Blaug, 'The Myth of the Old Poor Law and the Making of the New', *Journal of Economic History*, 23 (1963), pp. 151–84; Mark Blaug, 'The Poor Law Report Reexamined', *Journal of Economic History*, 24 (1964), pp. 229–45; Ursula R. Q. Henriques, *Before the Welfare State: Social Administration in Early Industrial Britain* (Longman, London, 1979), p. 24.

58 J. R. Poynter, *Society and Pauperism: English Ideas on Poor Relief, 1795–1834* (Routledge & Kegan Paul, London, 1969), pp. xviii–xxv, 245–7.

59 Lynn Hollen Lees, *The Solidarities of Strangers: The English Poor Laws and the People, 1700–1948* (Cambridge University Press, Cambridge, 1998), p. 41.

60 Hilton, *The Age of Atonement*, p. 245.

61 S. E. Finer, *The Life and Times of Edwin Chadwick* (Methuen, London, 1952), pp. 72–5.

62 Nicholas C. Edsall, *The Anti-Poor Law Movement 1834–44* (Manchester University Press, Manchester, 1971), chs 2–8.

63 Derek Fraser, 'The English Poor Law and the Origins of the British Welfare State', in *The Emergence of the Welfare State in Britain and Germany*, ed. Wolfgang Mommsen (Croom Helm, London, 1981), pp. 9–31; Anne Digby, 'The Rural Poor Law', in *The New Poor Law in the Nineteenth Century*, ed. Derek Fraser (St Martin's, New York, 1976), pp. 149–70; Anne Digby, *Pauper Palaces* (Routledge & Kegan Paul, London, 1978).

64 Eric J. Evans, *The Forging of the Modern State* (Longman, London, 1988), p. 224.

65 Mitchell, *British Historical Statistics*, p. 605; Evans, *The Forging of the Modern State*, p. 225.

66 Karel Williams, *From Poverty to Pauperism* (Routledge & Kegan Paul, London, 1981), pp. 89, 102–4; Lees, *The Solidarities of Strangers*, pp. 178–210.

67 Margaret Crowther, *The Workhouse System 1834–1929: The History of an English Social Institution* (University of Georgia Press, Athens, 1981), pp. 42–4, 198–9; Sidney and Beatrice Webb, *English Local Government* (new edn, 11 vols, Archon Books Hamden, CN, 1963), vol. 10, pp. 55–6, 72–5; Finer, *The Life and Times of Edwin Chadwick*, pp. 84–6; Lees, *The Solidarities of Strangers*, p. 147.

68 David Roberts, 'How Cruel was the Victorian Poor Law?', *Historical Journal*, 6 (1963), pp. 97–106.

69 F. M. L. Thompson, *The Rise of Respectable Society* (Harvard University Press, Cambridge, MA, 1988), pp. 201–2; Geoffrey Finlayson, *Citizen, State, and Social Welfare in Britain 1830–1990* (Oxford University Press, Oxford, 1994), pp. 24–34.

70 Lees, *The Solidarities of Strangers*, ch. 5.

71 Finlayson, *Citizen, State, and Social Welfare*, pp. 62–3; Brian Harrison, *Peaceable Kingdom: Stability and Change in Modern Britain* (Oxford University Press, Oxford, 1982), p. 217; Anthony S. Wohl, *The Eternal Slum: Housing and Social Policy in Victorian London* (Edward Arnold, London, 1977), p. 141; Norman McCord, 'The Poor Law and Philanthropy', in *The New Poor Law*, ed. Fraser, pp. 91–3.

72 K. Theodore Hoppen, *The Mid-Victorian Generation 1846–1886* (Oxford University Press, Oxford, 1998), pp. 114–16.

73 V. A. C. Gatrell, 'Crime, Authority and the Policeman-State', in *The Cambridge Social History of Britain 1750–1950*, ed. F. M. L. Thompson (3 vols, Cambridge University Press, Cambridge, 1990), vol. 3, pp. 243–310.

74 Martin Wiener, *Reconstructing the Criminal: Culture, Law, and Policy in England, 1830–1914* (Cambridge University Press, Cambridge, 1990), pp. 141–56; Thompson, *The Rise of Respectable Society*, pp. 309–11, 315–16.

75 Robert D. Storch, 'The Plague of the Blue Locusts: Police Reform and Popular Resistance in Northern England, 1840–57', *International Review of Social History*, 20 (1975), pp. 61–90; Robert D. Storch, 'The

Policeman as Domestic Missionary: Urban Discipline and Popular Culture in Northern England, 1850–1880', *Journal of Social History*, 9 (1976), pp. 481–509; Bob Bushaway, *By Rite: Custom, Ceremony and Community in England 1700–1880* (Junction Books, London, 1982), pp. 242–5; Hugh Cunningham, 'The Metropolitan Fairs: A Case Study in the Social Control of Leisure', in *Social Control in Nineteenth-Century Britain*, ed. A. P. Donajgrodzki (Croom Helm, London, 1977), pp. 163–84, esp. pp. 163–5; David Taylor, *The New Police in Nineteenth-Century England: Crime, Conflict and Control* (Manchester University Press, Manchester, 1997), pp. 106–7.

76   J. M. Beattie, *Crime and the Courts in England 1660–1800* (Princeton University Press, Princeton, NJ, 1986), pp. 636–7.

77   Quoted in Michael Ignatieff, *A Just Measure of Pain: The Penitentiary in the Industrial Revolution, 1750–1850* (Pantheon, New York, 1978), p. 177.

78   Ignatieff, *A Just Measure of Pain*, ch. 7.

79   Michael Ignatieff, 'State, Civil Society and Total Institutions: A Critique of Recent Social Histories of Punishment', in *Social Control and the State*, eds Stanley Cohen and Andrew Scull (Martin Robertson, Oxford, 1983), pp. 75–105; Lucia Zedner, *Women, Crime, and Custody in Victorian England* (Oxford University Press, Oxford, 1991).

80   Henriques, *Before the Welfare State*, pp. 183–4.

81   Judith Walkowitz, *Prostitution and Victorian Society: Women, Class, and the State* (Cambridge University Press, Cambridge, 1980); Stefan Petrow, *Policing Morals: The Metropolitan Police and the Home Office 1870–1914* (Oxford University Press, Oxford, 1994), pp. 120–2.

82   Sydney Checkland, *British Public Policy 1776–1939* (Cambridge University Press, Cambridge, 1983), pp. 152–3; Mary Lyndon Shanley, *Feminism, Marriage, and the Law in Victorian England, 1850–1895* (Princeton University Press, Princeton, NJ, 1989), ch. 1.

83   Margot Finn, 'Women, Consumption, and Coverture in England, *c.*1760–1860', *Historical Journal*, 39 (1996), pp. 703–22; Margot Finn, 'Working-Class Women and the Contest for Consumer Control in Victorian County Courts', *Past & Present*, 161 (1998), pp. 116–54.

84   Gail L. Savage, ' "Intended Only for the Husband": Gender, Class, and the Provision of Divorce in England, 1858–1868', in *Victorian Scandals: Representations of Gender and Class*, ed. Kristine Garrigan (Ohio University Press, Athens, 1992), esp. pp. 26–8.

85   Wally Seccombe, 'Patriarchy Stabilised: The Construction of the Male Breadwinner Norm in Nineteenth-Century Britain', *Social History*, 11 (1986), pp. 53–76; Mariana Valverde, ' "Giving the Female a Domestic Turn": The Social, Legal, and Moral Regulation of Women's Work in British Cotton Mills, 1830–1850', *Journal of Social History*, 21 (1988), pp. 619–34; Sonya Rose, *Limited Livelihoods: Gender and Class in Nineteenth-Century England* (University of California Press, Berkeley, 1991), pp. 50–72; Pat Thane, 'Women and the Poor Law in Victorian and Edwardian England', *History Workshop*, 6 (1978), pp. 29–51.

86   Tholfsen, *Working-Class Radicalism in Mid-Victorian England*, pp. 179–89.

87   James Hinton, *Labour and Socialism: A History of the British Labour Movement 1867–1974* (University of Massachusetts Press, Amherst, 1983), ch. 3; Jonathan Spain, 'Trade Unionists, Gladstonian Liberals and the Labour Law Reforms of 1875', in *Currents of Radicalism*, eds Biagini and Reid, pp. 109–33.

88   James E. Cronin, *The Politics of State Expansion: War, State and Society in Twentieth-Century Britain* (Routledge, London, 1991), p. 24; Neville Kirk, *The Growth of Working-Class Reformism in Mid-Victorian England* (University of Illinois Press, Urbana, 1985), pp. 267–301.

89   Karl Polanyi, *The Great Transformation: The Political and Economic Origins of Our Time* (Beacon, Boston, 1944), p. 141.

90   Quoted in *Report on the Sanitary Condition of the Labouring Population*, ed. M. W. Flinn (Edinburgh University Press, Edinburgh, 1965), p. 39.

91   Harold Perkin, 'Individualism versus Collectivism in Nineteenth-Century Britain: A False Antithesis', *Journal of British Studies*, 17 (1977), pp. 105–18; Henry Parris, 'The Nineteenth Century Revolution in Government: A Reappraisal Reappraised', in *The Victorian Revolution: Government and Society in Victoria's Britain*, ed. Peter Stansky (New Viewpoints, New York, 1973), pp. 29–60, esp. p. 54; W. L. Burn, *The Age of Equipoise: A Study of the Mid-Victorian Generation* (Norton edn, New York, 1965), pp. 134–5, 220; Arthur J. Taylor, *Laissez-Faire and State Intervention in Nineteenth-Century Britain* (Macmillan, London, 1972), pp. 36–7; Patrick Atiyah, *The Rise and Fall of Freedom of Contract* (Oxford University Press, Oxford, 1979), p. 231; William C. Lubenow, *The Politics of Government Growth* (David & Charles, Newton Abbot, 1971), pp. 83–4.

92   Flinn, ed., *Report on the Sanitary Condition of the Labouring Population*; Finer, *Life and Times of Edwin Chadwick*, pp. 216–19.

93   Christopher Hamlin, *Public Health and Social Justice in the Age of Chadwick: Britain, 1800–1854* (Cambridge University Press, Cambridge, 1998).

94   Fraser, *The Evolution of the British Welfare State*, pp. 82–5.

95   Fraser, 'The English Poor Law and the Origins of the British Welfare State', in *The Emergence of the Welfare State*, ed. Mommsen, pp. 9–31.

96   Oliver MacDonagh, 'The Nineteenth-Century Revolution in Government: A Reappraisal', in *The Victorian Revolution*, ed. Stansky, pp. 5–28; Oliver MacDonagh, *A Pattern of Government Growth 1800–1860* (MacGibbon & Kee, London, 1961); G. Kitson Clark, ' "Statesmen in Disguise": Reflexions on the History of the Neutrality of the Civil Service', in *The Victorian Revolution*, ed. Stansky, pp. 61–92, esp. pp. 84–5; G. M. Young, *Victorian England: Portrait of an Age* (Oxford University Press, Oxford, 1980), p. 46; Burn, *The Age of Equipoise*, esp. pp. 224–5.

97   See e.g. Jenifer Hart, 'Nineteenth-Century Social Reform: A Tory Interpretation of History', *Past & Present*, 31 (1965), pp. 39–61; Parris, 'The Nineteenth-Century Revolution in Government: A Reappraisal Reappraised'.

98   See e.g. G. F. A. Best, *Shaftesbury* (Batsford, London, 1964).

99   David Roberts, 'Tory Paternalism and Social Reform in Early Victorian England', in *The Victorian Revolution*, ed. Stansky, pp. 147–68; David

Roberts, *Paternalism in Early Victorian England* (Rutgers University Press, New Brunswick, NJ, 1979), esp. pp. 206–9, 271–2; David Roberts, *Victorian Origins of the British Welfare State* (Yale University Press, New Haven, 1960), pp. 65–6; Ashley, quoted in Geoffrey Finlayson, 'Shaftesbury', in *Pressure from Without in Early Victorian England*, ed. Patricia Hollis (Edward Arnold, London, 1974), pp. 159–82, esp. p. 167.

100 Cecil Driver, *Tory Radical: The Life of Richard Oastler* (Oxford University Press, Oxford, 1946); J. T. Ward, *The Factory Movement 1830–1855* (Macmillan, London, 1962).

101 Hilton, *The Age of Atonement*, pp. 212–13.

102 R. G. Kirby and A. E. Musson, *The Voice of the People: John Doherty 1798–1854: Trade Unionist, Radical and Factory Reformer* (Manchester University Press, Manchester, 1976); Weaver, *John Fielden*.

103 Oliver MacDonagh, *Early Victorian Government 1830–1870* (Holmes & Meier, London, 1977), pp. 48–51; Henriques, *Before the Welfare State*, pp. 79–87.

104 Weaver, *John Fielden*, pp. 274–87.

105 MacDonagh, *Early Victorian Government*, pp. 72–4; Fraser, *The Evolution of the British Welfare State*, p. 27.

106 Robert Gray, *The Factory Question and Industrial England, 1830–1860* (Cambridge University Press, Cambridge, 1996), esp. pp. 71–2, 95–6.

107 Roberts, *Victorian Origins*, pp. 87–95; Harold Perkin, *Origins of Modern English Society* (ARK Paperbacks edn, London, 1985), pp. 438–42; H. W. Arthurs, *Without the Law: Administrative Justice and Legal Pluralism in Nineteenth-Century England* (University of Toronto Press, Toronto, 1985), pp. 130–1.

108 Ursula Henriques, 'Jeremy Bentham and the Machinery of Social Reform', in *British Government and Administration*, eds H. Hearder and H. R. Loyn (University of Wales Press, Cardiff, 1974), pp. 169–86, esp. pp. 175–7; Roberts, *Victorian Origins*, pp. 106–9.

109 Norman McCord, 'Some Limitations of the Age of Reform', in *British Government and Administration*, eds Hearder and Loyn, p. 198.

110 P. W. J. Bartrip, 'State Intervention in Mid-Nineteenth Century Britain: Fact or Fiction?', *Journal of British Studies*, 23 (1983), pp. 63–83, esp. pp. 76–7. See also P. W. J. Bartrip, 'British Government Inspection, 1832–1875: Some Observations', *Historical Journal*, 25 (1982), pp. 605–26, esp. pp. 612–13.

111 Perkin, *Origins of Modern English Society*, pp. 331–8.

112 Roberts, *Victorian Origins*, pp. 318–20.

113 Most notably A. V. Dicey, *Lectures on the Relation Between Law and Public Opinion in England, during the Nineteenth Century* (Macmillan, London, 1905); Parris, 'The Nineteenth-Century Revolution in Government: A Reappraisal Reappraised'; Hart, 'Nineteenth-Century Social Reform'; David Roberts, 'Jeremy Bentham and the Victorian Administrative State', *Victorian Studies*, 2 (1959), pp. 193–210; Henriques, 'Jeremy Bentham and the Machinery of Social Reform'.

114 Flinn, ed., *Report on the Sanitary Condition of the Labouring Population*, pp. 27–9.

115 Perkin, *Origins of Modern English Society*, pp. 267–9.
116 David Roberts, 'The Utilitarian Conscience', in *The Conscience of the Victorian State*, ed. Peter Marsh (Syracuse University Press, Syracuse, NY, 1979), pp. 39–72, esp. pp. 58–66.
117 S. E. Finer, 'The Transmission of Benthamite Ideas', in *Studies in the Growth of Nineteenth-Century Government*, ed. Sutherland, pp. 11–32; Kitson Clark, 'Statesmen in Disguise'.
118 Mandler, *Aristocratic Government in the Age of Reform*, pp. 247–66.
119 Anthony S. Wohl, *Endangered Lives: Public Health in Victorian Britain* (Harvard University Press, Cambridge, MA, 1983), pp. 148–50.
120 Christopher Hamlin, 'Edwin Chadwick and the Engineers, 1842–1854: Systems and Anti-Systems in the Pipe-and-Brick Sewers War', *Technology and Culture*, 33 (1992), pp. 680–709.
121 Royston Lambert, 'A Victorian National Health Service: State Vaccination, 1855–71', *Historical Journal*, 5 (1962), pp. 1–18.
122 Quoted in Fraser, *The Evolution of the British Welfare State*, p. 69. See also Royston Lambert, *Sir John Simon 1816–1904 and English Social Administration* (MacGibbon & Kee, London, 1963).
123 This and the following paragraph rely on Fraser, *The Evolution of the British Welfare State*, pp. 60–4.
124 Wohl, *Endangered Lives*, pp. 101–2.
125 Ibid., p. 170.
126 Henriques, *Before the Welfare State*, pp. 123–5.
127 See e.g. Joshua Toulmin Smith, *A Letter to the Metropolitan Sanitary Commissioners* (London, 1848), p. iv.
128 Wohl, *The Eternal Slum*, pp. 73–4.
129 Enid Gauldie, *Cruel Habitations: A History of Working-Class Housing 1780–1918* (George Allen & Unwin, London, 1974), pp. 276–7.
130 Wohl, *The Eternal Slum*, pp. 139–45, 188–99.
131 Maxine Berg, *The Machinery Question and the Making of Political Economy 1815–1848* (Cambridge University Press, Cambridge, 1980), pp. 250–2, 296–7.
132 Paul Richards, 'The State and Early Industrial Capitalism', *Past & Present*, 83 (1979), pp. 91–115.
133 Hoppen, *The Mid-Victorian Generation*, p. 110.
134 Roberts, *Victorian Origins*, pp. 272–3.
135 Hoppen, *The Mid-Victorian Generation*, p. 123.
136 Ibid., pp. 107–8.
137 The Webbs, *English Local Government*, vol. 1, pp. 557–8, 605–6.
138 Bryan Keith-Lucas, *The Unreformed Local Government System* (Croom Helm, London, 1980), p. 102.
139 David Eastwood, *Government and Community in the English Provinces, 1700–1870* (Macmillan, London, 1997), pp. 110–11; Eastwood, *Governing Rural England*, conclusion.
140 Derek Fraser, ed., *Municipal Reform and the Industrial City* (Leicester University Press, Leicester, 1982), pp. 2–3; Biagini, *Liberty, Retrenchment, and Reform*, pp. 320–1.

141 W. H. Greenleaf, *The British Political Tradition* (3 vols, Methuen, London, 1983, 1987), vol. 3, pp. 52–3.

142 See e.g. P. W. Musgrave, *Society and Education in England since 1800* (Methuen, London, 1968), pp. 21–38; Eric Midwinter, *Nineteenth-Century Education* (Longman, London, 1970), pp. 37–8; Michael Sanderson, *Education, Economic Change and Society in England 1780–1870* (Macmillan, London, 1983), p. 59ff; John Lawson and Harold Silver, *A Social History of Education in England* (Methuen, London, 1973), p. 290ff.

143 E. P. Hennock, 'Finance and Politics in Urban Local Government in England, 1835–1900', *Historical Journal*, 6 (1963), pp. 212–25; E. P. Hennock, *Fit and Proper Persons: Ideal and Reality in Nineteenth-Century Urban Government* (Edward Arnold, London, 1973); V. A. C. Gatrell, 'Incorporation and the Pursuit of Liberal Hegemony in Manchester 1790–1839', in *Municipal Reform*, ed. Fraser, pp. 16–60, esp. pp. 51–2; Brian Barber, 'Municipal Government in Leeds 1835–1914', in *Municipal Reform*, ed. Fraser, pp. 104–5.

144 Anthony Howe, *The Cotton Masters 1830–1860* (Oxford University Press, Oxford, 1984), pp. 154–60.

145 Theodore Koditschek, *Class Formation and Urban-Industrial Society: Bradford, 1750–1850* (Cambridge University Press, Cambridge, 1990), p. 321.

146 See esp. Derek Fraser, 'Joseph Chamberlain and the Municipal Ideal', in *Victorian Values: Personalities and Perspectives in Nineteenth-Century Society*, ed. Gordon Marsden (Longman, London, 1990), pp. 135–46.

147 F. M. L. Thompson, 'Town and City', in *The Cambridge Social History*, ed. Thompson, vol. 1, pp. 1–86, esp. pp. 64–71.

Chapter 4   The Making of the Social-Service State, 1880–1939

1 Jose Harris, *Private Lives, Public Spirit: Britain 1870–1914* (Penguin, London, 1993), pp. 216–17.

2 K. Theodore Hoppen, *The Mid-Victorian Generation 1846–1886* (Oxford University Press, Oxford, 1998), p. 124.

3 Quoted in Gertrude Himmelfarb, *Poverty and Compassion: The Moral Imagination of the Late Victorians* (Alfred A. Knopf, New York, 1991), p. 309.

4 Martin Wiener, *Reconstructing the Criminal: Culture, Law, and Policy in England, 1830–1914* (Cambridge University Press, Cambridge, 1990), pp. 186–7, 338; Jose Harris, 'The Transition to High Politics in English Social Policy', in *High and Low Politics in Modern Britain*, eds Michael Bentley and John Stevenson (Oxford University Press, Oxford, 1983), pp. 58–79, esp. pp. 70–1.

5 M. E. Rose, *The Relief of Poverty, 1834–1914* (Macmillan, London, 1972), p. 28.

6 Jose Harris, *Unemployment and Politics: A Study in English Social Policy 1886–1914* (Oxford University Press, Oxford, 1972), pp. 35–7; Rose, *The Relief of Poverty*, pp. 28–9.

7 Anthony S. Wohl, *The Eternal Slum: Housing and Social Policy in Victorian London* (Edward Arnold, London, 1977), pp. 210–30.

8 Reba Soffer, *Ethics and Society in England: The Revolution in the Social Sciences 1870–1914* (University of California Press, Berkeley, 1978), ch. 4; Harris, *Unemployment and Politics*, pp. 1–2; Sydney Checkland, *British Public Policy 1776–1939* (Cambridge University Press, Cambridge, 1983), pp. 175–6.

9 Melvin Richter, *The Politics of Conscience: T. H. Green and his Age* (Weidenfeld & Nicolson, London, 1964); Harold Perkin, *The Rise of Professional Society: England since 1880* (Routledge, London, 1989), pp. 124–7; Himmelfarb, *Poverty and Compassion*, ch. 17; Patrick Atiyah, *The Rise and Fall of Freedom of Contract* (Oxford University Press, Oxford, 1979), p. 585; David Nicholls, 'Positive Liberty, 1880–1914', *American Political Science Quarterly*, 56 (1962), pp. 114–28.

10 Himmelfarb, *Poverty and Compassion*, ch. 16.

11 Derek Fraser, 'The English Poor Law and the Evolution of the British Welfare State'; Karel Williams, *From Poverty to Pauperism* (Routledge & Kegan Paul, London, 1981), pp. 107–44; Lynn Hollen Lees, *The Solidarities of Strangers: The English Poor Laws and the People, 1700–1948* (Cambridge University Press, Cambridge, 1998), pp. 280–1; Michael Rose, 'The Crisis of Poor Relief in England 1860–1890', in *The Emergence of the Welfare State in Britain and Germany*, ed. Wolfgang Mommsen (Croom Helm, London, 1981), pp. 50–70, esp. pp. 60–1; A. M. McBriar, *An Edwardian Mixed Doubles: The Bosanquets versus the Webbs* (Oxford University Press, Oxford, 1987), pp. 43–4.

12 Margaret Crowther, *The Workhouse System 1834–1929: The History of an English Social Institution* (University of Georgia Press, Athens, 1981), pp. 222–3.

13 Paul Johnson, 'Risk, Redistribution and Social Welfare in Britain from the Poor Law to Beveridge', in *Charity, Self-Interest and Welfare*, ed. Martin Daunton (UCL Press, London, 1996), pp. 225–48, esp. pp. 237–8.

14 Harris, *Unemployment and Politics*, pp. 42–3, 141–2; Pat Thane, *Foundations of the Welfare State* (Longman, London, 1982), pp. 10–11; Himmelfarb, *Poverty and Compassion*, pp. 123–5; Gareth Stedman Jones, *Outcast London* (Pantheon, New York, 1971), pp. 312–14.

15 G. R. Searle, *The Quest for National Efficiency* (University of California Press, Berkeley, 1971), pp. 54–5. See also Bernard Semmel, *Imperialism and Social Reform: English Social-Imperial Thought 1895–1914* (Harvard University Press, Cambridge, MA, 1960); H. C. G. Matthew, *The Liberal Imperialists* (Oxford University Press, Oxford, 1973).

16 Bentley B. Gilbert, *The Evolution of National Insurance in Great Britain: The Origins of the Welfare State* (Michael Joseph, London, 1966), ch. 2.

17 Quoted in Perkin, *The Rise of Professional Society*, p. 59.

18 Mark Mazower, *Dark Continent: Europe's Twentieth Century* (Alfred A. Knopf, New York, 1998), pp. 96–7.

19 Wiener, *Reconstructing the Criminal*, esp. pp. 259–62; Stefan Petrow, *Policing Morals: The Metropolitan Police and the Home Office 1870–1914* (Oxford University Press, Oxford, 1994).

20 Jeffrey Weeks, *Sex, Politics and Society: The Regulation of Sexuality since 1800* (Longman, London, 1989), pp. 86–103.

21 V. A. C. Gatrell, 'Crime, Authority and the Police-Man State', in *The Cambridge Social History of Britain 1750–1950*, ed. F. M. L. Thompson (3 vols, Cambridge University Press, Cambridge, 1990), pp. 263, 308–9.

22 Harris, *Private Lives, Public Spirit*, pp. 208–10.

23 David Taylor, *The New Police in Nineteenth-Century England: Crime, Conflict and Control* (Manchester University Press, Manchester, 1997), p. 106.

24 For a useful overview of electoral reform in this era, see Harris, *Private Lives, Public Spirit*, pp. 190–1.

25 This paragraph relies on James E. Cronin, *The Politics of State Expansion: War, State and Society in Twentieth-Century Britain* (Routledge, London, 1991), ch. 3.

26 James Cronin, 'The British State and the Structure of Political Opportunity', *Journal of British Studies*, 27 (1988), pp. 199–231, esp. p. 215.

27 See esp. A. M. McBriar, *Fabian Socialism and English Politics 1884–1918* (Cambridge University Press, Cambridge, 1962).

28 Henry Pelling, *The Origins of the Labour Party 1880–1900* (Oxford University Press, Oxford, 1965), pp. 118–19.

29 Arthur Marwick, 'The Labour Party and the Welfare State in Britain, 1900–1948', *American Historical Review*, 73 (1967), pp. 380–403; Kenneth D. Brown, *Labour and Unemployment 1900–1914* (Rowman & Littlefield, Totowa, NJ, 1971), pp. 170–1.

30 Ross McKibbin, *The Ideologies of Class: Social Relations in Britain, 1880–1950* (Oxford University Press, Oxford, 1994), p. 3.

31 Richard Price, *Labour in British Society: An Interpretive History* (Croom Helm, London, 1982), esp. pp. 71–93; James Hinton, *Labour and Socialism: A History of the British Labour Movement 1867–1974* (University of Massachusetts Press, Amherst, 1983), ch. 4; McKibbin, *The Ideologies of Class*, pp. 18–39; John Belchem, *Class, Party and the Political System in Britain 1867–1914* (Blackwell, Oxford, 1990), pp. 70–1.

32 Paul Johnson, *Saving and Spending: The Working-Class Economy in Britain 1870–1939* (Oxford University Press, Oxford, 1985), esp. pp. 14, 193–4; Geoffrey Finlayson, *Citizen, State, and Social Welfare in Britain 1830–1990* (Oxford University Press, Oxford, 1994), p. 127; Thane, *Foundations of the Welfare State*, pp. 28–9.

33 Martin Pugh, *State and Society: British Political and Social History 1870–1992* (Arnold, London, 1994), pp. 45–6; J. S. Hurt, *Elementary Schooling and the Working Classes 1860–1918* (Routledge & Kegan Paul, London, 1979); Ellen Ross, *Love and Toil: Motherhood in Outcast London, 1870–1918* (Oxford University Press, New York, 1993), pp. 24–5; Hugh Heclo, *Modern Social Politics in Britain and Sweden: From Relief to Income Maintenance* (Yale University Press, New Haven, 1974), pp. 89–90.

34 See Henry Pelling, *Popular Politics and Society in Late-Victorian Britain* (Macmillan, London, 1968), pp. 1–18; Pat Thane, 'The Working Class and State "Welfare" in Britain, 1880–1914', *Historical Journal*, 27 (1984), pp. 877–900.

35 See e.g. Stuart Hall and Bill Schwartz, 'State and Society, 1880–1930', in *Crises in the British State 1880–1930*, eds Mary Langan and Bill Schwartz (Hutchinson, London, 1985); John Saville, 'The Welfare State: An Historical Approach', *New Reasoner*, 3 (1957–8), pp. 1–24.

36 Quoted in Derek Fraser, *The Evolution of the British Welfare State* (Macmillan, London, 1973), p. 129.

37 Paul Smith, ed., *Lord Salisbury on Politics* (Cambridge University Press, Cambridge, 1972), intro.; Peter Marsh, *The Discipline of Popular Government: Lord Salisbury's Domestic Statecraft, 1881–1902* (Harvester Press, Hassocks, Sussex, 1978).

38 McBriar, *An Edwardian Mixed Doubles*, pp. 52–3.

39 Harris, 'The Transition to High Politics in English Social Policy', pp. 63–6.

40 Ibid., pp. 58–63.

41 Jose Harris, 'Society and State in Twentieth-Century Britain', in *The Cambridge Social History*, ed. Thompson, vol. 3, pp. 63–118, esp. pp. 65–70.

42 Pat Thane, 'Government and Society in England and Wales, 1750–1914', in *The Cambridge Social History*, ed. Thompson, vol. 3, p. 44.

43 Harris, *Private Lives, Public Spirit*, p. 191.

44 P. J. Waller, *Town, City, and Nation: England 1850–1914* (Oxford University Press, Oxford, 1983), pp. 300–13.

45 Quoted in Derek Fraser, 'Joseph Chamberlain and the Municipal Ideal', in *Victorian Values: Personalities and Perspectives in Nineteenth-Century Society*, ed. Gordon Marsden (Longman, London, 1990), p. 145.

46 See e.g. John Davis, *Reforming London: The London Government Problem, 1855–1900* (Oxford University Press, Oxford, 1988), chs 5–6. For a more negative assessment, see Susan Pennybacker, *A Vision for London 1889–1914: Labour, Everyday Life and the LCC Experiment* (Routledge, London, 1995).

47 See esp. Pat Thane, 'Labour and Local Politics: Radicalism, Democracy and Social Reform, 1880–1914', in *Currents of Radicalism*, eds Eugenio Biagini and Alastair Reid (Cambridge University Press, Cambridge, 1991), pp. 244–70.

48 Waller, *Town, City, and Nation*, pp. 256–7; Martin Daunton, 'Housing', in *The Cambridge Social History*, ed. Thompson, vol. 2, pp. 195–250, esp. pp. 226–7; Martin Daunton, *House and Home in the Victorian City: Working-Class Housing 1850–1914* (Edward Arnold, London, 1983), pp. 201–2.

49 See esp. Avner Offer, *Property and Politics 1870–1914* (Cambridge University Press, Cambridge, 1981).

50 A. T. Peacock and Jack Wiseman, *The Growth of Public Expenditure in the United Kingdom* (2nd edn, George Allen & Unwin, London, 1967), p. 208.

51 E. P. Hennock, 'Finance and Politics in Urban Local Government in England, 1835–1900', *Historical Journal*, 6 (1963), pp. 212–25, esp. pp. 224–5; G. C. Baugh, 'Government Grants in Aid of the Rates in England and Wales, 1889–1990', *Historical Research*, 65 (1992), pp. 215–37, esp. pp. 216–20.

52 Paul Kennedy, *The Rise and Fall of the Great Powers* (Unwin Hyman, London, 1988), p. 224.

53 Lance Davis and Robert A. Huttenback, *Mammon and the Pursuit of Empire: The Political Economy of British Imperialism, 1860–1912* (Cambridge University Press, Cambridge, 1986), p. 304.

54 Kennedy, *The Rise and Fall of the Great Powers*, pp. 203–9; William H. McNeill, *The Pursuit of Power: Technology, Armed Force, and Society since A.D. 1000* (University of Chicago Press, Chicago, 1982), pp. 286–7.

55 Patrick O'Brien, 'The Costs and Benefits of British Imperialism 1846–1914', *Past & Present*, 120 (1988), pp. 163–200, esp. pp. 186–8, 193–4.

56 Harris, 'The Transition to High Politics in English Social Policy', pp. 76–8; E. H. H. Green, *The Crisis of Conservatism: The Politics, Economics and Ideology of the British Conservative Party, 1880–1914* (Routledge, London, 1995), pp. 48–51.

57 Green, *The Crisis of Conservatism*, esp. pp. 22–3, 155–6, 192–3, 206, 261–2, 327–9.

58 See esp. Anthony Howe, *Free Trade and Liberal England 1846–1946* (Oxford University Press, Oxford, 1997), pp. 230–52, 272; Bruce K. Murray, *The People's Budget 1909–10: Lloyd George and Liberal Politics* (Oxford University Press, Oxford, 1980), pp. 23–37.

59 Checkland, *British Public Policy*, pp. 176–7.

60 Thane, *Foundations of the Welfare State*, pp. 87–8.

61 Thane, 'Government and Society', p. 59; H. V. Emy, *Liberals, Radicals and Social Politics 1892–1914* (Cambridge University Press, Cambridge, 1973), pp. 233–4.

62 Murray, *The People's Budget*, pp. 310–11.

63 O'Brien, 'The Costs and Benefits of British Imperialism', pp. 194–5.

64 F. M. L. Thompson, 'English Landed Society in the Twentieth Century', *Transactions of the Royal Historical Society*, 5th ser., 40 (1990), pp. 1–24; 6th ser., 1 (1991), pp. 1–23; 6th ser., 2 (1992), pp. 1–21; 6th ser., 3 (1993), pp. 1–22.

65 Doreen Collins, 'The Introduction of Old Age Pensions in Britain', *Historical Journal*, 8 (1965), pp. 246–59; Thane, *Foundations of the Welfare State*, pp. 82–4; Heclo, *Modern Social Politics*, p. 156.

66 Thane, *Foundations of the Welfare State*, pp. 85–7; J. R. Hay, *The Origins of the Liberal Welfare Reforms 1906–1914* (Macmillan, London, 1975), pp. 54–7; Gilbert, *The Evolution of National Insurance*, chs 6–7; Johnson, 'Risk, Redistribution and Social Welfare', pp. 236–7.

67 Thane, *Foundations of the Welfare State*, pp. 94–7; David Sutton, 'Liberalism, State Collectivism and the Social Relations of Citizenship', in *Crises in the British State*, eds Langan and Schwartz, pp. 74–5.

68 Jean S. Heywood, *Children in Care* (3rd edn, Routledge & Kegan Paul, London, 1978), pp. 108–9; George Behlmer, *Child Abuse and Moral Reform in England, 1870–1908* (Stanford University Press, Stanford, 1982), pp. 220–3.

69 David Powell, *British Politics and the Labour Question, 1868–1990* (St Martin's, New York, 1992), p. 35; Henry Pelling, *A History of British Trade*

Unionism (Macmillan, London, 1963), pp. 130–1; Checkland, *British Public Policy*, pp. 225–6.

70　Powell, *British Politics and the Labour Question*, p. 36.

71　Jane Morgan, *Conflict and Order: The Police and Labour Disputes in England and Wales, 1900–1939* (Oxford University Press, Oxford, 1987), pp. 17, 280.

72　Roger Davidson, 'Llewellyn Smith, the Labour Department and Government Growth 1886–1909', in *Studies in the Growth of Nineteenth-Century Government*, ed. Gillian Sutherland (Routledge & Kegan Paul, London, 1972), pp. 227–62; Keith Middlemas, *Politics in Industrial Society: The Experience of the British System since 1911* (André Deutsch, London, 1979), pp. 58–64; Joe White, '1910–1914 Reconsidered', in *Social Conflict and the Political Order in Modern Britain*, eds James E. Cronin and Jonathan Schneer (Rutgers University Press, New Brunswick, NJ, 1982), p. 87; Checkland, *British Public Policy*, p. 209.

73　See esp. Checkland, *British Public Policy*, pp. 219–21.

74　Harris, *Unemployment and Politics*, pp. 159, 289; Lord Askwith, *Industrial Problems and Disputes* (Harper & Row, New York, 1974), pp. 278–9; Checkland, *British Public Policy*, pp. 215–17.

75　Michael Freeden, *The New Liberalism: An Ideology of Social Reform* (Oxford University Press, Oxford, 1978). See also Paul Addison, *Churchill on the Home Front* (Pimlico, London, 1993), pp. 60–1; Emy, *Liberals, Radicals and Social Politics*, p. 104ff.

76　Quoted in Brian Harrison, *The Transformation of British Politics 1860–1995* (Oxford University Press, Oxford, 1996), p. 69.

77　Thane, *Foundations of the Welfare State*, pp. 88–90, 139; Harris, *Unemployment and Politics*, pp. 258–81; McBriar, *An Edwardian Mixed Doubles*, chs 8–11; Lees, *The Solidarities of Strangers*, pp. 320–2.

78　Pat Thane, 'Non-Contributory versus Contributory Pensions 1878–1908', in *The Origins of British Social Policy*, ed. Pat Thane (Croom Helm, London, 1978), pp. 84–106.

79　Arthur Marwick, *Britain in the Century of Total War: War, Peace and Social Change, 1900–1967* (Bodley Head, London, 1968), pp. 33–5; Harris, *Unemployment and Politics*, pp. 349–56; Howe, *Free Trade and Liberal England*, pp. 250–2; John Saville, 'The British State, the Business Community and the Trade Unions', in *The Development of Trade Unions in Great Britain and Germany, 1880–1914*, eds Wolfgang Mommsen and H.-G. Husung (Allen & Unwin, London, 1985), pp. 315–24.

80　McKibbin, *The Ideologies of Class*, pp. 18–39.

81　David Vincent, *The Culture of Secrecy: Britain 1832–1998* (Oxford University Press, Oxford, 1998), p. 141.

82　Belchem, *Class, Party and the Political System*, p. 5; Pelling, *A History of British Trade Unionism*, pp. 127–8.

83　Pat Thane, 'Women and the Poor Law in Victorian and Edwardian England', *History Workshop*, 6 (1978), pp. 29–51, esp. pp. 32–3, 48–9.

84　Ross, *Love and Toil*, ch. 7.

85　Harris, 'Society and State', pp. 65–7.

86   J. M. Winter, *The Great War and the British People* (Macmillan, London, 1986), p. 75; Arthur Marwick, *The Deluge: British Society and the First World War* (Bodley Head, London, 1965), p. 290.

87   This paragraph follows J. M. Bourne, *Britain and the Great War 1914–1918* (Edward Arnold, London, 1989), pp. 177–8.

88   Kennedy, *The Rise and Fall of the Great Powers*, p. 274.

89   Cronin, *The Politics of State Expansion*, pp. 2–3.

90   David Cannadine, *The Decline and Fall of the British Aristocracy* (Picador, London, 1992), p. 111. See also W. A. Armstrong, 'The Countryside', in *The Cambridge Social History*, ed. Thompson, vol. 1, pp. 87–154, esp. pp. 136–7.

91   Marwick, *The Deluge*, p. 191; Arthur Marwick, *War and Social Change in the Twentieth Century* (Macmillan, London, 1974), pp. 58–9; Cronin, *The Politics of State Expansion*, pp. 60–1; Fakhi Shehab, *Progressive Taxation* (Oxford University Press, Oxford, 1953), pp. 258–9; B. E. V. Sabine, *A History of Income Tax* (George Allen & Unwin, London, 1966), pp. 151–3; Forrest Capie and Geoffrey Wood, 'Money in the Economy, 1870–1939', in *The Economic History of Britain since 1700*, eds Roderick Floud and Donald McCloskey (2nd edn, 3 vols, Cambridge University Press, Cambridge, 1994), pp. 217–46, esp. pp. 232–3.

92   See e.g. Thomas C. Kennedy, 'Public Opinion and the Conscientious Objector, 1915–1919', *Journal of British Studies*, 12 (1973), pp. 105–19; Marwick, *The Deluge*, pp. 81–2; Bourne, *Britain and the Great War*, pp. 212–13.

93   See e.g. F. S. L. Lyons, *Culture and Anarchy in Ireland 1890–1939* (Oxford University Press, Oxford, 1979); Charles Townshend, *Political Violence in Ireland: Government and Resistance since 1848* (Oxford University Press, Oxford, 1983); Charles Townshend, *The British Campaign in Ireland 1919–21* (Oxford University Press, Oxford, 1975); David Fitzpatrick, *Politics and Irish Life 1913–1921* (Gill & Macmillan, Dublin, 1977).

94   Cronin, *The Politics of State Expansion*, pp. 71–2.

95   For an excellent overview of these governmental changes, see Harris, 'Society and State', pp. 71–2.

96   See e.g. Chris Wrigley, 'The Ministry of Munitions', in *War and the State: The Transformation of British Government, 1914–1919*, ed. Kathleen Burk (George Allen & Unwin, London, 1982), pp. 32–56; Bourne, *Britain and the Great War*, pp. 188–91; Jose Harris, *William Beveridge: A Biography* (Oxford University Press, Oxford, 1977), pp. 208–9.

97   See e.g. Susan Pedersen, *Family, Dependence, and the Origins of the Welfare State* (Cambridge University Press, Cambridge, 1993), pp. 83–5; Marwick, *The Deluge*, pp. 208–9.

98   Middlemas, *Politics in Industrial Society*, pp. 75–6; Cronin, *The Politics of State Expansion*, pp. 45–6; Jose Harris, 'Bureaucrats and Businessmen in British Food Control, 1916–1919', in *War and the State*, ed. Burk, pp. 135–56, esp. p. 135; D. J. Oddy, 'Food, Drink and Nutrition', in *The Cambridge Social History*, ed. Thompson, vol. 2, pp. 251–78, esp. p. 262; Marwick, *The Deluge*, pp. 195–6; McNeill, *The Pursuit of Power*, p. 343.

99   See e.g. Duncan Tanner, *Political Change and the Labour Party, 1900–1918* (Cambridge University Press, Cambridge, 1990), pp. 352–5; Marwick, *Britain in the Century of Total War*, pp. 105–7; Pedersen, *Family, Dependence, and the Origins of the Welfare State*; Ross McKibbin, *The Evolution of the Labour Party 1910–1924* (Oxford University Press, Oxford, 1974), pp. 238–40.

100   Marwick, *War and Social Change*, p. 70; Marwick, *Britain in the Century of Total War*, pp. 123–5.

101   Pedersen, *Family, Dependence, and the Origins of the Welfare State*, pp. 107–13.

102   H. C. G. Matthew, J.A. Kay, and Ross McKibbin, 'The Franchise Factor in the Rise of the Labour Party', *English Historical Review*, 91 (1976), pp. 723–52; Susan Kingsley Kent, *Sex and Suffrage in Britain, 1860–1914* (Princeton University Press, Princeton, 1987), esp. pp. 82–5, 221–2.

103   R. H. Tawney, 'The Abolition of Economic Controls, 1918–1921', *Economic History Review*, 13 (1943), pp. 1–30.

104   Bourne, *Britain and the Great War*, p. 193.

105   I owe this list of factors to Harris, 'Society and State', pp. 82–3.

106   Rodney Lowe, 'The Erosion of State Intervention in Britain, 1917–24', *Economic History Review*, 2nd ser., 31 (1978), pp. 270–86.

107   Henry Roseveare, *The Treasury 1660–1870* (George Allen & Unwin, London, 1973), pp. 187–9.

108   Tawney, 'The Abolition of Economic Controls'; Peter Cline, 'Winding Down the War Economy: British Plans for Peacetime Recovery, 1916–19', in *War and the State*, ed. Burk, pp. 157–81; Sutton, 'Liberalism, State Collectivism and the Social Relations of Citizenship'.

109   Max Beloff, 'The Whitehall Factor: The Role of the Higher Civil Service 1919–39', in *The Politics of Reappraisal, 1918–1939*, eds Gillian Peele and Chris Cook (St Martin's, New York, 1975); Roger Davidson and Rodney Lowe, 'Bureaucracy and Innovation in British Welfare Policy 1870–1945', in *The Emergence of the Welfare State*, ed. Mommsen, pp. 263–95, esp. pp. 280–2.

110   Harris, 'Society and the State', pp. 75–7; Rodney Lowe, *Adjusting to Democracy: The Role of the Ministry of Labour in British Politics, 1916–1939* (Oxford University Press, Oxford, 1986), pp. 8–11.

111   Philip Williamson, 'The Doctrinal Politics of Stanley Baldwin', in *Public and Private Doctrine*, ed. Michael Bentley (Cambridge University Press, Cambridge, 1993), pp. 181–208; David Jarvis, 'The Shaping of Conservative Electoral Hegemony, 1918–39', in *Party, State and Society: Electoral Behaviour in Britain since 1820*, eds Jon Lawrence and Miles Taylor (Scolar, Aldershot, 1997), pp. 131–52.

112   Susan Howson, *Domestic Monetary Management in Britain 1919–38* (Cambridge University Press, Cambridge, 1975), pp. 140–3; Robert Skidelsky, *Politicians and the Slump: The Labour Government of 1929–1931* (Macmillan, London, 1967), pp. 2–3; P. J. Cain and A. G. Hopkins, *British Imperialism: Crisis and Deconstruction 1914–1990* (Longman, Harlow, 1993), pp. 40–1;

Thane, *Foundations of the Welfare State*, pp. 165–6; Checkland, *British Public Policy*, pp. 291–4.

113 Ross McKibbin, *Classes and Cultures: England 1918–1951* (Oxford University Press, Oxford, 1998), esp. pp. 269–75.

114 Hinton, *Labour and Socialism*, pp. 109–15.

115 Powell, *British Politics and the Labour Question*, pp. 82–4; Hinton, *Labour and Socialism*, p. 141.

116 Alec Cairncross and Barry Eichengreen, *Sterling in Decline* (Blackwell, Oxford, 1983), pp. 17–19, 102; Forrest Capie, *Depression and Protectionism* (Gregg, Aldershot, 1994); G. C. Peden, *British Economic and Social Policy: Lloyd George to Margaret Thatcher* (Philip Allan, London, 1985), pp. 100–1.

117 Checkland, *British Public Policy*, pp. 312–14; Peden, *British Economic and Social Policy*, pp. 102–3; Sidney Pollard, *The Development of the British Economy* (3rd edn, Edward Arnold, London, 1983), pp. 82–8.

118 John Stevenson, *Social Conditions in Britain Between the Wars* (Penguin, Harmondsworth, 1977), p. 16.

119 Michael Stewart, *Keynes and After* (2nd edn, Penguin, Harmondsworth, 1972), pp. 96–115; S. N. Broadberry, *The British Economy Between the Wars: A Macroeconomic Survey* (Blackwell, London, 1986), pp. 154–5; Peden, *British Economic and Social Policy*, pp. 74–8, 109–10; Skidelsky, *Politicians and the Slump*, pp. 16–17; Mark Thomas, 'The Macro-Economics of the Inter-War Years', in *The Economic History of Britain*, eds Floud and McCloskey, vol. 2, pp. 320–58, esp. pp. 356–7.

120 See esp. Skidelsky, *Politicians and the Slump*, p. 69; K. O. Morgan, *Labour in Power 1945–1951* (Oxford University Press, Oxford, 1985), pp. 11–13.

121 McKibbin, *The Ideologies of Class*, pp. 224–6; Barry Eichengreen, 'The Inter-War Economy in a European Mirror', in *The Economic History of Britain*, eds Floud and McCloskey, vol. 2, pp. 291–319, esp. p. 311; Robert Skidelsky, 'Keynes and the Treasury View: The Case For and Against an Active Employment Policy in Britain 1920–1939', in *The Emergence of the Welfare State*, ed. Mommsen, pp. 167–87, esp. pp. 185–7.

122 Harris, *William Beveridge*, pp. 352–3.

123 Alan Deacon, *In Search of the Scrounger: The Administration of Unemployment Insurance in Britain 1920–1931* (University of Leeds Press, Leeds, 1976), pp. 17–18; Heclo, *Modern Social Politics*, pp. 90, 110–12.

124 Skidelsky, *Politicians and the Slump*, p. 282.

125 Deacon, *In Search of the Scrounger*, p. 9.

126 Noreen Branson and Margot Heinemann, *Britain in the 1930s* (Praeger, New York, 1971), pp. 22–50.

127 Alan Deacon and Jonathan Bradshaw, *Reserved for the Poor: The Means Test in British Social Policy* (Martin Robertson, Oxford, 1983), pp. 26–8.

128 Alun Howkins and John Saville, 'The Nineteen Thirties: A Revisionist History', in *The Socialist Register*, eds Ralph Miliband and John Saville (Merlin Press, London, 1979), pp. 89–100.

129 Pedersen, *Family, Dependence, and the Origins of the Welfare State*, esp. pp. 304–8; Jane Lewis, 'Models of Equality for Women: The Case of State

Support for Children in Twentieth-Century Britain', in *Maternity and Gender Policies: Women and the Rise of the European Welfare States*, eds Gisela Bock and Pat Thane (Routledge, London, 1991), pp. 73–92, esp. pp. 82–3; Pat Thane, 'Visions of Gender in the Making of the Welfare State', in *Maternity and Gender Policies*, eds Bock and Thane, pp. 93–118, esp. p. 112.

130   Thane, *Foundations of the Welfare State*, p. 170; Hinton, *Labour and Socialism*, pp. 122–3.

131   McKibbin, *Classes and Cultures*, p. 38; G. F. Shirras and Laszlo Rostas, *The Burden of British Taxation* (Cambridge University Press, Cambridge, 1942), p. 58.

132   Peden, *British Economic and Social Policy*, pp. 78–80.

133   B. R. Mitchell, *British Historical Statistics* (Cambridge University Press, Cambridge, 1988), pp. 590–1.

134   Peacock and Wiseman, *The Growth of Public Expenditure*, pp. 190–1.

135   Hinton, *Labour and Socialism*, pp. 122–3.

136   Peacock and Wiseman, *The Growth of Public Expenditure*, pp. 164–6.

137   McBriar, *An Edwardian Mixed Doubles*, pp. 303–5, 366–7; Bentley B. Gilbert, *British Social Policy 1914–1939* (Cornell University Press, Ithaca, NY, 1970), p. 235; Branson and Heinemann, *Britain in the 1930s*, pp. 222–5; Noreen Branson, *Popularism* (Lawrence & Wishart, London, 1979).

138   McKibbin, *Classes and Cultures*, pp. 206–9; Gillian Sutherland, 'Education', in *The Cambridge Social History*, ed. Thompson, vol. 3, pp. 119–70, esp. pp. 162–7; Thane, *Foundations of the Welfare State*, pp. 151–2; P. W. Musgrave, *Society and Education in England since 1800* (Methuen, London, 1968), pp. 81–2, 98; Perkin, *The Rise of Professional Society*, pp. 248–9.

139   Johnson, 'Risk, Redistribution and Social Welfare', p. 239.

140   Branson and Heinemann, *Britain in the 1930s*, p. 227.

141   Johnson, 'Risk, Redistribution and Social Welfare', pp. 244–5; Martin Daunton, 'Introduction', in *Charity, Self-Interest and Welfare*, ed. Daunton, pp. 1–22, esp. pp. 9–10; Frank Prochaska, *The Voluntary Impulse: Philanthropy in Modern Britain* (Faber and Faber, London, 1988), p. 88.

142   John Burnett, *A Social History of Housing 1815–1970* (David & Charles, London, 1978), pp. 236–43; Stevenson, *Social Conditions*, pp. 177–8.

143   McKibbin, *Classes and Cultures*, p. 73.

144   Mark Swenarton, *Homes Fit for Heroes: The Politics and Architecture of Early State Housing in Britain* (Heinemann, London, 1981).

145   Baugh, 'Government Grants in Aid of the Rates', pp. 235–6.

146   Lord Hewart, *The New Despotism* (Cosmopolitan, New York, 1929); W. H. Greenleaf, *The British Political Tradition* (3 vols, Methuen, London, 1983, 1987), vol. 3, pp. 540–56; E. L. Hasluck, *Local Government in England* (Cambridge University Press, Cambridge, 1936), p. 17.

147   Peacock and Wiseman, *The Growth of Public Expenditure*, pp. 106–8.

148   Thane, 'Visions of Gender'; Michael Savage, 'Urban Politics and the Rise of the Labour Party, 1919–1939', in *State, Private Life and Political Change*, eds Lynn Jamieson and Helen Carr (St Martin's Press, New York, 1990), pp. 37–51, esp. pp. 28–9; F. M. L. Thompson, 'Town and City', in *Cambridge Social History*, ed. Thompson, vol. 1, pp. 1–86, esp. pp. 78–80.

Chapter 5   Total War and Cradle-to-Grave Welfare, 1939–1979

1   See e.g. Paul Addison, *The Road to 1945* (2nd edn, Pimlico, London, 1994), p. 33.

2   Quoted in Rodney Lowe, *The Welfare State in Britain since 1945* (Macmillan, London, 1993), p. 14.

3   See Lowe, *The Welfare State*, p. 14.

4   Arthur Marwick, *Britain in the Century of Total War: War, Peace and Social Change, 1900–1967* (Bodley Head, London, 1968), p. 257; Arthur Marwick, *War and Social Change*, pp. 114–15; Peter Howlett, 'The Wartime Economy, 1939–1945', in *The Economic History of Britain since 1700*, eds Roderick Floud and Donald McCloskey (2nd edn, 3 vols, Cambridge University Press, Cambridge, 1994), vol. 3, pp. 1–31, esp. p. 29.

5   D. J. Oddy, 'Food, Drink and Nutrition', in *The Cambridge Social History of Britain 1750–1950*, ed. F. M. L. Thompson (3 vols, Cambridge University Press, Cambridge, 1990), p. 263.

6   Steven Broadberry and Peter Howlett, 'The United Kingdom: "Victory at all Costs"', in *The Economics of World War II*, ed. Mark Harrison (Cambridge University Press, Cambridge, 1998), pp. 43–80, esp. p. 57.

7   Marwick, *Britain in the Century of Total War*, pp. 291–3.

8   J. M. Winter, *The Great War and the British People*, pp. 39–40; W. K. Hancock and M. M. Gowing, *The British War Economy* (HMSO, London, 1949), pp. 464–5.

9   See e.g. James Cronin, *Labour and Society in Britain, 1918–1979* (Batsford, London, 1984), pp. 117–18; James E. Cronin, *The Politics of State Expansion: War, State and Society in Twentieth-Century Britain* (Routledge, London, 1991), pp. 145–6; Keith Middlemas, *Power, Competition and the State* (3 vols, Macmillan, London, 1986–91), vol. 1, pp. 344–6.

10 Henry Pelling, *A History of British Trade Unionism*, pp. 220–1; David Powell, *British Politics and the Labour Question, 1868–1990* (St Martin's, New York, 1992), pp. 109–10.

11 See Corelli Barnett, *The Audit of War: The Illusion and Reality of Britain as a Great Nation* (Macmillan, London, 1986).

12 W. D. Rubinstein, *Capitalism, Culture, and Decline in Britain 1750–1990* (Routledge, London, 1993), pp. 21–2; Mark Harrison, 'The Economics of World War II', in *The Economics of World War II*, ed. Harrison, pp. 21–2; Marwick, *Britain in the Century of Total War*, pp. 276–7.

13 Howlett, 'The Wartime Economy', pp. 16–17; B. E. V. Sabine, *A History of Income Tax* (George Allen & Unwin, London, 1966), pp. 296–7; E. A. Wright, *Britain in the Age of Economic Management* (Oxford University Press, Oxford, 1979), p. 135; George Shirras and Laszlo Rostas, *The Burden of British Taxation* (Cambridge University Press, Cambridge, 1942), pp. 26–7; Pat Thane, *Foundations of the Welfare State* (Longman, London, 1982), pp. 262–3.

14 Roger Middleton, 'The Size and Scope of the Public Sector', in *The Boundaries of the State in Modern Britain*, eds S. J. D. Green and R. C. Whiting (Cambridge University Press, Cambridge, 1996), pp. 89–145, esp. p. 98.

15 Jose Harris, 'Society and State in Twentieth-Century Britain', in *The Cambridge Social History*, ed. Thompson, vol. 3, pp. 63–118, esp. p. 94.

16 Scott Newton, *Profits of Peace: The Political Economy of Anglo-German Appeasement* (Oxford University Press, Oxford, 1996), pp. 202–3; John Stevenson, ' "Planners' Noon"? The Second World War and the Planning Movement', in *War and Social Change: British Society in the Second World War*, ed. H. L. Smith (Manchester University Press, Manchester, 1986), pp. 58–77, esp. pp. 66–7; Addison, *The Road to 1945*, p. 118; Jose Harris, 'Political Ideas and the Debate on State Welfare 1940–45', in *War and Social Change*, ed. Smith, pp. 233–63, esp. pp. 236–7.

17 Jose Harris, *William Beveridge: A Biography* (Oxford University Press, Oxford, 1977), ch. 16; Harris, 'Political Ideas', pp. 246–9.

18 Richard Titmuss, *Problems of Social Policy* (HMSO, London, revised edn, 1970), pp. 506–15.

19 Jose Harris, 'Did British Workers Want the Welfare State? G. D. H. Cole's Survey of 1942', in *The Working Class in Modern British History: Essays in Honour of Henry Pelling*, ed. Jay Winter (Cambridge University Press, Cambridge, 1983), pp. 193–214, esp. pp. 213–14.

20 Jose Harris, 'Some Aspects of Social Policy in Britain During the Second World War', in *The Emergence of the Welfare State in Britain and Germany*, ed. Wolfgang Mommsen (Croom Helm, London, 1981), pp. 247–62, esp. pp. 248–9, 256–7.

21 Ben Pimlott, 'The Myth of Consensus', in *Echoes of Greatness*, ed. Lesley M. Smith (Macmillan, Basingstoke, 1988), pp. 129–42; Stephen Brooke, *Labour's War: The Labour Party during the Second World War* (Oxford University Press, Oxford, 1992), esp. pp. 4–6, 171, 342–3; Paul Addison, *Churchill on the Home Front* (Pimlico, London, 1993), p. 440.

22 Thane, *Foundations of the Welfare State*, pp. 264–5; Addison, *The Road to 1945*, p. 21.

23 Addison, *The Road to 1945*, pp. 264–5; Addison, *Churchill on the Home Front*, pp. 383–4; K. O. Morgan, *Labour in Power 1945–1951* (Oxford University Press, Oxford, 1985), pp. 38–9; Brooke, *Labour's War*, pp. 229–30; Ina Zweiniger-Bargielowska, 'Explaining the Gender Gap: The Conservative Party and the Women's Vote, 1945–1964', in *The Conservatives and British Society, 1880–1990*, eds Martin Francis and Ina Zweiniger-Bargielowska (University of Wales Press, Cardiff, 1996), pp. 194–224, esp. pp. 196–209.

24 Ross McKibbin, *The Ideologies of Class: Social Relations in Britain, 1880–1950* (Oxford University Press, Oxford, 1994), p. 302; James Cronin, 'The British State and the Structure of Political Opportunity', *Journal of British Studies*, 27 (1988), pp. 199–231, esp. pp. 228–9.

25 Morgan, *Labour in Power*, pp. 170–4; Hugh Heclo, *Modern Social Politics in Britain and Sweden: From Relief to Income Maintenance* (Yale University Press, New Haven, 1974), p. 147; Lynn Hollen Lees, *The Solidarities of Strangers: The English Poor Laws and the People, 1700–1948* (Cambridge University Press, Cambridge, 1998), p. 328.

26 Rudolf Klein, *The Politics of the National Health Service* (Longman, London, 1983), pp. vii, 1–2; Morgan, *Labour in Power*, pp. 158–63; Harold Perkin, *The Rise of Professional Society: England since 1880* (Routledge, London, 1989), pp. 346–8; Marwick, *Britain in the Century of Total War*, pp. 342–4; Jose Harris, ' "Contract" and Citizenship', in *The Ideas that Shaped Modern Britain*, eds David Marquand and Anthony Seldon (Fontana, London, 1996), pp. 122–38, esp. p. 137.

27 Henry Pelling, *The Labour Governments 1945–51* (Macmillan, London, 1984), pp. 110–13; Morgan, *Labour in Power*, pp. 163–70.

28 Morgan, *Labour in Power*, pp. 138–9; R. Kelf-Cohen, *British Nationalisation 1945–1973* (St Martin's, New York, 1973), pp. 265–8; Leslie Hannah, 'The Economic Consequences of the State Ownership of Industry, 1945–1990', in *The Economic History of Britain*, eds Floud and McCloskey, vol. 3, pp. 168–94, esp. pp. 172–80.

29 Alec Cairncross, *Years of Recovery: British Economic Policy 1945–51* (Methuen, London, 1985); Alec Cairncross, 'Economic Policy and Performance, 1945–1964', in *The Economic History of Britain*, eds Floud and McCloskey, vol. 3, pp. 32–66, esp. pp. 46–9; Morgan, *Labour in Power*, chs 8–9; Pelling, *The Labour Governments*.

30 Steven Fielding, Peter Thompson, and Nick Tiratsoo, *'England Arise!' The Labour Party and Popular Politics in 1940s Britain* (Manchester University Press, Manchester, 1995).

31 Zweiniger-Bargielowska, 'Explaining the Gender Gap'.

32 Morgan, *Labour in Power*, pp. 182–3.

33 C. A. R. Crosland, *The Future of Socialism* (Jonathan Cape, London, 1956), p. 65.

34 Cairncross, 'Economic Policy and Performance, 1945–1964', p. 35; Alan Milward, *The European Rescue of the Nation-State* (University of California Press, Berkeley, 1992), pp. 21, 41–2; Jim Tomlinson, 'British Economic Policy since 1945', in *The Economic History of Britain*, eds Floud and McCloskey, vol. 3, pp. 255–83, esp. p. 264; Michael Pinto-Duschinsky, 'Bread and Circuses? The Conservatives in Office, 1951–1964', in *The Age of Affluence 1951–1964*, eds Vernon Bogdanor and Robert Skidelsky (Macmillan, London, 1970), pp. 78–116, esp. pp. 88–9.

35 E. H. H. Green, 'The Conservative Party, the State, and the Electorate, 1945–64', in *Party, State and Society: Electoral Behaviour in Britain since 1820*, eds Jon Lawrence and Miles Taylor (Scolar, Aldershot, 1997), pp. 176–200, esp. pp. 178–9, 196.

36 Milward, *The European Rescue of the Nation-State*, pp. 33–5.

37 Dennis Kavanagh, *British Politics: Continuities and Change* (Oxford University Press, Oxford, 1985), pp. 183–4.

38 P. J. Cain and A. G. Hopkins, *British Imperialism: Crisis and Deconstruction 1914–1990* (Longman, Harlow, 1993), pp. 234, 265–6, 275–7, 290–1; Paul Kennedy, *The Rise and Fall of the Great Powers* (Unwin Hyman, London, 1988), pp. 367–8; Martin Chick, *Industrial Policy in Britain 1945–1951: Eco-*

nomic Planning, Nationalisation and the Labour Governments (Cambridge University Press, Cambridge, 1998), p. 39; Cairncross, *Years of Recovery*, pp. 230–1; Harold Wilensky, *The Welfare State and Equality* (University of California Press, Berkeley, 1975), pp. 75–9; D. C. Watt, *Succeeding John Bull: America in Britain's Place 1900–1975* (Cambridge University Press, Cambridge, 1984), pp. 149–51; Anthony Seldon, 'Ideas are not Enough', in *The Ideas that Shaped Post-War Britain*, eds Marquand and Seldon, pp. 257–89, esp. pp. 260–1; C. J. Bartlett, *The Long Retreat* (Macmillan, London, 1972); Michael Mann, *States, War and Capitalism* (Blackwell, Oxford, 1988), p. 27.

39   Lowe, *The Welfare State*, pp. 336–7.

40   Paul Johnson, 'The Welfare State', in *The Economic History of Britain*, eds Floud and McCloskey, vol. 3, pp. 284–317, esp. p. 284.

41   All percentages in this and the following paragraph are drawn from Lowe, *The Welfare State*, p. 124.

42   Harris, 'Society and State', p. 108, n. 116.

43   J. F. Sleeman, *The Welfare State: Its Aims, Benefits and Costs* (Allen & Unwin, London, 1973), pp. 66–7; R. M. Page, 'Social Welfare since the War', in *The British Economy since 1945*, eds N. F. R. Crafts and N. W. C. Woodward (Oxford University Press, Oxford, 1991), pp. 443–94, esp. p. 463; Michael Sanderson, *Educational Opportunity and Social Change* (Faber, London, 1987), pp. 62–3; W. H. Greenleaf, *The British Political Tradition* (3 vols, Methuen, London, 1983, 1987), vol. 3, pp. 424–5; Pauline Gregg, *The Welfare State* (University of Massachusetts Press, Amherst, 1969), pp. 304–5; Peter Gosden, *The Education System since 1944* (Martin Robertson, Oxford, 1983), p. 137.

44   Sleeman, *The Welfare State*, p. 79; Anne Digby, *British Welfare Policy: Workhouse to Workfare* (Faber and Faber, London, 1989), pp. 80–1.

45   Ross McKibbin, *Classes and Cultures: England 1918–1951* (Oxford University Press, Oxford, 1998), p. 534.

46   Morgan, *Labour in Power*, p. 90.

47   Gillian Sutherland, 'Education', in *Cambridge Social History*, ed. Thompson, vol. 3, pp. 119–70, esp. p. 168; Sanderson, *Educational Opportunity and Social Change*, pp. 47–51; McKibbin, *Classes and Cultures*, pp. 226–7, 269–71.

48   Johnson, 'The Welfare State', pp. 309–10.

49   Harris, ' "Contract" and "Citizenship" ', p. 130; Vic George and Paul Wilding, *Ideology and Social Welfare* (Routledge & Kegan Paul, London, 1976), pp. 121–5; Peter Baldwin, *The Politics of Social Solidarity: Class Bases of the European Welfare State 1875–1975* (Cambridge University Press, Cambridge, 1990), p. 19; John Saville, 'The Welfare State: An Historical Approach', *New Reasoner*, 3 (1957–8), pp. 1–24, esp. pp. 20–4; Thane, *Foundations of the Welfare State*, pp. 254, 289; Page, 'Social Welfare since the War', pp. 490–1.

50   Harris, *William Beveridge*, pp. 448–9; Johnson, 'The Welfare State', p. 290; Digby, *British Welfare Policy*, pp. 68–9, 129–30; Page, 'Social Welfare since the War', p. 485; A. B. Atkinson, *Poverty in Britain and the Reform of Social Security* (Cambridge University Press, Cambridge, 1969), p. 24; Alan

Deacon and Jonathan Bradshaw, *Reserved for the Poor: The Means Test in British Social Policy* (Martin Robertson, Oxford, 1983), pp. 108–9, 130–2, 196–9; David Vincent, *Poor Citizens: The State and the Poor in Twentieth-Century Britain* (Longman, London, 1991), pp. 142–3.

51   A. W. Dilnot, J. A. Kay, and C. H. Morris, *The Reform of Social Security* (Oxford University Press, Oxford, 1984), pp. 18–19; Vincent, *Poor Citizens*, pp. 172–3; Brian Abel-Smith and Peter Townsend, *The Poor and the Poorest* (G. Bell and Sons, London, 1965), esp. pp. 63–7; Peter Townsend, *Poverty in the United Kingdom: A Survey of Household Resources and Standards of Living* (University of California Press, Berkeley, 1979), p. 915; Johnson, 'The Welfare State', pp. 301–2; Peter Clarke, *Hope and Glory: Britain 1900–1990* (Penguin, Harmondsworth, 1996), pp. 305–6.

52   Kenneth O. Morgan, *The People's Peace* (2nd edn, Oxford University Press, Oxford, 1999), pp. 424–5.

53   Johnson, 'The Welfare State', pp. 302–5.

54   Henry Phelps Brown, *Egalitarianism and the Generation of Inequality* (Oxford University Press, Oxford, 1988), pp. 329–31.

55   Johnson, 'The Welfare State', p. 292; J. C. Kincaid, *Poverty and Equality in Britain* (Penguin, Harmondsworth, 1973), pp. 73–7; Deacon and Bradshaw, *Reserved for the Poor*, pp. 151–3.

56   See e.g. Peter Abel-Smith, 'Whose Welfare State?', in *Conviction*, ed. Norman Mackenzie (MacGibbon & Kee, London, 1959), pp. 55–73; Robert E. Goodin and Julian Le Grand, *Not Only the Poor: The Middle Classes and the Welfare State* (Allen & Unwin, London, 1987); Julian Le Grand, *The Strategy of Equality* (George Allen & Unwin, London, 1982).

57   Barry Supple, 'British Economic Decline since 1945', in *The Economic History of Britain*, eds Floud and McCloskey, vol. 3, pp. 318–46, esp. pp. 320–4; N. F. C. Crafts and N. W. C. Woodward, 'Introduction and Overview', in *The British Economy*, eds Crafts and Woodward, pp. 1–24, esp. p. 8.

58   Supple, 'British Economic Decline', pp. 343–5.

59   Jim Tomlinson, 'British Economic Policy since 1945', in *The Economic History of Britain*, eds Floud and McCloskey, vol. 3, pp. 275–83; Robert Millward, 'Industrial and Commercial Performance since 1950', in *The Economic History of Britain*, eds Floud and McCloskey, vol. 3, pp. 123–67, esp. pp. 158–62; J. D. McCallum, 'The Development of British Regional Policy', in *Regional Policy*, eds Duncan Maclennan and John Parr (Martin Robertson, Oxford, 1979), pp. 3–42, esp. pp. 35–8.

60   Cronin, *The Politics of State Expansion*, pp. 16–17, 241–2; James Hinton, *Labour and Socialism: A History of the British Labour Movement 1867–1974* (University of Massachusetts Press, Amherst, 1983), pp. 190–1.

61   Morgan, *The People's Peace*, pp. 243–98; Sidney Pollard, *The Development of the British Economy, 1914–1990* (4th edn, Edward Arnold, London, 1992), pp. 408–9; Dennis Kavanagh and Peter Morris, *Consensus Politics from Attlee to Thatcher* (Blackwell, Oxford, 1989), pp. 38–9; T. J. Hatton and Alec Chrystal, 'The Budget and Fiscal Policy', in *The British Economy*, eds Crafts and Woodward, pp. 52–88, esp. pp. 68–71; Dennis Kavanagh, *Thatcherism*

and British Politics: The End of Consensus? (Oxford University Press, Oxford, 1987), p. 125.

62 David Marquand, *The Unprincipled Society* (Jonathan Cape, London, 1988), pp. 48ff.

63 Cronin, 'The British State and the Structure of Political Opportunity', pp. 229–30; Samuel H. Beer, *Britain Against Itself: The Political Contradictions of Collectivism* (W. W. Norton, New York, 1982); Harris, 'Society and the State', p. 115; Kavanagh, *British Politics: Continuities and Change*, pp. 166–71; Dennis Kavanagh, 'The Heath Government, 1970–1974', in *Ruling Performance: British Governments from Attlee to Thatcher*, eds Peter Hennessy and Anthony Seldon (Blackwell, Oxford, 1987), pp. 216–40, esp. pp. 234–5; Anthony H. Birch, *The British System of Government* (9th edn, Routledge, London, 1993), p. 116; J. J. Richardson and A. G. Jordan, *Governing Under Pressure: The Policy Process in a Post-Parliamentary Democracy* (Martin Robertson, Oxford, 1979), pp. 44–54; Perkin, *The Rise of Professional Society*, pp. 9–11.

64 Peter Jenkins, *The Battle of Downing Street* (Charles Knight, London, 1970); Morgan, *The People's Peace*, pp. 300–5; Leo Panitch, *Social Democracy and Industrial Militancy* (Cambridge University Press, Cambridge, 1976), pp. 258–9; R. Richardson, 'Trade Unions and Industrial Relations', in *The British Economy*, eds Crafts and Woodward, pp. 439–40.

65 See e.g. Desmond Hamill, *Pig in the Middle: The Army in Northern Ireland, 1969–1985* (Methuen, London, 1985); Jack Holland, *Too Long a Sacrifice: Life and Death in Northern Ireland since 1969* (Dodd, Mead, New York, 1981).

66 David Butler and Anne Sloman, *British Political Facts 1900–1975* (4th edn, St Martin's, New York, 1980), pp. 264–5; Robert Taylor, *The Fifth Estate: Britain's Unions in the Seventies* (Routledge & Kegan Paul, London, 1978), p. 240.

67 Greenleaf, *The British Political Tradition*, vol. 3, pp. 566–7, 628–9; Gillian Peele, 'The Developing Constitution', in *Trends in British Politics since 1945*, eds Chris Cook and John Ramsden (Macmillan, London, 1978), pp. 1–27, esp. pp. 10–14; Marwick, *Britain in the Century of Total War*, pp. 396–7; Michael Hill, *The State, Administration, and the Individual* (Rowman & Littlefield, Totowa, NJ, 1976), pp. 157–9.

68 Greenleaf, *The British Political Tradition*, vol. 3, pp. 339–40.

69 Hugh Heclo and Aaron Wildavsky, *The Private Government of Public Money* (University of California Press, Berkeley, 1974); David Heald, *Public Expenditure: Its Defence and Reform* (Martin Robertson, Oxford, 1983), pp. 151–73.

70 See esp. Peter Hennessy, *Whitehall* (Secker & Warburg, London, 1989); Peter Kellner and Lord Crowther-Hunt, *The Civil Servants: An Inquiry into Britain's Ruling Class* (Macdonald General Books, London, 1980).

71 G. C. Baugh, 'Government Grants in Aid of the Rates in England and Wales, 1889–1990', *Historical Research*, 65 (1992), pp. 215–37, esp. pp. 225–8; Bryan Keith-Lucas and Peter G. Richards, *A History of Local Government in the Twentieth Century* (George Allen & Unwin, London, 1978),

pp. 47–53, 127–31, 149–51; Alex Henney, *Inside Local Government: A Case for Radical Reform* (Sinclair Browne, London, 1984), pp. 57–8, 157, 280–1; William Hampton, *Local Government and Urban Politics* (2nd edn, Longman, London, 1991), pp. 22–50; Douglas Ashford, *British Dogmatism and French Pragmatism* (George Allen & Unwin, London, 1982), pp. 251–66; Brian Harrison, *The Transformation of British Politics 1860–1995* (Oxford University Press, Oxford, 1996), p. 119; C. D. Foster, R. A. Jackman, and M. Perlman, *Local Government Finance in a Unitary State* (George Allen & Unwin, London, 1980), pp. 127–31; Clifford Pearce, *The Machinery of Change in Local Government 1888–1974* (George Allen & Unwin, London, 1980), pp. 8–9.

72 See esp. Vernon Bogdanor, *Devolution* (Oxford University Press, Oxford, 1979); Michael Hechter, *Internal Colonialism: The Celtic Fringe in British National Development, 1536–1966* (Routledge & Kegan Paul, London, 1978), ch. 5.

73 Quoted in Derek W. Urwin, *The Community of Europe: A History of European Integration since 1945* (Longman, London, 1991), p. 31.

74 John Pinder, *European Community: Building of a Union* (Oxford University Press, Oxford, 1991); Urwin, *The Community of Europe*; Uwe W. Kitzinger, *The Politics and Economics of European Integration: Britain, Europe, and the United States* (Frederick A. Praeger, New York, 1964); N. Piers Ludlow, *Dealing with Britain: The Six and the First UK Application to the EEC* (Cambridge University Press, Cambridge, 1997).

75 Harris, 'Society and State', pp. 109, 111.

76 See e.g. David Vincent, *The Culture of Secrecy: Britain 1832–1998* (Oxford University Press, Oxford, 1998), pp. 254–6.

77 Heclo, *Modern Social Politics*, p. 326.

78 Jose Harris, 'Political Thought and the State', in *The Boundaries of the State*, eds Green and Whiting, pp. 15–28.

79 Paul Johnson, 'Some Historical Dimensions of the Welfare State "Crisis"', *Journal of Social Policy*, 15 (1986), pp. 443–65, esp. pp. 454–5.

80 Vincent, *Poor Citizens*, pp. 176–81; Patrick Dunleavy, *The Politics of Mass Housing in Britain, 1945–1975* (Oxford University Press, Oxford, 1981); John Burnett, *A Social History of Housing 1815–1970* (David & Charles, London, 1978), pp. 286–9; John R. Short, *Housing in Britain: The Post-War Experience* (Methuen, London, 1982), pp. 168–9.

81 Hugh Heclo, 'Toward a New Welfare State?', in *The Development of the Welfare State in Europe and America*, eds Peter Flora and Arnold J. Heidenheimer (Transaction, London, 1981), pp. 383–406, esp. pp. 399–401.

82 Charles Feinstein, 'Success and Failure: British Economic Growth since 1948', in *The Economic History of Britain*, eds Floud and McCloskey, vol. 3, pp. 95–122; Peter A. Hall, *Governing the Economy: The Politics of State Intervention in Britain and France* (Oxford University Press, Oxford, 1986), esp. pp. 37–8.

83 Hall, *Governing the Economy*, pp. 98–9; Lowe, *The Welfare State*, pp. 76–8; Kavanagh, *Thatcherism and British Politics*, pp. 160–5.

84 See esp. Ramesh Mishra, *The Welfare State in Crisis: Social Thought and Social Change* (St Martin's, New York, 1984), ch. 2.
85 Quoted in Kavanagh, *Thatcherism and British Politics*, pp. 127–8.
86 S. N. Broadberry, 'Unemployment', in *The British Economy*, eds Crafts and Woodward, pp. 212–35, esp. p. 233.
87 Morgan, *The People's Peace*, pp. 382–433; Phillip Whitehead, *The Writing on the Wall: Britain in the Seventies* (Michael Joseph, London, 1985), pp. 282–4; Phillip Whitehead, 'The Labour Governments, 1974–1979', in *Ruling Performance*, eds Hennessy and Seldon, pp. 241–73; Robert Taylor, 'Industrial Relations', in *The Ideas that Shaped Post-War Britain*, eds Marquand and Seldon, pp. 88–121, esp. pp. 108–9; Hall, *Governing the Economy*, pp. 94–5.

Chapter 6   The Limits of State Power, 1979 to the Present

1 Dennis Kavanagh, *Thatcherism and British Politics: The End of Consensus?* (Oxford University Press, Oxford, 1987), pp. 304–5; Ramesh Mishra, *The Welfare State in Crisis: Social Thought and Social Change* (St Martin's, New York, 1984), intro.
2 Eric J. Evans, *Thatcher and Thatcherism* (Routledge, London, 1997), p. 26; Edgar Wilson, *A Very British Miracle: The Failure of Thatcherism* (Pluto Press, London, 1992), pp. 67–9.
3 Jim Tomlinson, *Public Policy and the Economy since 1900* (Oxford University Press, Oxford, 1990), pp. 295–6, 312.
4 Hugo Young, *One of Us: A Biography of Margaret Thatcher* (revised edn, Pan Books, London, 1990), pp. 316–17; Peter Clarke, *Hope and Glory: Britain 1900–1990* (Penguin, Harmondsworth, 1996), p. 393.
5 Tomlinson, *Public Policy and the Economy*, pp. 332–5; T. J. Hatton and Alec Chrystal, 'The Budget and Fiscal Policy', in *The British Economy since 1945*, eds N. F. R. Crafts and N. W. C. Woodward (Oxford University Press, Oxford, 1991), pp. 72–3; Nicholas Timmins, *The Five Giants: A Biography of the Welfare State* (Fontana, London, 1995), pp. 393–4; Ian Gilmour, *Dancing with Dogma* (Simon & Schuster, London, 1992), p. 120; Young, *One of Us*, p. 535.
6 See esp. Beatrix Campbell, *Wigan Pier Revisited: Poverty and Politics in the Eighties* (Virago, London, 1984).
7 Jim Tomlinson, 'British Economic Policy since 1945', in *The Economic History of Britain*, eds Roderick Floud and Donald McCloskey (2nd edn, 3 vols, Cambridge University Press, Cambridge, 1994), pp. 255–83, esp. p. 273.
8 Rodney Lowe, *The Welfare State in Britain since 1945* (2nd edn, Macmillan, Basingstoke, 1994), pp. 313–14; Young, *One of Us*, p. 197.
9 Leslie Hannah, 'Mrs. Thatcher, Capital-Basher?', in *The Thatcher Effect*, eds Dennis Kavanagh and Anthony Seldon (Oxford University Press, Oxford, 1989), pp. 38–48, esp. pp. 38–9; Peter A. Hall, *Governing the Economy: The Politics of State Intervention in Britain and France* (Oxford University Press, Oxford, 1986), pp. 128–9.

10   William Brown, 'The Changed Political Role of Unions under a Hostile Government', in *Trade Unions in British Politics*, eds Ben Pimlott and Chris Cook (2nd edn, Longman, London, 1991), pp. 274–85, esp. pp. 275–6; E. A. Reitan, *Tory Radicalism* (Rowman & Littlefield, Lanham, MD, 1997), pp. 165–6.

11   Roger Geary, *Policing Industrial Disputes: 1893 to 1985* (Cambridge University Press, Cambridge, 1985), ch. 7; David Powell, *British Politics and the Labour Question, 1868–1990* (Macmillan, Basingstoke, 1992), pp. 140–2; Raphael Samuel, Barbara Bloomfield, and Guy Boanas, *The Enemy Within: Pit Villages and the Miners' Strike of 1984–5* (Routledge & Kegan Paul, London, 1986), p. 16.

12   Powell, *British Politics and the Labour Question*, p. 142; Brown, 'The Changed Political Role of Unions', pp. 276–9.

13   Leslie Hannah, 'The Economic Consequences of the State Ownership of Industry, 1945–1990', in *The Economic History of Britain*, eds Floud and McCloskey, vol. 3, pp. 168–94, esp. pp. 181–2; Dennis Swann, *The Retreat of the State: Deregulation and Privatization in the UK and the US* (University of Michigan Press, Ann Arbor, 1988), p. 231.

14   Simon Jenkins, *Accountable to None: The Tory Nationalization of Britain* (Hamish Hamilton, London, 1996), p. 23.

15   Nicolas Spulber, *Redefining the State: Privatization and Welfare Reform in Industrial and Transitional Economies* (Cambridge University Press, Cambridge, 1997), p. 87.

16   John Kay, Colin Mayer, and David Thompson, 'Introduction', in *Privatisation and Regulation: The UK Experience*, eds John Kay, Colin Mayer, and David Thompson (Oxford University Press, Oxford, 1986), pp. 1–32, esp. pp. 2–3.

17   Reitan, *Tory Radicalism*, pp. 159–63; Kenneth O. Morgan, *The People's Peace* (2nd edn, Oxford University Press, Oxford, 1999), p. 523; Evans, *Thatcher and Thatcherism*, p. 121.

18   Jenkins, *Accountable to None*, pp. 31–4; Patrick Birkinshaw, Ian Harden, and Norman Lewis, *Government by Moonlight: The Hybrid Parts of the State* (Unwin Hyman, London, 1990), pp. 1–4, 278–9.

19   Martin Daunton, 'Housing', in *The Cambridge Social History of Britain 1750–1950*, ed. F. M. L. Thompson (3 vols, Cambridge University Press, Cambridge, 1990), vol. 2, pp. 195–250, esp. pp. 249–50; Lowe, *The Welfare State*, pp. 337–9.

20   John Hills and Christine Mullings, 'Housing: A Decent Home for All at a Price within their Means?', in *The State of Welfare: The Welfare State in Britain since 1974*, ed. John Hills (Oxford University Press, Oxford, 1990), esp. p. 149.

21   Peter Hennessy, 'The Civil Service', in *The Thatcher Effect*, eds Kavanagh and Seldon, pp. 114–23, esp. pp. 115–19.

22   Lowe, *The Welfare State*, p. 314; Hennessy, 'The Civil Service', pp. 118–19; Evans, *Thatcher and Thatcherism*, pp. 57–8.

23   Paul Anderson and Nyta Mann, *Safety First: The Making of New Labour* (Granta Books, London, 1997), pp. 184–5; Howard Glennerster and

William Low, 'Education and the Welfare State: Does It Add Up?', in *The State of Welfare*, ed. Hills, pp. 28–87, esp. pp. 34–5; Gilmour, *Dancing with Dogma*, p. 167.

24   Timmins, *The Five Giants*, pp. 483–7; Peter Scott, 'Higher Education', in *The Thatcher Effect*, eds Kavanagh and Seldon, pp. 198–212, esp. pp. 205–8; Reitan, *Tory Radicalism*, pp. 177–8.

25   Lowe, *The Welfare State*, pp. 331–3; Evans, *Thatcher and Thatcherism*, pp. 66–9; Howard Glennerster, *British Social Policy since 1945* (Blackwell, Oxford, 1995), pp. 205–8, 225–6; Dennis Kavanagh and Peter Morris, *Consensus Politics from Attlee to Thatcher* (Blackwell, Oxford, 1989), p. 87; Anne Digby, *British Welfare Policy: Workhouse to Workfare* (Faber and Faber, London, 1989), pp. 121–2.

26   Quoted in Paul Johnson, 'The Welfare State', in *The Economic History of Britain*, eds Floud and McCloskey, vol. 3, pp. 284–317, esp. pp. 297–8.

27   Jenkins, *Accountable to None*, p. 10; G. C. Peden, 'Economic Knowledge and the State in Modern Britain', in *The Boundaries of the State in Modern Britain*, eds S. J. D. Green and R. C. Whiting (Cambridge University Press, Cambridge, 1996), pp. 170–90, esp. pp. 175–6.

28   Lowe, *The Welfare State*, pp. 320–9. See also Ray Hudson and Allan M. Williams, *Divided Britain* (2nd edn, John Wiley & Sons, Chichester, 1995), pp. 271–2.

29   Glennerster, *British Social Policy*, pp. 180–3, 214–19.

30   David Willetts, 'The Family', in *The Thatcher Effect*, eds Kavanagh and Seldon, pp. 262–73, esp. p. 267; Andrew Gamble, *The Free Economy and the Strong State* (2nd edn, Macmillan, Basingstoke, 1994), pp. 243–4.

31   Ivor Crewe, 'Values: the Crusade that Failed', in *The Thatcher Effect*, eds Kavanagh and Seldon, pp. 239–50, esp. pp. 243–4; Glennerster, *British Social Policy*, pp. 226–7.

32   Glennerster, *British Social Policy*, pp. 221–2.

33   Howard Glennerster, 'Health and Social Policy', in *The Major Effect*, eds Dennis Kavanagh and Anthony Seldon (Macmillan, London, 1994), pp. 318–31, esp. pp. 320–1.

34   Glennerster, *British Social Policy*, pp. 232–3.

35   Timmins, *The Five Giants*, pp. 503–7.

36   Paul Johnson, 'Inequality, Redistribution and Living Standards in Britain since 1945', in *Welfare Policy in Britain: The Road from 1945*, eds Helen Fawcett and Rodney Lowe (Macmillan, Basingstoke, 1999), pp. 18–33, esp. pp. 21–2.

37   See Will Hutton, *The State We're In* (Jonathan Cape, London, 1995), pp. 170–1.

38   Johnson, 'Inequality', pp. 26–32. See also Glennerster, *British Social Policy*, p. 178.

39   Digby, *British Welfare Policy*, p. 110.

40   Kavanagh, *Thatcherism and British Politics*, p. 231.

41   Hills and Mullings, 'Housing', pp. 167–8.

42   Hugo Young, *Thatcherism: Did Society Survive?* (Catholic Housing Aid Society, London, 1992), pp. 2–5.

43   Jenkins, *Accountable to None*, pp. 5–6.

44   Gamble, *The Free Economy and the Strong State*, p. 251.

45   Tony Travers, 'The Threat to the Autonomy of Elected Local Government', in *The New Centralism: Britain Out of Step in Europe?*, eds Colin Crouch and David Marquand (Blackwell, Oxford, 1989), pp. 3–20, esp. pp. 9–11; K. Newton and T. J. Karran, *The Politics of Local Expenditure* (Macmillan, London, 1985), p. 122; Malcolm Grant, 'Central–Local Relations: The Balance of Power', in *The Changing Constitution*, eds Jeffrey Jowell and Dawn Oliver (2nd edn, Oxford University Press, Oxford, 1989), pp. 247–72, esp. pp. 271–2; Colin Crouch and David Marquand, 'Foreword', in *The New Centralism*, eds Crouch and Marquand, pp. vii–xi; Stuart Lansley, Sue Goss, and Christian Wolmar, *Councils in Conflict: The Rise and Fall of the Municipal Left* (Macmillan, London, 1989), pp. 56–7.

46   Evans, *Thatcher and Thatcherism*, pp. 62–4; Lansley, Goss, and Wolmar, *Councils in Conflict*, pp. 183–6; Gilmour, *Dancing with Dogma*, pp. 218–19; Jenkins, *Accountable to None*, pp. 59–60.

47   Jenkins, *Accountable to None*, p. 61.

48   Max Beloff and Gillian Peele, *The Government of the UK: Political Authority in a Changing Society* (2nd edn, Weidenfeld & Nicolson, London, 1985), pp. 358–9; Charles Townshend, *Making the Peace: Public Order and Public Security in Modern Britain* (Oxford University Press, Oxford, 1993), pp. 132–53; K. D. Ewing and C. A. Gearty, *Freedom Under Thatcher: Civil Liberties in Modern Britain* (Oxford University Press, Oxford, 1990), pp. 18–19, 103–5; Anderson and Mann, *Safety First*, pp. 248–9, 260–9.

49   David Vincent, *The Culture of Secrecy: Britain 1832–1998* (Oxford University Press, Oxford, 1998), pp. 262–5, 308–9; Wilson, *A Very British Miracle*, pp. 135–7, 175–9; Charles Townshend, 'State and Public Security', in *The State: Historical and Political Dimensions*, eds Richard English and Charles Townshend (Routledge, London, 1999), pp. 171–2; Townshend, *Making the Peace*, p. 189.

50   J. M. Ross, 'The Road to Constitution', in *National Identities: The Constitution of the United Kingdom*, ed. Bernard Crick (Blackwell, Oxford, 1991), pp. 151–6; Will Hutton, *The State to Come* (Vintage, London, 1997), pp. 63–4; Ewing and Gearty, *Freedom Under Thatcher*, pp. 6–7; Ian Harden and Norman Lewis, *The Noble Lie: The British Constitution and the Rule of Law* (Hutchinson, London, 1986), pp. 6–7; Anthony Lester, 'The Constitution: Decline and Renewal', in *The Changing Constitution*, eds Jowell and Oliver, pp. 345–70, esp. pp. 368–9; Ferdinand Mount, *The British Constitution Now: Recovery or Decline?* (Heinemann, London, 1992), pp. 2–3.

51   Quoted in Vernon Bogdanor, *Power and the People: A Guide to Constitutional Reform* (Gollancz, London, 1997), p. 12.

52   Quoted in Cosmo Graham and Tony Prosser, 'Introduction: The Constitution and the New Conservatives', in *Waiving the Rules: The Constitution under Thatcherism*, eds Cosmo Graham and Tony Prosser (Open University Press, Milton Keynes, 1988), p. 13.

53   Tom Nairn, *The Enchanted Glass: Britain and its Monarchy* (Hutchinson Radius, London, 1988), pp. 155–6; Hutton, *The State We're In*, pp. 3–4;

David Eastwood, 'The State We Were In: Parliament, Centralization and English State Formation', in *The State*, eds English and Townshend, pp. 18–43, esp. pp. 26–7, 34–8.

54 For useful assessments, see Vernon Bogdanor, *The Monarchy and the Constitution* (Oxford University Press, Oxford, 1995); Frank Prochaska, *Royal Bounty: The Making of a Welfare Monarchy* (Yale University Press, New Haven and London, 1995).

55 For this list of factors I am indebted to Chris Pierson, *The Modern State* (Routledge, London, 1996), pp. 123–5.

56 Colin Hay, *The Political Economy of New Labour: Labouring Under False Pretences?* (Manchester University Press, Manchester, 1999), pp. 183–4; Hutton, *The State We're In*, pp. 15–17.

57 Young, *One of Us*, pp. 183–91.

58 Quoted in Hugo Young, *This Blessed Plot: Britain and Europe from Churchill to Blair* (Overlook Press, Woodstock, NY, 1998), p. 347. See also Sean Greenwood, *Britain and European Cooperation since 1945* (Blackwell, Oxford, 1992), pp. 112–15; Derek W. Urwin, *The Community of Europe: A History of European Integration since 1945* (Longman, London, 1991), pp. 230–41.

59 Young, *This Blessed Plot*, pp. 368–70; Greenwood, *Britain and European Cooperation*, pp. 115–17.

60 Michael Chisholm, *Britain on the Edge of Europe* (Routledge, London, 1995), pp. 5–6; Allan M. Williams, *The European Community: The Contradictions of Integration* (2nd edn, Blackwell, Oxford, 1994), p. 144; Young, *This Blessed Plot*, pp. 365–6, 436–40.

61 For a convenient overview of the debate, see Hutton, *The State to Come*, pp. 93–8.

62 Eric Hobsbawm, 'An Afterword: European Union at the End of the Century', in *European Integration in Social and Historical Perspective, 1850 to the Present*, eds Jytte Klausen and Louise A. Tilley (Rowman & Littlefield, Lanham, MD, 1997), pp. 267–76.

63 Quoted in Brian Harrison, *The Transformation of British Politics 1860–1995* (Oxford University Press, Oxford, 1996), p. 399.

64 For sensible remarks on this subject, see e.g. David Coombes, 'Europe and the Regions', in *National Identities*, ed. Crick, pp. 134–5; Alan Milward, *The European Rescue of the Nation-State* (University of California Press, Berkeley, 1992), pp. 346–7, 446–7; Chisholm, *Britain on the Edge of Europe*, pp. 6–7; Hutton, *The State to Come*, pp. 11–12.

65 Anderson and Mann, *Safety First*, pp. 97–8; *Guardian*, 25 August 1999, p. 1; Hay, *The Political Economy of New Labour*, pp. 137–8.

66 Stephen Driver and Luke Martell, *New Labour: Politics After Thatcherism* (Polity, Cambridge, 1998), pp. 113, 162–4; Ruth Levitas, *The Inclusive Society? Social Exclusion and New Labour* (Macmillan, Basingstoke, 1998), pp. 112–13, 128–37; Jim Tomlinson, 'Economic Policy: Lessons from Past Labour Governments', in *New Labour in Power: Precedents and Prospects*, eds Brian Brivati and Tim Bale (Routledge, London, 1997), pp. 11–33,

esp. pp. 15–16, 20–2; Anderson and Mann, *Safety First*, pp. 199–202, 387–8; Hay, *The Political Economy of New Labour*, pp. 136–40.

Conclusion

1 Philip Harling and Peter Mandler, 'From "Fiscal–Military" State to *Laissez-faire* State, 1760–1850', *Journal of British Studies*, 32 (1993), pp. 44–70, esp. pp. 48–9, 57.

2 Roger Middleton, 'The Size and Scope of the Public Sector', in *The Boundaries of the State in Modern Britain*, eds S. J. D. Green and R. C. Whiting (Cambridge University Press, Cambridge, 1996), pp. 89–145, esp. p. 95.

3 Harling and Mandler, 'From "Fiscal–Military" State to *Laissez-faire* State', p. 57.

4 Middleton, 'The Size and Scope of the Public Sector', pp. 92–110.

5 G. C. Baugh, 'Government Grants in Aid of the Rates in England and Wales, 1889–1990', *Historical Research*, 65 (1992), pp. 215–37, esp. pp. 225–8.

6 Jan-Erik Lane, David McKay, and Kenneth Newton, *Political Data Handbook: OECD Countries* (Oxford University Press, Oxford, 1997), pp. 100, 105–6.

Index